INDIAN AND FAR EASTERN RELIGIOUS TRADITIONS

RELIGION AND MAN

Under the General Editorship of
W. RICHARD COMSTOCK

INDIAN AND FAR EASTERN RELIGIOUS TRADITIONS

ROBERT D. BAIRD
University of Iowa

ALFRED BLOOM
University of Hawaii

Harper & Row, Publishers
New York, Evanston, San Francisco, London

Cover photo: Allen Hagood, National Park Service

RELIGION AND MAN:
INDIAN AND FAR EASTERN RELIGIOUS TRADITIONS

Copyright © 1972 by Harper & Row, Publishers, Inc.

Printed in the United States of America. All rights reserved. No part of this book may be used or reproduced in any manner whatsoever without written permission except in the case of brief quotations embodied in critical articles and reviews. For information address Harper & Row, Publishers, Inc., 49 East 33rd Street, New York, N. Y. 10016.

Standard Book Number: 06-040448-5

Library of Congress Catalog Card Number: 72-185898

INDIAN AND FAR EASTERN RELIGIOUS TRADITIONS

PART ONE

INDIAN RELIGIOUS TRADITIONS
ROBERT D. BAIRD

If the study of religion is characterized as the study of what is ultimately important to persons and communities, then the study of Indian religious traditions is the study of what has been and is of ultimate importance to Indians. One could begin such a discussion with a series of generalizations about "Hinduism," "Buddhism," "Jainism," or the "Indian Mind." By the end of our study, most if not all such generalizations would have been proven false. Instead, we will approach the study of religion in India with the openness that is necessary if one is to grasp the rich variety of religious expressions. We will find an interesting combination including imports from other lands as well as indigenous developments. Hence, we are not suggesting that what we will consider is "typically" or "essentially" Indian. Even the possibility of sifting an "essence" from the variety here presented is questionable.

RELIGION IN THE VEDIC PERIOD

PRE-VEDIC RELIGION

About one thousand years before the Aryans (see pp. 116 ff.) entered India through the northwest mountain passes, twenty-five hundred years before the Christian era, there existed a highly developed civilization now known as the Indus Valley Civilization. Excavations in the area centering around the once large cities of Mohenjo-Daro on the Indus river and Harappa on the Ravi river give evidence of an awareness of city planning and the existence of comfortable and spacious domestic dwellings.

While no written documents have been uncovered, archeological remains in the form of figurines, seals, and other objects have raised the question of the relationship between the religion of these early inhabitants and religious expressions found in later periods. It has been tempting to see more in the remains than the evidence clearly warrants. Nevertheless, certain finds are remarkable because they emphasize aspects of religious expression that came to be important in later India, but which were apparently of little significance in the Vedic literature (see pp. 117 ff.), the assumed source of most later Indian religious expressions.

No building has been found that can be clearly identified as a temple. In the Vedic period sacrifices took place in open fields, not in temples. Unlike the Vedic period, though, which gives no clear evidence of having made anthropomorphic images of the deities worshiped, the Indus Valley has yielded figurines which seem to have had religious significance.

Although some may simply be toys with no religious meaning, numerous female figurines appear to be representations of the mother goddess. Laden with ornaments, with protruding breasts and ample hips, they seem to connote fertility, and suggest the existence of a fertility cult. Others, either pregnant or with children in their

4 INDIAN RELIGIOUS TRADITIONS

Horned deity surrounded by animals. (Courtesy of the New Delhi Museum.)

arms, may be ex-voto offerings or examples of sympathetic magic. The generally accepted view, however, is that they represent the Great Mother Goddess who is still worshiped in India. The abundance of female figurines is particularly significant when one couples the present prevalence of the Mother Goddess in India with the slight attention given to female deities in the *Rigveda* (see p. 118). Perhaps the historical antecedents of the worship of the Mother in India are pre-Aryan and pre-Vedic.

In one of the seals there is a seated figure which has been designated a "proto-type of Shiva."[1] According to the most common interpretation, the seal contains a human form with three visible faces seated in a yogic posture. The figure is surrounded by an elephant, a tiger, a rhinoceros, and a buffalo. A pair of horns resembling the trident of Shiva crowns his head. A striking coincidence occurs here since the later Shiva is three-faced, is called the lord of beasts (*pashupati*), and the great ascetic (*mahayogi*). The relationship must be considered a problematic one that has not been substantiated.[2]

The worship of animals and trees has also been inferred from some of the finds. The pipal tree (since honored because under it the Buddha is held to have achieved enlightenment) was apparently sacred in the Indus Valley Civilization as evidenced by its association with the figures of deities on seals. Although not all the animals represented on the seals may be sacred, some seem to be. The rhinoceros, tiger, and bison are frequently depicted as feeding from troughs. These are not simply feeding troughs, but food offerings to appease wild animals, since oxen, which are presumed to have been domesticated, are never shown feeding from them. On one seal a god in a yogic position has a canopy of snakes over him, anticipating the *nagas* (serpent deities) of later Indian mythology. (Vishnu, as well as other later deities—indeed, even the Buddha—is often pictured with snake hoods extending over his head.)

Numerous cone-shaped objects have been found which seem to be *lingas* and point to the possible worship of the phallus. Whether other ring-shaped stones are *yonis* is a matter of debate. Since the worship of the linga is later connected with Shiva, and since such worship is absent from the *Rigveda,* the idea of a historical connection is tempting, even if only a possibility.

Several finds have indicated presence of the swastika symbol, although the meaning of it for the Indus Valley Civilization is not definitely known. It is also commonly found in later Indian temple structures.

COMING OF THE ARYANS

In the area from Poland to Central Asia there were large numbers of seminomadic peoples who in the early part of the second millennium B.C. migrated eastward and southward. Some stayed in what is now Iran and others moved as far as India, entering the land

---

1. Sir John Marshall, ed., *Mohenjo-Daro and the Indus Civilization,* London, Arthur Probsthain, 1931, vol. 1, p. 52.

2. For a critique of this interpretation and a counterproposal, see Herbert P. Sullivan, "A Re-examination of the Religion of the Indus Civilization," in *History of Religions,* vol. 4, no. 1, 1964, pp. 115–125.

through the Kyber Pass in the northwest mountains. They were not accustomed to urban living as were many of the inhabitants of the Indus Valley Civilization, but they were not barbarians. These invaders, who reached India about 1500 B.C., called themselves Aryas (a term that has since been Anglicized as Aryans). That this name also survived in Iran will surprise no one who is familiar with the numerous parallels between the religion of the *Rigveda* and the ancient Iranian religion.

Sir Mortimer Wheeler, who excavated in the Indus Valley, believes that the invading Aryans overthrew Harappa.[3] Although nomadic, the Aryans were militarily advanced. They first took the surrounding villages, and refugees apparently fled to the cities for protection. The cities then became overcrowded causing the previously existing order and planning to collapse. The cities, particularly Harappa, were walled as a defense from the attacks. When the cities were finally seized, most of the inhabitants of Mohenjo-Daro fled, but skeletons found on the steps of a well and in other unexpected places indicate that some may have been overtaken and killed in flight.

The Aryans arrived with a patrilinear system of tribal organization ← *patriarchy* and a rather well-defined priesthood. They had developed a poetic technique in the composition of hymns in praise of their gods which were chanted at sacrifices. For some time these hymns were remembered by families of priests, and a sacredness was attached to them. Even minor alterations were not permitted and they were passed on with remarkable accuracy. This collection of hymns was later committed to writing and it gives us the first substantial body of Indian texts for religious interpretation. At this point archeological evidence is slight compared with that available for the Indus Valley Civilization, but written evidence of the religion of the Indo-Aryan people of the Vedic age is quite full. With the Brahmanas, Aranyakas, and Upanishads (see pp. 120 ff.), it is possible to construct with a certain degree of accuracy the beliefs and cult practice of the Vedic period.

Two words of caution are in order. The first is that the texts which have come to us are quite clearly the work of a priestly class and hence may or may not reflect what the people actually believed and practiced. At least we can say that the texts reflect the priestly ideal which was held before the people (we will see that the *Atharvaveda* is one possible exception). A second point is that due to the lack of historical allusions in the texts themselves, it is difficult, if not impossible, to date specific texts with any degree of accuracy. The best that can be given is a relative chronology placed within centuries.

RELIGIOUS LITERATURE IN THE VEDIC PERIOD

The term *veda* means knowledge, and, in the present context, it bears the special connotation of sacred knowledge. The ancient Vedas contain the priestly tradition which the Aryans brought into

3. Sir Mortimer Wheeler, *The Indus Civilization,* 3rd ed., London, Cambridge University Press, 1968.

India and developed in the course of centuries on Indian soil. The Vedas have been and still are considered *shruti* ("that which is heard," and hence not of human origin) by many Indians. They are revelation, not in the sense that they contain truths revealed by a Supreme Being, but in that they are eternal truth "seen" or "apprehended" by the *rishis* or seers. The Vedas are to be distinguished from another class of sacred writings often designated as *smriti* ("that which is remembered," and hence of human origin). *Smriti*, then, is human commentary on *shruti*, and generally includes all non-Vedic literature.

The Vedic texts include Samhitas or collections of basic verses; the Brahmanas, which are theological and ritual commentaries on the Samhitas, written in prose; the Aranyakas ("forest texts") and Upanishads which follow the Brahmanas and are commentaries of a mystical and philosophical nature.

In the course of time there developed four distinct collections (Samhitas) for specific purposes. The *Rigveda* (*Riksamhita*) is the oldest and is basic to the others. Consisting of 1028 hymns, it has a total of 10,462 verses divided into ten books. Most of the hymns of the *Rigveda* are addressed to specific deities and are basically poetic in form like the following one addressed to Agni the fire god:

Agni I praise, the household priest,
God, minister of sacrifice,
Invoker, best bestowing wealth.

Agni is worthy to be praised,
By present as by seers of old:
May he to us conduct the gods.

Through Agni may we riches gain,
And day by day prosperity
Replete with fame and manly sons.

The worship and the sacrifice,
Guarded by thee on every side,
Go straight, O Agni, to the gods.

May Agni, the invoker, wise
And true, of most resplendent fame,
The god, come hither with the gods.

Whatever good thou wilt bestow,
O Agni, on the pious man,
That gift comes true, O Angiras.

To thee, O Agni, day by day,
O thou illuminer of gloom,
With thought we, bearing homage, come:

To thee the lord of sacrifice,
The radiant guardian of the Law,
That growest in thine own abode.

So, like a father to his son,
Be easy of reproach to us;
Agni, for weal abide with us.[4]

The second Veda is a collection of sacrificial formulae (*yajus*) called the *Yajurveda* (*Yajuhsamhita*). Since this Samhita contains verses from the *Rigveda*, it must have been composed later than the *Rigveda*. Contained in this collection are instructions regarding the times and materials for sacrifice, the construction of the fire altar, and formulae for the soma sacrifice (see p. 127).

The third Veda contains melodies (*samans*) and is therefore called the *Samaveda* (*Samasamhita*). These are largely verses taken from the *Rigveda*, some 1810 of them, and are set to music. As the *Yajurveda* was composed for ritual purposes, these verses were meant to be chanted at the soma sacrifice.

The fourth Veda is the *Atharvaveda* (*Atharvasamhita*)—a collection of magical formulae (*atharvan*). Sometimes mention is made of the three Vedas, excluding the *Atharvaveda* collected at a later date. It is probably not accurate, however, to restrict the materials of the *Atharvaveda* to a single period, since the magic and charms more likely existed side by side with the high cult as is the case today. This collection contains prayers for long life and prayers to cure sickness and demonic possession. There are curses upon demons, sorcerers, enemies, as well as charms to secure love. As a collection of magical charms, the *Atharvaveda* was probably more the possession of the laity. The following is a charm for perfect health.

From thy eyes, thy nostrils, ears, and chin—the disease which is seated in thy head—from thy brain and tongue I do tear it out.

From thy neck, nape of thy neck, ribs, and spine—the disease which is seated in thy fore-arm—from thy shoulders and arms do I tear it out.

From thy heart, thy lungs, viscera, and sides; from thy kidneys, spleen, and liver do we tear out the disease.

From thy entrails, canals, rectum, and abdomen; from thy belly, guts, and navel do I tear out the disease.

From thy thighs, knees, heels, and the tips of thy feet—from thy hips I do tear out the disease seated in thy buttocks, from thy bottom the disease seated in thy buttocks.

From thy bones, marrow, sinews and arteries; from thy hands, fingers, and nails I do tear out the disease.

The disease that is in thy every limb, thy every hair, thy every joint; that which is seated in thy skin, with Kasyapa's charm, that tears out, to either side do we tear it out.[5]

4. *Rigveda* I.1, from A. A. Macdonell, *Hymns of the Rigveda*, London, Oxford University Press, n.d., pp. 72–73.
5. *Atharvaveda* II.23, from Maurice Bloomfield, trans., *Hymns of the Atharvaveda*, Delhi, Motilal Banarsidass, 1964 (first published 1897), pp. 44–45.

Collections of accepted interpretations (*brahmanas*) by the Brahmans or priests developed. They were collections of theological statements arising from scholastic controversy, some of which relate to the stanzas of the Samhitas while others describe and explain the rites. Following the divisions of the priestly cult, the Brahmanas are classified according to the Veda to which they refer and out of which they grew, and are related to the growing specialization of the priesthood. The Brahmanas connected with the *Rigveda* are intended for the *hotri* ("pourer" of oblation—reciter of the verses of the *Rigveda*); those attached to the *Yajurveda* are for the *adhvaryu*, who is responsible for the manual operations of the sacrifice. The Brahmanas attached to the *Samaveda* are for the *udgatri*, who sings the hymns at the soma sacrifice. Since all the other Samhitas had Brahmanas attached to them, it was not long before one was also attached to the *Atharvaveda*. The Brahmanas began as liturgical appendices to the Samhitas, but later became independent. Most important is the *Shatapatha Brahmana*, the "Brahmana of the hundred ways," consisting of one hundred lectures. It is more elaborate than most of the other Brahmanas, dealing in detail with the nature of vegetable offerings, the soma sacrifice, fire offerings, rites connected with the king, and the elaborate horse sacrifice.

The Aranyakas are "texts of the forest." They are secret and perhaps dangerous because of their magical power, and therefore must be kept from the public and read in forests.[6] Concerned neither with the performance nor the explanation of sacrifice, the Aranyakas explicate its mystical meaning and symbolism. As such they form a natural transition to the Upanishads, the oldest of which are included in or appended to the Aranyakas, and the line of demarkation is not always easily determined.

The Brahmanas emphasized ritualism. The Aranyakas are an admission that the exceedingly detailed and complex sacrificial rituals could not be expected of all; they emphasize meditation rather than ritual performance. The Aranyakas helped to bridge the apparent gap between *karmamarga* (the way through works, i.e., through sacrifice) and *jnanamarga* (the way through knowledge, i.e., through meditation), by showing the mystical, symbolic, and meditative meaning of the sacrifices.

The most ancient Upanishads are closely connected with the Aranyakas. Continuing the mystical tendency, they discuss the symbolism of melodies and words, expound the theory of breathing, and move into cosmological theories of the Atman-Brahman theme. It is commonly accepted that *upanishad* is derived from *sad*, "to sit," *upa*, "nearby," and *ni*, "devotedly." In the Upanishads themselves the term is usually synonymous with "secret" (*rahasya*). Hence the term which etymologically means "to sit nearby" (as a teacher and student for instruction) came to refer to the secret instructions imparted at such private meetings. The texts probably began in the

---

6. Louis Renou, *Vedic India*, Calcutta, Susil Gupta (India), Private Limited, 1957, trans. from French by Phillip Spratt (1st French ed. 1947), pp. 32–33.

form of short philosophical statements. These statements were communicated from teacher to pupil, the communication being preceded and followed by expository discourses. In time the discourses assumed a definite shape and when committed to writing, resulted in the Upanishads as we now know them. The heterogeneity of thought in the Upanishads suggests that they contain the views of a series of teachers, old and new ideas mingled in a single Upanishad. When the texts were finally brought together and arranged, the Upanishads were appended to the Brahmanas. Standing thus at the end of the Vedas, they came to be known as *vedanta* (*veda*, "knowledge" + *anta*, "end"), and later the term which first indicated position came to imply aim or fulfillment much as the English term "end" serves both meanings. Although the number of Upanishads exceeds two hundred there are about ten principle ones.

It is repeatedly stated in the Upanishads that the teachings contained therein are a mystery and that much care should be taken to keep them from the unworthy lest they become misused and misunderstood. In the *Prashna Upanishad,* six pupils go to a great teacher seeking instruction in the highest reality. He asks them to live with him for a year, apparently with the purpose of watching them to ascertain their fitness to receive the teaching. In the *Katha Upanishad,* when Naciketas wants to know whether or not the soul survives after death, Yama (god of the dead) does not reply until he has tested the sincerity and strength of the mind of the young inquirer. Even in the earlier Upanishads, such a point of view is assumed. "Verily, a father may teach this Brahma to his eldest son or to a worthy pupil, (but) to no one else." [7]

The following chart of Vedic literature may be useful in summarizing the relationship of the various texts to each other, particularly in seeing which Brahmanas and Upanishads are attached to which Samhitas.[8]

Samhitas	Brahmanas	Aranyakas	Upanishads
Rigveda	Aitareya Kaushitaki	Aitareya Kaushitaki	Aitareya Kaushitaki
Yajurveda	Taittiriya	Taittiriya	Taittiriya Mahanarayana Kathaka Maitrayaniya Shvetashvatara
	Shatapatha	Brihad	Brihadaranyaka Isha
Samaveda	Pancavimsha Chandogya Talavakara		Chandogya Kena
Atharvaveda	Gopatha		Mundaka Prashna Mandukya

7. R. C. Zaehner, *Hindu Scriptures,* New York, Dutton, 1966, p. 86. *Chandogya* III.11.4.
8. R. De Smet and J. Neuner, eds., *Religious Hinduism,* Allahabad, St. Paul Publications, 1964, p. 32.

The date of the texts can be affixed in terms of a relative chronology. *Rigveda* is older than any of the other Samhitas, since the others presuppose it. Nevertheless, the question of dating is complicated when one distinguishes the compilation of the *Rigveda,* which may have taken place about the time of the Brahmanas, from its composition, which took place earlier. Vedic writers considered the matters being explicated as timeless and independent of historical events and chronology. Nevertheless, the Vedic literature was probably composed as a whole after the entry of the Aryans into India (c. 1500 B.C.), and before the arrival of the Buddha (563–483 B.C.), since some of the geographical locations, animals, etc., mentioned in the *Rigveda* are Indian.

It is difficult to date the Brahmanas, but they must come after the Samhitas. The somewhat modern grammar used in them would date them after the *Rigveda,* perhaps 1000 to 800 B.C. One might well follow the dating scheme of J. A. B. Van Buitenen.

Rigveda—1400 B.C.
Yajurveda—1400–1000 B.C.
Samaveda—1400–1000 B.C.
Atharvaveda—1200 B.C.
Brahmanas—1000–800 B.C.
Aranyakas—800–600 B.C.
Oldest Upanishads (*Brihadaranyaka, Chandogya, Taittiriya*)—600–500 B.C.
Early metrical Upanishads (*Shvetashvatara, Katha*)—500–300 B.C.
Other Upanishads rarely older than 300 B.C.[9]

GODS OF THE RIGVEDA

Consisting primarily of hymns addressed to various deities in vogue, the *Rigveda* offers considerable information on how the gods were viewed. But due to the lack of any probable chronology, it is impossible to trace their historical development with any degree of accuracy. Nor should one expect a consistently developed mythology in which certain gods are assigned certain areas of sovereignty. Rather, it is a collection of hymns addressed to gods whose functions and characteristics overlap. Max Müller, trying to avoid calling the religion of the *Rigveda* either monotheism or polytheism, used the term "henotheism" for the tendency to ascribe all power to the specific deity that was uppermost in the mind of the worshiper at a given time. There is in the *Rigveda* a tendency, found in later Indian mythology, to ascribe attributes of other gods to the particular deity being addressed.

Although many of the deities reflect an early worship of the powers inherent in nature, the deities of the *Rigveda* do not represent mere nature worship. While there is no strong evidence for the use of images at this time, many of the nature powers are described in anthropomorphic terms. Sky and sun gods are particularly prevalent.

9. J. A. B. Van Buitenen, "Vedic Literature," in *Civilization of India Syllabus,* Madison, Wis., University of Wisconsin Press, 1965.

In spite of the fact that the hymns of the *Rigveda* are a priestly work produced chiefly for use with the sacrifices, not all hymns reveal a clear sacrificial orientation. Since the hymns represent a considerable period of development prior to their present written state, one should not be surprised to find some hymns which carefully reflect a particular sacrificial situation and others which portray a more general type of outpouring. There is hardly a god in the *Rigveda* who is so insignificant that he does not receive homage from the other deities.

Taking into account that one cannot decide which deities were important by the number of hymns addressed to them or the frequency with which they are mentioned, it is perhaps significant that Indra is addressed alone in some 250 hymns (approximately one-fourth of the hymns of the *Rigveda*) and is addressed jointly with other deities in some fifty more.

Although there is reason to suppose that Indra had storm-god connections and hence had a basis in one of the forces of nature as did many of the other Vedic deities, he is frequently described anthropomorphically. He has a body, hands, legs, lips, jaws, and even a beard. His exploits are superb and began when at birth he emerged from the womb through his mother's side—a motif later added to the birth of the Buddha. As protector of the warrior class, he is considered somewhat dangerous and unpredictable. His overindulgence in soma makes him all the more able to engage in mighty exploits, including those of the lover.

Indra's connection with the warrior class is supported by his superlative exploits. He carries a thunderbolt (*vajra*) and through drinking soma amasses power and energy to slay Vritra the serpent and to release the pent-up waters. The serpent may be a reference to the demon of drought who is pierced by the lightning accompanying a thunder storm. Both Indra and Vritra are furnished with *maya,* a term signifying occult, superhuman power. *Maya* later came to mean trick, magic, or illusion and was used to express the cosmic illusion of the phenomenal world in Advaita philosophy (see p. 188). Indra as the war god of the Vedic Indians humbled the Dasyas, their Dravidian foes, and gave the Dasyas' possessions to his own worshipers.

Sometimes found in association with Indra are the Maruts. They travel through the sky in golden chariots drawn by horses. Clothed in rain, they direct and create the storm. Although they recognize Indra as their superior and help him in his wars, they are terrifying and sometimes malevolent. Later, in the Brahmanas, they abandon him and become hostile.

Although mentioned in only a few Vedic hymns, Rudra is of interest because of the possible connection with the later deity Shiva. Armed with bows and arrows, he is a deity to be feared. Yet he redresses wrongs, dwells in the forest, and has dominion over animals. He is sometimes described as fierce and as destructive as a wild beast, one to whom the title *shiva* ("auspicious") was attached, perhaps euphemistically.

Of high cultic significance, Agni the fire god is addressed in some two hundred hymns. Indeed, all but two of the books of the *Rigveda* begin with an Agni hymn. Because of his connection with the sacrificial fire, Agni dwells in the fire pit (*vedi*) where he is kindled every morning. This pit is the "navel of the earth." Because of the use of *ghee* (clarified butter) in the sacrifices, Agni is called butter-backed and butter-haired, and since ghee, as a drink of the gods, is poured into the sacrificial fire with a spoon, Agni is labeled "one whose mouth is a spoon." The elaborate sacrificial rituals of Vedic times required several priests who specialized in certain aspects of the ritual. Knowing and performing the functions of each, Agni is the archetypal priest, the divine counterpart of the earthly priesthood. Agni is also called lord of the house (*grihapati*), an aspect reflecting an earlier setting in which he was more the center of domestic life than of sacrificial cult. As a dispeller of darkness he repels enemies who might attack at night. He banishes illness and puts demons to flight. Agni is all-seeing, taking account of the wicked deeds of men. He is sometimes besought for forgiveness.

Of comparable importance among the cult deities is Soma. Some 120 hymns are addressed to Soma, and the ninth book of the *Rigveda* seems to be a collection of some hymns which were brought together from their previous places in other books. It is necessary to distinguish between soma the plant, soma the exhilarating juice that is prepared with pressings from the plant, and soma the heavenly nectar of which the plant juices are the embodiment. Soma is seen as a protector from accident, illness, or trouble and as the giver of joy, comfort, riches, and long life. One who fears an enemy in battle can gain strength and help by drinking soma. Its preparation involved pressing the stalks of the soma plant and straining the liquid through a sieve of woolen cloth. Hymns were composed to praise the tawny color as well as the movement and sound of the liquid. Indra sometimes drank pure soma, but most of the deities, as well as men participating in the sacrifice, drank it mixed with milk, curd, or grain. Although all the gods had a share in the soma offering, Indra and Vayu seem to have received a much larger portion. In both the *Avesta* and the *Rigveda* soma (hoama in the *Avesta*) is important enough to suggest it was part of the pre-Indian Aryan heritage.

In the *Rigveda,* solar deities and sky gods dominate the scene. Most clearly related to the sun is Surya, also a name for the sun. An all-seeing god, he beholds the good and evil deeds of men. He rides in a car drawn by steeds who are unyoked at sunset. Since Surya appears after dawn, he is described as the child of Dawn (Ushas). The lack of a consistent mythology is brought to the fore by the fact that Surya is also described as a young man who follows the maiden "Dawn." In the *Rigveda,* Ushas is one of the few female deities and she is consistently portrayed as a delightful and beautiful maiden. Sometimes Ushas is depicted as the wife of Surya. Indeed, they are also considered brother and sister, since in some hymns both are regarded as the children of Dyaus (sky deity, counterpart to the Greek deity Zeus).

Also sons of Dyaus are the Ashvins ("possessors of horses").

These sons are twins who make their home in the heavens where they journey in a golden chariot drawn by birds or horses. In ritual they are worshiped in the morning because of their connection with the rising sun. When they yoke their car in the morning, Ushas (Dawn) is born.

A most famous verse, named "Gayatri" because of its poetic form, is addressed to Savitri and is repeated from memory by devout Brahmans every day:

*May we attain that excellent
Glory of Savitri the god,
That he may stimulate our thoughts.*

Rigveda III.62.10

A solar deity, Savitri is the golden deity, possessed of golden arms and equipped with a golden car and golden yoke pins. At evening he impels all creatures to go to sleep and in the morning he stirs them to awaken for a working day. Some of his functions overlap with those of Surya in the morning and with those of Ratri (night) in the night, a fact which again reinforces the view that the *Rigveda* contains no completely consistent mythology.

There are several other deities connected with the sun, but one more should be isolated because of his later significance rather than for his relative importance in the *Rigveda*. Vishnu was later included as the preserver in the so-called triad of gods which also include Brahma (the creator) and Shiva (the destroyer) (see p. 173). One of Vishnu's chief characteristics was his "three steps," which probably referred either to the three stations of the sun (sunrise, zenith, sunset) or to his encompassing of the three regions (earth, middle air, heaven).

Varuna, the sovereign of the cosmic order, creates and rules through *rita* (cosmic and ethical order, the later extension of which is *dharma*). As sovereign of the universe, he controls the appearance and movement of the heavenly bodies. Rain falls from the sky at his command. Varuna is omniscient, knowing the flight of the birds in the sky. No creature winks without his knowledge. His sovereignty and knowledge extend to the ethical realm. It is this ethical dimension which distinguishes him from the other Vedic deities and has led some to point out his affinity with the Hebrew Yahweh. As the support of *rita* (cosmic and ethical order), all decrees and statutes proceed from his holy will. Varuna knows the secret violations of that will, which are caused by thoughtlessness, weakness of the will, bad example, dice, anger, or wine. Specific prohibitions exist against deception and gambling, or, if one cannot keep from the latter, against cheating at dice.

Sin against the moral precepts laid down by Varuna might result in disease or even in falling out of fellowship with Varuna. In each of the hymns addressed to him, Varuna is entreated to release the sinner from the penalty of his faults.

In the *Rigveda* deification extended to rivers, mountains, and even to the sacrificial implements. An example of this is Sarasvati, a goddess of the river who is another of the few female deities of the *Rigveda* and one who would later become the goddess of learning.

While there was in general a positive attitude toward the deities, some were feared for their malicious deeds. The *rakshas* were demons who walked by night, assumed many forms, and interfered with sacrifices by eating meat and drinking milk set aside for the sacrifice. There were *gandharvas,* spirits of the clouds and waters who guarded the Soma and sometimes monopolized it. The *apsaras* or water nymphs were the *gandharvas'* wives; they wielded magical powers and symbolized fecundity.

In the pre-Vedic Iranian period *Asuras* were a class of deities alongside the *devas*. In Iran the *Asuras* won an ascendancy (cf. the prime deity Ahura Mazda) while the *devas* became known as demons. In India the reverse occurred. The *devas* were the deities, and since the *asuras* were their enemies, they became demons. In the earlier part of the Vedas, *asuras* are favorable and the term is applied to Varuna. Later in the *Yajurveda* and the *Atharvaveda* they become enemies of the gods and are lowered to the level of demons.

CULT PRACTICE

Sacrifice was central to the cult. As early as the *Rigveda,* there probably were both domestic sacrifices performed by the head of the house around a domestic fire as well as more elaborate sacrifices performed in public often sponsored by a king or some other official. The latter rites are elaborately detailed in the Brahmanas, while for the former we are dependent on the *Grihya Sutras,* a body of texts which were not composed until the post-Vedic period (500–200 B.C.).

The sacrifices of the Vedic cult did not take place in temples, but in the house of the sacrificer or on altars on a level spot of ground covered with grass. The dimensions of the altars and the methods of construction were prescribed in great detail. The offering consisted in what men themselves enjoyed eating: milk, ghee, and cakes of barley or rice. The ancient Vedic worshipers do not appear to have been vegetarians or to have held to the later doctrine of *ahimsa* (noninjury) which would have excluded animal sacrifice. In addition to animal sacrifices there is some evidence of human sacrifice, which was considered the most efficacious of all.

While some of the less complicated sacrifices required only one priest, there was a development which led to various priests performing different parts of the sacrifice. The growing complexity of the sacrifice itself seemed to have required such specialization. The most important priest was the Hotri, whose chief duty came to be the recitation of stanzas of the *Rigveda*. The Adhvaryu was responsible for the manual operation of the sacrifice; he tended the fires, prepared the altar, utilized the utensils, and cooked the oblations. The Brahman came to be the overseer of the cult; he ordered the various performances and was aware of the expiation to be performed in case of error in the sacrifice. In addition there was the

Udgatri, or singer of those portions of the *Samaveda* used during the soma sacrifice.

At first the sacrifices were primarily means whereby the favor of the gods could be obtained. As time passed and as the sacrifices became more elaborate, the sacrifice became more a powerful mystery. Through the sacrifice the priest created the world anew and men came to believe that the order of nature ultimately rested on the perfect performance of the sacrifice. The result was that the gods themselves became dependent on the sacrifice, and, since the sacrifice depended upon the accuracy of the priestly class, the Brahmans became more powerful than any earthly king or even any god. Special honoraria always accompanied the sacrifices and were given to the priests in the form of cows, gold, clothes, a horse, or other valuable objects. The Vedic sacrifice presents itself in the form of a drama with the priests as actors, and with portions of the sacrifice set to music with interludes and climaxes.

The soma sacrifice (*agnishtoma*) is named in praise of Agni, perhaps because the last of the hymns used on that day is addressed to Agni. This sacrifice was performed each spring and involved certain preliminary operations, such as the consecration of the area and the participants. The soma was ceremoniously purchased, altars were built, and preparations for the sacrifice were made for three days. The sacrifice proper was accomplished in one day. It consisted of three pressings of the soma: morning, noon, and evening, of which the noon pressing was the climax of the sacrifice. In addition to vegetable and animal sacrifices, the pressing of the soma from the soma plant, and the drinking of it by the officiant, the noon pressing was also the time when the honoraria were distributed. The sacrificer might give up to one thousand cows or even all of his wealth—sometimes even his daughter who might marry one of the priests. The worshipers, having drunk the invigorating soma, saw visions of the gods and experienced sensations of power. They even identified themselves with the gods.

Among the Vedic rituals, most impressive was the horse sacrifice (*ashvamedha*). It was a demonstration of triumph indulged in by a king, thereby manifesting his royal authority. Although the sacrifice itself lasted for three days, the preparatory ceremonies extended for a year or even two. After preparatory oblations, a prize horse was left to run at large for a year while further preparatory activities took place. During this time the king and his army followed the horse, claiming all territory through which it passed. At the end of the year the horse returned, and, while there were numerous animal and soma sacrifices, the horse was finally sacrificed by strangulation. The horse sacrifice was, among other things, a popular festival to obtain prosperity for the kingdom and for the subjects.[10]

In addition to the public rites, there were domestic ones. For the most part, domestic rites consisted of a series of small sacrifices with simple ceremonies involving offerings of a vegetable nature,

---

10. Benjamin Walker, *Hindu World: An Encyclopedic Survey of Hinduism,* London, G. Allen, 1968, vol. I, p. 458.

and only rarely involving animals. It was the master of the house who normally performed these rites and it was his responsibility, along with his family and his pupil, to maintain the fire.

There were also sacred events (*samskaras*) which followed members of the three upper classes from conception to death. Each transitory phase of life was fraught with danger, which made it essential to perform special rites to counteract evil influences. The number of such threshold rites was at one time quite large.

> *Nearly every formal observance was referred to as a samskara and was attended by fire and water rituals, prayers and sacrifices, oblations, lustrations and other ceremonies, regulated by ancient taboos. Stress was laid on proper orientation, mantras, auspicious times and so on, many details of which were preserved in the later samskaras. The number of samskaras was gradually reduced from over 300 to about 40, then to 18 or even 10.*[11]

In terms of the life cycle, the first ceremony had to do with conception, and was followed, in the third month of pregnancy, with a ceremony to ensure the birth of a male offspring. Between the fourth and eighth month of the first pregnancy the husband would stand behind the wife, and, in the "parting of the hair" ceremony, would part the hair of the wife, starting at the front of the head and moving backward. Tying green fruit from the *udambara* twig around the wife's neck was intended to ensure fertility to her and exuberance and heroism in the child. Another ceremony was performed immediately after birth. The father would smear the child's tongue with a mixture of butter, curds, and honey taken from a golden spoon, and the navel cord was cut. Other rites were intended to endow the child with wealth and intelligence. Ten days after birth came the naming ceremony, and usually in the third year (for the Brahman), fifth year (for the Kshatriya), or seventh year (for the Vaishya), the tangled hair was moistened and the rite of tonsure took place.

Of prime importance was the initiation rite (*upanayana*). According to class, this was to take place in the eighth (Brahman), eleventh (Kshatriya), or twelfth (Vaishya) year. While the three upper classes all had such a rite, it became much more significant for the Brahman. Prior to the initiation he was classless. In the *upanayana* rite, the young male was endowed with the sacred thread and was taught the famous "Gayatri" stanza from the *Rigveda*. A period of studentship was thus initiated, during which time the youth lived with his teacher and served him. In exchange for his instruction, the young man begged for food and brought fuel for the sacred fire. Not until he had gone through the *upanayana* rite was the boy permitted to study the Vedas. This ceremony, which involved the shaving of the head, bathing, and being clothed in a new garment, is still practiced today, although it is modified because of the availability of education in public schools. When the boy returned to the world after his period as a student, he participated in a rite of return, the main feature of which was a ceremonial bath.

---

11. Ibid., p. 315.

Upanayana rite as performed in Bombay in 1965. (Photo by Robert D. Baird.)

A series of ceremonies in honor of the male ancestors also formed an important part of Vedic ritual. Offerings were made to the *pretas,* spirits who had lately departed, and also to the *pitris,* who were distant and more mythical ancestors. The continuing homage to the dead from generation to generation depended on the continuation of the family line and emphasized the importance of male offspring.

When death occurred, the hair and nails of the person were cut off and the body was washed, annointed, and clothed in a new garment. It was placed on the funeral pyre and the wife of the deceased was made to accompany her husband's body on the pyre. During this period, the wife would arise and leave the pyre before the conflagration (*Rigveda* IX.18.8). The practice of *sati* (see p. 238), or the immolation of the widow with her husband, does not seem to have been practiced in Rigvedic times. After the burning of the corpse, the mourners bathe and offer libations of water. Certain Rigvedic verses indicate that the fire conducts the *pretas* to the company of the *pitris.* Later a ceremony was developed for this purpose and took place on the twelfth day after death, or at the end of a year from death. When the dead was added to the group of *pitris,* his great-grandfather was dropped, since the number of *pitris* honored always remained at three. Offerings to the *pitris* are made at regular monthly intervals.

Renunciation was not a popular ideal in the *Rigveda.* The hymns of the *Rigveda* include prayers for sons, wealth, or military victory. In the period of the *Rigveda* men were generally not dissatisfied with life as they experienced it. The ideal of four stages in life (*ashramas*) did not develop until the period of the Upanishads, when the path of renunciation became popular. Some of the earlier Upanishads stress the conflict between the family life and the idea of asceticism and renunciation of the world which came to be the means for religious realization. The later development of the doctrine of *ashramas* is an attempt to combine within one orthodoxy these two opposing positions, making place for the contemplative life and the secular life in one system. The division came to involve, successively, life as a student (*brahmacarin*) which began at the time of initiation, the life of the householder (*grihastha*), and the life of the recluse or forest dweller (*vanaprasthya*). There was added the fourth stage of the *atyashramin,* or "he who is beyond the *ashramas.*" Such persons were later called *sannyasins,* although the term is not used in the Vedic literature.

The religious convictions expressed in the designation of four *ashramas* were also revealed in the recognition of four broad social groups. As early as the purusha hymn of the *Rigveda* the division of society into classes was given religious sanction. In the Vedic period there were two main groups in society, the Aryas and the Dasyus or Dasas. The former were sacrificers and worshipers of the fire, were fair, and probably corresponded to the invaders. The Dasas were dark-skinned and were criticized because they worshiped the phallus. This, coupled with the fact that the term for class (*varna*) means color, indicates a certain class distinction on the basis of color. The *Rigveda* narrates how Indra killed the Dasyus and protected the Arya color, and how he trampled down the caves of the Dasa color (*Rigveda* III.34.9; II.12.4). In time the Aryas came to have Dasa wives or mistresses.

As early as the *Rigveda,* a threefold division existed among the Aryas. Although the terminology varies, these divisions correspond to the classes of the Brahman, Kshatriya, and Vaishya. They do not seem at this time to have developed into rigid castes (*jati*) with proscription against intermarriage and interdining. These three classes were somewhat occupationally determined along the lines of intellectual progress, military might, and cattle prosperity, and in that order of social status. These professions do not seem to have been hereditary although there must have been the natural tendency to follow in the path of one's father. These classes continued to be fluid in the periods of the Brahmanas and Upanishads. The view of later periods that the teaching and study of the Vedas was the exclusive privilege of the Brahmans was a Brahman point of view which was not universally held in the Vedic age. Some of the authors of the Vedic hymns were Kshatriyas, and in the Upanishads, heredity received more emphasis, but was not rigidly followed. There seems to have been intermarriage, particularly among the three Aryan classes, and occasionally between them and the Shudras, which was the name given to the Dasas. Interdining took place but there was a proscription against using food cooked by a Shudra for the sacrifice.

While there are exceptions in which women were held to have had the knowledge of Brahman,[12] in general women had a low social position, perhaps equivalent to that of the Shudra. A woman did not have inheritance rights, and there was no initiation (*upanayana*), for women did not study the sacred texts. Society was male-oriented and a male child was more important than a female one because of the necessity of carrying on the family line and continuing the religious ceremonies for one's ancestors.

DEVELOPMENT OF RELIGIOUS THOUGHT

By the end of the Rigvedic period there was a growing tendency to seek for some unifying principle in the *Rigveda*. This tendency is already present in the henotheistic tendencies of the *Rigveda*, but the last book contains hymns that move toward a theistic interpretation. The title *Prajapati* (Lord of Beings), which originally was a title for other deities, came to refer to a separate deity who was above all, and responsible for the creation and governing of the universe (*Rigveda* X.121). Similar characteristics are attributed to *Vishvakarman* (All Creator) (*Rigveda* X.82.3). This does not represent a monolithic development, but illustrates varied attempts to find an explanation of the universe. That these efforts were still far from unified is clearly indicated in one hymn which ends its speculation about the origins of the universe with an expression of profound uncertainty.

> *Then neither Being nor Not-being was,*
> *Nor atmosphere, nor firmament, nor what is beyond.*
> *What did it encompass? Where? In whose protection?*
> *What was water, the deep, unfathomable?*
>
> *Neither death nor immortality was there then,*
> *No sign of night or day.*
> *That One breathed, windless, by its own energy:*
> *Nought else existed then.*
>
> *In the beginning was darkness swathed in darkness;*
> *All this was but unmanifested water.*
> *Whatever was, that One, coming into being,*
> *Hidden by the Void,*
> *Was generated by the power of heat.*
>
> *In the beginning this (One) evolved,*
> *Became desire, first seed of mind,*
> *Wise seers, searching within their hearts,*
> *Found the bond of Being in Not-being.*

---

12. It is necessary to distinguish several words which look somewhat alike. In this text, *Brahma* (Brahmā) is the creator god, *Brahman* (Brahman) is the principle of Ultimate Reality so basic to Shankara and found in many earlier texts (i.e., Upanishads), *Brahman* (Brāhman) is the priestly class. When the diacritical marks are removed the last two (Ultimate Reality or priestly class) must be distinguished by context. There are also the *Brahmanas* (Brāhmaṇas) which are a body of vedic texts. In some books members of the priestly class are referred to as *Brahmins*.

Their cord was extended athwart:
Was there a below? Was there an above?
Casters of seed there were, and powers;
Beneath was energy, above was impulse.

Who knows truly? Who can here declare it?
Whence it was born, when is this emanation.
By the emanation of this the gods
   Only later (came to be),
Who then knows whence it has risen?

Whence this emanation hath arisen,
Whether (God) disposed it, or whether he did not—
Only he who is its overseer in the highest heaven knows,
(He only knows), or perhaps he does not know! [13]

Most of these more speculative hymns are found in the tenth book of the *Rigveda*, which is admittedly later than the rest. In one of these hymns the high place of sacrifice is assumed and the creation of the world is depicted in terms of a sacrifice of primal man (X.90). There is little to suggest that the doctrines of rebirth and karma were known at this time or that the later notions of Atman and Brahman were part of the religious views (see p. 189).

By the time of the Brahmanas, sacrifice became more important than the gods themselves who were frequently presented as the exemplary performers of the sacrificial rituals. It was commonly assumed that sacrifice was eternal like the Vedas. Not only was the world created by an original sacrifice, but the natural laws of the physical world were maintained by the proper enactment of sacrifices. Although it may not be possible to trace historical dependence, the concept of *rita* in the *Rigveda* and the absolute dependableness of the sacrifices in the Brahmanas paved the way for the development of the doctrine of karma, which assumed a dependable causal connection within the spiritual order.

The conception of Brahman, which in later Vedanta and in some strains of the Upanishads is the only Real, was earlier connected with sacrifices. Das Gupta (an Indian scholar) indicates that some of the earlier meanings of the term are food for the food offering, the chant of the sama singer, a magical formula or text, duly completed ceremonies, and simply "great." [14] By the time of the *Shatapatha Brahmana,* Brahman is declared to be the moving force behind everything.

There is a debate among scholars regarding the point of continuity or discontinuity between the Samhitas and the Brahmanas and Upanishads. Undoubtedly there is considerable religious difference. But the question of whether those responsible for the Upanishads rejected sacrifices in favor of meditation is unanswerable in those

---

13. *Rigveda* X.129. R. C. Zaehner, *Hindu Scriptures,* New York, Dutton, 1966, Everyman's Library, pp. 11–13.

14. Surendranath Das Gupta, *A History of Indian Philosophy,* London, Cambridge, 1963 (first published in 1922), vol. I, p. 20.

terms, since several attitudes exist in the Upanishads themselves. While the later Indian philosophical systems have committed themselves to a unified interpretation of the Upanishads, such unanimity did not exist in the upanishadic period, for religious speculation was still quite fluid. In some passages there is strong rejection of sacrificial methods, while in others there is an attempt to make the transition to meditative internalization less abrupt. The *Brihadaranyaka Upanishad* which was attached to the *Shatapatha Brahmana* proceeds by transforming the horse sacrifice, elaborately described in the *Shatapatha Brahmana,* into a meditational device. Hence it is implicitly admitted that it is either impossible or undesirable to perform the sacrifice itself, but that the same result can be assured by meditating on the correspondences between various portions of the horse and the various parts of the universe. Such a revaluation of this ancient sacrifice makes the transition easier than if the sacrifice were simply rejected. That many of the existing Upanishads were originally embedded as literary documents in the Brahmanas indicates that there was no sudden break but rather a gradual reinterpretation which took place while the sacrifices continued to exert their influence.

As interest moved from the sacrifice to the forms of meditation, an understanding of particular correspondences between the sacrifice and aspects of the human body or the universe considered as Brahman became indispensable. In the important Upanishads the search for this basic reality, Brahman, was intensified. One encounters sages who move from place to place in search of a competent teacher to instruct them in the nature of Brahman. While the *Rigveda* seemed to move in the direction of a supreme being outside of man or the universe as the explanation of the world, the upanishadic seers looked within man and found there a substance or essence of the universe (Brahman). But this point was not reached without considerable effort. Many visible objects such as the sun, or even the wind, were considered for this honor and found to be inadequate. The search continued for that which was unchangeable. Brahman was identified as *prana* (vital breath in man) and various passages labor to show that *prana* was superior to other physical organs and therefore that meditation on *prana* led to the best results.

Dissatisfaction with any identification of Brahman with the elements of the physical world led some to conclude that positive definitions of Brahman were impossible. By whatever means they tried to give form to the Ultimate Reality, they failed. Some therefore concluded that all positive attributions were erroneous and that only negative statements could be made. In the *Brihadaranyaka Upanishad* (IV.15.5) Yajnavalkya says that "He the atman is not this, not this (neti . . . neti). He is inconceivable, for he is not changed, untouched, for nothing changes him." In the *Katha Upanishad* (III.15) it is stated: "That which is inaudible, intangible, invisible, indestructible, which cannot be tasted, nor smelt, eternal, without beginning or end, greater than the great, the fixed. He who knows it is released from the jaws of death." The implication to be drawn from this line of thought in a later period was that ultimate realization is best explained by remaining silent.

In the *Rigveda* and somewhat in the Brahmanas the ideal aimed at is length of days on earth, and life in heaven in companionship with the gods. In the Brahmanas one begins to hear more about "re-death" (*punarmrityu*), which was feared because it would end that enjoyable life after death.[15] Hence means were sought to avoid this "re-death" by religious and magical means. In the early Upanishads, such a concern is absent, for life after death is not regarded as somehow different from the present earthly life. In the course of Indian history, this notion was transformed into the well-known belief in reincarnation or the transmigration of souls from one body to another. It was believed that a person lived a series of lives in the condition of man, an animal, or even as a *deva* (god) in one of the numerous heavens.

The condition of each succeeding rebirth was determined by the relative balance of good and bad deeds in previous existences. This points to an early belief in the doctrine of karma by which man's relation to morality (*dharma*) determines his destiny. "The two went away and deliberated. What they said was *karma* (action). What they praised was *karma*. Verily, one becomes good by good action, bad by bad action."[16] While such a belief could logically offer the reassurance that one's situation is never hopeless and that, being based on one's previous deeds one's predicament is surely just, in fact the opposite was not infrequently the case. Disease, suffering, and bondage to the continual course of migration was man's lot.

Continued existence in successive states of reincarnated life came to be thought of as an unfortunate entanglement in the endless wheel of time. The goal for which man longed was no longer reincarnation in a more blissful state of existence, but release from the entire web of endless births and rebirths.

He, however, who has no understanding,
Who is unmindful and ever impure,
Reaches not the goal,
But goes on to reincarnation (samsara).[17]

Although in the Upanishads man longed for release from *samsara*, it was recognized that release was not easy. It was only possible for a few and then only after considerable study and discipline. One did not treat the truth lightly, but only instructed those who were clearly worthy. Worthiness often implied the willingness to detach oneself from otherwise normal life patterns. Existence as a householder was both distracting and transitory.

Thus arose the ideal norm of the wandering monk (samnyasin, bhiksu, muni), *the homeless ascetic, living on alms, cut off from*

15. Franklin Edgerton, *The Beginnings of Indian Philosophy*, London, G. Allen, 1965, p. 29.
16. *Brihadaranyaka Upanishad* III.2.13. Robert Ernest Hume, *The Thirteen Principal Upanishads*, Madras, Oxford University Press, 1949, p. 110.
17. *Katha Upanishad* VI.7. Hume, op. cit., p. 352.

> family ties, possessions, and all worldly life. He stood outside of everything, even of caste; a member of any caste, or of none, might become a truth-seeking mendicant.[18]

Even ascetic practices (*tapas*) were sometimes utilized, although it would be left to the Jainas (see p. 153) to emphasize that as a primary method.

Nevertheless, liberation is the ideal in the Upanishads; emancipation or *moksha* is the state of infinity that is attained when one comes to know the identity of Atman and Brahman. The ceaseless course of transmigration is only for those who do not know their true nature. *Moksha* is the elimination of all duality. Hence it is not that *we know,* for such a statement sustains a distinction between the knower and the object known. Instead, we are pure knowledge itself. Such emancipation is not a new acquisition, nor the result of some action, but always exists as the truth of our nature. The meditative practices are only methods used by people in a state of ignorance whereby they uncover their true selves. Yet even this type of language, indeed all language, is inadequate, since it is structured in terms of subject and object. The state is therefore inexpressible.

We are all emancipated already, but just "as he who does not know the place of a hidden treasure fails to find it, though he passes over it constantly, so all these creatures fail to find the world of Brahman, though they daily (in deep sleep) enter into it; for by unreality are they turned aside" (*Chandogya Upanishad,* VIII.3.2). In this enlightened state all desire, hope, and fear are obliterated. The loss of individuality involves the loss of suffering and pain. Likewise, all works no longer have any effect. Such knowledge is a matter of immediate intuition and hence cannot be doubted—it is self-authenticating. And, this awareness eliminates rebirth which is merely part of the world of ignorance.

---

18. Edgerton, op. cit., p. 32.

RELIGION IN THE POST-VEDIC PERIOD

The sixth century B.C. was a time of religious change. Even in the Upanishads the emphasis on sacrifice was questioned either through outright rejection or through reinterpretation. In general the Upanishads represent the Brahmanical attempt at adjusting to the mounting criticism of the sacrificial system and the growing rigidity of the caste system.

The Brahmanical religious system was challenged by numerous sects which arose and lapsed, never to be heard from again. Teachers appeared, propounding doctrinal theories accompanied by certain methods for the realization of their ideal. Such men were often ascetics, or homeless wanderers who accumulated a group of followers bound together in a search for the Real. They wore the yellow robe of the ascetic and, in contrast with the earliest forest dweller who probably lived on wild fruit and roots, were dependent on the householders for their daily food.

These homeless ones were called various names such as *shramanas* (ascetics) or *bhikshus* (almsmen). The followers of the Buddha preferred the latter, while other groups chose other terms. Of all the teachers who accumulated groups of disciples, two have had lasting importance in India or throughout Asia. One was Gotama (Pali form of Sanskrit Gautama), who, as the Buddha, became an object of faith, or the teacher of the path to the elimination of suffering. After his doctrine and appeal died out in India, it continued to be the faith of millions throughout Southeast Asia, Tibet, China, and Japan. The other teacher was Mahavira, from whom the present Jain community received inspiration.

BUDDHA AND THE PALI TRADITION

Sometime in the sixth century B.C. within the present boundary of Nepal, an individual was born who was to have an influence throughout India, Asia, and, as of the twentieth century, throughout the world. Known commonly by his title Buddha ("Enlightened One"), Siddhattha Gotama would live, according to all traditions, a full life of eighty years. His dates are variously given, but can be taken as 563–483 B.C.

Not only is the date of the Buddha somewhat uncertain, but one's ability to write a historically reliable life of the Buddha, or to describe the original teachings of the Buddha himself, is hampered by the nature of the available documents. The Buddha wrote nothing himself, and the various texts which have come to us all date a few hundred years after the death of the Buddha and are the result of the work of certain schools or sects and hence bear their doctrinal marks.

The texts themselves indicate that shortly after the death of the Buddha there existed numerous schools which differed on matters of practice and doctrine. While the standard number is eighteen, we know of some thirty-five sects by name alone. The Pali Canon, which is the scriptural corpus of the so-called Theravada Buddhists of Ceylon and Southeast Asia, is the preserved canon of one of these schools.

In order to understand better what these documents can reveal and how far back toward the Buddha they can take us, we must indicate the contents of the Pali Canon and other important works which are acceptable within this tradition. The following canon was preserved in Pali, a language akin to Sanskrit. It is held sacred even today by that community called Hinayana, or "little vehicle," by their Mahayana competitors, or self-named Theravada, or the "way of the elders." This canon, called the *Tipitaka* (Sanskrit *Tripitaka*), or "three baskets," contains the following:

A. *Vinaya-Pitaka*. A basket of discipline which contains the rules for the monastic order, the Sangha.
   1. *Sutta-vibhanga,* or "principles" within which is the *Patimokkha* (Sanskrit *Pratimoksha*), some 252 rules which are recited at fortnightly confessions by the monks.
   2. *Mahavagga* (major division) contains rules for entry into order, and regulations for the behavior of the monks. It also enumerates rules for the rainy season and gives a short account of the Buddha's life.
   3. *Cullavagga* (minor division) includes further information about life in the Sangha, reasons for exclusion, manner of ordination for nuns, and accounts of the first two councils.
B. *Sutta-Pitaka* (Sanskrit *sutra*). The word *sutta* means thread, and while it refers to aphoristic statements in the Brahmanical sutras, it here consists of five collections (*nikayas*) of dialogues supposed to have been uttered by the Buddha and arranged according to length.
   1. *Digha-nikaya* contains thirty-four "long *suttas*" including the

important *Mahaparinibbanasutta* which gives account of the death of the Buddha.
2. *Majjhima-nikaya* includes 152 *suttas* of "medium length" which tell of the Buddha's austerities, enlightenment, and early teachings.
3. *Samyutta-nikaya* (kindred sayings) includes 2889 *suttas* in fifty-six groups among which are the Deer Park Sermon and discourses on the chain of causation and other doctrinal matters. These are arranged in a further fivefold classification.
4. *Anguttara-nikaya* (gradual sayings) includes 2308 *suttas* in eleven sections which are arranged according to number from discourses dealing with one thing up to lists of eleven things.
5. *Khuddaka-nikaya* (minor discourses) are fifteen books of short discourses among which are the *Jataka*, or stories of the previous births of the Buddha, and the *Dhammapada*, the "Path of Truth."

C. *Abhidhamma-Pitaka* includes seven books which deal with further doctrinal refinements of a rather technical nature. This includes the *Kathavatthu* (points of controversy) in which Theravada doctrine is expounded over against other "false" views.

Later texts highly honored in the Southern School are the *Milindapanha* ("Questions of King Milinda," c. A.D. 100), in which King Menander has his questions satisfactorily answered by the monk Nagasena and is finally converted; the *Dipavamsa* (c. fourth century A.D.), a history of the island (Ceylon); the *Mahavamsa* (c. fifth century), or great chronicle of Ceylon; and the *Visuddhimagga* ("The Path of Purity"), an exposition of the Buddha's doctrine by Buddhaghosha in the fourth century A.D.

In addition to the Pali texts, there are numerous Sanskrit texts which are more relevant for understanding Mahayana interpretations of the Buddha's doctrine. The Pali Canon is generally dated earlier than the Sanskrit manuscripts. Even the Pali Canon, however, was not reduced to written form until some time after the Buddha. At the time of King Ashoka (274–236 B.C.) it seems that the *Abhidhamma* was not yet committed to writing, since only the *Dhamma* (i.e., *Sutta-Pitaka*) and the *Vinaya* are mentioned. It also seems that the *Vinaya* developed gradually, perhaps the *Patimokkha* being composed within fifty years of the Buddha. The sections which deal with the Buddha's life could not have been written for one to two hundred years after the time of the Buddha. Further, the canon represents only one school of thought. The best procedure one can follow is to describe the tradition and use it to reach the beliefs and practices of the early followers of the Buddha. While such followers may be accurately describing the life and teachings of the Buddha, there is little chance at present to verify this historically. By examination of layers of tradition within the Pali Canon, and by comparisons with other canons, one can project partial traditions into the oral period prior to the dated manuscripts, but this can only point to a possible (not even probable) account of the life and teachings of the Buddha.

It is the tradition of the Theravada community that the entire *Tipitaka* was recited at the First Council, which reportedly took place at Rajagaha right after the death of the Buddha, and that the entire *Tipitaka* was transmitted by memory until it was written down early in the sixth century after the Buddha (c. 25 B.C.) in Ceylon.[1] It appears, however, that certain portions were written down prior to that time. Nevertheless, if one is to accept the *Tipitaka* as straightforward accounts of the life and teachings of the Buddha, one must accept the reliability of the oral tradition. There is considerable evidence that the cult and imagination of the devotees was at work in the formulation of the canonical materials.[2]

It is fruitless to try to empty the accounts of the Buddha of the miraculous or unusual. Even in the relatively early *Mahaparinibbanasutta* the miraculous occurs, and in the earliest texts the devotion of the Buddha's followers has left its mark on the accounts of his life. While the miraculous element increases in time, even the Theravada community presents the Buddha in a remarkable light.

TRADITION ON THE LIFE OF THE BUDDHA

As seen in the *Tipitaka,* the life of the Buddha has an end, but no appropriate beginning. Since the very term "Buddha" means "enlightened one," there can be many Buddhas but only one Siddhattha Gotama. It was eons ago, through the existence of an ascetic named Sumedha and in the presence of a previous Buddha Dipankara, that the Buddha who now concerns us took the vows of a Bodhisattva (a Buddha to be) and thereby initiated the discipline that would eventually lead him to Buddhahood. In the Tushita heaven from which he was reborn as Shakyamuni, he himself determined the time and place of his birth. It was in the Shakya clan and into the family of the king that he was born. In a dream, King Shuddhodhana's first wife, Maya, received Gotama into her body in the form of a white elephant (symbol of perfect wisdom and royal power). He was born in Lumbini in the foothills of the Himalayas, within the present boundary of Nepal.

When the child was born, the trees of Lumbini Park burst into bloom. Gods and men worshiped him with scented garlands. After birth the child was taken to the palace where his horoscope was told. It was determined that he would become either a "universal monarch," or a *tathagata* (one who has thus come) or *arhat* (one who is worthy to be honored). Yashodhara, his future wife, thousands of other personages of noble and servant birth, and even Kanthaka, the Bodhisattva's future steed, were born at the same time as the Buddha.

---

1. Bhikkhu J. Kashyap, "Origin and Expansion of Buddhism," in Kenneth W. Morgan, ed., *The Path of the Buddha,* New York, Ronald, 1956, p. 38.
2. Sukumar Dutt, *The Buddha and Five After-Centuries,* London, Luzac & Company Limited, 1957.

Gotama was cared for by thirty-two nurses and was provided with three palaces (one each for the hot, cool, and rainy seasons), and four pleasure parks at each of the cardinal points at the edge of the city. Every conceivable gratification was provided, including fragrant flowers, luxurious couches, women, dancing, singing, and instrumental and orchestral music. Numerous guards were provided for his protection.

One might well wonder why the young prince, surrounded by luxury and married to a lovely wife who had just given birth to his son Rahula (bond), would leave this for the life of a monk. The religious community explained this with the legend of the four passing sights through which Gotama, who had been shielded from all unpleasantness throughout his youth, saw successively an old man wrinkled, toothless, and bent over a stick; a diseased man with fever; and a corpse wrapped in cloth being carried in procession to the funeral pyre. Finally he saw a monk, serenely begging with bowl in hand. It was this conjunction of experiences which caused Gotama to search for the means whereby a man could maintain serenity in face of the greatest evils of existence—old age, sickness, and death.

Gotama began his search with what is called in the tradition the great renunciation. As the household slept, he took a final look at his sleeping wife and child and left for the courtyard where his groom and horse were waiting. A large retinue of gods and men assisted him, even to keeping the hoofs of Kanthaka from pounding the ground. They assisted him until he stopped at daybreak. Then he dismissed the numerous gods, tore off his princely garments which he exchanged for the clothes of a huntsman, and cut off his hair with a sword. No longer the prince, he was now a wandering seeker after enlightenment, one in a long tradition extending before and after him in India to the present day.

Transformed thus from a layman to a mendicant, the Buddha put aside his resplendent jewelry, including the heavy earrings which left his ears distended because of their heavy weight. This deformity was captured by later sculpture and interpreted by the Chinese and Tibetans as a sign of wisdom. Although he is reported to have cut his hair, artists continued to present the Buddha with his hair tightly curled, one of the thirty-two traditional marks of a great man. His dismissal of the gods is also significant for the Theravada community, because they believed that salvation could be achieved only by personal effort without the help of men or gods.

Gotama studied under Alara Kalama, but the lessons were not to his taste. The biographers present the Buddha as omniscient; he knew all the answers before they were given to him. Having practiced yoga, he tried ascetic austerities. Even with his foreknowledge that this was not the way, he engaged in such austerities in order to lead blind humanity through the authority of experience. His meditational practices and dietary abstentions were so severe that his body wasted away until it was unable to bear his spirit.

Like dried canes now became my arms and legs, withered through this extremely scanty diet; like the foot of a camel be-

came my buttock; like a string of beads became my spinal column with the vertebrae protruding. Just as the roof-beams of an old house sharply protrude, so protruded my ribs; just as in a deep well the little water-stars far beneath are scarcely seen, so now in my eye-balls the sunken pupils were hardly seen; just as a gourd freshly cut becomes empty and withered in the hot sun, so now became the skin of my head empty and withered. When I wished to touch my belly, I reached to the back of my spine, and when I wished to touch my spine, I again reached to the belly,—thus near had come my belly to my spinal column. To reinforce this body, I chafed the limbs with the hand and the badly rooted hair fell from the skin. So strangely was the pure color of my skin affected by the scanty diet that some said, "The ascetic Gotama is black," while others said, "The ascetic Gotama is yellow." Then this thought came to me: This is the uttermost; beyond this one cannot go.[3]

In addition to limiting his diet, he practiced complete immobility, seeking neither shade nor sunshine, nor shelter from wind or rain. He did not move as much as a finger to protect himself from horse-flies, mosquitos, or reptiles. Realizing that his body and mind were impoverished, he ceased his fast in an effort to restore his strength, an act which resulted in the break with the five ascetics who had thus far accompanied him and who now thought he was going back on his intentions. These five would later hear his first sermon near Benares and become his disciples.

Taking some strands of kusha grass for a seat, he sat facing the west and resolved: "Upon this seat, though my body dry up and my skin, my bones and my flesh be dissolved—without having reached enlightenment, no matter how long and difficult to reach, I shall not stir from this seat." A. Foucher comments:

He did not have to go to such lengths. His studies, quickly ended, took a year; his fruitless austerities cost him six years; his complete success was to come in twenty-four hours. The following day the rising sun would shine, not upon one ascetic among others, but upon a unique Being without equal anywhere in the world; for it is one of the dogmas of Buddhism that in a given time and universe there can exist only one Buddha.[4]

His later followers described the struggle that was his that night in terms of a conflict between himself and Mara, the tempter. A theme for the artist, Mara's assault launched an army of repulsive monsters, ghosts, devils, and other hideous figures. The attack was, of course, brushed aside by the Buddha. He reached his right hand downward toward the earth in the earthwitnessing *mudra* (symbolic position of the hands). The response of earth to his victory is contained in the words: "It is true, O great man, it is true; it is as you say and I am the eyewitness." At the sight of this miraculous appa-

---

3. Sukumar Dutt, op. cit., p. 39.
4. A. Foucher, *The Life of the Buddha, According to the Ancient Texts and Monuments of India,* Middletown, Conn., Wesleyan University Press, 1963, abridged translation by Simone Brangier Boas., p. 107.

rition, Mara's army scattered in flight. Next ensued the three watches of the night, a process in which Gotama came to know the twelvefold chain of causation and its meaning (see p. 145).

Gotama achieved enlightenment as dawn broke. Mara tempted the Buddha to go immediately into *Parinibbana* (see p. 149), but he resisted the temptation. His struggle with Mara symbolizes the conflict between existence in the world and the Nibbanic experience which takes one out of the world. A similar struggle was experienced by the monastic order that produced the Pali Canon.

The Buddha's hesitation to preach the *Dhamma,* or truth, to others was based upon the fact that it was difficult to understand and that it took moral effort beyond the grasp of the average man. However, Gotama's concern for humanity overcame the more selfish motive, which suggested that he simply enter *Parinibbana.*

Gotama traveled to what is now Sarnath, four miles north of Benares and about 130 miles west of Gaya, the spot of his enlightenment. The five ascetics who had left him previously saw him approaching from a distance and vowed not to rise or offer him a seat, food, or respect. In spite of their resolve, the manner of his personal presence caused them to do precisely what they vowed not to do. After his sermon, which is referred to as the turning of the wheel of the *Dhamma,* they became his first converts. This encounter shows that Gotama was not immediately successful, since he had already traveled some 130 miles from Gaya and had encountered a number of persons along the way. His Deer Park Sermon contained the four noble truths and the noble eightfold path. The following is the content in skeletal form.

1. Life is suffering (*dukkha*).
2. The cause of this suffering is grasping or desire (*tanha*).
3. Suffering can be eliminated when desire is extinguished.
4. Desire can be eliminated through the eightfold path, consisting of
    a. Right understanding;
    b. Right aspiration;
    c. Right speech;
    d. Right conduct;
    e. Right vocation;
    f. Right effort;
    g. Right mindfulness;
    h. Right concentration.

After considerable success at winning converts, some seven years after enlightenment he returned to his native city where he conferred ordination on his son Rahula, his half-brother Nanda, and numerous other candidates. His death was the result of a meal of dried boar's flesh (or perhaps some kind of roots) which, according to tradition, resulted in a frequently recurring case of dysentery. Of course, a Buddha cannot simply die. During the night he went through a series of mystical states of trance prior to entering *Parinibbana* and complete bliss.

DOCTRINE ACCORDING TO THE PALI TRADITION

While the Pali tradition was only one of several stemming from the Buddha, it exerted considerable influence and still dominates Southeast Asia. The Theravada community attributes this system of thought to the Buddha, and it is for that reason that they profess it as their own.

The Pali Canon consistently portrays the Buddha as uninterested in purely metaphysical or philosophical questions. He is portrayed as an intensely practical person whose ultimate concern is the alleviation of suffering and rebirth. He who will not tend to the problem of suffering until he has had his metaphysical questions adequately answered is like a man who has been wounded by a poisoned arrow and refuses to allow its removal until he knows what kind of arrow it is, the caste, height, name, color, and other details about the one who shot it, and the type of bow and bowstring that was used. In this futile concern with irrelevant questions, he dies.

All of the theoretical analysis which follows should be interpreted in the light of this dominant emphasis on the practical function of truth. The acquisition of right views about ourselves and the world has as its purpose the elimination of suffering through the experiential realization of the truth of these views.

Three Marks (Lakkhana) of Existence

As one surveys man and the world, there are three characteristics of all existence.[5] This is set forth in the *Anguttara-Nikaya* III.134 as follows:

> *Whether Buddhas arise, O priests, or whether Buddhas do not arise, it remains a fact, and the fixed and necessary constitution of being that (1) All its constituents are transitory. (2) All its constituents are misery. (3) All its elements are lacking in an Ego. This fact a Buddha discovers and masters, and when he has discovered and mastered it, he announces, teaches, publishes, proclaims, discloses, minutely explains, and makes it clear, that all the constituents of being are transitory, are misery, and are lacking in an Ego.*

One mark of all existence, then, is *anicca* (Sanskrit *anitya*), or impermanence. Everything, according to the *Tipitaka*, is transitory. In the Upanishads the search was for Being, and Brahman or Atman was considered the only thing that abides. The emphasis of the *Tipitaka* is on the phenomenal world and its constant flux.

> *We are deceived if we allow ourselves to believe that there is ever a pause in the flow of becoming, a resting place where positive existence is attained for even the briefest duration of time. It is only by shutting our eyes to the succession of events that we come to speak of things rather than of processes. The quickness or slowness of the process does not affect the generalization.*[6]

---

5. Edward Conze, *Buddhist Thought in India,* London, G. Allen, 1962, pp. 34 ff.
6. Ananda Coomaraswany, *Buddha and the Gospel of Buddhism,* New York, Harper & Row, 1964, first published in 1916, p. 95.

A second mark of all existence is *anatta* (Sanskrit *anatman*). It is not unrelated to the doctrine of impermanence, for if impermanence is the rule, then it follows that there can be no permanent self or Atman. One of the false notions under which we labor is that there is an abiding "I." Instead of thinking of the self as a distinct and continuing entity, we are instructed that the empirical self is compounded and temporary. It is at any moment merely the conjunction of five *khandhas* (Sanskrit *skhandhas*), or groups which are continually restructured according to the law of *kamma*. There is one physical *khandha* and four of a mental nature:

1. *Rupa* (form) is the material or physical aspect of the empirical being. *Rupa* is capable of refinements, and in higher beings is so subtle that it approaches the immaterial.

2. *Vedana* (sensations) are the result of the contact of senses with the external world. This includes both physical and psychical sensibilities and they can be classified as pleasant, unpleasant, or neutral.

3. *Sanna* (Sanskrit *sanjna*) is the power which produces conceptions of physical objects within the human psyche. There are six, which correspond to the six sense organs (five ordinary sense organs plus the *citta*, or mind, which receives impressions from the other senses).

4. *Sankara* (Sanskrit *samskara*), or impulses, refer to all active dispositions, tendencies, impulses, volitions, strivings, emotions whether conscious or repressed.

5. *Vinnana* (Sanskrit *vijnana*) or consciousness is the most important since the others depend on it. This is the psychic power of discrimination and hence is more akin to intelligence than mere consciousness.

All the facts of experience involving ourselves or objects in relation to us can be understood in terms of the *khandhas*. There is no self existing independently of the *khandhas*. In the *Milindapanha*, Nagasena illustrates this doctrine by indicating that the term "chariot" is merely a convention for referring to the pole, axle, wheels, chariot body, and banner staff in a certain conjunction. Neither one of these components is the chariot, nor is the chariot something else outside of them. Likewise, the use of the term "self" is only a convention and has no more reality than the chariot conceived as an entity distinct from its physical parts.

A third mark of existence is *dukkha* (suffering). Life is characterized by suffering or "ill," that is, it is out of joint. One can begin with the rather obvious point that sickness, old age, death, and separation from what one loves are causes of suffering. But the point of this doctrine is that all of life is suffering. Those who have come to a high level of realization through meditation will sense this more clearly than others. Existence is suffering because we cling to things which are transitory and confuse the impermanent *khandhas* with a permanent self which is, as we have learned, nonexistent. The full realization of this characteristic of existence is reserved for the Arhat. Because only holy men are sure of it, it is sometimes called a "holy truth."

> *The Arhat is so much more sensitive than we are, makes so much greater demands than we do. No one minds feeling an eye-lash on the palm of his hand, but everyone is irritated when it drops into his eye; just so the ordinary person is insensitive to the ills of the conditioned, whereas they torment the sage. Saints suffer more intensely in the highest heaven than fools in the most terrible hells.*[7]

Dependent Origination (Paticcasamuppada)

The doctrine of *paticcasamuppada* (Sanskrit *pratityasamutpada*), or dependent origination, was thought basic to the doctrine of the Buddha by the Theravada community. It is also called the wheel of causation, or the doctrine of causation, and is mentioned either in terms of the complete twelve causes (*nidanas*) or in partial form in no less than ninety-six suttas. The importance of the twelve causes is that they are an expansion of the last two noble truths of the Buddha's Deer Park Sermon—namely the cause of suffering and the method for the elimination of suffering. The causes are not always listed as twelve, but the following came to be accepted as standard.

1. Ignorance (*avijja*) is the first link and the primary root of all evil and suffering. It is ignorance of the true doctrine as found in the four noble truths and the three marks of existence that cause all of man's sorrow and suffering.

2. Volitional activities (*sankara*) include all moral and immoral actions of body, mind, and speech. Both moral and immoral actions are included, for all such distinctions are part of our state of ignorance which true insight eliminates. Ignorance is the cause of these activities.

3. Consciousness (*vinnana*) is consciousness which is linked with another existence, and this is caused by the moral and immoral activities of a being and hence leads to rebirth.

4. Name and form, or mind and matter (*nama-rupa*), are the kamma-determined results of mental and physical phenomena, and are the result of relinking consciousness.

5. Sense fields (*salayatana*) refer to the six senses together with their objects. These sense fields of operation arise as the result of the existence of mind and matter.

6. Contact (*phassa*) refers to the sensory and mental impressions which result from the contact between the senses and objects of sense.

7. Feeling (*vedana*) comes through sensory and mental impressions, and can be classified as favorable, unfavorable, or neutral.

8. Craving or desire (*tanha*) arises as the result of pleasant sounds, tastes, smells, sights, objects of touch, or thought.

9. Attachment (*upadana*) is the result of grasping or craving. The four types of attachment are to sensuality, to false views, to wrong rites and ceremonies, and to self-deception.

10. Becoming (*bhava*) is the process which stems from attachment and results in another rebirth.

---

7. Edward Conze, op. cit., p. 36.

11. Rebirth (*jati*) is the result of the process of becoming which stems from attachment.

12. Old age and death (*jaramarana*) result from the fact of being born, for without rebirth there would be no old age, sickness, or death.

Not infrequently the Buddha indicates that the list can be reversed, a fact that emphasizes its intensely practical purpose: without rebirth there would be no death, without becoming there would be no rebirth, and so on until without ignorance there would be no moral or immoral activities.

The doctrine of the twelve causes is an attempt to show that there is no first cause, that everything, including our suffering and rebirth, is dependent on something else, which, if eliminated, will also eliminate the problem. Ignorance is more of a logical starting point than a chronological one. If ignorance were eliminated, so would all suffering and rebirth be eliminated.

> *For the Blessed One in his discourses on the round of rebirth was accustomed to choose from Dependent Origination two of the factors of being as his starting points: either, on the one hand, ignorance, as when he says, "As I have told you, O priests, the first beginning of ignorance cannot be discerned, nor can one say, 'Before a given point of time there was no ignorance, it came into being afterwards.' Nevertheless, O priests, it can be discerned that ignorance possesses a definite independence": or, on the other hand, desire for existence, as when he says, "As I have told you, O priests, the first beginning of desire for existence cannot be discerned, nor can one say, 'Before a given point of time there was no desire for existence, it came into being afterwards.' Nevertheless, O priests, it can be discerned that desire for existence possesses a definite dependence."* [8]

Kamma and Rebirth

Kamma (Sanskrit *karma*) is what governs the changing processes of the phenomenal world, particularly the continuously regrouping *khandhas*. *Kamma* refers to a deed, but also to its result. According to the *Samyutta-Nikaya*, the result is inevitable.

> *According to the seed that's sown,*
>   *So is the fruit ye reap therefrom.*
> *Doer of good will gather good,*
>   *Doer of evil, evil reaps.*
> *Sown is the seed, and thou shalt taste*
>   *The fruit therof.*

Kamma operates in an impersonal and impartial manner, characterized by neither love nor hate. Not only is *kamma* operative in the moral realm in that one becomes what he does, but there is a connection between the moral and the physical so that good or evil

---

8. Quoted in Henry Clarke Warren, *Buddhism in Translations*, New York, Atheneum Publishers, 1963, reprint, p. 171.

deeds have a certain physical effect as well. This is portrayed in the *Milindapanha*.

> *Why is it Nagasena, that all men are not alike, but some are short-lived, some are long-lived, some sickly and some healthy, some ugly and some beautiful, some without influence and some of great power, some poor and some wealthy, some lowborn and some highborn, some stupid and some wise?* [9]

Nagasena replied that just as different vegetables are produced by different seeds,

> *Just so . . . are differences you have mentioned among men to be explained. For it has been said by the Blessed One: Beings, O Brahmin, have each their own karma, are inheritors of karma, belong to the tribe of their karma, are relatives by karma, have each their own karma as their own protecting overlord. It is karma that divides into high and low and the like divisions.* [10]

The abode of one's birth is determined by one's *kamma* as well. This can best be illustrated with a quote from the *Majjhima-Nikaya* I.389.

> *(1) If a man produces injurious aggregations of body, speech, and mind, he is reborn in an injurious world. There he is affected by injurious impressions, and feels injurious feelings extremely painful, such as do those who are beings in Hell. Thus the rebirth of a creature is due to the creature. It is through what he does that he is reborn. Thus beings are the heirs of their karma.*
>
> *(2) If a man produces a non-injurious aggregation of body, speech, and mind, he is reborn in a non-injurious world. There he is affected by non-injurious impressions, and feels non-injurious feelings extremely pleasant, such as do the wholly-bright gods.*
>
> *(3) If a man produces an injurious and non-injurious aggregation of body, speech, and mind, he is reborn in a world both injurious and non-injurious. He is affected by both kinds of impressions and feelings, such as human beings, some gods, and some beings in states of punishment.*
>
> *(4) When the intention is directed to the abandonment of black karma with black ripening, or white karma with white ripening, and of black-white karma with black-white ripening, this is called neither black nor white, producing neither black nor white karma. It tends to the destruction of karma.* [11]

One can be born in various heavens and hells as well as in human form, and one's *kamma* in a previous existence determines the locus of the birth. Not all *kamma* produces its effect in the same life in which the deed is done. Some ripens in the same life, some

---

9. T. W. Rhys Davids, trans., *The Questions of King Milinda*, New York, Dover, 1963 (first pub. as vol. XXXV of S. B. E.), vol. I, p. 100.

10. Ibid., p. 101.

11. Quoted in Edward J. Thomas, *The History of Buddhist Thought*, London, Routledge, 1933, pp. 112–113.

in the next, and some in successive births. Furthermore, some *kamma* is more weighty and takes precedence over other *kamma*. Examples of this are matricide, patricide, murder of an Arhat, wounding a Buddha, or causing a schism in the Sangha.

What one does at the moment of death determines the future birth, since one cannot at that time act out of character but must act in terms of the habitual *kamma* which has been developing a certain character throughout life. While the Buddha's doctrine of *kamma* has at times led to fatalism, it can also be an incentive for the future, knowing that what one will be is presently being determined by acts.

The Pali tradition also affirmed belief in rebirth, although it rejected the concept of transmigration because of its rejection of permanence. The latter seemed to imply that there was something that transmigrates. The Buddha, having rejected the concept of Atman held by the Upanishadic seers, posed a problem that was dealt with by such later thinkers as the author of the *Milindapanha*. If there is nothing permanent, and if there is no permanent entity which is reborn, how can one still hold to the doctrine of rebirth? The *Milindapanha* uses analogies to explain that just as there is a causal connection within a life as the *khandhas* continuously regroup from one moment to another, so there is a causal connection from one life to the next. Just as one is neither identically the same person from one moment to another, nor for that matter an entirely different one, but is at any moment whatever the kammic force makes him be, so is the same principle applied to the transition from one life to another.

> Said the king: "Bhante Nāgasena, does rebirth take place without anything transmigrating (passing over)?"
>
> "Yes, your majesty. Rebirth takes place without anything transmigrating."
>
> "How, bhante Nāgasena, does rebirth take place without anything transmigrating? Give an illustration."
>
> "Suppose, your majesty, a man were to light a light from another light; pray, would the one light have passed over (transmigrated) to the other light?"
>
> "Nay, verily, bhante."
>
> "In exactly the same way, your majesty, does rebirth take place without anything transmigrating."
>
> "Give another illustration."
>
> "Do you remember, your majesty, having learnt, when you were a boy, some verse or other from your professor of poetry?"
>
> "Yes, bhante."
>
> "Pray, your majesty, did the verse pass over (transmigrate) to you from your teacher?"
>
> "Nay, verily, bhante."
>
> "In exactly the same way, your majesty, does rebirth take place without anything transmigrating."
>
> "You are an able man, bhante Nāgasena."
>
> (*Milindapanha* LXXI.16)

It is the view of the Pali Canon that through meditation one can develop a memory of one's past lives. That is what the Buddha himself came to see when he achieved enlightenment. The Buddha saw first one life, then two, and so on up to a hundred thousand and more. The *Jataka* tales refer to these previous births.

The Buddha is depicted as rejecting the concept of caste, the authority of the Vedas, and the efficacy of the sacrifices. However, although the Buddha's doctrine of *anatta* was in tension with the popular beliefs in *kamma* and the rebirth of the soul, they were evidently so much a part of the Indian thought patterns at that time that the Buddha maneuvered and transformed part of them rather than overtly rejecting them as a whole. His own solution was to reject the notion of the transmigration of a substantial soul, but to retain the belief in *kamma* and rebirth in the ways indicated above. This fact illustrates how commonly held the doctrines of *kamma*, rebirth, and transmigration of the soul must have been at that time.

Nibbana

The suffering that is inherent in existence is only eliminated when one achieves the state of *Nibbana* (Sanskrit *Nirvana*).[12] *Nibbana* cannot be accurately described since it transcends all the distinctions which are inherent in language. *Nibbana* means the absence of craving and involves the extinction of hatred, lust, or ignorance. In *Nibbana* there is no birth, old age, sickness, death, or defilement. It is a state utterly incomparable with any state in phenomenal existence. It is for this reason that most statements about *Nibbana* are negative ones. This is not to be taken to imply that *Nibbana* is negative or annihilating. The *Tipitaka* refers to it as Highest Refuge, Safety, Unique, Absolute Purity, Supramundane, Security, Emancipation, Peace. The Sanskrit term *Nirvana* means "the blowing out." But this is not annihilation or the blowing out of all existence, but the blowing out of suffering and desire.

Nibbana is achievable in this life. It is a condition in which passion is destroyed, but the *khandhas* remain. The person in this state of realization while living is an Arhat, the ideal of the Pali Canon. When an Arhat dies he reaches the state of *Parinibbana,* a state in which the *khandhas* do not remain. In the *Suttas* the Buddha is sometimes asked whether or not the Buddha or an Arhat exists after death. In such cases the Buddha held that such speculative questions are unprofitable in contributing to the alleviation of suffering. Furthermore, as the question is framed, it is impossible to answer. It is like asking where the fire goes when it goes out.

Nibbana is called the "Uncompounded Element" in the *Abhidhamma,* and in the *Milindapanha* it is one of two things that are causeless (the other being space).

While the *Tipitaka* makes such attainment the goal, and the Arhat the one who has so realized it, there is also the idea that the struggle to realize *Nibbana* is long and extends over several births. This

---

12. Since this is a discussion of the Pali tradition, we are using the Pali term *Nibbana* instead of the Sanskrit *Nirvana.*

route is described as breaking the ten fetters.[13] Special names were affixed to those who had made progress in breaking the fetters and who were therefore closer to *Nibbana* by degrees. The *Sotapanno* is one who has entered the stream and is on his way to *Nibbana,* having broken the first three fetters. He will be reborn on earth or in heaven not more than seven times before he achieves *Nibbana.* The *Sakadagamin* is the once returner who will be born once more in this world and then attain *Nibbana.* He has broken the first three fetters, and has reduced four and five (lust and anger) to a minimum. The *Anagamin* is one who will not return, having freed himself from the first five fetters. He will not be reborn in this world or in a sensuous heaven, but will be reborn in a Brahma world only once. Finally, the *Arhat* has eliminated all evil and impurity, has attained *Nibbana,* and will not be reborn.

LIFE IN THE SANGHA

It was common for those seeking wisdom and release to group themselves around a teacher. Numerous disciples followed the Buddha, and in his own lifetime the beginnings of the *Sangha,* or Order, appeared. At first the *bhikkhus* appear to have spent nine months of the year as wanderers, living in a community only during the rainy season. After Buddha's death there was no central authority to bind together the various communities that existed in scattered places. Sites first used as rain retreats were donated by lay followers as places for monastic dwelling.

The early laws of the Sangha were probably the *Patimokkha,* recited at the fortnightly confessions of the *Uposatha* service. According to the *Tipitaka,* the Buddha determined all the laws of the *Vinaya* during his lifetime, but it is more likely that some of the minor rules in the *Patimokkha* were framed and added in the course of time. The three refuges, I take refuge in the Buddha, the Dhamma, and the Sangha, seem to have originated after the Buddha's death, since it is improbable that anyone would have thought of taking refuge in the Sangha so long as the Buddha was living. The *Vinaya* that we have is from the school responsible for the Pali Canon, but there are many other versions belonging to different schools. Since there was no central authority, even the decisions supposed to have been made at the First Council at Rajagaha could not command universal acceptance—each community accepted as much or as little as it chose.

Actually, the Sangha was a body of *bhikkhus* who formed a common life free from the cares of food and clothing so that they could concentrate on Arhatship.

Two ceremonies were part of the admission. The preparatory ordination (*Pabbajja,* or outgoing) represented going forth from the world and was symbolized when the novice had his head shaven, was robed in yellow, and recited the three refuges and the ten pre-

---

13. These are: belief in the existence of the self, doubt, trust in ceremonies of good works, lust, anger, desire for rebirth in worlds of form, desire for rebirth in formless worlds, pride, self-righteousness, ignorance.

Ajanta caves. Inhabited by Buddhist monks from the second century B.C. to the seventh century A.D. (Photo by Robert D. Baird.)

cepts.[14] Full membership in the circle of the *bhikkhus* came with the *Upasampada* (the arrival). For this the candidate had to be at least twenty years old, and was introduced to the chapter by a learned and competent monk who asked those in favor of his admission to signify such by their silence. This request was repeated three times and if there were no objections the *Upasampada* was complete. The newly admitted *bhikkhu* had a preceptor who instructed him and upon whom he waited.

As an individual the *bhikkhu* may possess three robes, a girdle for the loins, an alms bowl, a razor, a needle, and a water strainer so as not to injure unnecessarily any forms of life in the water that he might drink. As a group the Sangha could have other possessions and property which expanded in quantity as the laity fulfilled their obligations of giving.

There were four offenses (*parajikas*) which could mean the expulsion of a *bhikkhu* from the Sangha, but only on his confession of an offense, which he was morally obliged to offer. These offences were sexual intercourse, theft, knowingly depriving a creature of life, and boasting of some superhuman perfection.

An order of nuns (*bhikkhunis,* Sanskrit *bhikshunis*) was formed, but only after considerable hesitation on the part of the Buddha. There seems to have been some fear that the *bhikkhunis* would try to usurp the power of ruling the order, and so they were subordinated to the *Bhikkhu-Sangha*. The *bhikkhuni* was required to bow reverently before every *bhikkhu* even if he had only been ordained for a day, and she for many years. She could never scold or revile a *bhikkhu,* nor ever accuse a *bhikkhu,* although a *bhikkhu* might scold, revile, or accuse a *bhikkhuni*.

While the Sangha was the heart of this community it could only be sustained by the existence of lay devotees, men (*upasakas*) and women (*upasikas*). The *upasaka* could take the threefold refuge, al-

---

14. The ten precepts are to abstain from destroying life, stealing, impurity, lying, intoxicants, eating at forbidden times (*bhikkhus* eat one main meal before noon), dancing, music and theaters, garlands, perfumes and ornaments, high or large beds, accepting gold or silver.

though this did not imply living the life of a *bhikkhu*. He might not even be exclusively devoted to the teaching of the Buddha. The *upasaka* would keep the first five, or sometimes eight (especially at certain times), of the precepts. On full-moon days he took the vow of eight precepts and stayed at the temple because of the difficulty of fulfilling such vows at home. While it might be possible for a devout *upasaka* to achieve *Nibbana* at death, his more normal goal was to accumulate merit for a better birth through living a moral life and through giving alms to the *bhikkhus*. The *bhikkhus* do not beg for their own sake, but offer the *upasakas* and *upasikas* the opportunity to give, and hence increase their merit.

MORAL PRECEPTS

Since *Nibbana* is the goal, and is characterized by nonattachment, it is natural that actions which come closest to this goal are desirable. In the good life one moves from various degrees of attachment to detachment. Hence *sila* (morality), while part of the relative distinctions which are ultimately erroneous, plays an important role for one on the road to *Nibbana*. *Sila* is represented by the ten precepts that are followed by the *bhikkhus,* and the five or eight that are accepted by the *upasakas* and *upasikas*.

There seem to be three broad steps in the path to perfection: *sila, samadhi* (concentration), and *panna* (Sanskrit *prajna*—insight or wisdom). *Sila* is the first step toward the goal. However, the mental attitude is more important than the deed itself. The *Abhidhamma,* for example, spends considerable time on the analysis of mental states, but practically none on social problems. In the proscription against killing, the consummation of the act is less significant than the intent to do so. Anger and greed are wrong because they indicate attachment.

In addition to the ten precepts there is also *dana-sila* (giving), the merit of which is increased by the closeness of the gift to *Nibbana*. Hence the Sangha is a rich field of merit.

The so-called four immeasurables (*apramanani*), however, come closer to the heart of Theravada morality. They are called this because of their desirable universal extension. (1) *Metta* (loving kindness) is a benevolent harmlessness which begins with one's own feelings and is radiated to others until it is extended to the whole world. Even if one does not enter directly into action to cure the ills of the world, he can have an effect by radiating *metta*. Such activity can turn aside the rush of a wild elephant or stop the bite of a venomous serpent. It can be practiced by both *bhikkhu* and *upasaka*. The more one approximates *Nibbana,* the more he turns from direct action to the radiation of universal good will. (2) *Karuna* (compassion) involves pity or helpful sympathy without the emotional factor which would imply attachment. The mere extension of emotion is sentimental. *Karuna,* however, does not distinguish between one's own suffering and another's; it involves a compassion for others who are caught in the same rounds of birth and rebirth as oneself. (3) *Mudita* (sympathetic joy) is the counterpart of *karuna,* for one has the capacity for joy in the success of another. (4) *Upekha* (equanimity) is the closest to *Nibbana*. The others seem to have an element of attachment involved in them, but the closer they come to *Nibbana*, the more they approximate equanimity or the quality of neutrality and nonattachment. The "perfect deed" is characterized by *upekha*. While the basis for an active social ethic is slight in the Pali Canon, Buddhists in Southeast Asia today are busy reinterpreting their tradition to give basis for a "Buddhist" approach to economics, politics, or world peace. Such a concern is part of their attempt to emerge from domination by the colonial powers and show that one can deal with contemporary problems in terms of one's indigenous tradition.

MAHAVIRA AND THE JAINAS

There is evidence that the Jain religious community is at least as old as the Buddha, but it would be historically safer to say that the Jainas existed as contemporaries of the followers of the Buddha.

Vardhamana, as Gotama, was a Kshatriya (see p. 130) and is reported to have been born near Vaishali. Some of the details of his life are similar to those of Gotama and this has led some scholars to claim that we are dealing with a single individual. Such a view is no longer held. Vardhamana is better known by his epithet *Mahavira* (great hero) just as Gotama has come to be remembered as the Buddha. Jainas are followers of the *Jina*, which means victor or conqueror and is an appellation given to one who has attained *moksha*, or enlightenment. Mahavira was raised in luxury, and did not enter a state of homelessness until his parents died of voluntary starvation, an accepted manner of death for those who had completed prescribed austerities. After twelve years of austerities, similar to those which proved unsatisfactory for the Buddha, Vardhamana became the *Jina*, or conqueror. After thirty years of teaching and organizing he was finally liberated by death at the age of seventy-two. At that time his *jiva* (in this system a term referring to the "soul") went to the top of the universe where it is no longer touched by prayers or requests. The Jainas hold that *moksha* is a matter of personal effort and in this they agree with the Pali Canon.

According to the Jainas, however, their religion is eternal and Mahavira is not the founder, but the last in a long line of *Tirthankaras* ("fordfinders" who have achieved Nirvana at death). The twenty-third *Tirthankara* was Parshva, who is said to have lived about two hundred and fifty years before Mahavira and is generally accepted as a historical figure. It is the position of the Jainas that Mahavira did not found a new religion, but merely revived one that existed from eternity. As one goes back toward the first *Tirthankara Rshabha*, however, the time spans between *Tirthankaras* become unbelievably long and the physical dimensions of the *Tirthankaras* and their life spans become increasingly immense. Although all of the *Tirthankaras* have been released from the world and have no attachment to nor influence over worldly cares, the Jainas have made them objects of worship. The *Tirthankaras* are regarded as gods, as indeed, are all people potentially, and all liberated souls actually. They are worshiped in image form and in elaborate temples. All of the *Tirthankaras* were Kshatriyas according to the tradition, but the first twenty-two *Tirthankaras* are generally not believed to have any historical base.[15]

Doctrinal Summary While the Upanishads were moving toward the affirmation that Being was One in the Atman-Brahman doctrine, and the Buddhists of the Pali tradition were denying any reality to permanence in favor of a view characterized by becoming and change, the Jainas proposed a view that rejected both as absolute systems and affirmed them as partial truths. The Jainas have come to be known for their doctrine of *syadvada,* or the doctrine of maybe. In terms of a seven-fold formula, they supported their view that every proposition is only conditional and no proposition can be either absolutely affirmed, or absolutely negated. In each case the assertion is prefaced with "maybe," "somehow," or "in a certain sense."

1. Maybe (somehow) a thing exists.
2. Maybe (somehow) a thing does not exist.
3. Maybe (somehow) a thing both exists and does not exist.
4. Maybe (somehow) a thing is indescribable.
5. Maybe (somehow) a thing exists and is indescribable.
6. Maybe (somehow) a thing does not exist and is indescribable.
7. Maybe (somehow) a thing both exists and does not exist and is indescribable.

In the first assertion we choose to make a statement of affirmation about a pot (or some other thing) according to its "substance, place, time, and nature."[16] But since the pot does not exist in the form of another substance, place, time, or nature, the second negating statement can also be made. Since the existence and nonexistence of the pot are intimately bound together, the third assertion becomes possible. But, if one wants to emphasize both existence and nonexistence as primary modifications and do this simultaneously, one is affirming the indescribability of the pot. But the pot is not indescribable in every way, for total inexpressibility would deny us the right to even describe it with the word "inexpressible." The last three assertions are merely the combination of indescribability (the fourth) with the first three.

The doctrine of *syadvada* has been criticized because it supposedly makes it possible to offer contradictory statements about the same object. But the Jainas reply that only according to this doctrine are contradictions avoided, since all statements are made only from a point of view and not absolutely.

Jaina logic admits that contradictory statements cannot be made about the same thing in the same sense at the same time and place, but stresses the fact that contradiction can be avoided only

---

15. For a list of the twenty-four *Tirthankaras* with their ages, sizes, and other details, see Jack Finegan, *The Archeology of World Religions,* Princeton, N.J., Princeton University Press, paperback edition, 1965, vol. I, p. 190.

16. *Syadvadamanjari,* quoted in S. Radhakrishnan and Charles A. Moore, *A Source Book in Indian Philosophy,* Princeton, N.J., Princeton University Press, 1957, p. 264.

by their own doctrine of syādvāda, *in which every statement is made only from a particular point of view. The charge of contradiction lies, if at all, at the door of the absolutist, who affirms or denies a statement about a thing from no point of view, as it were, which, according to the Jaina logician is impossible.*[17]

According to the Jainas, the entire universe can be explained in terms of two categories: *jiva* and *ajiva*. The *jiva* refers to the conscious and the *ajiva* to the unconscious. The *jiva* means the living principle, but in this system it seems equivalent to the soul or permanent spiritual aspect of man. In man the *jiva* is joined with matter or *ajiva*, which obscures the infinite intelligence and power which characterize the *jiva* as such. These characteristics are obscured during *samsara* (successive states of rebirth) but are not destroyed. The *jiva* acts and is acted upon. It is, curiously enough, capable of changing its size to fit the physical object it inhabits, thus illuminating the whole of the space. Hence the unalterable nature of the *Atman* which is affirmed in the Upanishads is denied by the Jainas in the doctrine of the *jiva*. Also, there are an infinite number of *jivas* which are eternal (as is matter) and although in their liberated state they are identical with one another (although sometimes they vary in size), they are not reduced to One as is the case with the Atman-Brahman doctrine of the Upanishads. The goal is to subdue the material element of one's being and hence eliminate its unhappy influence so that *jiva* may rise unfettered in its purity and excellence to the top of the universe.

The category of *ajiva* is distinguished from *jiva* in that *ajiva* lacks life and consciousness. *Ajiva* includes space, time, and matter (also *dharma* and *adharma*, which indicates the ability to rest and move). Matter is eternal and consists of atoms which are not visible to the senses except in combinations which form our objects of sense. The Jainas hold, however, that in addition to animals and plants, also the smallest particles of the elements such as earth, fire, water, and wind, are endowed with *jivas*. Matter is equally real with the spiritual order, but impedes the brilliance of the latter.

Knowledge constitutes the very essence of the *jiva*. It is capable of knowing anything unaided and with precision, and it is only through the interference of karma that omniscience is not actually operative. Instead of explaining lack of knowledge as the result of ignorance (*avidya*), as does the Pali Canon and some passages of the Upanishads, the Jainas explain this lack of knowledge as the result of karma. Karma is elaborately classified in types by the Jainas, but is invariably conceived as a subtle matter which permeates the *jivas* and hence weights them down. If, through the appropriate means, the influx of karma is stopped and the permeating karma is worked out, the individual becomes a *kevalin* (omniscient one), as did Mahavira while he was still living. At death the *jiva* is released from the bondage of the body and rises until it reaches beyond the *lokakasha* (place of space) to the top of the universe, where it rests in eternal bliss. In that state the knowledge of the *jiva* is not ham-

17. Radhakrishnan and Moore, op. cit., p. 262.

pered, it is void of cares for worldly affairs, and the only influence it continues to exert is the one of example. The *jiva* is able to exist between enlightenment and the attainment of godhead (all *jivas* are gods although there is no supreme Creator God) without any fresh influx of karma. He is at this time called an Arhat (as in the Pali Canon) and this corresponds to the *jivan-mukti* (one liberated while living) of Shankara (see p. 188) or the attainment of *Nibbana* as distinct from *Parinibbana* in the Pali Canon.

Laity and the Order

Like the division among the followers of the Buddha of the *bhikkhus* (and *bhikkhunis*) and the *upasakas* (and *upasikas*), so among the Jainas the highest calling is to the order of *yatis* (strivers) while the lower calling is less demanding for the *shravakas* (hearers, referring to laity). For both *yatis* and *shravakas* one reaches the state of liberation by the three jewels, a phrase common to the Pali Canon. The three jewels are right faith (in Mahavira and his teaching), right knowledge (in terms of correct doctrine), and right conduct.

Right conduct was similar in principle for *yatis* and *shravakas*, but the former pursued the rules more intensely. For the *yatis* there are five vows. The first was the vow of *ahimsa* (noninjury), which avoided injury to any form of life. Since there were *jivas* in even the smallest particles of matter, the *yati* went to every possible precaution to avoid injury. He would strain his water, he would cover his mouth with a cloth when speaking, so as not to risk injury to the air, and he would look six feet ahead of him when walking, to avoid stepping on any form of life. He had a soft broom which he used to brush the place before sitting or before laying an object down. He would engage in no swift movements and would often hesitate to scratch an itch for fear of causing injury to an unseen guest. The householder tried to take every precaution to avoid such injury, but he seldom went to the length of the *yatis*.

The Jainas have avoided agriculture because of the possibility of injury to worms or other sentient beings living in the soil. They also avoided butchering and fishing. To escape from such occupations many of them moved into commerce and banking, where they are a prosperous and respected community today. They have also maintained hospitals for sick and feeble animals and birds, and have placed numerous bird feeders in the streets and in various other places throughout communities where the Jainas exist in substantial numbers. Such expressions of *ahimsa* still exist today.

The doctrine of *ahimsa* is interpreted as extending not only to physical injury, but also to psychological or emotional injury by thought, word, or deed. In the twentieth century the Jainas feel that if the doctrine of *ahimsa* were heeded, the world could be saved from self-destruction.

A second vow is not to speak untruths, even in jest. This also means not to cause others so to speak, nor to consent to the lies of others. A third vow is against greed and is a promise to take nothing that is not given. Again, this vow implies that one will not cause others to be avaricious, nor will one be a party to others who do so. A fourth vow is to observe chastity. For the *yatis* this means re-

Puja scene inside Jain Temple, Ahmedabad. (Photo by Robert D. Baird.)

nouncing all sexual pleasures, while for the householder, it is taken to mean fidelity in marriage. The fifth vow is the most radical in that it involves the renouncement of all attachments. This renunciation extends to all sensual pleasures, such as gratifying sounds, sights, textures, odors, and flavors. Nonattachment means that one would neither love nor hate any object. Nonattachment was also a significant part of Pali Buddhist morality. For the householder this vow involved checking greed through placing a limit on one's wealth and giving away the excess.

Actually, the householder had twelve vows. These included the above five in their modified form, and the following: (6) to avoid temptation by refraining from unnecessary travel, (7) to limit the number of things in daily use, (8) to be on guard against evils that can be avoided, (9) to keep specific times for meditation, (10) to impose special periods of self-denial, (11) to spend occasional days as monks, and (12) to give alms in support of the *yatis*.

For one who has gone through the various forms of self-denial, who has undertaken penance for twelve years and is ripe for Nirvana, death by starvation might be the culmination. But this was never to be used as a means of circumventing the need for a long period of austerities. Extreme self-imposed austerities were repudiated by the Buddha, but were considered by Mahavira and the Jainas to be the most successful means of stopping the influx of karma, expelling karma that adheres to the *jiva,* and attaining release. Jaina saints who attain release are distinguished by names which were also common among the followers of the Buddha, such as Buddha, Kevalin, Tathagata, Arhat, and Jina. But while the followers of the Buddha tended to use the terms Buddha, Arhat, and Tathagata, the Jainas favored the term Jina (conqueror). The idea that *Tirthankaras* appear periodically in history is a form of the view

Inside scene of Dilwara Temple, Mt. Abu. (Photo by Robert D. Baird.)

which is also expressed in the concept of the appearances of numerous Buddhas, or the descents of Vishnu or Krishna in the *Bhagavad Gita.*

Sectarianism It seems that shortly after the death of Mahavira, the community split into several sects. Numerous divisions exist today. In broad terms there are two important sects, the *Digambaras* ("clothed in space") and the *Shvetambaras* ("white-clothed"). The *Digambaras* contend that perfection could not be reached by anyone who wore clothing. Nudity was part of several sects in this period and was practiced by Mahavira, but was condemned by the Buddha. The *Digambaras* also deny that sanctity can be attained by women and hold that perfected saints, such as *Tirthankaras,* live without food.

The *Shvetambaras* hold that one can attain Nirvana even though clad. They also allow women to enter the monastic order under the assumption that they have a possibility of attaining Nirvana. Another sect, the *Sthanakavasis,* are opposed to the use of images. Since they have no temples, they worship anywhere, principally through acts of meditation.

Jaina Temples Images of the *Tirthankaras* are housed in imposing temples. The images so resemble each other that it is difficult to see any differences from one *Tirthankara* to another. The *Digambara* images are always without ornamental glass eyes and are unclothed. The *Shvetambara* images are more elaborately decorated and often clothed. Since there is no priesthood to care for the worship of the images, this service is performed by *Shravakas* or sometimes even by Brahmans who are hired by the Jainas to tend to the temple duties. The *Tirthankaras* receive the same kind of worship as do the other popular deities of the *bhakti* movement: Vishnu, Krishna, Shiva, and the Buddha (see pp. 160 ff.).

The carvings in the temples on Mt. Abu in Gujarat, on Mt. Girnar, or the temple on Mt. Satrunjaya near Palitana, are outstanding. The Jainas are still numerous in Gujarat, and there are a few in the south of India. They number about one and one-half million. At Sravanabelgola there is a fifty-six-foot image of a naked saint, exposed to the elements of the heat or rain. With vines growing up his arms, he stands in utter detachment to the world. Pilgrims come to this site frequently and a large festival is held every twelve years.

BHAKTI MOVEMENTS

As early as 500 B.C. there were tendencies which later developed into what is known as the *bhakti* movement. *Bhakti,* often translated "devotion," includes faith, love, surrender, and devotional attachment. *Bhakti* is a religious orientation which is common in association with theism. As devotion to a personal deity, it is expressed in *puja,* which means adoration or worship on the theoretical level. Concrete expressions of *puja* include the offering of fruit or flowers to the deity and circumambulating the temple. In both terms, *puja* and *bhakti,* a personal relationship and an attitude of reverential dependence is implied. Devotees can be seen in the temples bowing or prostrate before the image enshrined there. While the supreme object of *bhakti* and *puja* is the deity itself, parents or elders, spiritual teachers and holy men, and even the motherland, have been objects of devotion to some extent.

Perhaps the most concise and systematic accounts of *bhakti* theology are to be found in the *Narada Bhakti Sutras* and the *Shandilya Sutras*. While these are not much older than the twelfth century A.D., they articulate a religious orientation which is approximated in various degrees by other movements in India. For these sutras, *bhakti* is neither knowledge, nor the following of ritual acts, nor belief in a system. It is affection and submission to a person. *Bhakti* is not preliminary to something else, but is an end in itself. It is surrender (*prapatti*) to no earthly object but to God only. *Bhakti* can be directed not only to the Adorable One (*Bhagavan*), but to any of his incarnations (*avataras*) which are the result of his pure compassion. *Bhakti* is higher than external observances and activities and higher than philosophical meditiation. Since it involves submission on man's part, it also implies divine grace.

Bhakti is classified as lower or imperfect when it is motivated by worldly concerns such as sickness, danger, or the desire for some favor such as the birth of a male child. Even this, however, is to be cultivated by listening to and singing the praises of the Lord, through offerings of flowers and food to the image, and through prostration before and circumambulation of the image. One is counseled to worship the Lord in the form of one's friend or master. Later works divide imperfect *bhakti* into eighty-one degrees.

In addition to imperfect or lower *bhakti*, there is higher *bhakti*. This is completely selfless and involves single-hearted attachment to God, all other affections having been destroyed. Higher *bhakti* is not the result of human striving, but of pure grace. Such *bhakti* is not the means to liberation; it is liberation.

Some scholars would like to find the roots of *bhakti* as early as the *Rigveda*. But, with few exceptions, the attitude of the Vedic man to his deities was not one of devotional attachment. Likewise, there are *bhakti* tendencies in some of the Upanishads, such as the *Shvetashvatara*. But this view does not dominate the Upanishads and is more commonly found in the later ones than in the early ones.

In the *Bhagavad Gita*, the doctrine of *bhakti* is taught. But the *Gita* is a transitional document not always consistent with itself. It begins with an emphasis on disciplined action (*karmayoga*), and ends with the superiority of devotion (*bhakti*) to *Krishna*. Though the *Gita* contains references in which *bhakti* is seen as the means to knowledge, subordinating it to *jnanayoga,* or the way to God through knowledge, its more characteristic emphasis is that *bhakti* itself is liberation.

In its fully developed form, *bhakti* is a highly articulate theological system which can be used to justify the tendency of many to express ultimacy in terms of intense love or devotion to a personal god.

BUDDHA BHAKTI

One need not argue whether *bhakti* began within the Buddhist fold or whether it was pre-Buddhist. Regardless of when the system began, one can detect a devotion to the Buddha which developed almost immediately after his death and which reached its logical fulfillment in the Mahayana systems of grace and the attainment of salvation by faith in Amitabha Buddha.

There were no temples during the lifetime of the Buddha. After his death his remains were distributed to various places and enclosed in *stupas*—originally funerary mounds that later became more elaborate and central to worship and devotion. Artists capitalized on *stupas* and created elaborately sculptured gateways which depicted certain scenes and episodes from the traditional life of the Buddha.

At first the Buddha's presence was depicted with a wheel to symbolize turning the wheel of the law, or a tree (the Bodhi tree), or a footprint of the Buddha. Later the sculptor became bolder in his representation of the Buddha and created images of him either meditating or teaching in seated or standing posture.

Devotees would come from some distance to offer flowers and walk around the *stupa*. At some of the more important sites, the path of circumambulation was enclosed with a stone railing at-

Great Stupa, Sanchi. In existence at the time of Ashoka. (Photo by Robert D. Baird.)

tached to the lofty gates which were erected at each of the cardinal points. Wood or stone umbrellas were placed above the *stupa,* and if its relics were of the Buddha or some other important person, several umbrellas appeared above each other. The *stupa* at Sanchi has three umbrellas while a *stupa* nearby, supposedly containing the relics of two important disciples, has only one umbrella.

The growing *bhakti* attitude toward the Buddha can be seen not only in the increasing elaborateness of the artistic forms, but also in the type of literary productions stemming from the Mahayana groups. The lives of the Buddha become more elaborate and supernatural. The *Mahavastu* (second century B.C.) tells us little that is new about the life of the Buddha, but a different emphasis is apparent. Here the Buddha not only decides to be born in India, and determines the other details of his birth, but he is pictured as a superman superior to the world. He is a great magician who can touch the sun or moon with his hand. *Bhakti* comes to the fore when adoration of the Buddha produces enough merit to achieve Nirvana. An offering of flowers or circumambulation of the *stupa* earns for the devotee an infinite reward. Later portions of the *Mahavastu* contain references to images of the Buddha with a halo, such as appears in Indo-Greek art in the first century A.D. The role of the Bodhisattva, or Buddha-to-be, is elaborated with devoted concern in terms of ten stages (*bhumis*) through which the Buddha-to-be must go in order to reach the brink of Nirvana.

The *Lalitavistara,* another late life of the Buddha, also glorifies his nature. Here Buddha's life on earth is described as the diversion or sport (*lalita*) of a supernatural being. As a Bodhisattva in the Tushita heaven, all the gods, including Brahma, do homage to him. In Vaishnava works the same picture is painted, with the single exception that Vishnu replaces Buddha. And, when the boy Bodhisattva was brought to the temple by his foster mother, all the images of the gods fell down before him.

Another sutra of considerable importance for Mahayana which reflects the *bhakti* attitude to the Buddha is the *Lotus of the True Law* (*Saddharmapundarika*). In the process of trying to bring the followers of the Pali tradition over to the new way of looking at the Buddha and his doctrine, the Buddha appears as an eternal personage. The tradition of his earthly life and the attainment of Nirvana is conceded, but is seen as a device (*upaya,* or skill in means) to lead people to the higher doctrine (*Mahayana*). The doctrine of Nirvana which the Buddha taught in the Pali Canon was only a means of attracting those weary with suffering. All the beliefs of the Pali Canon are admittedly true, but only as appearance and not as reality. As the sutra opens, the Buddha is surrounded by twelve hundred Arhats, eighty thousand Bodhisattvas, numerous gods led by Shakra (Indra) and Brahma, and various other beings numbering in the millions. The Buddhas are mentioned and are portrayed in such a way that they rival other Indian gods who are also objects of *bhakti*. In some chapters the Bodhisattvas are given such prominence and worship that even the Buddhas recede into the background. Mention is made throughout the sutra of the adoration of relics and the worship of images which are found at *stupas* and in magnificent temples or monasteries.

Buddha *bhakti* perhaps reaches its peak in the *Sukhavativyuha,* or description of the land of bliss. There had developed a belief in numerous Buddhas, and the worlds over which they exerted influence. Amitabha, sometimes called Amitayus (Infinite Life), ruler of the Western Paradise, became particularly popular. The *Sukhavativyuha* exists in a longer form and in a later condensed form. The longer one was translated into Chinese about A.D. 170, but the date of its original composition is unknown. These books contain a description of the land of bliss where all sorts of pleasures abound. If anything deemed necessary is missing, one can have it merely by wishing. Furthermore, the element of *bhakti* reaches its peak when one learns that entrance can be gained into this perfect land by prayer to Amitabha. Even a single thought or repetition of the name Amitabha will suffice. Such were the happy results of a transfer of merit from Amitabha. Having practiced virtues and sacrifice through innumerable lives, Amitabha had acquired a store of merit which he could transfer to devotees in compensation for their demerits.

The flowering of Buddha *bhakti* thus involved a modification in the traditional view of karma held by the Theravada camp, the followers of the Pali tradition. They held that the Buddha taught that one could only save himself through self-effort since the Buddha had entered *Parinibbana*. This emphasis on self-effort was now replaced by a doctrine of grace which included the notion that merit could be transferred from the Buddha to the follower who adopts the way of love and devotion.

KRISHNA BHAKTI

Certainty about the origin of the devotion to Krishna is not possible. Krishna is mentioned only a few times prior to the *Mahabharata,* an epic which was in the process of being written and edited from 400 B.C. to A.D. 400. In the *Mahabharata,* Krishna appears substantially as a human hero. The *Bhagavad Gita,* which forms only a small portion of that epic (which is three and one-half times the length of the Christian Bible), presents Krishna as the Supreme God, who, if made the object of devotion, will save men. In this work Krishna is sometimes seen as having all the features that Brahman had in the Upanishads, but with the theistic flavor which permeates the *Gita.*

The *Gita* begins on the battlefield, and in places teaches that disciplined action, that is, action done in a nonattached manner, without concern for the fruits of the action, is the most adequate path to liberation. Nevertheless, the climax of the *Gita* is chapter 11 where the devotee Arjuna is given a mystical vision of Lord Krishna. All of the emphases of *bhakti* are present. The key is devotion and faith toward the Lord (*Bhagavan*). The vision is seen as given to those who are devoted to him and it is given out of Krishna's free grace. The interpretation of karma which emphasizes self-effort is somewhat set aside. Although the *Gita* teaches that action is inevitable and that bad karma is the result of attached action, it is stated elsewhere in this work that one who is devoted to Krishna will not be reborn.

While some interpreters hold that in the *Gita* Krishna is an incarnation (*avatara*) of the god Vishnu, this is hardly the impression conveyed by a careful reading of the text. Krisha appears in the *Gita* as the Supreme God. Vishnu is mentioned in only two passages and there, merely as a title applied to Krishna, perhaps in the way that various Vedic gods were given the qualities of other deities when they became the object of praise.

The tales of Krishna are more fully developed in the fourth-century addition to the *Mahabharata,* the *Harivamsa,* and in the medieval *Bhagavata Purana*. No longer the teacher of the *Gita,* now Krishna's exploits as a child, or as a lover, are portrayed. Tradition says he was born at Mathura, where an edifice marks his birthplace today. His father was Vasudeva, a name by which Krishna was also known. Krishna performed miracles as a child, killing demons and sheltering the *gopis* (cowherd lasses) by holding Mount Govardhana over their heads with his finger. He also stole butter and sweets in childhood. He is pictured in adolescence as a lover who had numerous love affairs with the cowherd lasses. On one occasion he hid the clothes of the *gopis* while they bathed in the river at a spot that is pointed out by temple priests today (it must be said that different priests point to different spots). While he had amorous affairs with numerous *gopis,* his favorite came to be Radha. They are often pictured together, Krishna playing his flute with Radha by his side in a moonlit garden.

In Mathura, the cruel king Kamsa issued an order to kill all the children of Devaki (Krishna's mother), since it was prophesied that her eighth child would kill him. Krishna's father saved his son from

Seventeenth-century miniature, probably from Jaipur, depicting Krishna and the gopis. (*Courtesy of the Museum of Fine Arts, Boston.*)

such a fate, and as he carried him across the Jumna river the water gradually subsided so that it never touched the child.

From the sixth to the ninth centuries there was a series of twelve poet-saints who significantly influenced South Indian religious life. They were called the *Alvars,* or those who are immersed in God. More devotional than theological, they sang about the lives of Krishna and Rama throughout South India. *Bhakti* lauds various types of love toward the deity, such as that between father and child, mutual friendship, and that between the lover and the beloved. The *Alvars* expressed their basic devotion to God in terms of friendly love (*sakhya*), a servant's devotion to his master (*dasya*), a mother's affection for her son (*vatsalya*), a son's respect for his father (*pitribhakti*), and also a woman's love for her beloved (*madhurya*). The *Alvars* were followed by a series of theologians called *Acharyas* who provided a philosophical basis for *bhakti* and theism. Ramanuja was one in this succession.

Surrender to God, or *prapatti*, is an aspect which is emphasized in the hymns of the *Alvars*. *Prapatti* involves a sense of absolute humility and the willingness to give up anything that is against God's will. It also involves faith that God will protect his devotees.

In South India during the twelfth or fourteenth centuries, Nimbarka identified Krishna with Brahman, the essence of the universe. Other *bhakti* philosophers in the south (Ramanuja and Madhva) had been devoted to Krishna, but had placed little emphasis on the cowherd element and had ignored Radha. For Nimbarka, Radha was the eternal consort of Krishna and was incarnate like him at Vrindavan. Nimbarka was emphatic in his worship of Krishna and his consort Radha, even to the exclusion of other gods. His sect became popular in the north as well, and the success of the *bhakti* movement there is dependent on him to a large degree.

In the fifteenth century, Vallabha founded a school which emphasized the grace of god coming through devotion as a cause of liberation. Vallabha and descendants of his who headed this community were considered as incarnations of Krishna. Vallabha ultimately settled in Benares where he wrote a commentary on the *Bhagavata Purana*.

After the death of Vallabha his seven sons wandered throughout India gaining proselytes. Their sect attached itself to the adolescent Krishna, whose amorous sport with the *gopis* is the theme of the tenth chapter of the *Bhagavata Purana*. The *guru* of this sect was considered to be the manifestation of Krishna. Imitation of Krishna's amorous deeds was taken quite seriously, and union with Krishna was sought through intercourse with the *guru*. Husbands accepted this role for their wives and daughters. The male worshiper would sometimes drink water wrung from the wet garments of the *guru*, eat portions of his food, or chew again the betel spit from his mouth.[1] This is not the first time that union with the God was to be attempted through sexual union.

The worship of Krishna has been strong in Bengal, appearing in literary form as early as the twelfth century with the *Gitagovinda* of Jayadeva. A movement which stems from Chaitanya (1486–1533) places considerable emphasis on the cowherd manifestation of Krishna and on the *gopi* Radha. Although not the originator of the movement, Chaitanya's personality was so forceful that even within his lifetime he was considered an incarnation of Krishna by some, while others thought of him as Krishna himself. Still others saw him

---

1. The leaf of the betel vine is covered with lime, sprinkled with areca nut, folded over, and fastened with a clove. This is chewed, and the saliva and mouth become a brilliant red in the process.

as the ultimate form of the divine—Radha and Krishna in a single body.

While Chaitanya was no theologian, he sensed the importance of his movement and sent theologians to Vrindavan to establish an *ashram* (monastery) to shape the formal doctrine of the sect. These theologians were anxious to show that Krishna was not merely an *avatara* of Vishnu, as held by some, but the Supreme God himself.

One of the questions considered was the question of the nature of the love of the *gopis,* who were married women, for Krishna. One interpretation was that since the *gopis* were married and belonged to another, their love for Krishna was all the more pure and ideal. If they were his own, the relationship might have resulted in self-centered desire. But it is precisely because it is love for one who belongs to another that the love is so intense and yet so unselfish. The pain of separation from their beloved draws the *gopis'* interest away from worldly concerns and leads them to meditation on Krishna which is the heart of *bhakti.*

One can still walk along the Jumna and visit temples in Vrindavan and Mathura which are dedicated to Krishna and Radha. The images here may be plain or elaborate. Sometimes they are placed in a swing so that devotees can rock them. Special festivals are held in their honor.

RAMA BHAKTI

There are two Indian epics, the *Mahabharata* and the *Ramayana.* The *Ramayana* was substantially complete as early as the fourth century B.C. It contains seven chapters but it is generally agreed that the first and the last are later additions. Apart from a few editorial editions, Rama is presented in chapters 2 through 6 as a great hero, but still a man. Most of the Vedic gods are mentioned and Vishnu and Shiva hold positions of prime importance. In chapters 1 and 7, however, Rama becomes an incarnation of Vishnu just as Krishna came to be. It was perhaps some time in the second century B.C. that this divine Rama became embodied in the written tradition.

The *Ramayana* centers around Rama who won the hand of Sita in an archery contest. Rama and Sita were banished to a life in the forest because of a favor promised to Dasharatha's second queen. Disguised as an ascetic, the demon king Ravana came to their hermitage and carried Sita away in his aerial car to his island kingdom of Lanka (Ceylon). Rama and his brother Lakshmana sought for her, but were unsuccessful until aided by Hanuman, brave leader of the monkeys. Leaping over the straits and building a causeway of stones to Ceylon, they slew Ravana and rescued Sita. Although Sita lived a chaste life in the palace of her abductor, her purity was questioned and she went through several ordeals to prove her innocence. As a final proof she called on her mother Earth to swallow her. The earth opened and she disappeared. This epic has so endeared itself to the hearts of numerous Indians that they not only worship Rama, but see Rama and Sita as the ideal divine couple. Indians have even built shrines to Lakshmana and Hanuman.

Street temple to Hanuman, Agra. (Photo by Robert D. Baird.)

Shrines, particularly to Hanuman, abound in the north today. He is usually painted orange and given a muscular physique. So popular is Rama that friends often greet each other in his name.

Ramananda lived in the fifteenth century and exerted considerable influence on the course of religious history in the north. Ramananda worshiped Rama and Sita alone. He also disregarded caste to an extent beyond some of the other *bhaktas*. It is common in *bhakti* to hold that a man can achieve release through devotion to God regardless of his caste. But Ramananda went so far as to include among his disciples a woman, a Muslim, and an outcaste. His concern to speak to the common people led him to speak and write in the vernacular rather than in Sanskrit. A sect stemming from him is called the *Ramanandis* or sometimes the *Ramawats.* United in their faith in the one personal God whom they call Rama, they hold that *bhakti* consists in perfect love toward God and that all men are brothers.

Ramananda had reportedly broken with his teacher because of staunch regulations about abstentions and because of proscriptions about eating with persons of other castes. The worship of Rama was free of the erotic tendencies that one finds in Krishna worship. Through Ramananda and his disciples the worship of Rama was spread throughout northern and central India.

Kabir, one of the important figures in Ramananda's school, objected to ceremonies and rejected caste. Holding that Rama is a spirit, Kabir concluded that he could not be worshiped in images but only through prayer. Furthermore, God is not the exclusive right of Hindus or Muslims. Kabir was of importance to the Sikh community (see p. 211) which attempted to bring together some of the chief tenets in the Hindu and Muslim creeds and hence eliminate some of the tension between the two communities.

Perhaps no one has been more influential in spreading the worship of Rama than the poet Tulsi Das (1532–1623). Tulsi married and lived a householder's life, later to become a sannyasin, to go on pilgrimages throughout India, and finally to settle in Benares. Although he wrote more than twenty formal works, his most famous and influential was his *Ramacharitmanas* ("The Lake of Rama's Deeds"). Based on the standard *Ramayana*, it was written in Hindi and has probably had the popular appeal in supporting devotion to Rama that the *Gita* or the *Bhagavata Purana* has had for Krishna. The poet exhibits deep feeling in his tender description of Rama's character. Tulsi lays great stress on the repetition of the name of *Rama* for the cultivation of *bhakti*. He urges the control of the senses and dedication of all actions to God.

In Tulsi the grace of Rama reigns supreme. Tulsi leaves the door open to approach God through various ways. Once man has begun the search, God will mercifully do the rest. Even the demon king Ravana is ultimately saved, emphasizing the compassion and mercy of God. Rama meets the Brahman Valmiki in the forest and inquires as to a suitable place to build a dwelling where he may live with his wife Sita and his brother Lakshmana. The following reply of Valmiki captures the spirit of Tulsi's devotion:

> Listen, O Rāma, now I shall tell you
> Where you should live with Sītā and Lakṣmaṇa:
> Those whose ears, like unto the sea,
> By the stories of your life, like unto various rivers,
> Are always being filled, but are never satisfied;
> Their hearts are your home.
>
> Those whose eyes, being like the cātaka bird;
> Are ever longing for the rain-cloud of the vision of God,
> O giver of joy, O Lord of the Raghus,
> Live in their hearts with your brother and Sītā.
>
> Your good name, being like the Mānasa lake,
> Those whose tongues, like the swans,
> Pick up the pearls of your divine qualities,
> Live in their hearts, O Rāma.
>
> He who can smell only the fragrant offering to God,
> He who offers his food to you before eating it,
> He whose very clothes and jewels are consecrated to the Lord,
> He whose head bows down to Brāhmaṇas, gods, and guru,
> With love and great humility,
> Whose hands daily worship the feet of Rāma,
> Who depends in his heart on Rāma and looks to no one else,
> Whose feet ever walk to the holy places of pilgrimage,
> O Rāma, live in their hearts.
>
> Those who desire only devotion to God as the fruit of all their
>   good deeds in the world,

Live in the temple of their hearts, O Sītā, and you two sons of Raghu.
Those who have neither desire nor anger, nor pride, nor deceit, nor delusion,
Who neither covet nor lament, and are without attachment or aversion,
Who have neither hypocrisy, arrogance, nor deceit,
O Rāma, live in their hearts.

Those who are loved by all and are well-wishers of all,
Who are the same in sorrow and happiness, praise and blame,
Who speak sweet words of truth, having pondered well on them,
Who, sleeping or awake, seek refuge in thee,
Who look upon the wives of others as their own mothers,
And on the wealth of others as the worst poison,
Who rejoice to see the prosperity of others, and grieve greatly in their diversity,
They who love you more than life,
Their hearts are auspicious places for you to live in.

Those who look upon you as master, friend, father,
Mother, and teacher, to whom you are all in all,
Dwell in the temple of their hearts,
Both ye brothers with Sītā.
Those who never wish for anything,
Who love you quite naturally,
Live in their hearts forever,
There is your home.[2]

VISHNU BHAKTI Krishna-Vasudeva was the founder of the Bhagavata religion and was eventually deified himself. In the course of time this deity was identified with Vishnu, a solar deity who was of minimal significance in the *Rigveda* but who came into more prominence in the Brahmanas, during which time the cult of Vishnu became known. By the fourth century B.C., it appears that the two most popular deities were Vishnu and Shiva. By the period of the *Puranas* (A.D. 300–1200), Vishnu had expanded his scope and dominance, chiefly by reason of the doctrine of *avataras*.

Theistic trends were commonly found to grow outside the influence of the Brahmans. When a local deity became sufficiently prominent, the Brahmans would attempt to bring such worship into their orbit of influence, either by indicating that the local deity was really Vishnu under a different name, or that he was an *avatara* (incarnation or descent) of Vishnu. This process has been called Brahmanization because it was a means of bringing the deities under Brahmanic control. This can also be called Sanskritization, since it was

2. *Ayodhyakanda*, 127.2–131. Quoted in H. Bhattacharyya, ed., *The Cultural Heritage of India*, Calcutta, The Ramakrishna Mission Institute of Culture, 1956, vol. IV, pp. 404–405.

a process whereby local deities were brought into the orbit of a widely accepted notion of orthodoxy.[3]

In the *Puranas,* Vishnu came to have numerous *avataras.* Although the traditional list contains ten, some list over twenty. These incarnate deities not only extended the worship of Vishnu, but also expanded his nature as well. The traditional list of ten *avataras* includes both human and animal forms.

1. The Fish (*Matsya*). In the form of a fish Vishnu saved Manu (the progenitor of the human race) from a destructive flood. Recognizing the divinity of a fish that had grown so large that only the ocean could contain it, Manu worshiped the fish and was told of the coming flood. Manu boarded a ship that he had built for his family. Vishnu appeared in the sea as a fish with a huge horn to which the ship was tied until the waters subsided. Vishnu is also said to have saved the Vedas from the flood by assuming this form.

2. The Tortoise (*Kurma*). Vishnu appeared in this form to retrieve some things that were lost in the deluge. Placing himself (as a tortoise) at the bottom of the sea of milk, he served as a base for Mount Mandara. Twisting the serpent Vasuki around the mountain as a rope, the gods then pulled the serpent, thus churning the sea and recovering the desired objects. These included Amrita (water of life which renewed the gods), Lakshmi the goddess of wealth, and other deities and valuable objects.

3. The Boar (*Varaha*). When the earth was dragged to the bottom of the sea by the demon Hiranyaksha, Vishnu as the Boar killed the demon and raised the earth to its former position. This *avatara* may stem from a divine boar which was originally a tribal totem.

4. The Man-Lion (*Narasimha*). A demon had become invulnerable. He could not be killed by day or by night, by man or by beast, inside or outside of the temple. When this demon sought to kill his own son because he worshiped Vishnu, his destruction was sealed. Vishnu took the form of a Man-Lion (neither man nor beast) and came forth from a pillar of the temple (neither inside nor outside of the temple) at sunset (neither day nor night). Thus was the demon destroyed.

5. The Dwarf (*Vamana*). Through countless devotions and austerities a demon named Bali had gained dominion over the three worlds. In order to restore such power to the gods from whom it had been taken, Vishnu appeared in the form of a dwarf. He asked Bali to grant him as much land as he could traverse in three steps. Once the request was granted, Vishnu assumed gigantic form and in two strides restored heaven and earth. He graciously left Bali in control of the infernal regions.

6. Rama with the Ax (*Parashurama*). Here Vishnu took the form of a Brahman who destroyed the Kshatriyas because of their arrogant

---

3. "Sanskritization, then, refers to a process in the Indian Civilization in which a person or a group consciously related himself or itself to an accepted notion of true and ancient ideology and conduct." J. A. B. Van Buitenen, "On the Archaism of the *Bhagavata Purana*," in Milton Singer, ed., *Krishna: Rites, Myths, and Rituals,* Honolulu, East-West Center Press, 1966, p. 35.

dominance. This *avatara* is not to be confused with the Rama of the *Ramayana*.

7. Rama. This is the Rama whose story is the theme of the *Ramayana*. Vishnu took this form in order to destroy the demon Ravana.

8. Krishna. Vishnu took the form of Krishna in order to kill the demon Kamsa.

9. Buddha. Vishnu took this form to destroy the wicked who rejected the Vedas. By so doing he established the authority of those sacred writings.

10. Kalki. This *avatara* is future. At the end of the present Kali age, Kalkin will come, mounted on a white horse. He will judge the wicked, reward the good, and set up a new age.

Since Krishna was one of the most popular deities, it was only a matter of time before he would also be identified as an *avatara* of Vishnu. As we have seen in our discussion of Krishna, there are explicit cases where the identification of Krishna as an *avatara* of Vishnu is resisted and Krishna is proclaimed as the Supreme Being. Likewise Rama was destined to be drawn into orbit, although not until considerably later. There were also those such as Tulsi Das who proposed the worship of Rama and Sita to the exclusion of the other *avataras* of Vishnu.

Even the Buddha, who rejected the authority of the Vedas, the Brahmanical authority, and the efficacy of the sacrifices, was taken into the fold as an *avatara*. In this way the Brahmans could admit his religious significance in the light of his strong following, and at the same time denounce his teachings. The Brahmans held that Vishnu became the Buddha in order to delude the wicked by leading them to deny the Vedas and the efficacy of the sacrifices, thereby assuring their damnation. In this way the destruction of the wicked would be an example to others. Until recently the temple of the Buddha at Budhgaya was run by Brahmans and the Buddha was the object of *puja* just as any other deity might be—much to the chagrin of contemporary Buddhists.

The difficulty with most discussions of Vishnu is that they take the interpretative position of the Vaishnava (i.e., devotees of Vishnu), and fail to recognize that not infrequently the effort to incorporate other religious expressions in this manner was resisted. Although it is usually stated that Vaishnavas comprise the largest group of Indian devotees, it must quickly be added that by far the largest number of such Vaishnavas are devotees of Krishna or Rama.

Vishnu is usually pictured with his vehicle the bird Garuda or with his wife Lakshmi or Shri, the goddess of wealth. While in the *Puranas* a triad of gods is mentioned, Brahma the creator, Vishnu the preserver, and Shiva the destroyer, those who are devoted to Vishnu commonly set this triad aside and focus on Vishnu as the Lord of creation, preservation, and destruction.

Today Vishnu is worshiped at Puri in Orissa as Lord Jagannath, whose car festival is well known. In it Lord Jagannath is carried in a huge car from the temple to his summer palace, and is later returned. In Maharashtra he is worshiped as Vithoba, where a sect has grown into significant proportions. In the south he is worshiped on a mountain near Tirupati. There a seven-foot, four-armed image is enshrined in a large temple. This is a common place for devotees to go on a pilgrimage, and is so sacred to them that non-Hindus are not permitted to enter the temple. Such is also the case at the Jagannath temple in Puri.

SHIVA BHAKTI

Shiva, meaning "auspicious," was a euphemistic epithet given to the Rigvedic Rudra. As Rudra, Shiva inspires more fear than love. He is conceived as the destroyer when in the company of Brahma and Vishnu. As the great ascetic, Shiva is often depicted with a garland of skulls and surrounded with ghosts and demons.

> On the high slopes of the Himālayan Mount Kailāsa, Śiva, the great yogī, sits on a tiger skin, deep in meditation and through his meditation the world is maintained. He is depicted thus as wearing his long matted hair (jaṭā) in a topknot, in which the crescent moon is fixed, and from which flows the sacred river Ganges. In the middle of his forehead is a third eye, emblem of his superior wisdom and insight. His neck is black, scarred by a deadly poison which was the last of the objects churned from the cosmic ocean, and which he drank to save the other gods from destruction. Snakes, of which he is the lord, encircle his neck and arms. His body is covered with ashes, a favorite ascetic practice. Beside him is his weapon, the trident, while near him are his beautiful wife Pārvatī and his mount, the bull Nandi.[4]

Shiva is also the lord of animals and the lord of dance. As Nataraja, his dance supports the rhythm of the universe. Powerful and creative, he is worshiped most commonly in the form of the linga (i.e., a representation of the male sexual organ). In the innermost heart of the Shaiva temple is the linga. Nandi the bull stands outside the inner sanctum, his eyes fixed on this most sacred symbol, the linga, which is even more commonly used than anthropomorphic representations of the deity.

In the *Shvetashvatara Upanishad*, bhakti is enjoined to Shiva. The final verse of this Upanishad states that the truths contained therein are to be told to a "high-minded man who feels the highest devotion (*bhakti*) for God and for his *guru* as for God." As early as the second century B.C., the grammarian Patanjali mentions a Shiva-bhagavata sect. In their attempts to spread the influence of Shiva, the devotees identified him with local deities as the followers of Vishnu had done. Shiva is even given *avataras* in imitation of the doctrine held by Vaishnavas, but they never played the significant role which they did for Vishnu. In the case of Vishnu, the *avataras*, particularly Krishna and Rama, were more prominent than Vishnu himself. Such is not the case for Shiva.

While followers of Shiva have had a greater tendency toward ad-

---

4. A. L. Basham, *The Wonder That Was India*, New York, Grove Press, Inc., 1959 (first published 1954), p. 307.

Sixteenth-century southern Indian copper figure of Shiva as Nataraja. (Courtesy of the Museum of Fine Arts, Boston.)

vaitin views (see p. 188) than the *bhaktas* previously considered, there have still been those whose message was devotional and emotional rather than meditative. The Vaishnava Alvars have their counterparts in the Shaiva Nayanars. Some sixty-three of them produced hymns of a devotional nature. Some of these hymns form the *Devaram,* the first of twelve canonical books called *Tirumurai* which are considered by some Shaivites (Shaiva Siddhanta) as *shruti* (see p. 118). This shows that sometimes in theory and often in practice the Vedas are not the supreme authority. These hymns are not an attempt at a systematic theology but an account of a vivid experience. Optimism reigns as God's mercy and grace are pro-

Shaiva priest in Poona. Nandi is facing the inner shrine where there is a Shiva Linga. (Photo by Robert D. Baird.)

claimed. Devotion to Shiva is useful for all. Shiva exists everywhere and appears even to the illiterate if, as a true *bhakta,* his mind is intent on Shiva's love and service.

The prominence given to grace cannot be ignored. When man realizes his condition, the freely given grace of God seems even more wonderful.

Thou gav'st thyself, thou gainest me;
which did the better bargain derive?
Bliss found I in infinity;
but what didst thou from me derive?

In South India there developed a theological tradition called Shaiva Siddhanta. The first systematic attempt to state the beliefs of Tamil Shaivism is the *Shiva-jnana-bodham* of Meykandar in the first half of the thirteenth century. Meykandar's position is realistic and theistic. Shiva is the *guru* par excellence whose grace illuminates the intellect when one submits to the teachings of the human *gurus.* Shiva, the soul of man, and the bonds of ignorance are all considered real. Karma and *maya* are not evils, but agencies used by Shiva for the purification of the soul from ignorance. The three paths of service, worship, and meditation are proposed, but all are to be animated by *bhakti*. This makes the soul open to Shiva's grace, by which union with him is possible. Shiva imparts divine knowledge (*patijnana*) by way of intuition to highly advanced souls. To those less advanced, he works through a human *guru,* which explains the concern of the *bhakta* to meet a *guru* through whom Shiva can give divine knowledge. Liberation is union with Shiva, but not a complete cessation of separateness. Shiva is bliss itself, while

Shaiva priests in Srirangam Shiva Temple, southern India. (Photo by Robert D. Baird.)

the soul can only enjoy bliss. Hence in this emphatically *bhakti* system theism is maintained.

The Kashmir brand of Shaivism is quite different. It appears just before the ninth century. Here Shiva is merely a form for presenting *advaita* philosophy (see p. 188). Shiva is the underlying reality of the universe, the world being an emanation from him. While the world is quite real inasmuch as it has the reality it appears to possess, it is illusory in the sense that Shiva, the prime reality, remains unaffected by change in the sensible world. In its true nature the soul is identified with Shiva, but by reason of its ignorance it considers itself finite and imperfect. The awakened soul realizes its true nature as Shiva through *bhakti* worship and devotion.

SHAKTI BHAKTI

Shakti worship is worship of the deity's power in the form of his consort. This has taken various forms, from simply representing the deity with his consort to singling her out as the chief object of worship. Although erotic practices might well be expected, not all Shaktism is erotic, and some forms are highly philosophical. Rites and rituals of a sacramental and magical nature accompanied with diagrams and gestures comprise a wide-ranging practice which has not been sufficiently studied for us to get an overview or a very penetrating understanding. The texts which describe the elaborate rites and theories connected with Shaktism are called *Tantras*.

Although the Mother Goddess seems to have been venerated in the Indus Valley Civilization, little place is given to goddesses in the Vedic literature. Female deities were probably worshiped to some extent on the popular level from earliest times, but in the fourth century they came to be worshiped in special temples, and from the sixth to the tenth centuries the cult association with Shakti worship became elaborately developed. Worship of the Mother Goddess grew in importance until early in the Muslim period.

While devotion of a sort was directed to Sarasvati, the wife of Brahma, and to Lakshmi, the wife of Vishnu, Shakti is most commonly worshiped as the wife of Shiva. Since the name Shakti has been used to identify a number of local goddesses, the name of Shiva's consort varies in different locales. Her most common names are Durga, Kali, Parvati, and Uma.

The concept underlying worship of Shakti is that since the eternal Shiva is inactive while his wife is Shakti or pure activity, the creation of the world and the work of grace and liberation are her functions. Hence Shakti becomes more important than Shiva himself, who is static and ineffective without his wife.

The Shaktas (devotees of Shakti) made use of adoration *mantras,* which were brief expressions of reverence for the goddess. The Shaktas also made use of diagrams of mystic import (*mandalas*), ritual gestures with the fingers (*mudras*), and ritual movements of the hands (*nyasa*) for bringing the goddess into the body.

The worship of Shakti became particularly significant from A.D. 550 to 900, when an elaborate cult developed. Some of it was closer to *bhakti* principles than were other parts. It was the view of the Shaktas that in the *kali* (black) age in which we now exist, their methods were the only adequate ways to liberation. One of the means was the public worship of the goddess in temples. Offerings to the goddess were vegetable, animal, or human. Tradition indicates that Hsüan tsang, a Chinese pilgrim, was almost sacrificed to Durga. Human sacrifice was abolished by the British, and even animal sacrifice has since been made illegal by the State of Madras. While the vegetable offerings were laid before the image, animals were sacrificed in the temple courtyard some distance from the image.

A second method was circle worship (*cakra-puja*), sometimes called left-handed tantra. An equal number of men and women meet secretly at night and sit in a circle. The goddess is represented in the center of the circle by a yoni (i.e., a mystical sign representing the female sexual organ.) In addition to the repetition of *mantras,* the participants partake of the five *tattvas* (sometimes called the five M's, since each begins with that letter in Sanskrit): wine, meat, fish, parched grain, and sexual intercourse.

A third method was meditative exercises or discipline (*sadhana*), intended to bring the participant to perfection. Finally, there was the use of sorcery and spells. As with other sects, the Shaktas advised those who wanted to make real spiritual progress to select a *guru* and undertake initiation.

The worship of the goddess was also found among the followers of the Buddha. These same principles were implied in the tantric texts which appeared in the sixth and seventh centuries. The Buddhas and Bodhisattvas came to be seen as inert while their wives were active and wide-awake. Hence, in addition to the three traditional bodies of the Buddha (see pp. 184 ff.), tantrism taught that there was a fourth body, the *vajrasattva,* whereby the Buddha embraced his Shakti, *Tara* or *Bhagavati.*

Perhaps the best known goddess in India today is Kali, the Shakti of Shiva, who is worshiped in her own right. In Bengal, particularly in the Kalighat Temple in Calcutta, devotees fall before her image on their bellies, often with sighs and groans of devotion. Goats are sacrificed to her in the courtyard. The image of Kali is similar to the description in the *Kali Tantra*.

> *Most fearful, her laughter shows her dreadful teeth. She stands upon a corpse. She has four arms. Her hands hold a sword and a head and show the gestures of removing fear and granting boons. She is the auspicious divinity of sleep, the consort of Śiva.*
>
> *Naked, clad only in space, the goddess is resplendent. Her tongue hangs out. She wears a garland of heads. Such is the form worthy of meditation of the Power of Time, Kālī, who dwells near the funeral pyres.*[5]

Thus portrayed, Kali manifests both the powers of destruction and grace. All the pleasures of the world are transient, while only Kali is permanent and can grant happiness. Why is she black? Because she is the ultimate energy. Colors are distinctions, while in Kali all colors dissolve into shapelessness and darkness.

ATTEMPTS AT SYNTHESIS

While it was common to place other deities in a hierarchy beneath one's chief deity, and sometimes to even move toward monotheism, there were also attempts to synthesize the deities without placing one above another. Such an attempt at synthesis can be illustrated on three levels.

There is the attempt to combine male and female. Not only can one find images that are half male and half female, but Shiva and Shakti are sometimes portrayed in this manner. As common as the worship of Shiva in the form of a linga is the worship of Shakti in the form of a yoni. Sometimes one finds the linga and yoni as part of a single representation. In this way the male and female aspects of the universe are united in one artistic representation. This was also seen in the unification of Krishna and Radha in a single person.

The two most popular deities by far are Vishnu and Shiva. Therefore, it should not be surprising that there would be an effort to combine the two of them. This was done in the form of the deity Harihara (or Shankara-Narayana), that is, Vishnu and Shiva combined. A hymn is addressed to him and is contained in the *Harivamsa*. There is evidence that he was rather widely worshiped in the Deccan and in South India. Various local village deities have been assimilated with him.

Another form of synthesis is to combine gods into groups. Some temples are dedicated to the five deities Shiva, Vishnu, Durga, Ganesha, and Surya. The *trimurti* of Brahma, Vishnu, and Shiva is another example of such grouping. This triad is not nearly as important for Indian devotion as has sometimes been suggested.

---

5. Quoted in Alain Danielou, *Hindu Polytheism*, London, Routledge, 1964, p. 496.

Nevertheless, it is another manifestation of the attempt at synthesis. In this context Brahma is the Creator, Vishnu the Preserver, and Shiva the Destroyer. These are dominant characteristics in the deities considered individually; but as separate objects of devotion, each one assumes all three characteristics. As a matter of fact, Brahma never had a large cult or following of his own, but did find his place in various pantheons.

RELIGIOUS SYSTEMS

The discussion of Indian religious or philosophical systems often includes a description of the six "orthodox" systems: the Nyaya, Vaisheshika, Sankhya, Yoga, Purvamimamsa, and Uttaramimamsa (or Vedanta). These systems are called "orthodox" because they each rely, at least in word, on the authority of the *Vedas*. The systems of the Jainas, the Pali Canon, and the Carvakas (materialists) are then considered "heterodox," because they reject Vedic authority.

The historian of religions, however, cannot present his material as either "orthodox" or "heterodox," regardless of how strong or prominent the majority party happens to be. His goal is not to interpret material according to some standard of "orthodoxy," however arrived at, but to seek to understand the religions of as many persons and groups as possible.

The Indian philosophical tradition is exceedingly complex and varied. Some of the systems exist today while others exerted their main influence in past ages. We will discuss several attempts at religious systematization. In each case the system is religious because it is a systematic articulation of what someone believes ought to be ultimately important for man. The first two systems to be considered (Madhyamika and Yogacara) are variations of what is usually called "Mahayana Buddhism" in distinction from the "Theravada Buddhism" represented in the Pali Canon.

MADHYAMIKA Some time in the middle or toward the end of the second century A.D., there lived a South Indian Brahman named Nagarjuna, whose religious system was called Madhyamika because it was the "middle way" between realism and nihilism, the views, respectively, that phenomena are real and that nothing exists.[1] Having been raised in

---

1. For a fuller exposition of Madhyamika, cf. T. R. V. Murti, *The Central Philosophy of Buddhism,* London, G. Allen, 1955; K. Venkata Ramanan, *Na-*

a Brahman family, Nagarjuna received thorough religious instruction. According to legendary accounts, he was renowned for his learning and his superhuman powers by the time he reached manhood. He and three companions studied magic and learned to make themselves invisible. They used this knowledge to enter the palace where they seduced women. Their escapades were discovered and Nagarjuna's companions were slain. Nagarjuna concluded that the root of suffering was lust. He went to a mountain *stupa* and took the rites of going forth (*pabbajja*). It is reported that in ninety days he mastered the *Tipitaka* and then turned to the Mahayana scriptures. He is remembered as an avid debater who always won his debates.

The *Vajracchedika* or Diamond Cutter Sutra, and the *Ashtasahasrika Prajnaparamita Sutra,* were systematized by the Madhyamika school of thought. The former argues for the negation of all phenomenal distinctions, while the latter emphasizes the perfection of nondual wisdom. Nagarjuna's system is a commentary on such and other *prajnaparamita* sutras.

Although the Madhyamika was intended to be an authentic understanding of the thought of the Buddha, it differs from the doctrine of the Pali Canon which also proposes to present the teachings of the Buddha. Nagarjuna's system is not an ontological system, but a system of dialectic intended as a means to realization.

Important for understanding Nagarjuna is his understanding of the silence of the Buddha. As early as the Pali Canon there are accounts which indicate that the Buddha would not answer certain types of questions. These came to be called the fourteen Inexpressibles, and are as follows:

1. Whether the world is eternal, or not, or both, or neither;
2. Whether the world is finite (in space), or infinite, or both, or neither;
3. Whether the Tathagata exists after death, or does not, or both, or neither;
4. Whether the soul is identical with the body or different from it.

There is no reason why the last statement could not also contain four alternatives, but in the dialogues of the Buddha it usually does not. In refusing to answer such questions, was the Buddha agnostic to, or innocent of, metaphysics?

According to Nagarjuna, the Buddha's silence was much more sophisticated than any of the above-proposed answers. For the Buddha, the Real actually transcended all thought and rational categories. He was convinced that any view about the Real that was presented could be shown to be logically absurd, since such categories of thought, while applicable to the phenomenal world, are not applicable to the Real.

Considering all such metaphysical speculations as dogmatism

garjuna's Philosophy as Presented in the Maha-Prajnaparamitasastra, Tokyo & Rutland, Vt., Charles E. Tuttle Co., 1966; Richard H. Robinson, *Early Madhyamika in India and China,* Madison, Wis., University of Wisconsin Press, 1967; Frederick J. Streng, *Emptiness: A Study in Religious Meaning,* New York and Nashville, Abingdon, 1967.

(*dhitthi-vada*), the Buddha consistently avoided falling into the same net by refusing to answer such questions. Any answer that might be given in response to such inquiries would be inadequate. Hence the Buddha rejected all views, and by not offering in their place an alternative view, raised the more basic question of the relation of Reality to all viewpoints. The silence of the Buddha implies the recognition that the Unconditioned Reality is indescribable.

Madhyamika is a system, not in offering an articulate ontology but in the sense that it offers a critique of all other systems of ontology. This critique goes deeper than a mere refutation of alternatives, for it tends thereby to show that when it comes to a question of Reality, the conflict is in reason itself. Madhyamika utilizes the *reductio ad absurdum* to show the logical absurdity of all metaphysical statements. But, by refuting other points of view Madhyamika does not propose its own point of view in terms of reason and logic. On the other hand, it is not, simply by reason of its refutation of all other views, nihilism. Madhyamika's criticism of all views might be called *upaya,* or the means to a spiritual end. If Reality transcends all language and reason, then only by the repudiation of all such views can Reality appear.

By the time of Nagarjuna, the upanishadic view that the Real was the Atman was well developed. This view attempted to solve the problem of suffering by arguing that only the permanent is Real, that the changing things to which we cling are not Real. On the other hand, the Pali Canon solved the problem of suffering in the reverse manner by denying any permanence and affirming a world of constant flux. Hence there was no Atman and no Brahman. All of the human experiences could be accounted for without positing a permanent entity within. But the Pali Canon did not question the reality of the *khandhas* which it used to account for human experience. It also broke things down into *ayatanas* (sense organs and sense data) and *dhatus* (ultimate elements of existence), of which there were six (earth, fire, water, air, space, and consciousness).

The Madhyamikas question the doctrine of the *khandhas.* How can one, on the basis of the *khandhas* alone, explain the grouping of the *khandhas,* since this is not an inherent feature of the *khandhas* themselves? Furthermore, the constant regrouping of the *khandhas* from one moment to another involves one in all the problems associated with the doctrine of causation (see p. 183). The *dhatus* were taken as radical elements which were irreducible. But to be a basic element distinguishable from other such basic elements, each must have a specific character which distinguishes it from others. In the *Abhidhamma,* such *dhatus* are given characteristics which distinguish them. The earth is characterized by hardness, for example. The Madhyamika philosopher asks if there is anything which differentiates hardness from earth. If the answer is no, then it is not possible to distinguish one *dhatu* from another. If there is a distinction between the *dhatu* earth and its hardness, then it is asked if the earth could exist prior to its hardness. If the answer is affirmative, then the *dhatu* could exist without its distinctive property and hence would itself be nondescript, and a nondescript entity is a nonentity. Hence we end with no distinctions to apply. Without a nature of their own, the *dhatus* are nothing in themselves. And, the same argument applies to the *khandhas*.

If the view contained in the Pali Canon is contradictory, so is the substance view of the Upanishads. If the Atman were identical with the states of existence, it would have to be subject to birth and death. The Pali view that all we have are changing *khandas* offends the moral sense by having the deeds of one "person" become results which affect another "person," hence putting the responsibility of a deed on one who did not commit it. If, however, one says that the Atman as an eternal substance exists independently of the changing states, then it should be perceivable apart from those states, but this is not so. The only conclusion, according to Nagarjuna, is that the self is neither different from nor identical with the states of existence. Furthermore, there is no self apart from the states, nor can one say it is nonexistent.

The doctrine of causation (*paticcasamupada*) is basic to an understanding of Pali Buddhist thought. The doctrine is used to show that nothing is independent of everything else, but that everything has a cause and thus arises from another. But Nagarjuna argued that by maintaining that there is essential difference between cause and effect, one is arguing that the effect is totally different from the cause. The implication is that anything should be able to produce anything, hence enabling anything to arise anywhere and at any time. To insist on the essential difference between cause and effect means to give up the notion of causation.

To hold to the identity of cause and effect by arguing that things are produced out of themselves, as does the Sankhya philosophy,[2] would avert the problem but would introduce another, namely the loss of a meaningful distinction between cause and effect if they are identical. Hence this view is also self-contradictory, since one cannot retain the notion of cause without introducing the differences.

When the Jainas try to combine the two views by maintaining the continuous and emergent aspects, they fall into still greater problems, since the Real must then have two different aspects. If we admit that we are unable to explain the relationship between these two aspects, then we have admitted what the Madhyamika position is trying to say—that it is beyond reason.

The alternative of the skeptics and materialists is quickly disposed of by Nagarjuna. Theirs is the view that things appear by chance. He merely asks for the reason for the assertion that things arise at random. If an answer is given, it refutes itself by admitting that the conclusion is arrived at causally. If no answer is given, the statement is ignored since it is merely dogmatically stated.

According to Nagarjuna, the meaning of the doctrine of causation is that things depend on each other and have no reality of their own. Hence it teaches that they are *shunya* (empty). If there is any

---

2. A philosophical position that is realistic and dualistic, holding that both spirit and matter are eternal and real.

term used for Reality, it is *Shunyata* (void or emptiness) which is the disavowal of all views about Reality.

The foregoing is not mere idle argumentation, but has relationship to a religious goal. For Nagarjuna, the Real is not produced, but is known by being uncovered. The refutation of views performs this service. After negating all views, the intellect becomes so pure that it is indistinguishable from the Real. Madhyamika seems to have a preference for speaking of the Ultimate in epistemological rather than in metaphysical terms. Hence Madhyamika refers to *Prajna* which is nondual intuition of the Real or *Prajnaparamita,* the perfection of wisdom.

Prajna, however, is a particular knowledge which does not participate in the dualistically conceived knowledge of our phenomenal existence. In this lower knowledge there is always a distinction between the subject and the object known. *Prajna* is immediate, intuitive, nondual, and contentless. When it arises, after all dualistic views are eliminated through criticism, there is no change ontologically, but only in terms of our apprehension. The mind is free of all impediments, all suffering and pain. This *Prajna* is the same as *Shunyata.* The one indicates that it is perfect nondual wisdom, while the other indicates that it is void of all views. *Tathata* is another term applied to the Real, which means "thatness" or "suchness" and indicates that the Real is the way it is without distinctions.

We have previously noted the growing emphasis on the Buddha as an object of worship and devotion (*bhakti*). The Buddha had also been called *Tathagata,* or "one who has thus come." In time *Tathagata* came to be more than merely a term for an enlightened being. *Tathagata* came to be closer to a Perfect Being or God. This is taken into the Madhyamika system as a personalized aspect of *Shunyata.* This is also part of the element of grace and mercy which seems so foreign to the Pali Canon, but which came to be a feature of later interpretations of the Buddha's teaching. Hence the *Tathagata* can be spoken of in personal terms. *Tathagata* engages in various activities for the salvation of men and assumes forms out of his infinite compassion to save all beings out of his free grace. There is no limit to the number of *Tathagatas* or to the forms they may assume. The number of Buddhas is numerous and the idea that they may arise according to human needs is a doctrine that is paralleled in the *Bhagavad Gita* with reference to Krishna. Nevertheless, in all of this, Nagarjuna remains firm in his position that the Real is indescribable and best expressed in silence. Hence, although in one sense *Prajnaparamita* is equated with *Tathagata,* this would only be from the relative point of view, for *Prajna* is silence and cannot be said to be born or to assume forms or to be compassionate.

Even Madhyamika, which emphasized the emptiness of all views, incorporated the doctrine of the three bodies of the Buddha. This *Trikaya* doctrine became a way of organizing the images under which the Buddha had come to be conceived. Buddhology had developed to such an extent that the Gautama of history was of less concern than other Buddhas.

The first body, or *Dharmakaya,* is the cosmic body, the essential nature of the Buddha and one with the Absolute. Although the *Dharmakaya* is closest to *Shunyata,* it is still personal, with innumerable merits and powers, and is indeed an object of devotion. The arising of the *Dharmakaya* from *Shunyata* is inexplicable, for ultimately *Shunyata* is void of all views or dualistic conceptions. The second body, *Sambhogakaya,* is the "body of bliss." A reflection of the *Dharmakaya* in the material world, it is the form in which the Buddha appears at the beginning of the Mahayana *sutras* with innumerable rays shooting from his body and accompanied by innumerable spiritual beings and Bodhisattvas. He is endowed with thirty-two primary and eighty secondary marks of beauty and excellence. The *Nirmanakaya* is an apparitional body which the Buddha assumed in order to save beings from misery. The *Nirmanakaya* is a manifestation of *Sambhogakaya* in the world and corresponds to the historical Gautama and other Buddhas of history. Buddhas and Bodhisattvas are forms chosen by *Tathagata* to help men. They are deliberate descents of Divinity. But all of this is a concession to ignorance.

The *Trikaya* doctrine is more than mere speculation. It was a functional way of uniting various aspects of thought and devotion that had developed around the memory of the Buddha, though Theravadins were inclined to minimize such forms of devotion. The Madhyamikas, however, held to the view that *all* is void, and hence could not propose that such practices and developments were inferior forms of expression. Such a proposal would impute to them a qualified reality, and to other views a higher degree of reality. But since *all* views are void, they could accept such devotional expressions as part of the skill in means (*upaya*) which was possessed by Buddhas and Bodhisattvas. In the *Diamond Sutra* it is stated that once one recognizes that there is no Bodhisattva, no dharmas, no Nirvana, and no beings to be led to Nirvana, then one can speak of them. Once it is recognized that all such designations are empty, then they can be used as "skill in means" (*upaya*). One example of such argumentation is the following:

> *The Lord asked: What do you think Subhuti, is the Tathagata to be seen through his possession of marks?—Subhuti replied: No indeed, O Lord. And why? This possession of marks, O Lord, which has been taught by the Tathagata, as a no-possession of no-marks this has been taught by the Tathagata. Therefore, it is called "possession of marks."* [3]

According to Nagarjuna, one does not distinguish the phenomena from *Shunyata* since *Shunyata* is actually the real nature of the phenomena. *Shunyata* is known through the appearances which are *upaya* (means or devices) for reaching the Absolute. There is no fall and recovery, since Nirvana does not cease. All that is necessary for the apprehension of the Real is the dissolution of false views. This is why Madhyamika is not nihilism, for if there were nothing, no

---

3. Edward Conze, *Buddhist Wisdom Books,* London, G. Allen, 1958, pp. 60–61 (emphasis added).

views would be false. Views are false only because they falsify the Real.

If the Real is *Shunyata*, then the appearances are due to *avidya*, or ignorance. It might be asked if *avidya* is real or unreal. One view is to say that if *avidya* is really the cause of the unreal, it must itself be real for the unreal cannot be a cause. Nagarjuna argues that *avidya* is unreal, otherwise its products would have to be real. Furthermore, *avidya* has no beginning, but it does have an end in *Prajna*.

There are three movements on the route to realization. The first is dogmatism (*drishti*), the second is criticism of all views, and the third is *Prajna*, or intuitive knowledge. The dogmatism of views is necessary as a means, for one would never see the conflict without at least two views. As a result of this conflict one comes to an awareness of the fact that the Absolute is *Shunyata*, void of all views, transcending reason and thought. Hence the criticism culminates in *Prajna*.

YOGACARA

This school of thought existed from the second century A.D. After its chief fourth-century systematizers, Asanga and Vasubandhu, it came to be the dominant school of thought, eclipsing Madhyamika among the professed followers of the Buddha. Born into a North Indian Brahman family, Asanga was one of three brothers, all of whom were originally known by the name of Vasubandhu. The oldest later acquired the name of Asanga. The youngest is not part of this study since no doctrinal importance attaches to him. All of the brothers were converted to the Sarvastivadin school,[4] but Asanga was the first to move over to a Mahayana position. As a Sarvastivadin, the second brother, Vasubandhu, is credited with several works of significance. Asanga exerted considerable effort and subtlety to convert him to Mahayana. Toward the latter part of his life, Vasubandhu also came to believe in Amitabha and looked forward to rebirth in his Western Paradise.

In addition to the designation of Yogacara, this school is called *Vijnanavada*, or the viewpoint that only consciousness is Real. It is because of this basic doctrine that the school has been characterized as subjective idealism. The independent existence of objects is rejected in favor of pure thought. The denial of the independent existence of external objects is not just part of an abstract philosophical system, but becomes a new way of stating man's problem and attempting a solution. Man's problem is that he projects objects independent of thought, and he will not be liberated as long as he conceives of a subject and an object. Liberation for the Pali Canon and the Madhyamika also was an experience of nonduality and hence eliminated the distinction of subject and object. But this time there exists an ontology which emphasizes mind and attempts a solution not by seeing that there is no ego and that all is flux, or as

---

4. This school held to the reality of the past, present, and future and developed a canon (not presently available to us) that seems to have been somewhat parallel to the Pali Canon.

Madhyamika did by seeing the inherent contradictions in all views and thereby transcending this dualism in *Prajna*, but rather by withdrawal of the senses from supposed external objects until there is thought only.

The Yogacarins used several arguments to defend their idealistic point of view, but the most significant for their entire viewpoint were those which were based on experience. Their appeal was not to common sense experience which would seem to belie a view that rejects the reality of external objects, but the experience of the Buddhas and those who have not achieved complete awareness, however, could approximate it through various steps and levels of meditation. This meditative process was designed to make the practitioner perceive that in realization there is nothing apart from thought.

The Yogacarins are called so because of the emphasis they place on meditative and yogic practices. They represent a reaction against what they consider an overemphasis on the logical process by the Madhyamika dialectic which had little concern for the practice of meditation and the various states of trance which result therefrom. The Yogacarins did not reject the notion of the void, but called it thought. Once one comes to realize that all is thought, all external objects are dissolved. Of course, the implication of Madhyamika is accepted that thought is "really no thought." This is the case since it is the pure subject free from all objects.

By talking of the Absolute as Nirvana (blowing out), or *Shunyata*, transcendence is preserved by reverting to negative designations. The Yogacarins, however, wanted to emphasize the locus of this transcending experience. One cannot achieve this nondual experience through introspection, since as soon as we thus turn in toward the subject, it becomes the object of thought. But by "ruthless withdrawal from each and every object, in the introversion of trance, one could hope to move toward such a result." [5] In this way the problem of grasping is also solved, since there is no grasping when there is nothing to be grasped. Instead of removing the object of desire through analyzing away both subject and object in terms of a world of flux, or by showing the utter irrationality of all views, this school removed the object of desire by withdrawing from it in meditation.

Everything, then, is only mind and our illusion consists in projecting real external objects. This is not merely abstract speculation any more than was the analysis found in the Pali Canon. It is true that these texts can appear to be involved in barren intellectual hairsplitting, but here, as in previous interpretations of the Buddha's teachings, the practical result of liberation is the goal.

The highest insight is reached when everything appears as sheer hallucination. The Yogācārins based this conviction not merely on a number of logical arguments which proved the impossibility of

---

5. Edward Conze, *Buddhism: Its Essence and Development,* New York, Harper Torchbooks, 1959, pp. 166–167.

an external object, but on the living experience of ecstatic meditation.[6]

The Yogacarins are also noted for their doctrine of the "store consciousness" (*alaya-vijnana*). Interpreters of the teachings of the Buddha had been plagued with the opposition of common sense observation to the doctrine of *anatta*. Although the Pali Canon and most later interpreters disavowed permanence or the existence of the person as a sustained entity, certain doctrines crept in which appear to compromise the radical nature of impermanence as a universal characteristic of existence. One early school, the *Pudgalavadins* (those who believe in a person), spoke of a principle called the *pudgala*, or person, which was neither different nor not-different from the *khandhas*. Hence they brought in the notion of a person, while simultaneously affirming the Pali analysis of man. The Yogacarins' concept of the "store consciousness" serves a similar function in attempting to account for the awareness that some of our past experiences are stored up for a time, only to come to fruition in a later life. This consciousness is the basis of all of our acts of thought, and accounts for deeds which do not reach immediate fruition. Once this doctrine was conceived, however, it led to considerable metaphysical speculation regarding the relation of the physical world to the store consciousness in terms of emanations. While the Yogacarins did emphasize liberation in their yogic concerns, they also interpret the Buddha and his teachings considerably differently than does the Pali Canon. The Pali tradition as well as Madhyamika had disavowed metaphysical questions. The Yogacarins developed a full ontological system. Along with the Madhyamikas, they elaborated the *Trikaya* doctrine. The *Lankavatara Sutra* comes closest to embodying their doctrinal position.

ADVAITA VEDANTA This position is called *Vedanta* because it is based on the Upanishads which come at the end of the *Veda,* and *Advaita* because it is a nondual (*a + dvaita*) system. Shankara (788–820), with whom this system is commonly associated, was the son of a *Shivaguru* and was born in the Malabar country of the Deccan. He was considered an *avatara* of Shiva, and accounts of his life contain references to miraculous deeds. At the age of eight he became an ascetic, and he is said to have written his commentary on the *Brahma Sutras* at the age of twelve. He traveled throughout India, engaging his opponents in debate, and established four monasteries (*maths*) which still exist today: Badarinath in the Himalayas; Dwaraka on the west coast; Puri on the east coast; and Shringeri in Mysore State.

Since Shankara believed himself to be interpreting *Shruti,* most of his position is found in his commentaries, which include digressions in which he attempts a refutation of all opposing positions. His main commentary is on the *Brahma Sutras*. Of considerable importance also are his commentaries on ten Upanishads, particularly the

6. Ibid., p. 168.

Chandogya and the *Brihadaranyaka,* a commentary on the *Gita,* and a more systematic treatise called *Upadeshasahasri* ("A Thousand Teachings"). The various philosophical schools based on *Vedanta* all regarded the *Brahma Sutras* as condensations of the teachings of the Upanishads, and the differences of opinion arose about the *meaning* of the sutras and the upanishadic texts to which they refer.

Shankara did not originate the *advaita* position which was already rather well worked out by his teacher's teacher Gaudapada. Gaudapada, however, was explicitly dependent on the Madhyamika and Vijnanavada systems of the Buddhists, while Shankara harshly rejects such formulations even though he was accused of being a "crypto-Buddhist." *Advaita* continued to develop after Shankara, his followers splitting philosophical hairs in an attempt to perfect his system.

The basic question to be considered here has to do with the nature of Brahman. Brahman, or Ultimate Reality, is pure consciousness devoid of all attributes (*nirguna*) and devoid of all categories of the intellect (*nirvishesha*). There is no distinction between Atman and Brahman. Brahman is nondual (*advaita*), transcending the distinctions between knower, knowledge, and known. And since there is ultimately no duality, Brahman alone is ultimately Real. Transcending all categories, Brahman can best be described in negative terms. Positively the best one can do is to say that Brahman is pure consciousness, pure existence, and pure bliss. By stating the matter this way, one is denying that Brahman is a substance that has such qualities in favor of the position that existence and consciousness and bliss are one. In Brahman all intellectual distinctions end.

Metaphysical Questions

Associated with Brahman is its potency, or *maya,* which allows Brahman to appear as qualified Lord (*Ishvara*) who is the creator, preserver, and destroyer of the world, which is his appearance. In this state one often refers to *Saguna Brahman,* or Brahman with qualities as distinct from *Nirguna Brahman,* without qualities. *Nirguna Brahman* is ultimately a designation which describes a state of immediate experience of the plenitude of Being rather than being a mere concept.

In much Indian thought one must get used to thinking in terms of levels of being rather than in terms of whether something is real or unreal. Some entities are more real than others, and this is ultimately determined by their degree of participation in Brahman, Brahman alone being ultimately Real. Shankara's system can be understood in terms of three such levels.

1. Reality (*sat paramarthika*). The whole truth and the sole Reality.
2. Appearance (*vivarta*). Illusory and characterized by change.
    a. Phenomenally real (*vyavaharika*). Ordinary waking experience. Religiously speaking it is the theistic religious experience.

b. Illusory existent (*pratibhasika*). The illusion of dreams and other illusory experience.
3. Unreality (*asat*). The level of logical contradictions.

These levels are to be understood in terms of the principle of devaluation (*badha,* or contradiction). This is the process whereby we devalue a previously approved object in light of new experience. In this scheme the levels of appearance are not unreal (*asat*), since they do not consist in logical contradictions, but neither are they Real, since they can be devalued by experience of the Real. They have the level of appearance or phenomenal "reality" but ultimately they can be devalued. The level of appearance does not *in fact* have an objective counterpart, but the level of *asat* cannot *in principle* have a counterpart.

The world is appearance (*vyavaharika*). It has a practical reality, but does not qualify for the designation "Real" since it can be devalued. It is real only so long as we are in a state of ignorance and so long as knowledge does not dawn. In describing the relationship of the world to Brahman, several terms are used which are almost identical in meaning. It is *maya* in that it is not what it appears to be, *avidya* in that it is based on ignorance, *adhyasa,* in that it is a superimposition such as when one mistakes a rope for a snake at dusk, and *vivarta* in that it is merely appearance. In his ignorance, man takes the world for what it is not—the Real.

Ultimately the doctrine of *maya* is inexplicable. *Maya* itself is not Real, for it exists on the level of appearance and has no existence apart from Brahman. On the other hand, one cannot say it is unreal, since it projects the world of appearance. Such conflicts led Nagarjuna to ultimate silence and the rejection of all logic. Shankara, by holding that *maya* has only a phenomenal and relative character, is saying nearly the same thing, and the similarity led to the accusation of his being a "crypto-Buddhist." When right knowledge appears, ignorance and *maya* are removed.

Shankara held to the view that the cause alone was real and that the effects were false (*satkaryavada*). This is the view of causation which states that the effect (*karya*) is existent (*sat*) in the material cause and is not a novel thing. The process of the imaginary attribution of something where it does not exist is *adhyasa* (superimposition). As Nagarjuna, Shankara rejected the view that things arise by chance. But since Brahman alone is Real, he was forced to take the view that there is no change in substance and hence no change in Reality. Change belongs to the level of appearance. While we must, on this level, live as though things change, when knowledge dawns, we will see that such views are due to our ignorance.

Psychological Questions

The levels of the phenomenal and the Real are equally relevant for an examination of human nature. To begin with, there is the supreme Atman (*Paramatman*). Atman fits into the level of the Real, and hence is pure, undifferentiated, self-shining consciousness. Atman transcends all such distinctions as subject and object, time, space, or thought. Atman cannot be an object knowable by the mind or perceivable by the senses, since thought functions only through forms and multiplicity. Thought is a process, while Atman is a state. Atman is not different from Brahman, which means that in the depth of man's being, he is not different from Reality.

On the phenomenal level is the *jiva* which represents the individual human person, the phenomenal self which is a combination of reality and appearance. *Jiva* is reality to the extent that Atman is its ground, but it is appearance since it is finite, conditioned, and relative. Hence the individual self is empirically real for it is part of our experience, but it is transcendentally unreal for the only Real is the Atman which is not different from Brahman. Unlike the Pali tradition, man's problem is not that he holds to permanence when all is change, but that he identifies the change, of which the *jiva* is a part, with the Real. The consciousness of human limitation is grounded in ignorance. The Atman is essentially unlimited and Real.

Epistemological Questions

Reason does not occupy a primary place in the system of Shankara. The value of reason is that it is a necessary tool for assisting us to understand *Shruti*. The ultimate truth cannot be known by reason alone since it transcends reason which is part of the realm of appearance. What one debater shows to be reasonable can be shown by a more expert debater to be false. The ultimate truth is found in *Shruti*.

This means that Shankara was not compelled to show that his metaphysical system was completely and compellingly rational. Its truth depended on *Shruti*. If his position could be shown to be faithful to *Shruti* and if its apparent contradictions could be explained away without flying in the face of experience, there was little more for him to do. In the final analysis, his position would only be convincing to those who had achieved realization. As one moves up the levels of being and has the corresponding experiences, thus devaluing lower levels of existence, he becomes more convinced of the truth of the formulation. Absolute certainty comes only at that point at which the request for certainty is meaningless. In the final analysis, it is realization which clinches the matter. But, one must hasten to add, when that occurs, Shankara's entire system is devalued and seen for what it actually is—part of the level of appearance.

Liberation and Ethics

Perfection is possible in this life. When one comes to the realization that he is Brahman, he is a *Jivanmukta,* one who is liberated while living. Although living, the *Jivanmukta* does not identify himself with the body, which he realizes is only appearance. The world still appears for him, but he is not deceived by it. He is not affected by the world's misery and has no desire for the world's objects.

The reason why one can be liberated and still continue a bodily existence is explained by distinguishing three kinds of karma. There is karma that has brought forth its effects, karma that still lies accumulated, and karma that is gathered in this life. Knowledge of Reality (*Jnana*) destroys accumulated karma and makes it impossible to gather more karma in this life. But the karma that has already borne its effects in having produced the body must run its natural course.

This karma ceases when its force is exhausted just as the turning wheel of the potter comes to a full stop only when its momentum is spent. When the body perishes, the *Jivanmukta* is said to attain the disembodied state of liberation called *videhamukti*.

The role of ethics must also be placed in terms of the levels of being. If Brahman is beyond all distinctions, this includes ethical distinctions as well. The *Jivanmukta* is above all distinctions of good and evil. He is not susceptible to moral judgments. While he would probably not involve himself in the world of moral distinctions since he is not touched by sorrow or desire, neither would he be inclined to commit murder or other acts which would seem to presume egoism.

On the lower level of the phenomenal world, moral distinctions are necessary for ordering existence. In general one might say that those actions which lead to the highest good, or *moksha,* and tend to minimize ego involvement are good. On the other hand, those acts which lead to ego involvement are bad. All the acts of the *jiva* are to some extent involved in selfish desire, a fact which makes ethical virtues desirable on the lower level. Shankara generally accepts the *Dharmashastras* for ordering the phenomenal world. Yet it must be admitted that in terms of the Real, all such distinctions could be devalued.

VISHISHTADVAITA

From the time of the *Gita,* and even before, one can see evidence of the growth of the *bhakti* movement. Alongside the *bhakti* movement was the development of an articulate *advaita* position based on the Upanishads and culminating in the thought of Shankara. Shankara systematized his position prior to the composition of the *Bhagavata Purana* which systematized the *bhakti* of that time. With arguments which convinced many, Shankara relegated *bhakti* to the lower level of appearance. His view continues to dominate philosophy departments in India today. Nevertheless, *bhakti* was not easily relegated as merely preliminary to a nondual system. Many *bhaktas* did not find such a preliminary role for *Bhagavan* (the personal God and object of devotion) acceptable. The reaction against Shankara reached its peak in the writings of Ramanuja (1017–1137). Intending to remain loyal to the theism of the *bhakti* sects, Ramanuja attempted to offer a sound philosophical basis, which claimed the Upanishads and *Brahma Sutras* for its authority.

Ramanuja's position was furthered by the formation of a sect called *Shri-Vaishnavism* or *Shri Sampradaya*. This sect carried on many of Ramanuja's emphases. They developed the doctrine of *prapatti,* or submission to God, and opened Vedic knowledge even to Shudras (members of the lowest caste). Although in traditional fashion Shankara denied Vedic knowledge to those who were not of the twice born, Ramanuja admitted Jainas, Buddhists, Shudras, and even untouchables into his fold. Ramanuja also placed some emphasis on the use of images and included in his texts elaborate directions for the construction of temples and the various rituals associated with image worship.

Ramanuja rejected Shankara's doctrine of levels of reality. This rejection carried implications which made his view of Ultimate Reality, man, and liberation somewhat different from Shankara's. Ramanuja's view of Ultimate Reality is called *Vishishtadvaita,* or qualified nondualism. For him the Absolute is not distinctionless, but is qualified by diversity. It is a whole which consists of interdependent and interrelated elements. There is no undifferentiated pure consciousness. All knowledge involves distinctions. When the Upanishads speak of Brahman as devoid of qualities, they only mean that Brahman has no bad qualities and not that he has no qualities whatever.

Having rejected Shankara's distinction of levels of reality, it follows that he would also reject the distinction Shankara made between Brahman and Ishvara. For Ramanuja, Brahman is no formless entity, but a Supreme Person qualified by matter and souls, which are sometimes called his body. Ramanuja considers three things as ultimate and real: matter (*achit*), soul (*chit*), and God (*Ishvara*). While all three are real, the first two are dependent on God. Ishvara is Brahman. God manifests himself in various forms for his devotees: as the immanent soul of the universe; as the transcendent personal Lord; as creator, preserver, or destroyer; as *avatara* in human or animal form; as images enshrined in temples so that his devotees can see him physically.

Shankara's interpretation of *avidya* and *maya* is also rejected. *Maya* is the real power of God whereby he creates the world. There is no illusion involved since the world is also real. This position leaves open to Ramanuja a view of causation in which the effect is as real as the cause. For him, change is not apparent but real, being contained in the cause. Just as curd is a real transformation of milk, so an effect is as real as a cause.

Ramanuja spends considerable energy arguing against Shankara's view of *maya*. He asks, for example, where *maya* resides if it indeed exists? It cannot exist in Brahman without nondualism breaking down, nor in the individual self, which is mere appearance. Ramanuja concludes it is a pseudo-concept which exists in the mind of the *advaitin*. Furthermore, when Shankara maintains that *maya* is neither real nor unreal, he is merely engaging in intellectual gymnastics. Real and unreal are exhaustive and exclusive. A thing is either one or the other; no further alternative exists without the violation of well-established canons of logic.

Ignorance (*avidya*) is the cause of bondage, which means that the *jiva* wrongly identifies its reality with material objects such as the body. And, immediate intuitive knowledge is liberation. Souls are bound because of their ignorance and karma. While meditation is useful, it is subordinate to *bhakti* and is obtained by throwing oneself on the mercy of God. The highest *bhakti* only dawns by the grace (*prasada*) of God.

Liberation is not the realization that ultimately there is no distinction between Brahman and Atman, but the intuitive realization on the part of the soul that it is a mode of God. The liberated soul never becomes identical with Brahman. It is always finite while God remains infinite, and the soul does not share God's power as creator, preserver, and destroyer of the universe. For Ramanuja there is no possibility of liberation while one lives (*Jivanmukta*). As long as the soul remains associated with the body, it is clear that karmas persist and the soul cannot become pure.

Two centuries after Ramanuja, his followers divided into two schools. The Vadagalai, or northern school, held that one had to purify himself in order to receive divine grace. It maintained the need for man's cooperation with God in salvation and came to be known as the monkey school. Just as the monkey clings to the mother, so the devotee clings to God. While man casts himself entirely upon God, he does have to exert an effort to cling to him. The Tengalai, or southern school, magnified the importance of divine grace in liberation, and held that no individual effort was necessary for divine grace to dawn. This position came to be known as the cat view. As the mother cat lifts its kitten and carries it to a safe place without any effort from the kitten, so does God bestow his grace on man.

DVAITA Madhva lived during the thirteenth century and developed a system called *dvaita,* or dualism. He was born in a village near Udipi in South Kanara and died there as the head of a new order founded by him, called Brahma Sampradaya. As a young Sannyasin, he had been trained in Shankara's *advaita* but broke away to develop his own system, later converting his teacher. In order to propound his view, he relied on the whole *shruti* and *smriti*. While not neglecting the Upanishads, he utilized the Vedas and Brahmanas more than his predecessors and made heavy use of the Puranic literature, especially the *Bhagavata Purana* and *Vishnu Purana*. Being a strict Vaishnava, he held that Shaiva literature should be interpreted in the light of the conclusions of Vaishava literature.

Like Ramanuja, Madhva was devoted to Vishnu, but more particularly to his son Vayu, the wind god. In the present age Madhva held that liberation could only be acquired through Vayu, which meant through Madhva, since he was considered the god's incarnation. In the interest of *bhakti,* Ramanuja had proposed a qualified nondualism. Thus he was able to give some place to the prominent position of Shankara and the upanishadic passages which emphasized unity. On the other hand, Ramanuja preserved a place for *bhakti* by maintaining that the ultimate unity is a unity with distinctions. Madhva did not grant so much to unity. In his encounters with *advaitins,* particularly with the head of the Shankara monastery at Shringeri, the battle was fierce and they parted as enemies. Madhva called *advaitins* "deceitful demons." They reciprocated with a period of persecution in an attempt to destroy the movement.

While he was outspoken against the *advaitins,* Madhva did not speak against the followers of Ramanuja, even though his position differed from theirs. Madhva accused Shankara of being a "crypto-Buddhist" and actually teaching *Shunyavada* Buddhism (Madhyamika). Like Ramanuja, Madhva holds to three realities: God, souls, and matter. Hence the world is real and Shankara's doctrine of *maya* is rejected with many of the same arguments that were given by Ramanuja.

Madhva's view is *dvaita,* or dualism. He has no interest in holding things together in a unity, but stresses duality. For him there are five basic distinctions:

1. God is distinct from individual souls.
2. God is distinct from nonliving matter.
3. One individual soul is distinct from another.
4. Individual souls are distinct from matter.
5. When matter is divided, its parts are distinct from one another.

In each of the above cases Madhva goes somewhat further than Ramanuja and rejects Shankara altogether. Ramanuja held to the reality of God and the individual souls, but saw the latter as dependent on the former. While for Ramanuja, God is distinct from matter, the world was seen as the body which God animates. While individual souls were distinct for Ramanuja, they were identical when liberated. Madhva holds so strongly to the notion of distinctness that souls are not only numberless and atomic in size, but each is unique. Furthermore, while Ramanuja held that the liberated soul was like God except that it was finite and did not participate in the creation, preservation, and destruction of the world, Madhva stressed the difference between God and the liberated soul.

While believing that souls are unique, Madhva also classified them into three groups: those who are devoted to God alone and are destined to attain liberation; those who will never attain liberation and are destined to perpetual rebirth; and those who revile Vishnu and his devotees and are subject to damnation. In the whole history of Indian philosophy, this doctrine of damnation is peculiar to Madhva and the Jainas. It is more common to find the view that hells are temporary abodes where bad karma is allowed to spend itself, after which the soul progresses upward again.

Madhva's preference for difference also leads him to hold to degrees in the possession of knowledge and even in the enjoyment of bliss in liberated souls. No such doctrine is possible in Ramanuja since all liberated souls are identical, nor in Shankara since liberation is the elimination of all distinctions.

Worship of Vishnu takes place in three forms. It may involve putting on one's body the symbolic marks for Vishnu. The use of such *tilak* marks is practiced also by Shaivites who use ashes or paint to mark their foreheads and even their bodies and arms with horizontal marks. Vaishavas, on the other hand, are identified with vertical marks on their foreheads. But Madhva emphasized this somewhat more than others. He extended it to monks and laity. The marking involves two perpendicular lines meeting at the bridge of the nose, with a straight black line in the middle. Madhva also advocated naming one's sons after Vishnu, and worshiping him in word, thought, and deed.

8. *Samadhi* (concentration). Here the mind is so deeply absorbed in the object of contemplation that it loses the distinction between the subject and the object. While in *dhyana* meditation is intent, one is still conscious of a distinction between the object of meditation and the meditator. There is *conscious samadhi* (*samprajnata*) in which one is still conscious of the object of meditation even though the subject and object are fused together. In *unconscious samadhi* (*asamprajnata*), the fusion is so complete that consciousness of both subject and object is gone. "It is the highest means to realize the cessation of mental modifications which is the end. It is the ecstatic state in which the connection with the external world is broken and through which one has to pass before obtaining liberation." [11]

Up to the point of *samadhi,* one is engaged in a negative process of distinguishing the *purusha* from *prakriti,* but in the final state of realization, the positive nature of the eternal *purusha* manifests itself untainted by *prakriti.*

Each step toward *samadhi* is attended by supranormal powers. Yogins are said to be able to tame the most ferocious wild beast, see through solid objects, and pass through them as well. They can appear and disappear at will. They can know the past, present, and future immediately. It is tempting to be sidetracked by such "rewards" for one's diligence, but the texts continually warn that these are really hindrances to ultimate realization, since they have the power to become ends in themselves. Delight in such powers will prevent the yogin from reaching the goal. "They are by-products of the higher life. They are the flowers which we chance to pick on the road, though the true seeker does not set out on his travels to gather them. Only through the disregard of these perfections can freedom be gained." [12]

CARVAKA

One group that has been placed without the pale by those who accept the authority of the Vedas is called Carvaka. "The Cārvāka school has been the butt of ridicule for long. The very designations of its followers—cārvāka and lokāyata—have acquired a disparaging sense, much as the term 'sophist' did in ancient Greece, and have become bye-names for the infidel and the epicure." [13] The significance of the name Carvaka is uncertain, but another common name for the school, *lokayata,* has a meaning that is more clear. *Lokayata* indicates that this school holds that only this world (*loka*) exists and that there is no beyond.

There is reference to a sutra ascribed to Brihaspati who is described as a heretical teacher in the *Maitri Upanishad* (VII.9). However, that sutra is lost and fragments of its contents are found in the form of quotations in works that use them as a basis for the

---

11. Sharma, op. cit., p. 160.
12. Radhakrishnan, op. cit., p. 367.
13. M. Hiriyanna, *Outlines of Indian Philosophy*, London, G. Allen, 1932, p. 188.

refutation of the Carvaka system. Nevertheless, the view of this school can be described in broad outline.

For the Carvaka, the only valid source of knowledge is perception. They reject inference since it is based on universal connections which cannot be perceptually verified. Likewise, intuition, as well as the testimony of the Vedas, is rejected. It is this rejection of the Vedas that leads many to classify this school as "heterodox."

Since only perception is a valid source of knowledge, it follows that all "entities" which are not empirically verifiable are not real. There is no karma or rebirth, no supreme Ishvara, no divine providence or purpose in the world. The Vedic sacrifices are merely ways of keeping a priesthood employed, since there is nothing gained by such religious contortions. This view is described in the *Sarvadarshanasamgraha*:

> If you object that, if there be no such thing as happiness in a future world, then how should men of experienced wisdom engage in the Agnihotra and other sacrifices, which can only be performed with great expenditure of money and bodily fatigue, your objection cannot be accepted as any proof to the contrary, since the Agnihotra, &c., are only useful as means of livelihood, for the Veda is tainted by the three faults of untruth, self-contradiction, and tautology; then again the impostors who call themselves Vaidic (for Vedic) pandits are mutually destructive. . . . And to this effect runs the popular saying—
> The Agnihotra, the three Vedas, the ascetics three staves, and smearing oneself with ashes,—
> Brhaspati says these are but means of livelihood for those who have no manliness or sense.[14]

The entire universe is accounted for in terms of four basic elements: earth, water, fire, and air. Space (*akasha*), which is held to be an element by other schools, is rejected, since it is based on inference rather than perception.

There is no Atman or principle of permanence in man. What we experience as consciousness is simply the result of a certain conjunction of the four basic elements. Consciousness is always associated with the body and when the body disintegrates, consciousness disappears as well. Just as when someone chews a combination of betel leaf, areca nut, and lime, a red color appears in the mouth even though none of the ingredients possess the red color, so the combination of elements produces consciousness even though they do not separately possess it.

With the rejection of all of these supposedly religious doctrines and practices, what could be ultimately important for the Carvaka? What would characterize his life stance? If only the senses offer valid knowledge, and if the material world is all that exists, one should enjoy life to the fullest while it lasts. The Carvaka knows of no future rewards or punishments. His is an individual enjoyment of

---

14. S. Radhakrishnan and Charles A. Moore, *A Source Book in Indian Philosophy,* Princeton, N.J., Princeton University Press, 1957, pp. 229–230.

pleasure more than a concern for the most pleasure for the most people. The only real end for man is sensual enjoyment, the accumulation of wealth being a means to such an end. This is captured in a refrain.

While life is yours, live joyously;
None can escape Death's searching eye:
When once this frame of ours they burn,
How shall it e'er again return? [15]

Unlike most Indian religious systems, the Carvaka does not seek freedom from suffering. Pain is an inevitable characteristic of existence. But the possibility of future pain is no reason for denying ourselves pleasure.

The pleasure which arises to men from contact with sensible objects,
Is to be relinquished as accompanied by pain,—such is the reasoning of fools;
The berries of paddy, rich with the finest white grains,
What man, seeking his true interest, would fling away because covered by husk and dust? [16]

While the Carvaka orientation never gained wide and enduring philosophical acceptance, aspects of its viewpoint appear throughout Indian religious thought.[17] And, whatever the "orthodox" might have thought of it, it was a way of ordering life for some thinkers.

15. Ibid., p. 228.
16. Ibid., p. 229.
17. Cf. Dale Riepe, *The Naturalistic Tradition in Indian Thought*, Delhi, Motilal Bararsidass, 1961.

MEDIEVAL ARRIVALS

While the *bhakti* movement continued to spread, and articulate religious systems took on new completeness, several other religious traditions appeared which were to make their presence felt on Indian soil. Christians were present in India prior to the medieval period, but had no firm base until the arrival of Jesuit missions in the sixteenth century.

It is a mistake to call some of these religions non-Indian, since after centuries on the Indian subcontinent, they have been or are presently making an effort to share in Indian culture and national goals. Nor is it significant to point out that some of them came from outside the Indian borders, since that can be said for the religion of the Vedic Aryans. The Sikh tradition was formulated in India and the others were influenced in various ways by their new environment.

CHRISTIANS AND JEWS

If the tradition about Saint Thomas is reliable, Christian presence in India preceded its spread throughout Europe. Tradition states that about A.D. 52 Thomas landed in Cranganore, preached the Christian message, and established several churches on the Malabar coast. There is stronger historical evidence that in the fourth century, Christians migrated from Persia and Mesopotamia. By the sixth century, a church with clergy existed in Ceylon, Malabar, and in the Bombay area where bishops had been installed. The Christians on the Malabar coast were called "Christians of Saint Thomas" although they are now often spoken of as Syriac Christians because of their connection with Syriac-speaking churches in the East.

The largest portion of Indian Christians are Roman Catholics, who became influential because of the rise of Portuguese power in the early sixteenth century. Jesuit missions grew with such notable missionaries as Francis Xavier (1506–1552) and Robert de Nobili (1577–1656) who was successful in presenting the Christian message to the Indian intelligentsia. Colleges and seminaries were established, and a college bearing de Nobili's name still exists outside of Poona. While Jesuit missions declined in importance with the loss of Portuguese political influence, missions sponsored by other orders such as the Franciscans, Dominicans, Augustinians, and Carmelites followed. Catholics exist as a large minority force in the state of Kerala today.

In the seventeenth century and following, Protestant missions also contributed to the growing Christian presence. This development was given impetus in the north by the arrival of William Carey in 1793, and spread all over India with the support of foreign mission societies.

Christians, Protestant and Catholic alike, placed a high premium on education. Colleges and lower-level schools developed in number and quality.

> *In 1954, there were, under the auspices of the National Christian Council, 46 colleges, 448 high schools, 553 middle schools, and 103 teacher-training institutions in the whole of India. In 1951, the Roman Catholics had 42 colleges, 474 high schools, and 4,362 primary schools.*[1]

Medical missions also played an important role in spreading the Christian message. Considerable emphasis was placed on the care of those afflicted by leprosy and tuberculosis. As of 1956, there were over five hundred Christian-sponsored hospitals and dispensaries throughout India and Pakistan.

Christians also exerted considerable energy in work with outcasts and tribals. Many Hindus have interpreted this concern, and the mass conversions which sometimes resulted, as dishonest and not in the best national interest.

In South India the Church was fragmentized by reason of its associations with numerous foreign denominations. In 1947 India had some 150 missionary societies, with many of them at work in the south. Most of these missionary societies and the greater number of Protestant denominations merged in 1947 in the formation of the Church of South India. South Indian Christians have thus become a symbol of ecumenism for other Christians throughout the world.

Jews also settled in Malabar. The earliest reference to this community was in the tenth century, although tradition indicates a settlement of Jews at Cochin in the first century A.D. One group has, through intermarriage, taken on characteristic Indian features, while another has attempted to retain racial distinctiveness.

PARSIS In the beginning of the eighth century A.D., a community settled in western India and has remained there until the present. To under-

---

1. C. A. Abraham, "The Rise and Growth of Christianity in India," in *The Cultural Heritage of India,* Calcutta, The Ramakrishna Mission Institute of Culture, 1956, vol. IV, p. 565.

stant these people and the faith which they brought with them from Iran, it is necessary to go back to the seventh century B.C. and even earlier. These people are called Parsis because they migrated from Persia, or Zoroastrians because they trace their teachings back to Zoroaster. In the Bombay area the Parsis number about 100,000. There are about 20,000 in Iran, 6,550 in Pakistan, nearly 4,000 in Europe, a small group in Canada, and about 1,000 in the United States, Africa, and the Far East combined.

While some Parsis date Zoroaster as early as 6000 or 7000 B.C., thus making theirs a religion of great antiquity, most Western scholars would tend toward a seventh century B.C. date. Apart from the centuries between 331 B.C. when Alexander of Macedon defeated the last Achaemenian king and A.D. 220 which marks the beginning of the Sassanian dynasty, the Zoroastrian faith went through various changes but grew in influence because of the support of its kings. In A.D. 637 when the Arabs took Persia, the long Sassanian dynasty fell, and Zoroastrian faith ceased to be a favored religion.

During their long history in Persia, the followers of Zoroaster had developed a complicated system of ritual and scholastic distinctions which were more concerned with ritual purity than with ethical purity. The system of ritual taboos had become so complicated that only the priesthood was able to interpret it correctly.

Having lost their royal support, the Iranians found themselves at the mercy of the Arab Muslims. Persecution by them was one of the factors that led them to flee their homeland. Some went to China or westward, but a goodly number migrated to India where a permanent settlement was established at Sanjan in 716. There were migrations as early as 636, however, and the Parsis did not arrive in a single wave. Over the years they settled around Bombay and have been a highly successful business community.

The sacred writings of the Parsis are called the *Avesta,* or sometimes the *Zend-Avesta.* The word *zend* means "interpretation." Hence the *Zend-Avesta* refers to the *Avesta* plus certain commentaries or interpretations which have been added as time progressed. The meaning of the term *avesta* is either "knowledge" or "original text." The *Zend-Avesta* is a collection of diverse materials without any clear cohesion. The *Avesta* proper contains the *Yasna,* which is a liturgical book from which Parsi priests read while celebrating rituals that honor all the many deities of later Zoroastrians.

Zoroaster himself proclaimed a monotheistic faith in protest of the popular Iranian polytheism. The materials that are thought to go back to Zoroaster himself are called the *Gathas,* which are chapters 28–34 and 43–53 of the *Yasna.* These hymns are concerned with praising Mazda, Zoroaster's one deity, and they set forth the nature of the universal struggle between good and evil. Another part of the *Avesta* is the *Vispered* ("All the Lords"), a liturgical appendix to the *Yasna* which is addressed to numerous heavenly beings. It is a short liturgy and contains little that is not already in the *Yasna.* A third part of the *Avesta* is the *Vendidad,* a priestly code of ritual purification and taboos. The *Vendidad* is chronologically later than the

Gathas, which explains the strong emphasis on ritual purity. Also important for Parsi theology are the *Pahlavi* books written in a Persian variant called Pahlavi. These books were probably written in the ninth century A.D. and reflect the theology which developed in the last century of Sassanian rule.

Prior to the appearance of Zoroaster, the Iranians worshiped *daevas* (Sanskrit *devas*), or shining ones. Zoroaster considered *daevas* to be demons, but the people before him did not. The *daevas* were a class of beings closely resembling the early Vedic deities by reason of their common Aryan ancestry. In the *Rigveda* two classes of deities are distinguished: *asuras* and *devas*. In India the *asuras* came to be thought of as demons, while in Iran, because of Zoroaster, the *daevas* were considered demonic. Part of the elevation of the *asuras* was the place given to Ahura Mazda; he was elevated to the position of Supreme God by Zoroaster.

Besides the worship of ancestors as guardian spirits, the Iranians worshiped fire from antiquity. While Zoroaster himself prohibited the worship of fire, he retained it as a symbol of the deity. Parsis today keep fires burning continually in their temples, and five times daily the fire is ceremonially replenished with incense and sandalwood.

The counterpart of the Indian *Rita* is seen in the Iranian concept of truth or justice (*asha*), the basis of order in nature and in the society of men and gods.

The stories that cluster around the life of Zoroaster illustrate the faith of his followers. Demons tried to prevent the birth of Zoroaster and later attempted to injure his health. After birth the infant Zoroaster laughed instead of cried because the Lie Demon had been confounded. According to tradition, Zoroaster assumed the sacred thread (*kusti*) at the age of fifteen. At twenty he left his family in search for the meaning of life and at thirty he had a series of miraculous visions. The Archangel Vohu Manah (Good Thought) appeared to him as a figure nine times as large as a man. Vohu Manah ushered him into the presence of Ahura Mazda, who instructed him in the principles of the True Religion. Ten years later he won his first convert, but his most crucial convert was a prince Vishtaspa, who favored Zoroaster's faith.

In the *Gathas* one finds an ethical dualism in the form of an opposition between Truth (*Asha*) and the Lie (*Druj*). This conflict between truth and wickedness is portrayed without the possibility of compromise. Not being a philosophical work, the *Gathas* reflect the practical situation of their Persian setting—a pastoral community engaged in tilling the soil and cattle raising that was habitually threatened by a nomadic tribal society which destroyed men as well as cattle. This violence was merely part of a cosmic battle between good and evil, and those who followed the truth cultivated the soil and pulled the weeds.

> *The moral dualism between* Asha *and* Druj, *Truth and the Lie, Righteousness and Unrighteousness, which is so characteristic of the Gāthās can be seen as a universalization of a concrete political and social situation in which a peaceful, pastoral and cattle-*

breeding population was constantly threatened by the inroads of fierce nomadic tribes.[2]

Zaehner is even convinced that an actual state of war existed between the two parties.

Zoroaster saw no hope of compromising with evil. The enemy was to be either converted or defeated. To love one's enemy implied aligning oneself with him. As long as people are on the side of the Lie, they should be shown no mercy. Men are free to choose to be followers of either *Druj* or *Asha,* but so long as one follows *Druj* he is to be opposed. Nevertheless, the possibility of conversion is always present. Freedom is not philosophically defended but merely assumed.

Zoroaster also spoke out against a growing ritualism and against the slaughter of cattle for sacrificial purposes. The sacrifice seems to have been accompanied by drinking Homa juice (Indian Soma) resulting in ritual intoxication. Some of his opponents, therefore, were the priests who presided at these rituals. Zoroaster was firmly convinced that both cosmically and tactically, there were only two sides: Good and Evil. He was equally convinced that one had the freedom to choose on which side he would serve, that he had chosen the Good and that those who opposed him had chosen the Evil.

The greater cosmic conflict was between Ahura Mazda and Angra Mainyu, who was the chief personification of the Lie. In later thought, Ahura Mazda became assimilated with Spenta Mainyu (Holy or Bounteous Spirit), who was the protagonist against evil. Still later a metaphysical dualism developed to replace what was previously only an ethical dualism. There is some ambiguity within the early texts and even in the descriptions in the later tradition about the origin of evil. If one says that ultimately there is only one supreme deity, Ahura Mazda, then the question arises as to whether or not he is responsible for evil. On the other hand, if one proposes two eternal spirits such as Ahura Mazda and Angra Mainyu, he offers a metaphysical dualism which explains the problem of evil but offers no hope for its ultimate defeat.

In the *Gathas,* consideration is given to the Amesha Spentas, six divine abstractions which later came to be thought of as beings in their own right. For Zoroaster, they were aspects of God which man could share if he lived according to the truth. While the Amesha Spentas had no independent existence apart from God, his operations took place through them. One contemporary Parsi characterizes them as divine abstractions and lists them as follows:

1. *Vohu Manah,* The Good Mind;
2. *Asha Vahishta,* The Best Order, or Righteousness;
3. *Khshathra Vairya,* The Absolute Power;
4. *Armaiti,* High Thought, or Devotion;
5. *Haurvatat,* Perfection;
6. *Ameretat,* Immortality.

---

2. R. C. Zaehner, *The Dawn and Twilight of Zoroastrianism,* New York, Putnam, 1961, p. 34.

Zoroaster was convinced of the truth and finality of his teaching, having received it from Ahura Mazda himself. He was equally confident that Ahura Mazda would ultimately triumph over evil. He was eschatologically optimistic. In later theological thought, a well-worked-out eschatology developed. At the end of time, Saoshyans (savior) will renew all existence. The spirits of the dead will be raised, united with their bodies, and a mighty conflagration will take place. All men will wade through a stream of molten metal which will be as soothing as warm milk for the just, but will be a burning experience for the wicked. Sins will be purged and all creation will return to its maker. There is also an individual judgment which takes place at death, when the individual is judged at the Chinvat Bridge. In one account, the righteous soul is guided across the bridge by a beautiful maiden who is in reality his own good conscience. The wicked soul is met by an ugly hag who embraces him so that they fall into hell together (she is his own bad conscience). One's deeds, therefore, determine one's destiny. The question of the destiny of one whose good and evil deeds balanced inevitably arose, and it was said that they go to *Hamestakan*—an abode between earth and the stars.

Parsi fire temples have few external characteristics which distinguish them as temples. In Bombay they are identified by the symbol of Ahura Mazda on the outside. Inside the fire temple is an urn in the center of the room. The presiding priests wear a cloth covering their faces so that they will not breathe impurities into the fire, nor are they to cough or sneeze near the fire. Worshipers come at any time and after having washed the uncovered parts of their bodies, they give offerings of money and sandalwood to the priest. He in turn offers them some ashes from the sacred fire which they apply to their forehead. The worshiper bows and offers prayers toward the fire. I. J. S. Taraporewala indicates that the prophet chose fire as the chief symbol since it is the purest of God's creations. In the opinion of this contemporary Parsi, there are two other characteristics of fire which make the symbol meaningful: (1) fire has "the power of immediately transmuting everything it touches into a likeness of itself"; and (2) "the flames of fire always tend *upwards,* and thus aptly symbolize our yearning for the Higher Life." [3]

Fire is not to be contaminated by burning a dead body. If this does happen, the fire must be ceremonially purified, after which it becomes particularly sacred. The concern not to contaminate the sacred fire is also a reason why Parsis are not permitted to smoke. To draw impure air or breathe through the sacred fire would be a matter of disrespect. This does not mean that the community universally follows the precept.

Some fires are more holy than others; hence the temple in which they are housed becomes more important, as does the priest in charge of that temple. There are only eight first-grade temples in India, four of them being in Bombay. A first-grade temple requires

---

3. I. J. S. Taraporewala, *The Religion of Zarathushtra*, Bombay, Taraporewala, 1965, p. 41.

that the fire be filtered and brought together from seventeen sources. This includes fire from a thunderbolt igniting dry wood. Certain religious rituals are performed before the varying levels of fires.

The Parsis dispose of their dead by placing them in *dakmas,* or "towers of silence." There are scriptural prohibitions against cremation or burial in order not to pollute the fire or earth. Furthermore, it is considered a sin to waste the earth for cemeteries when it could be used to produce food. Although towers of silence are a curiousity to Westerners, they pose no embarrassment to Parsis.

The *dakma* itself is to be constructed on a hill, if possible, in an isolated locality where vultures may be attracted. The tower is constructed with three rows of niches, or *pavis*. The top circle is large and designed for men. The second row is smaller and for women, while the third is smaller still and intended for children. Each niche is separated by a passage where the bearers may walk. Large towers have some 450 niches. In the center is a pit which has a concrete or stone floor. When the bones are dried, they are thrown into the central pit where the action of sun and water pulverizes them. Burial of bones is permitted since they are not thought to be unclean, but no tomb is ever erected. The tower has an intricate drainage system whereby the water is filtered through four deep subterranean wells. When the body is taken into the towers, no one enters except the bearers and they must be purified. At a certain point in the cermony, non-Zoroastrians are no longer permitted to remain. The non-Parsi might break some of the detailed prescriptions for ceremonial purity since he is not familiar with them.

A leading Bombay priest, Dastur Dabu, justifies this method of disposing of the dead thus:

1. *It is charitable. A Parsi's last act on earth is the donation of his dead body to hungry birds, nature's appointed scavengers.*
2. *It is the speediest method of disposal. In about twenty minutes all flesh is devoured leaving only the bones exposed to the rays of the sun.*
3. *It is economical. Other methods require the purchase of ground, construction and maintenance of tombs, expanding cemeteries, and the purchase of fuel for cremation. The Parsi method is free. The same tower can accommodate hundreds of corpses and a small plot of ground is sufficient.*
4. *Rich and poor, humble and great are placed on the same platform without distinction. The garment and funeral procession are the same for all. There are no costly funerals or mourners. When the bones are dried up and begin to crumble under the rain and heat, they are put into the central pit where they are again mixed without distinction.*
5. *This is the most hygienic system. The corpse has no contact with residential surroundings; whatever water enters due to rain is diverted to four underground wells. There is no contamination of watermains nor is there any odor from burning flesh. "The towers of Bombay, having existed for centuries in the*

most fashionable locality, have never created any nuisance. Even during epidemics the towers receive sterilizing Sun's rays and are quite innocuous and safe."

6. *There is no false sentimentality. Death should be treated as the inevitable phenomenon that it is. Monuments that proclaim the deep sorrow of survivors are based on unnecessary sentimentality. The Parsi treats death in a sensible manner without a great deal of unnecessary fuss.*[4]

Initiation ceremonies in the Parsi community are called the *Naojote* ceremony and extend to girls as well as boys. The word *naojote* is composed of two words: *nao,* or new, and *zote,* or one who offers prayers. The ceremony is so named because after its performance the Parsi child is said to be responsible for offering prayers and observing religious customs and rites as a Zoroastrian.

After the ceremony the individual who is a Parsi by birth becomes a Zoroastrian by choice. The initiate is vested with a sacred shirt (*sudrah*), and the sacred thread (*kusti*). A Parsi without the sacred thread after the age of fifteen is out of the fold and considered likely to fall into evil ways. He is therefore initiated between the ages of seven and fifteen.

Toward the beginning of the twentieth century, Parsis were agitated over the question of admitting aliens into the community. Could one marry into the Parsi community? In 1905 the community at Bombay expressed its disapproval of admitting converts into the community. The law courts upheld this stand as follows.

The Parsi community consists of Parsis who are descended from the original Persian immigrants and who are born of both Zoroastrian parents and who profess Zoroastrian religion, the Iranis from Persia professing the Zoroastrian religion, who come to India either temporarily or permanently, and the children of Parsi fathers by alien mothers who have been duly and properly admitted into the religion.[5]

One section of the community was even opposed to admitting children of Parsi fathers and alien mothers. There was also a minority favoring the possibility of admitting persons who desired to join. That minority concedes, however, that such a provision is not likely to be permitted in the very near future, if at all.

MUSLIMS

While some Muslim contact with India resulted from small peaceful settlements, the main source of Muslim influence in India was the result of a series of invasions which culminated in 1526, a date which marks the beginning of the rule of the Mughals over North India. Mughal rule lasted until the death of Aurangzeb in 1707, after

---

4. Dastus Khurshed S. Dabu, *Message of Zarathushtra*, Bombay, The New Book Co. Private Ltd., 1959, pp. 120–121 *passim*.

5. *Dinsha Petit* v. *Jamsetji Jijibhai* (1909) 33 Bombay, as quoted in P. P. Balsara, *Highlights of Parsi History*, Bombay, 1966, p. 72.

which it slowly declined until the British gained control of India in 1858.

The first Muslim invasion occurred in the early eighth century when Muhummad Ibn Qasim marched into Sind. A limited Arab rule was extended until 1005 when the Arabs were overthrown by Mahmud of Ghazna, the ruler of a small Turkish kingdom in Afghanistan. Prior to the establishment of the Mughal regime, the kings who settled in Delhi did not always honor the judgments of their religious leaders, nor did they follow with great care the regulations of Islamic law.

The Mughals were more influenced by Persian than by Turkish culture which became the vehicle for their artistic expression. But since Muslims who had invaded India at various times were once Arabs, then Turks, and finally Persians, and since they did not come in one great invasion, they not only exerted influence on the Indians they found, but were influenced in return. The invaders were monotheistic and theoretically submitters to Allah. Their invasions and reign was marked by persecution, razing temples and images, offering of benefits to converts, and the imposition of burdens on non-Muslims.

All non-Muslims were required to pay a poll tax, which was lifted for converts. Idolators who opposed the Muslim armies were slaughtered and Brahmans were not infrequently massacred. One should neither underestimate the brutality which existed under monotheistic guise in order to tell a complimentary story, nor should one universalize the brutality so that the impression is left that Muslims never got along with their neighbors. In the reign of two Mughal rulers we have the two extremes typified.

While brutality was common during the reign of Akbar from 1556 to 1605, there were aspects of his rule which also indicated a spirit of tolerance. Akbar placed men of various religious persuasions in high government positions, after he had solidified his relations with his Hindu neighbors by marriage. He abolished the deeply resented poll tax even though it meant considerable loss of income.

Due to a spiritual crisis in 1578 (he had Sufi-type mystical experiences when a boy), Akbar built a hall in which religious debates were held. These debates began as Muslim theological discussions, but Akbar soon invited Brahmans, Jainas, and Parsis as well. He came to see that there were many men deserving of respect even though their religious allegiances varied. In addition to his religious motivation, there was probably the political desire to find a creed on which he could unite the diverse traditions of his kingdom. In 1579 he drew up an Infallibility Decree which made him the final arbiter in all matters of religious dispute. Later he promulgated a new creed which he called Divine Faith (*Din Ilahi*) which was an attempt to bring together what Akbar considered good in various religions. It was intended as a sort of religious fraternity within Akbar's court. This creed, however, died with its author.

At times Akbar showed hostility toward Islam, a tendency that made him less than popular with many Muslims. He had Sanskrit books translated into Persian, and incorporated many Parsi and

Taj Mahal, Agra. (Photo by Robert D. Baird.)

sectarian religious customs. Akbar worshiped the Sun and the Sacred Fire, forbade the slaughter of animals, wore sectarian marks on his forehead, and proclaimed religious toleration.

At one point Akbar sent to Goa for Catholic priests whom he engaged in debate. These priests were permitted to build a temple where Akbar attended Mass. The Mughal ruler admired the teachings and person of Jesus, but found the doctrines of the Incarnation and the Trinity unacceptable.

Akbar was followed by Jahangir (1605–1628) and then by Shah Jahan (1628–1659) who built the beautiful Taj Mahal as his wife's mausoleum.

Aurangzeb, the last of the powerful Mughal emperors, took the throne at the death of Shah Jahan. If Akbar illustrates the more pacificatory religious type, Aurangzeb typifies the more brutal features. Aurangzeb pledged himself to purge the land of "heretics" and "idolators." He curbed the extravagences of the Court, and suppressed many practices that he considered to be vices. Here is a description by a contemporary Muslim:

> *The Emperor, a great worshipper of God by temperament, is noted for his rigid attachment to religion. In his great piety he passes whole nights in the palace mosque and keeps the company of devout men. In privacy he never sits on a throne. Before his accession he gave in alms part of his food and clothing and still devotes to alms the income of some villages near Delhi and of some salt tracts assigned to his privy purse. He keeps fast throughout Ramazān and reads the holy Koran in the assembly of religious men with whom he sits for six or even nine hours of the night. From his youth he abstained from forbidden food and practices, and from his great holiness does nothing that is not pure*

and lawful. Though at the beginning of his reign he used to hear the exquisite voices of ravishing singers and brilliant instrumental performances, and himself understands music well, yet now for several years past, in his great restraint and self-denial, he entirely abstains from this joyous entertainment. He never wears clothes prohibited by religion, nor uses vessels of silver and gold. No unseemly talk, no word of backbiting or falsehood, is permitted at his Court. He appears twice or thrice daily in his audience chamber with a mild and pleasing countenance, to dispense justice to petitioners, who come in numbers without hindrance and obtain redress. If any of them talks too much or acts improperly he is not displeased and never knits his brows. By hearing their words and watching their gestures he says that he acquires a habit of forbearance and toleration. Under the dictates of anger and passion he never passes sentence of death.[6]

Aurangzeb demolished the schools and temples of the "infidels" and attempted to wipe out their teachings, which he considered destructive. He razed temples and had mosques erected in their places. One great temple, erected at the cost of over one million dollars, was destroyed, and jewels from the images were taken to Agra where they became part of the threshold of a mosque to be walked on by the true believers. Many Hindus were relieved of their government posts and the poll tax was imposed again. An appeal was made to Aurangzeb to soften his harsh actions as Akbar had done, but the plea went unheeded. Later in the seventeenth century in Maratha State, a Hindu state was set up through the military leadership of Sivaji. To this day he continues to be a Hindu hero because of his courageous leadership.

Muslims today engage in pilgrimages not only to Mecca, but also to the tombs and shrines of saints and heroes. Sometimes annual celebrations accompanied by fairs are held at the tombs of saints. Wreaths are laid, candles are burned, and costly drapes are placed over the tombs. Some pilgrims pray to the dead to help them in supplying their mundane needs, though such practice is opposed by the orthodox to little avail. Hindus visit the same tombs and offer the same reverence. Common religious practices in India have thus influenced the popular expression of Muslim faith.

In addition to this, there were more deliberate attempts to bring Muslims and Hindus together. One such effort grew into the religious tradition of the Sikhs.

SIKHS

Nanak (1469–1539), the first Sikh *guru*, was born some forty miles from Lahore in the Punjab area. Here the conflict between Hindus and Muslims had resulted in fighting and killing for centuries. Nanak was born into a *kshatriya* family. His father was rather low on the economic scale, being in the employ of a Muslim ruler. As a boy,

---

6. Quoted in H. G. Rawlinson, *India, A Short Cultural History*, New York, Praeger, 1952, first published in 1937, p. 343.

Nanak had meditative tendencies, and although he was married at the age of twelve, his religious tendencies were not abated. He left his wife and two children with his parents while he took a position in the district capital, but even there he could not keep his mind on his employment. He spent considerable time in the evenings singing hymns with a Muslim minstrel, Mardana.

One morning, while bathing in the river, he had a vision of God's presence. He was offered a cup of nectar which he accepted, and God said to him:

> I am with thee. I have made thee happy, and also those who shall take thy name. Go and repeat Mine, and cause others to do likewise. Abide uncontaminated by the world. Practice the repetition of My name, charity, ablutions, worship, and meditation. I have given thee this cup of nectar, a pledge of My regard.[7]

Tradition has it that Nanak responded with the words that introduce the *Japji*, which is repeated by devout Sikhs as a morning devotional prayer:

> There is but one God whose name is True, the Creator, devoid of fear and enmity, immortal, unborn, self-existent, great and bountiful. The True One was in the beginning, the True One was in the primal age. The True One is, was, O Nanak, and the True One also shall be.[8]

Tradition states that, after a full day's silence, Nanak uttered this pronouncement: "There is no Hindu and no Mussalman." Nanak then set out on an extended tour of northern and western India. To emphasize the basic unity of Muslim and Hindu teaching and practices, he even wore a unique garb which combined a Muslim headpiece and an Indian sectarian mark on his forehead, among other things.

In the *Adi Granth,* holy book of the Sikh community, are Nanak's teachings which attempt to combine, as did his garments, the faith of Hindus and Muslims. Nanak's belief in a single Creator God came from the Muslim side. In an attempt not to limit God to any one community, he avoided such names as Allah, Rama, Shiva, or Vishnu, simply calling God the True Name. Nanak's Creator God ordained that man be served by the lower forms of life in the creation, a notion which eliminated the need for vegetarianism.

Nanak also held to the doctrine of *maya,* in common with his Brahman neighbors. But although he retained the doctrine of *maya,* he did not follow its advaitin implications. The world, however, was ultimately unreal, God having created matter by drawing a veil over himself. In addition to this concept, Nanak believed in the law of karma, the doctrine of rebirth, and held that men prolonged the rounds of rebirth by living apart from God, thereby accumulating bad karma.

---

7. M. A. MacAuliffe, *The Sikh Religion: Its Gurus, Sacred Writings and Authors,* New Delhi, S. Chand & Co., 1963 reprint, vol. I, pp. 33–34.

8. Ibid., p. 35.

There was in Nanak a strong *bhakti* strain which comes through Kabir who preceded him, and Ramananda who preceded Kabir. Although simple repetition of the True Name is more efficacious than going on pilgrimages, bathing images, or bathing in sacred rivers, salvation was seen in terms of absorption into God, the True Name. The strong *bhakti* emphasis in Nanak would not allow him to espouse an ultimate elimination of individuality.

Nanak took a strong stand against both ritualism and asceticism. Since he was not a philosopher, he did not attempt to reconcile the apparent conflict between theism and *advaita*. *Bhakti* theologians solved this problem to their satisfaction by identifying Brahman with the Supreme Deity. By so doing they had to deny Shankara's doctrine of the levels of being as well as his view of *maya*. Shankara, on the other hand, solved the problem by relegating *bhakti* and the Supreme Deity to the preliminary level of the phenomenal world. Nanak was a mystic who felt his religion, not a theologian who made an intense effort to eliminate all logical conflicts.

The significant role of the *guru* was emphasized by Nanak and the community which followed him. The guidance of a *guru* was both necessary and sufficient to lead men to God. Those men who committed themselves to Nanak's teachings and became his followers were known as Sikhs, or disciples.

There was a succession of ten *gurus*, beginning with Nanak. Prior to his death, Nanak appointed one of his disciples as his successor. Angad, the second *guru*, devised a new script called *Gurmukhi*, in which he wrote the literature of his faith, and also began the compilation of the Sikh scriptures. At this stage these scriptures, which were later to be the *Adi Granth*, were mostly composed of the hymns of Nanak. Nanak's practice of operating a public kitchen where guests and friends could eat regardless of caste or religion was enlarged by Angad. Operating free kitchens in the Sikh gurdwaras (temples, literally, "gate of the *guru*") continues even today. Travelers who are hungry or weary can share a meal and obtain a place to lodge for the night.

Guru Angad selected as his successor Guru Amar Das (1479–1574), who prohibited the veiling and seclusion of women (*purdah*) as commonly practiced by Muslims. He also opposed the practice of widows throwing themselves on the funeral pyres of their husbands (*sati*). Amar Das continued the free kitchen and visitors accepted the hospitality of the *guru* by eating with the disciples. One of his visitors during this period was the Emperor Akbar.

The fourth *guru* was Guru Ram Das (1574–1581), who is remembered for having started the famous Golden Temple at Amritsar which remains today the center of the Sikh community. The temple is beautifully reflected in the artificial lake which surrounds it.

The fifth *guru*, Guru Arjan (1581–1606), completed the Golden Temple and installed in it the *Adi Granth* which he collated. The Muslim emperor Akbar, having been told by his advisers that the *Adi Granth* was a heretical book, examined it and found nothing that offended him. But Akbar died during the time that Arjan was *guru*, and his son Jahangir proved to be more cruel and fanatical.

Golden Temple, Amritsar. (Courtesy of the Government of India Tourist Office.)

Guru Arjan was tortured to death, but before he died he instructed the sixth *guru,* Guru Har Govind (1606–1646), to "sit fully armed on his throne and maintain an army to the best of his ability."

When Har Govind became *guru,* he wore two swords but would not wear the turban and necklace which had been symbolic of pacifying tendencies. He organized an army and drew to his side thousands of Sikhs who were willing to engage in battle. Hostility between Sikhs and Muslims continued to grow as the Muslims interpreted the Sikh presence as a political threat and a religious error. The Sikh movement, which began in an attempt to bring Muslim and Hindu together, was becoming a source of provocation for

Muslim hostility. Har Govind increased the missionary outreach of the Sikh community and was an able administrator as well.

The growing hostility continued during the period of the seventh *guru*, Har Rai (1630–1661), the eighth *guru*, Har K'ishan (1656–1664), and the ninth *guru*, Tegh Bahadur (1621–1675). Tegh Bahadur became a martyr for his faith as a victim of the fanaticism of Aurangzeb.

The tenth and final *guru*, Govind Singh (1666–1708), played a formative role in the military tendency of the Sikh community in the face of Muslim opposition. Convinced of his own divine authority, in 1699 he instituted the *Khalsa*, the Community of the Pure. Members were formally initiated with a baptism in which the initiates were required to drink and be sprinkled with sweetened water which had been stirred with a sharp sword. This nectar, *amrit*, was supposed to confer ceremonial purity and immunity in battle. Members of the casteless *Khalsa* changed their name to Singh ("Lion") and they repeated the battle cry of the Sikhs: "The pure are of God and the victory is to God." Their marks of identification were the five K's:

1. *Kesh,* or long hair, a sign of saintliness;
2. *Kangh,* a comb for keeping the hair tidy;
3. *Kach,* short drawers, insuring quick movement in battle;
4. *Kara,* a steel bracelet, signifying sternness and restraint;
5. *Kirpan,* or sword for defense.

Four further rules were prescribed for all members. They were not to cut any hair from the body; not to smoke, chew tobacco, or drink alcohol; not to eat the meat of any animal slaughtered by the Muslim method of bleeding to death; not to molest Muslim women, but to live a life of marital fidelity. The Sikhs were fearless fighting men, and their battles with Muslims were often brutal. Even after the Muslim threat had passed, the Sikhs continued their military prowess as honored members of the British army, and later, after Independence, in the Indian army.

Guru Govind Singh taught that after his death his followers were to regard the *Granth* as their *guru* and that there would be no further need for a human *guru.* Since that time there has been no human *guru* in the Sikh community, but the *Granth* has been worshiped as their one divine authority. In the Golden Temple and also in other gurdwaras as well, the *Sri Guru Granth Sahib* is enshrined with honor. On special occasions its words are read continuously day and night, and it is treated with all the care and reverence that a Vaishava might offer to an image of Vishnu. In the course of development from Guru Nanak through Guru Govind Singh, the community has undergone a transformation from pacifism to military emphasis.

Although Guru Nanak intended to bring together both Muslim and Hindu, it is almost prophetic that Muslims and Hindus quarreled over the disposal of his body at the time of death. Prior to his demise, the Muslims had proposed to bury him while the Hindus wanted to cremate him, but Nanak told the Hindus to place flowers on his right and the Muslims to place flowers on his left. Those whose flow-

Priest reading Adi Granth, Golden Temple, Amritsar. (Photo by Paul E. Pfuetze.)

ers remained fresh in the morning would have their way. On the morning following his death, they raised the sheet that had covered him to find the body gone. The flowers on both sides were fresh.

The story is intended to emphasize the unification of the two hostile religious groups, but it seems that their original hostility was more prophetic. By the reign of Guru Arjan, the *distinctiveness* of the Sikh community was emphatically stated. Guru Arjan is quoted as saying,

> *I have broken with the Hindu and the Muslim,*
> *I will not worship with the Hindu nor like the Muslim go to Mecca.*
> *I shall serve Him and no other.*
> *I will not pray to idols nor say the Muslim prayer.*
> *I shall put my heart at the feet of the one Supreme Being,*
> *For we are neither Hindus nor Mussalmans.*[9]

There has been a tendency for the Sikh community to absorb the practices of the Hindu community around them. Many of the youth have abandoned the distinctive symbols (five K's), and others have modified them by replacing the dagger with a small symbolic dagger on the wooden comb or by trimming the beard to improve its appearance. As the external symbols of the community are given up, there remains less to distinguish a Sikh from his Vaishvana neighbor. Hence many of the older generation place an emphasis on these externals as means of preserving their identity. One can find considerable literature emphasizing the glories of the Sikh tradition, the struggles with which it developed in the face of Muslim opposition, or the health value of long hair. One pamphlet, the result of research at a Human Hair Research Institute, emphasizes that on scientific grounds it can be shown that health depends upon

---

9. Khushwant Singh, *The Sikhs,* London, G. Allen, 1953, p. 27.

the solar rays of energy taken into the body through the hair. Hence, although the most healthy existence would be to live without clothing, without cutting the hair, and without washing the natural oils from the hair and skin too frequently, given the necessity of common decency, the Sikh alternative is the best.

There has been agitation for a Punjabi sabha, a political state with borders determined by the dominant use of Punjabi. The intent is to maintain a distinctive Sikh community; though it was the cause of bitter Hindu-Sikh communal controversy, a Punjabi sabha has been granted.

While the most famous gurdwara is the Golden Temple at Amritsar, there are numerous Sikh temples throughout India, particularly in the north. There the *Granth* is read, and each worshiper receives in his outstretched, cupped hands a portion of pudding which is eaten. Equal portions are given to all, symbolizing equality in the community. On holidays a mass meal may be eaten at the *langer,* or kitchen, of the gurdwara. Pilgrimages are important and devotees flock to important sites in Sikh history. The Sikhs are a hardworking people who have taken part in every level of Indian life. Nevertheless, the increasing inroads of secularism, a growing emphasis on externals of the faith, and the preservation of a distinctive identity make it difficult not to conclude that a significant religious shift has taken place. Whereas for Nanak, the ultimate matter was devotion to the True Name, for the present community, self-preservation appears to be somewhat more important. Nevertheless, there remain those who share Nanak's devotion to the transcendent ideal.

THE MODERN PERIOD

By 1818 the power of the British in India had spread from the Himalayas in the north to Cape Comorin in the south. After the Mutiny of 1857, the government was transferred from the East India Company to the British Crown. Peace was restored in 1858 and a unified system of administration was put into operation. The British were to continue in control until 1947 when political independence was achieved.

Although the British were in India primarily for economic reasons, their presence resulted in an Indian encounter with the West. It was originally the British policy to remain neutral on religious and cultural matters, but over the years a challenge to traditional values took both direct and indirect courses. During the eighteenth and nineteenth centuries grants were given by the British government through certain officials for the support of temples and mosques while under others missionary work was encouraged. In 1813 Parliament established a legal connection between the government of India and the Church of England.

One source of encounter was the challenge to various traditional practices by Christian missionaries. These missionaries spoke out against the practice of *sati* and were concerned about the fate of widows who were not permitted to remarry. They were disturbed also by the situation of children's marriage before the age of puberty, where the death of the boy would add to the number of young widows.

Western education also introduced Indians to new value systems. The scientific spirit drew Indians to the West, although attacks on polytheism and certain social practices were part of the encounter as well. In the early nineteenth century Indians were willing to look to the West for guidance and to accept its superiority; only later would they go through the stages of rejection, and then synthesis. Application of scientific knowledge to technological advance was also to be seen in marked contrast with predominantly village India.

GROWTH OF MOVEMENTS AND ORGANIZATIONS

The response to this encounter took the form of either vigorous reform or staunch defense, or various degrees between these two extremes.

Brahma Samaj

One of those organizations which has tended to favor more radical change is the Brahma Samaj. The term *Brahma* is an adjective formed from *Brahman* of the Upanishads, and *Samaj* means a society. In its varied history the Brahma Samaj has been strongly theistic; it has rejected polytheism, the worship of images, and sacrifice of animals; it has advocated the abolition of *sati,* child marriage, and polygamy. Still the very title of this organization indicates its intention of remaining firmly attached to its Indian past.

Ram Mohun Roy (1772–1833), who founded the Brahma Samaj in 1828, was born in a Bengali village and was married three times while still a child. At the age of twelve he left home, studied Persian and Arabic at Patna, engaged in Islamic studies, and then went to Benares where he studied Sanskrit. His first book, written in 1802 in Persian with an Arabic introduction, was a defense of monotheism. He studied Vaishnava, Tantric, Jain, and Buddhist positions, and was not content until he learned Hebrew, Latin, and Greek and had launched on a serious study of Christian literature.

In 1816 Ram Mohun published *Vedanta-sara* which attempted to find monotheism in the Vedanta point of view. Somewhat of a Unitarian, his contact with Christian missionaries led to some of his books, such as *The Precepts of Jesus, Appeal to the Christian Public,* and *The Ideal Humanity of Jesus.*

The Trust Deed for the Samaj temple indicates that the building was to be used for the worship and adoration of God without respect to the castes of worshipers. No images, pictures, or likenesses were to be permitted in the building. Sacrifices were also forbidden on the premises. Only sermons, hymns, and prayers that would strengthen the bonds of union among men of all religious creeds were to be used. Further, the Trust Deed warned against a contemptuous attitude toward the modes of worship of alien groups regardless of how illegitimate they might seem. The organization of the Samaj thus shows a social as well as a theistic orientation.

Ram Mohun contemplated a universal religion which he thought might some day have universal acceptance. This universal religion would include all that is common to all religions, with divisive elements omitted. Having found the Upanishads to teach monotheism, he was convinced that the notion of the one true God would be part of this common faith. This emphasis on the fundamental unity of all religions was also to be stressed by Ramakrishna, Vivekananda, Tagore, and Radhakrishnan, even though the nature and extent of that unity is diverse.

Devendranath Tagore (1817–1905), the father of the famous Bengali poet Rabindranath Tagore, succeeded Ram Mohun as head of the Brahma Samaj. He continued to support the Samaj opposition to idolatry. He also exerted caution to avoid undue Christian influence which might compromise the transcendence of God through incarnation, or *advaita* influence which might dissolve the difference between the worshiper and the Worshiped. Also, monotheism was strengthened by publishing an anthology of Upanishadic texts which he felt supported monotheism (*Brahma-Dharma*).

Since the Samaj had been little more than a weekly meeting, Devendranath saw the need, in 1843, for a structural organization and drew up a list of vows called the Brahma Covenant which was to be affirmed by members of the society. The main promises were to avoid idolatry and to worship God with love and obedience. Prayer and devotional exercises were introduced into the services of the Samaj and the direct communication of man with the Divine Being was stressed. Devendranath was less rationalistic than Ram Mohun.

Since the Vedas were considered the sole authority for the Samaj, the question of their infallibility was raised. A controversy arose which led to the sending of four individuals to Banaras to study and copy the Vedas and to report their findings. The result was the repudiation of the doctrine of the Vedas' infallibility and a new emphasis was placed on intuition.

Keshab Chandra Sen (1838–1884) joined the Samaj in 1857. Keshab held that the Brahma religion could be summed up in the two concepts of the fatherhood of God and the brotherhood of man. He was less concerned with theological controversy than with actual life. More than previous leaders, Keshab was enamored with Christ. He had to face mounting opposition from members who were anti-Hindu or anti-Christian. Such remarks as the following did not help to heal the rift: "Who rules India? Not politics or democracy, but Christ. None but Jesus ever deserved this bright, precious diadem—India. And Jesus shall have it!" [1]

Keshab even called himself a "servant of Jesus." Yet he emphasized religious unity and even Asian unity. Christianity was founded by Asians and the idea of a universal religion is a Christian idea. In 1869 the differences between the older members and the younger faction led by Keshab came to a head and resulted in the formation of the Brahma Samaj of India under Keshab. The older organization took the title Adi Brahma Samaj (original Brahma Samaj).

Keshab introduced a more devotional form of worship which included the singing of Vaishnava *bhajans.* Keshab himself became an object of devotion and was taken to task by the Adi Brahma Samaj. When Keshab failed to interfere with the devotion of his followers in his behalf, the cleavage between the two parties increased. Since he had previously opposed Hindu marriages because of their idolatrous connections, Keshab's integrity became suspect when he consented to the Hindu marriage of his daughter to the prince of Bihar. This led to a further split in the Samaj in 1878 when the dissenters organized the Sadharan Brahma Samaj, depreciated the cult of personalities, and reaffirmed their stand against idolatry. Social reform remained in the foreground in these concerns.

Keshab did not form the Brahma Samaj of India without a certain amount of sorrow, since it meant a break with his close friend De-

---

1. Quoted in V. S. Naravane, *Modern Indian Thought,* Bombay, Asia Publishing House, 1964, p. 43.

vendranath who became the leader of the Adi Brahma Samaj. Keshab was the last dynamic leader of the Brahma Samaj, which movement had pretty well spent its force by the time Keshab died. It exerted a powerful force for social reform in its day and based its social concerns on a faith in one Supreme Being. Frequently it gave evidence of concern for devotional life. While more radical than most movements in nineteenth-century India, the Brahma Samaj not only embraced the West or Christianity, but maintained a connection with its previous Indian tradition, however tenuous that connection became at times.

Mula Shanker (1824–1883) was dissatisfied with image worship in his early years and left his family to live the life of a wandering monk. Initiated into the Saraswati order of Sannyasins, he took the name by which he is commonly known, Dayananda Saraswati. In 1875 he founded the Arya Samaj as a universal religion open to anyone, regardless of caste or nationality. Dayananda held to the infallibility of the *Vedas* and used the slogan "back to the *Vedas.*" He rejected the polytheism and idolatry of the texts of the later Indian tradition such as the *Puranas,* holding they were immoral. In accepting the authority of the Vedas, many Indians included the Brahmanas and Upanishads. Dayananda limited his authority to the Vedic *samhitas.* He opposed the ritual of the Brahmanas and the *advaitin* tendencies of the Upanishads.

Arya Samaj

It was Dayananda's view that the Vedic hymns taught that there was only one God, who was to be worshiped spiritually and not by means of images. The various Vedic deities were interpreted merely as so many names for the one God rather than as reference to a variety of deities. Dayananda held to the doctrines of karma and rebirth and contended that they were also taught in the Vedas.

For Dayananda, the Vedas are the eternal utterances of God and hence contain no historical or temporary references. Those made to particular places or times are only apparent. The Vedas contain complete knowledge. Although the European has come upon the scene with impressive technological achievements brought about by science, this is much less impressive when one realizes that such accomplishments were already foreseen in the ancient Vedas.

> To him not only was everything contained in the Vedas perfect truth, but he went a step further, and by the most incredible interpretations succeeded in persuading himself and others that everything worth knowing, even the most recent inventions of modern science, were alluded to in the Vedas. Steam-engines, railways, and steamboats, were all shown to have been known, at least in their germs, to the poets of the Vedas.[2]

To become a member of the Arya Samaj one had to subscribe to ten fundamental principles.

---

2. Quoted in J. N. Farquhar, *Modern Religious Movements in India,* New York, Macmillan, 1919, p. 116.

1. God is the primary cause of all true knowledge, and everything known by its name.
2. God is All-Truth, All-Knowledge, All-Beatitude, Incorporeal, Almighty, Just, Merciful, Unbegotten, Infinite, Unchangeable, without a beginning, Incomparable, the Support of the Lord of All, All-Pervading, Omniscient, Imperishable, Immortal, Exempt from fear, Eternal, Holy, and the Cause of the Universe. To Him alone is worship due.
3. The Vedas are the books of true knowledge, and it is the paramount duty of every Ārya to read or hear them read, to teach and preach them to others.
4. One should always be ready to accept truth and renounce untruth.
5. All actions ought to be done conformably to virtue, i.e. after a thorough consideration of right or wrong.
6. The primary object of the Samaj is to do good to the world by improving the physical, spiritual, and social conditions of mankind.
7. All ought to be treated with love, justice, and due regard to their merits.
8. Ignorance ought to be dispelled and knowledge diffused.
9. No one ought to be contented with his own good alone, but everyone ought to regard his prosperity as included in that of others.
10. In matters which affect the general social well-being of the whole society, one ought to discard all differences and not allow one's individuality to interfere, but in strictly personal matters everyone may act with freedom.[3]

Their Sunday morning service had more affinity with a Protestant service with the singing of hymns, prayer, and a sermon, than it had with Vedic sacrificial worship. While certain of the laws of Manu were enjoined, child marriage was prohibited, although virgin widows and widowers were permitted to marry.

The Arya Samaj was strongly organized, and developed an antiforeign policy which led to the institution of the ceremony of *Shuddhi* for reclaiming those who left Hinduism and were later reconverted and purified. The Arya Samaj has been militantly antiChristian. It felt that having withstood the Muslims for hundreds of years, it could also withstand the Christian attack on their ancient religion.

Ramakrishna Movement

While the Ramakrishna movement established a tradition of social work and education, the man chiefly responsible for it was more of a contemplative than an activist. Gadadhar Chatterji (1836–1886) is known by the name he took as a sannyasin, Ramakrishna, or sometimes by his title Paramahamsa, which means "the highest swan." Unable to read or write, he could not be considered a scholar even though he showed considerable grasp of certain aspects of Indian philosophy and tradition. His only sayings have been collected and

---

3. Ibid., p. 120.

Dakshineshwar Temple. (Photo by Robert D. Baird.)

published by a follower in the volume *The Gospel of Sri Ramakrishna*. Ramakrishna was not responsible for the formation of the Ramakrishna Mission or the Order instituted by his successor Vivekananda.

To try to synthesize the thought of Ramakrishna would not only be difficult, but would also miss the real thrust of his life. He placed more stock in intuition than in intellect. Those who emphasize the latter are like men who go to an orchard and, instead of eating the mangoes, speculate about the number of branches on each tree and the number of leaves on each branch.

As early as the age of six, Ramakrishna was prone to mystic visions. At the age of seventeen he went to live with his brother who was the priest at the new temple at Dakshineshwar, north of Calcutta. Upon the death of his brother he became the priest, and spent considerable time in loving devotion to the goddess Kali. Ramakrishna is said to have been examined by a physician while in a trance, and no trace of pulse or heartbeat could be discerned.

Ramakrishna seems to have had a passion for as wide a variety of religious experiences as possible. He submitted to the disciplines of Tantra, and practiced *bhakti* by approaching God as parent, master, friend, child, and sweetheart. He devoted himself to Rama by playing the part of Hanuman even to the extent of climbing a tree, and, according to his devoted followers, growing the stub of a tail. Ramakrishna was initiated into *advaita* by Totapura, and in a surprisingly short time is said to have achieved *Nirvikalpa Samadhi,* the highest *advaita* experience.

Having practiced Muslim rites for a short time he also had visions of Jesus, and a picture of the Madonna with child once sent him into ecstacy. These experiences led him and his followers to conclude that they had ample proof of the basic unity of all religions.

Since Ramakrishna had all these mystical experiences, he was able to testify that they were not essentially different. Various religions and opinions are just so many streams which eventually merge into the same ocean. Ramakrishna used imagery and analogy to express himself rather than technical philosophical terminology. He did not see any point in making a great distinction between transpersonal Brahman and the personal God. No ultimate difference exists—any more than can be found between a diamond and its luster. If one has an instrument with seven holes, why should he always play a monotone? The entire throng of worshipers, whether Christians, Vaishnavas, Muslims, or Shaktas, are seeking the same God through different ways. As Ramakrishna put it, "You may eat your cake with icing either straight or sideways, it will taste sweet either way." [4]

In spite of the fact that some of Ramakrishna's actions might be considered irregular, those who came to know him were usually impressed. In his early years his family was concerned about his stability and encouraged his marriage in the hope that he might come down to earth from his mystic flights. Later Ramakrishna's wife joined him in a common spiritual quest, but they did not live together as husband and wife.

It was left to his disciple Narendranath Datta (1862–1902) to proclaim Ramakrishna's message literally around the world, to organize the movement, and to attach the social dimension by which the movement has been identified. Known as Vivekananda, Narendranath Datta was educated at Presidency College where he was exposed to Western education. At the time he met Ramakrishna, he was passing through an acute crisis of skepticism. He had read approvingly the works of J. S. Mill, Hume, and Herbert Spencer. He was impressed with Ramakrishna, and his own crisis coupled with poverty and the death of his father led him to attach himself to the Master.

After the teacher's death, Vivekananda gathered some disciples into a brotherhood in Banaras. Becoming a sannyasin, he wandered throughout India. In 1893 he came to Chicago for the World Parliament of Religions. His address there attracted much attention and he was heralded in the American and Indian press. Returning to India in 1897, he was enthusiastically received as he landed in Ceylon and traveled up the eastern coast of India. In 1897 he organized the Ramakrishna Mission and, one year later, the Belur Math where the Ramakrishna monks still reside.

While the Arya Samaj and the Brahma Samaj have dwindled in influence, the Ramakrishna Mission continues to contribute significantly to Indian life. The headquarters of the Mission are at Belur, north of Calcutta, and in other Indian cities there are Missions which have an organizational tie to the central headquarters. The movement has a press and publishes numerous books on Indian religion and culture.

---

4. Swami Nikhilananda, trans., *The Gospel of Sri Ramakrishna,* 4th ed., Madras, Sri Ramakrishna Math, 1964, p. 590.

Vivekananda considered himself an *advaitin,* but attempted to make his position understandable beyond academic circles. He preceded Radhakrishnan in arguing that to say that the world is *maya* is not an outright rejection of the universe nor is it equivalent to saying that the world does not exist. To designate the world as *maya* is not to say that it is illusion, but merely to indicate its relative reality. *Maya* indicates that the world is full of contradictions and, to that extent, can be considered unreal or illusory. But it is through *maya* that we come to the realization of Reality. Hence *advaita* does not imply inactivity or an attempt to escape from the world, but proposes to use the world as a means of transcending it.

Once it is emphasized that *maya* does not mean that the world is nonexistent, the qualified reality of the world is in turn emphasized in order to make room for social concern and activity. "The man who says that he will work when the world has become all good and then he will enjoy bliss, is as likely to succeed as the man who sits beside the Ganga and says, 'I will ford the river when all the water has run into the ocean.' " [5]

While he held a place for *jnanayoga* (the way of knowledge), and although this experience transcended reason, Vivekananda also held that no genuine inspiration contradicts reason. Inspiration sees things in flashes and is higher than reason, yet one must be on guard to distinguish inspiration from mere intellect or even deception. Vivekananda was particularly cautious with regard to occultism and mysticism, but he had no doubts about the authenticity of Ramakrishna.

Like many of those thinkers who have been characterized as "neo-advaitin," Vivekananda put considerable stock in science. Although he spoke out against Western materialism, he read in the sciences and not infrequently used scientific analogies to clarify and add weight to *advaita.* Vivekananda nevertheless did maintain the distinction to be taken up by Radhakrishnan, that India's role had been to stress the spirit while the West had concentrated on unraveling the forces of nature. He felt that nationalistic expressions of his day which attempted to lay the blame for India's ills at the door of religion were misplaced. India could not survive without religion since it had always been integrated with her destiny.

While an ardent defender of Vedanta, Vivekananda was not beyond attacking certain practices that he held were irrational or sentimental. He felt that it was sometimes necessary to abandon custom. There were certain ideas about food that he ridiculed. As for bathing ritual, if its merits were to be accepted we should expect a fish to reach Heaven before anyone else, since it bathes all the time.[6]

Vivekananda's *advaita* did not lead to inactive meditation, but was a call to action. He did not see knowledge, devotion, or action as three paths leading in different directions but as complements rein-

---

5. *Selections from Swami Vivekananda,* Calcutta, Advaita Ashrama, 1963, p. 146.

6. Cf. Naravane, op. cit., p. 101.

forcing each other. He placed stress on practical work, for liberation was never an escape from the world. The critics of *advaita* had contended that by declaring Brahman to be the sole Reality, a devaluation of human life had resulted. On the contrary, Vivekananda held that if man is identical with God he should seek to abolish the indignities of the world. "Religion is the manifestation of the Divinity already in man." [7]

Using Shankara's ultimate level in support of action on the relative level poses a difficulty, since ultimately such distinctions as "the world" do not exist. But a shift in emphasis has taken place coupled with a reinterpretation of the *advaitin* position. Vivekananda has attempted to make room for social concern and the dignity of the individual which is so commonly affirmed in the twentieth century.

Theosophical Society

The Theosophical Society was organized in New York in 1875 by Madame Blavatsky and Colonel Olcott. The latter was elected the first president and the former the corresponding secretary. In 1907, at the death of Colonel Olcott, Annie Besant became president.

In 1879 the founders moved their society to India, reportedly on orders from their Masters in Tibet, from which source Madame Blavatsky claimed to have received her first religious instructions. The Society was active in counteracting the work of Christian missionaries by emphasizing the long and valuable heritage of Indian culture and religion. In 1882 the headquarters were moved from Bombay to Adyar just outside Madras, where a spacious center is maintained today.

The Theosophical Society was consistently involved with the occult and miraculous. Followers believe that their leaders possess miraculous powers including the ability to produce material objects out of nothing. Attempts to expose these claims have been made, and while outsiders feel the exposition reasonably sure, devotees remain unconvinced.

Although Annie Besant was of English descent, she endeared herself to the Indians by proclaiming that India was her true land, because she lived a previous existence there. Mrs. Besant assumed Indian dress, sat cross-legged on the floor, and ate with the right hand in Indian style rather than with a knife and fork. She stirred Indians to maintain their Hinduism, and at the time when Hinduism was under attack from many sources, such encouragement from a Westerner was impressive to Indian ears.

Make no mistake. Without Hinduism India has no future. Hinduism is the soil into which India's roots are struck, and torn out of that she will inevitably wither, as a tree torn out of its place. Many are the religions and many are the races which are flourishing in India, but none of them stretches back into the far dawn of her past, nor is necessary for her endurance as a nation. Every one

---

7. *The Complete Works of Swami Vivekananda,* Calcutta, Advaita Ashrama, 1962, 8th ed., vol. IV, p. 358.

might pass away as they came, and India would still remain. But let Hinduism vanish, and what is she? A "geographical expression" of the past, a dim memory of her perished glory. Her history, her literature, her art, her monuments, all have Hinduism written across them. Zoroastrianism came for refuge and her sons have found asylum and welcome in India; but Zoroastrianism might pass, and India would remain. Buddhism was founded here, but Buddhism has disappeared and India remains. Islam came, a wave of conquest, and the Mussalmans form a part of the Indian people, and will share in the making of the future; yet Islam might pass, and India would remain. Christianity has come, and Christians rule the land and influence its steps; yet Christianity might pass and India would remain. India lived before their coming; India could live after their passing. But let Hinduism go, Hinduism that was India's cradle, and in that passing would be India's grave. Then would India with India's religion be but a memory, as are Egypt and Egypt's religion now. India would remain then as a subject for the antiquarian, the archaeologist, a corpse for dissection, but no longer an object of patriotism, no longer a Nation.[8]

Mrs. Besant started Central Hindu College which later became the nucleus of the present Banaras Hindu University. Although her political activities and her increased emphasis on the occult and clairvoyance lowered her esteem in Indian eyes, she is more remembered for her positive work in what D. S. Sarma has called the "renaissance of Hinduism." In 1943 a statue of Mrs. Besant was unveiled in the Madras Marina.

According to Theosophy, the Absolute emanates souls from within Itself. These souls or monads are of the same divine nature as the Absolute and therefore partake of *sat* (being), *cit* (intelligence), and *ananda* (bliss). In their present state the souls are dormant and unaware of their own potential and true nature. But they descend into matter (mineral, vegetable, and finally animal) and through a series of rebirths gain experience of themselves whereby they come to the level of "individualization." After individuation, at which point conscious evolution begins, the soul is no longer born into animal states since "no experience useful for the growth of the soul can be obtained through the small and primitive brains of animals." [9]

At the point of individuation, karma is operative. Karma means that when one does what is good and right, conditions result which aid in the soul's progressive realization and unfolding. Actions contrary to the divine will create conditions which thwart such progress. Karma is never punishment, but merely a means of learning what we are capable of becoming.

The purpose of rebirth is to provide the soul with all the experi-

---

8. "Address to Students at Central Hindu College," quoted in D. S. Sarma, *Hinduism Through the Ages,* Bombay, Bharatiya Vidya Bhavan, 1967, pp. 113–114.

9. C. Jinarajadasa, "What Theosophists Believe," in H. Bhattacharya, ed., *The Cultural Heritage of India,* Calcutta, The Ramakrishna Mission Institute of Culture, 1956, vol. IV, p. 642.

ences which will enable it to unfold its true nature. Once individuation is reached, one is born as male and female, and into various races and cultures. As one commits blunders by testing the Divine Law the soul gains illumination.

The goal of liberation (*moksha, Nirvana,* salvation) is not an escape from suffering nor is it the end of individual existence. In liberation, however, the soul is freed from all ignorance which surrounds it. Then rebirth is no longer necessary, but the soul continues to grow as it "becomes a larger embodiment of the wonders of Divinity." [10] Such beings participate in what is called "The Divine Plan."

Theosophy believes that there are *adepts* who are agents of the evolutionary process and who work under divine guidance for the benefit of man. The adepts are perfected men and they work together to assist in bringing about the divine evolutionary process ("The Divine Plan") in which souls progressively come to realize their true natures. The adepts are part of an organization called the "Great Hierarchy."

> *They form an organization called the Great Hierarchy or the Great White Brotherhood. They are not all of equal capacity, because some achieved liberation ages ago and others but recently, and therefore the former have a longer record of work and experience. But all of them are united by one will, which is to serve the plan of God for men. They are the flowers of the evolutionary process, since their consciousness is all the time in intimate communion with that of the Divinity.*[11]

These beings supervise all the processes of nature which we have become accustomed to call laws. They guide the origin and migration of races and provide men with great religious founders when it seems most beneficial. The universe, then, is in a process of unfolding the potential of the souls of men. Things are moving in a generally favorable direction. Life takes on an optimistic hue.

All religions are considered of value because they are derived from one source. Each religion thus fulfills a role in providing the transmigrating soul with a fullness of experience. Religiously, *bhakti,* yogic meditation, the example of Jesus, and the words of Muhammad are all divinely ordained means for the soul's progress to freedom.

The Theosophical Society headquarters has on its grounds a Catholic chapel as well as a Buddhist temple. People of all faiths are welcome and their library contains books from all religious traditions. With walled plaques symbolizing Christianity, Islam, Buddhism, Hinduism, and Judaism, the movement presents itself as taking the best of all faiths.

MODERN INDIAN THINKERS

In the nineteenth and twentieth centuries there emerged certain important Indian religious thinkers who cannot be dealt with in terms

---

10. Ibid., p. 644.
11. Ibid., p. 645.

of any particular institutional expression of religion. These thinkers represent an attempt to bridge the gap between technical philosophy and actual life and to place more emphasis on the relevance of religion for affirming the present existence rather than as a method for escaping from it.

A Bengali by birth, Rabindranath was raised in a home that was steeped in the Upanishads and the Vaishnava tradition. His father was Devendranath, whose Brahma Samaj attempted to reform Indian religion. While holding membership in the Adi Brahma Samaj and being an honorary member of the Sadharan Samaj, Rabindranath could not be contained in such organizations.

Rabindranath Tagore (1861–1941)

He was first a poet, the recipient of a Nobel Prize, and had an artistic view of the universe. Without degrading reason, he was more interested in apprehending the overarching harmony of a fluid universe.

> *My religion is essentially a poet's religion. Its touch comes to me through the same unseen and trackless channels as does the inspiration of my music. My religious life has followed the same mysterious lines of growth as my poetic life. Somehow they are wedded to each other.*[12]

Since he believed that truth lies primarily in relatedness, in seeing the harmony of apparently contrary forces, Tagore did not see the necessity of constructing a logically coherent philosophical system.

Tagore liked to see himself in the role of a reconciler of East and West. The historical influences upon him make this intention easily understandable. He often quotes from the Upanishads which had so deeply impressed his father. While the Upanishads were influential in Tagore's thought, he was inclined to interpret them theistically. Moreover, he felt there was in the Upanishads a positive element which enabled him to hold a decidedly affirmative view of life. Tagore's theistic leanings were probably due more to his Vaishnava upbringing than to any contact with Christians. His artistic nature made him more amenable to the *bhakti* ideal of devotion to God than to the *advaita* ideal of *Nirvikalpa Samadhi*. Since he held a complementary view of the world, he never felt compelled to reject Shankara's *advaita*. The influence of the Buddha as a force for cultural unity in Asia impressed him, but the Mahayana ideal of compassion touched him more than the less active ideal proposed in the Pali Canon.

Tagore was influenced by such Western thinkers as Benedetto Croce, Henri Bergson, Bertrand Russell, Albert Schweitzer, and John Dewey. As with other modern Indian thinkers, Tagore felt that science was Europe's greatest gift to humanity. He also emphasized that Christianity was originally an Asiatic religion. His thought was formed in an India where religious, cultural, and social changes

---

12. "The Religion of an Artist," in S. Radhakrishnan and J. H. Muirhead, eds., *Contemporary Indian Philosophy*, London, Allen & Unwin, 1936, p. 32.

were in process. His birth and privileged position enabled him to keep abreast of all such changes.

Tagore saw the universe through a universal principle of harmony and balance. God was a primary fact of experience and not a Being whose existence had to be proved. While Tagore's statements vacillated between theism and *advaita,* he seems to have emphasized the personalistic dimension. A personal God was not finite, nor did such a designation bring God down to man's level. While it did not exhaust the nature of God to speak of him as personal, it was the highest thing one could say about him.

Man is as real as God. Unwilling to side either with the *advaitins* or pluralists, Tagore held that the many are real without the organic unity of the whole being destroyed. While the one and the many are both real, it is impossible to explain how they are related. The doctrine of *maya* does not mean that the world is nonexistent, but points to the false belief that the world is independently real. Man, God, and the world find their reality in the harmonious interrelatedness of the three.

Tagore's joy came not by withdrawal from the world but in the discovery of the divine in nature and man. The universe was a symphony. The conviction that the universe was a creation of joy reinforced his certainty that God is love. Tagore could not accept the ideal of renunciation that had been so influential in India. For him escape from the world meant escape from God. He held that all work should be dedicated to God but the homeless mendicant was a denial of the God who created the world. "Deliverance is not for me in renunciation. . . . I will never shut the doors of my senses. The delights of sight and hearing and touch will bear thy delight." [13] Freedom does not come into being as the result of the cessation of action, but is achieved in action, just as joy is expressed through law.

Even death was seen affirmatively as God's messenger and the friend of man.

> Just as a child cries out when taken by its mother from her right breast but is immediately consoled when she puts it to her left breast, so death is nothing but a change in the arms of God.[14]

Tagore's stance might well be an aesthetic type of religion.

Mohandas Karamchand Gandhi (1869–1948)

Born into a Vaishya Vaishnava family in Kathiawad, Gandhi was married at the age of thirteen. He was permitted to sail across the sea to study law in England only after promising his mother than he would abstain from wine, meat, and women during his stay abroad. He returned to India in 1891 and then sailed to South Africa in 1893 where he struggled for the rights of Indians who were serving as indentured servants. In 1914 Gandhi entered the Indian political arena under Gokhale. At Gokhale's death, Gandhi was thrust into positions of leadership which culminated in the independence of India in Au-

---

13. Quoted in A. C. Underwood, *Contemporary Thought of India*, New York, Knopf, 1931, p. 173.
14. Ibid., p. 175.

gust 1947, and his assassination at the hand of a Hindu fanatic in January 1948.

Having grown to despise Western materialism, Gandhi wanted more than self-rule (*swaraj*). He wanted a revision of the social order so that the technological advances which crushed the spirituality of Europe would not do so to India. Gandhi feared that the victory of mechanized civilization would mean the death of spiritual values.

> *All modern machinery is of the devil. It enslaves those who use it. All India requires is her plough and spinning-wheel* (charka), *for on them her ancient prosperity was founded. It is curious to notice that Western medical science comes under the Mahatma's condemnation. It is materialistic, whereas according to Mr. Gandhi "disease is the result of our thoughts as much as our acts."* [15]

Gandhi retained a belief in transmigration and karma, placed an emphasis on the ascetic ideal, permitted worship of images as a means of religious concentration, taught sexual abstinence as a means to spiritual perfection, visited Hindu temples, taught the sanctity of the cow, and recognized the caste system. Through these beliefs Gandhi made contact with the Indian masses. Wavering at one time between Christianity and Hinduism, he came to consider himself a Hindu. Nevertheless, the Sermon on the Mount exerted considerable influence on him as did the *Bhagavad Gita*.

Ahimsa was a doctrine which led the Jainas to practice vegetarianism, among other things. While the term means noninjury, Gandhi gave it an additional meaning. He saw it not merely as a state of harmlessness, but as a positive state of love in which one did good even to the evildoer.

> *Literally speaking,* ahiṁsā *means non-killing. But to me it has a world of meaning and takes me into realms much higher, infinitely higher, than the realm to which I would go, if I merely understood by* ahiṁsā, *non-killing.* Ahiṁsā *really means that you may not offend anybody, you may not harbour an uncharitable thought even in connection with one who may consider himself to be your enemy. If we return blow for blow, we depart from the doctrine of* ahiṁsā. *But I go further. If we resent a friend's action or so-called enemy's action, we still fall short of this doctrine. But when I say, we should not resent, I do not say that we should acquiesce: but by resenting I mean wishing that some harm should be done to the enemy, or that he should be put out of our way, not even by any action of ours, but by the action of someone else, or say, Divine Agency. If we harbour even this thought we depart from the doctrine of* ahiṁsā. [16]

The term *satyagraha* (holding on to truth) was used by Gandhi in his South African campaign to describe the nonviolent agitation he was pursuing. While he could use this method for all nonviolent ac-

---

15. Ibid., p. 180.
16. "Address to the Y.M.C.A.," quoted in J. Neuner, ed., *Religious Hinduism*, Allahabad, St. Paul Publications, 1964, p. 298.

tion, it came to be associated with struggle in the political realm. Hence *satyagraha* stood for the struggle against what was considered an unjust law or regime through noncooperation and civil disobedience. Noncooperation meant the refusal to participate in the working of an unjust system and might involve boycott of schools, colleges, or government jobs. It implied for Gandhi, however, a "readiness to cooperate on the slightest pretext with the worst of one's opponents." [17] Civil disobedience is the breaking of an unjust law remaining ready to suffer the consequences. It involved going to jail, and Gandhi served some eight terms there himself.

The violation of law, however, is not to become contempt for law. Fasting was the ultimate weapon and was not to be used lightly. A fast should proceed in a religious spirit, never against an enemy, but against a "loved one." The object of such action is not to extract rights but to reform the individual or individuals involved. *Satyagraha* is not for the weak but for the strong. Resistance it is, but it must be nonviolent since the goal is dissolution of antagonisms, not antagonists. Nevertheless, if the choice were between violence and cowardice, Gandhi would choose violence. *Satyagraha,* if fully nonviolent, however, will infallibly be effective. While it may be difficult and even result in the loss of lives, no oppressors, regardless of their violence and ruthlessness, are beyond the reach of suffering love. The value of such suffering love Gandhi learned from Tolstoi.

Gandhi formed an Ashram near Ahmedabad and those who joined took eleven vows. Among these was the vow of *Brahmacarya*. Gandhi held that marriage was a barrier to the practice of *satyagraha* since husband and wife lavish on each other the love that they should devote to the world. Gandhi himself practiced married *brahmacarya,* or restraint in the married life. He insisted that the only legitimate means of birth control was self-control. He also held that man should work on a progressive reduction of his needs. To save what is not immediately needed is paramount to theft in the light of the starvation of others. In his diary he wrote: "Not to accumulate things not necessary for the day." He also taught the principle of *swadesi* by which only things produced in the immediate neighborhood would be used, thus explaining his use of homespun *khadar*.

Although he wore a political guise, Gandhi held that he was a religious man at heart. Hence the ultimate goal of *satyagraha* was *moksha*. But the immediate goal was *swaraj* (self-rule), which meant a complete social revolution. It meant political and economic decentralization whereby the state would give way to an enlightened anarchy in which everyone would be his own ruler. Being realistic enough to see the difficulty in this state, Gandhi held that the best government was the one which governed least. He envisaged a series of self-governing, self-sufficient villages, supported by cottage industries.

While he did not argue for the abolition of caste, he fought for the elimination of untouchability, calling such people *Harijans* (People of God). He identified with them, and also with widows whose plight he tried to alleviate.

---

17. Quoted in Neuner, op. cit., p. 299.

Sri Aurobindo Ghose (1872–1950)

Aurobindo was born into a Calcutta Brahman family much enamored with English education. To assure a minimum of contact with Indians, Aurobindo was sent to a convent school in Darjeeling at the age of five and to England at the age of seven. His education there included English literature and the Western languages, classical and modern. Fourteen years later, in 1893, he returned to India. There he served as a revenue officer, and as a professor and later Vice Principal of Baroda College until 1906. During this time, Aurobindo acquired a knowledge of Sanskrit, Indian culture, and the religious classics. He was influential in the nationalist movement, preaching nonviolence as an expedient. In 1908 while in prison as a consequence of his political activism, he received a vision of Krishna which led him, in 1910, to found an ashram at Pondicherry where he lived until his death on December 5, 1950. The ashram continues under the leadership of Mira Richard. Aurobindo's prison vision was described as follows.

> *I looked at the jail that secluded me from men and it was no longer by its high walls that I was imprisoned; no, it was Vasudeva who surrounded me. I walked under the branches of the tree in front of my cell but it was not the tree, I know it was Vasudeva, it was Sri Krishna whom I saw standing there and holding over me his shade. I looked at the bars of my cell, the very grating that did duty for a door and again I saw Vasudeva. It was Narayana who was guarding and standing sentry over me. Or I lay on the coarse blankets that were given me for a couch and felt the arms of Sri Krishna around me, the arms of my Friend and Lover. . . . I looked at the prisoners in the hall, the thieves, the murderers, the swindlers, and as I looked at them I saw Vasudeva, it was Narayana whom I found in these darkened souls and misused bodies.*[18]

Aurobindo's publications were voluminous and he also started a weekly magazine called *Arya* which aimed at "a systematic study of the highest problems of existence, and the formulation of a vast synthesis of knowledge, harmonizing the diverse religious traditions of humanity, occidental as well as oriental." [19] After 1926 Aurobindo was in seclusion and his contact with the outer world was through the Mother who virtually ran the Ashram.

His most widely known work, *The Life Divine,* contains a rather lengthy account of his philosophy. His thought is a reinterpretation of certain traditional themes in the light of modern thought (Western and Eastern). A coherence is supplied by the joint concepts of "involution" and "evolution." While Aurobindo is most interested in evolution and in the possible developments for humanity in the future, he believes that no evolution is possible without previous involution. Involution refers to the divine descent even to the world of matter. The utterly transcendent Eternal Spirit is beyond all description but it nevertheless descends into the lower realms of being

---

18. Quoted in Herbert Jai Singh, *Sri Aurobindo: His Life and Religious Thought,* Bangalore, Christian Institute for the Study of Religion and Society, 1962, p. 4.
19. Ibid., p. 5.

and then by evolution ascends until it returns to its source. In this descent the "Supermind" is the transition from the original unity to the multiplicity of the phenomenal world. The "Supermind" stands between the Supreme where there are no distinctions and the human Mind which is responsible for all the distinctions and mutations in existence.

Matter, the lowest level of being, is virtually devoid of consciousness, yet it is not merely what it appears to be, but is a low form of the Supreme. The characteristic stage of evolution reached by humans is Mind, which is preparatory to "Supermind." The Mind, however, interprets the truth of universal existence for practical purposes and since it is a fall from the Supermind, its salvation lies in returning to its original state.

The doctrine of karma points to the means whereby the soul grows through rebirth and the evolutionary process, rather than a series of rebirths where penalties from previous existences are experienced. The determining factor in the spiritual evolutionary process is not the law of karma, but the Spirit, which uses karma for its progressive upward development.

The doctrine of the resurrection of the body is rejected since death implies, in the evolutionary scheme, that the soul has outgrown the present body. Such a view is a divination of the present life rather than an escape from it. For Aurobindo the doctrine of *maya* does not teach that the world is illusion, but refers to the power of differentiation which gives form and shape to all phenomenal existence as it arises out of the indivisible unity of Brahman. Through the agency of *maya,* the world of the One becomes the world of the many. Hence the phenomena are not unreal, but the substantial form of Truth.

The practice of yoga is a method for awakening the potentiality for self-perfection which is latent in man. Yoga is not occult, but merely the intensification of Nature's ways for the perfection of man. The Yogi need not renounce the world. Hathayoga may perfect the body, but neglects the social sphere. Rajayoga aims at perfecting the senses, emotions, the mind, but puts too much emphasis on abnormal trances. The purpose of yoga should be to make the "spiritual life and its experiences fully active and fully utilizable in the waking state and even in the normal use of the functions." [20] Integral Yoga is the synthesis of all other yogas and aims at the divinization of the total life of man. This involves three steps: (1) surrendering oneself completely into God's hands; (2) watching with detachment the working of the divine in one's life—that is, the recognition that one's progress is not due to personal efforts, but to the Shakti working within; and (3) seeing the divine vision of the personal deity in everything. God's power manifests itself in the human life and man realizes that a "great power, not of our own, is thinking for us, feeling for us, acting for us, and that our heart and mind are being moved and motivated by it rather than ourselves." [21]

20. Ibid., p. 30.
21. Ibid., p. 32.

Historically, evolution proceeded from matter up to the present state of Mind. But a thin veil separates Mind from Supermind, and when that veil is removed, through the descent of the one the ascent of the other is achieved. Thus a higher level of humanity is attained whereby a newly constituted gnostic being is created who will be involved in action but indifferent to its fruits. The life of such a one is not governed by external laws but by the Divine Life within. This higher level of humanity will begin when groups of gnostic beings grow in different parts of the world. The number of such gnostic communities will gradually increase until humanity itself reaches a new level of human existence. The ashram at Pondicherry is a place where men and women of differing cultures live together to achieve that gnostic experience which Aurobindo envisaged.

While Aurobindo passed from a politically active life to the seclusion of the ashram at Pondicherry, Radhakrishnan moved from a position as professor of philosophy to President of India. A professional philosopher, and a defender of Hinduism, he was also concerned with showing that the Hinduism he defended was relevant to social and international problems. Radhakrishnan left his imprint upon the social, educational, and cultural development of his country. While holding that all religions are merely manifestations of *Sanatana Dharma* or eternal religion, he nevertheless leveled cogent attacks on phenomenal Christianity in the formulation of his staunch defense of Hinduism.

Sarvepalli Radhakrishnan (1888–   )

Born into a Telegu Brahman family, his traditional manner of life was challenged by the education he received in Christian missionary institutions such as Madras Christian College from which he graduated. Radhakrishnan has attempted to go back to the sources of his tradition (he has published books on the principal Upanishads, the *Bhagavad Gita,* and the *Brahma Sutra*) and to construct on such interpretations a Hinduism that will be relevant in a period that evidences pressing social and political problems. That he held a post at Oxford University and is the subject of one volume of the Library of Living Philosophers gives evidence that his intellectual stature has been recognized outside his native land.

Radhakrishnan has been sensitive to criticisms of Vedanta which characterize it as an attitude of world and life negation. Albert Schweitzer developed such an interpretation in his *Indian Thought and Its Development.* Radhakrishnan argues that such an oversimplification does not do justice to the complexity of Indian thought and practice.

Radhakrishnan's defense of "Hinduism" is closely connected with his interpretation and defense of Shankara. He argues that for Shankara, the doctrine of *maya* is not to be construed as illusionism nor is it to mean that the world is unreal. Ultimate Reality, or Brahman, is unitary to be sure, but Shankara accords the world and the phenomenal self a relative reality. The world is not independently real, but it is derived being. To point to the temporal character of the world is not to say it is unreal or that it has no meaning or significance.

Part of the concern to give meaning to the world and human activity is seen in Radhakrishnan's understanding of karma. Karma should not be interpreted pessimistically or deterministically. Karma has a past and a future. The past cannot be changed and while it affects man's present possibilities, it does not determine the future. Man remains free to act within the limits imposed by the past.

Life is like a game of bridge. The cards in the game are given to us. We do not select them. They are traced to past karma *but we are free to make any call as we think fit and lead any suit. Only we are limited by the rules of the game.*[22]

In addition to the interpretation of karma and *maya,* Radhakrishnan is able to emphasize certain other aspects of Indian thought and practice that give emphasis to meaningful activity in the world. There are the four aims of life: *artha* (material well-being), *kama* (normal use of the appetites and desires of man), *dharma* (duty of performing one's appointed place in the nature of things), and *moksha* (final liberation). Furthermore, there are four traditional stages in life through which one should go, which are an ever-present ideal even if not universally followed. The stage of the student is a time when one acquires the discipline of spiritual wisdom under the tutelage of a teacher. As a householder, a man is responsible for the continuity of the family. Radhakrishnan argues that the unmarried life was not an Indian ideal. The third stage of the forest dweller involves retiring from active life for meditation, but only after one's children are settled and one's social responsibilities are fulfilled. The sannyasin is the final stage where one has renounced all. But a sannyasin, says Radhakrishnan, is in the world and remains there without attachment. Thus we see that the four stages include a social orientation and concern for this world. Only at the end of life, after fulfilling all social obligations, does one retreat to the forest for spiritual realization.

The social system that Hinduism has devised also emphasizes its concern for the world. The caste system has been criticized by Westerners and Indians alike. Radhakrishnan rejects the numerous subcastes, and the rigid proscriptions against intermarriage and interdining, and the definition of caste by birth. He does this by distinguishing between class and caste. The caste spirit must go and mobility between classes must be allowed. The organization of society into four main classes of people according to their qualities (*gunas*) rather than according to birth is desirable. This social order is not only valid for Indians but has universal significance, because mankind is, in fact, divided by nature into four types. There are men of learning and wisdom (Brahmans), men of administrative ability (Kshatriyas) with heroic determination to carry out in the political realm the principles of the thinkers, men who engage in commerce and trade (Vaishyas) without whom society would collapse, and men whose contribution to society is manual labor and service (Shu-

---

22. S. Radhakrishnan, *An Idealist View of Life,* London, G. Allen, 1961, first pub. 1932, p. 279.

dras). Radhakrishnan sees no justification for the existence of outcastes. His system, however, is a spiritual democracy which enables men of equal capacities to work side by side rather than to be matched with unequals. The purpose of this arrangement is not to guarantee rights, but to clarify responsibilities and opportunities.

Radhakrishnan would stress unity rather than diversity. He speaks of Hindu unity, or Indian unity, sometimes of Asian unity, but most often of religious unity. He aligns himself with Ramakrishna and Vivekananda in holding that the different religions are only aspects of one eternal religion, *Sanatana Dharma*. But *Sanatana Dharma* turns out to be something closely related to Vedanta, even though it is thought to be the religion underlying all religions.

LAW AND RELIGIOUS REFORM

Pakistan, a state which was created in 1947 by the partition of India, later proclaimed itself an Islamic state, and in its 1956 Constitution required the head of the state to be a Muslim and required that laws enacted not be repugnant to the *Qur'an*. Burma, which was a province of India until 1937, declared itself a Buddhist state in 1961. India, however, has proclaimed herself a secular state, which has had implications for the religion of its citizens. Nevertheless, in spite of the avowed separation of religion from governmental control, the secular state has enacted laws which have had an effect on religious change. Some of the changes preceded India's independence in 1947, but instances of laws effecting religious change have increased since that time.

The ease with which Indians committed to a secular state depend on legislation to settle religious questions can be traced to several factors. First, it has been part of the past tradition in India for the king to promote religion by building pagodas or temples, and by maintaining the clerical class. This was true of the so-called Hindu kings, Buddhist monarchs, or Muslim rulers. Hence such state involvement is in keeping with traditional Indian conceptions and practices. In terms of the four classes, the Kshatriyas were to rule in keeping with the spiritual principles enunciated by the Brahmans.

Second, Indian religions have not had rigid ecclesiastical organizations. This is particularly true of the conglomeration of temples, orders, rites, and rituals that are sometimes classified as Hindu. Since the organizational structure for effective reform and ordered change do not exist as part of the religious entity, it is necessary for the state to step in and fill the void. Not infrequently this is welcomed by those involved. Buddhist monarchs were often responsible for the reform of the Sangha.

Third, there is the secularization of law. In the traditional sense, Hinduism and Islam saw personal law and social structure as an extension of religion, or better still, the distinction between religion and these dimensions is itself the result of secularization. Today, not only is there no unified personal Hindu law, but different laws for Muslims exist as well. Hence, Hindus, Buddhists, Christians, and Muslims are governed by different legal standards regarding marriage and divorce. One of the present goals is to arrive at a unified personal law for all Indians. But such an achievement means the secularization of law and the restriction of religion to the more personal sphere. This amounts to a redefinition of religion and is also a factor in the relationship of law to religious change.

Cases will now be considered where legislation has resulted in the suppression of practices previously considered religious, cases where legislation has regulated religious practices, and finally cases where legislation has directly engaged in reforming religion.

Suppression of Religious Practices

The suppression of certain religious practices deemed undesirable by ruling powers was effected before independence. One of the first cases of this type was the rendering illegal of the practice of *sati* in Bengal presidency in 1829 and in Bombay and Madras in 1830. *Sati,* a word which originally referred to a virtuous and chaste woman, came to refer to the self-immolation of a widow on the funeral pyre of her husband. While the ancient lawgivers considered this a virtuous act, it was not obligatory. In the early nineteenth century, however, there were strong social pressures upon widows to make such a sacrifice. *Sati* was more prevalent in Bengal than elsewhere, and in the early nineteenth century about five hundred cases of *sati* were reported in the Calcutta area each year. The reformer, Ram Mohun Roy, led an attack on the practice of *sati* which gained Indian support. The practice became illegal under Governor General William Bentinck.

Another practice which came under attack was that of sacrificing children to the river Ganges. In fulfillment of religious vows, a child would be cast into the Ganges if a previously barren woman were granted more than one child. In 1802 such acts, though religiously motivated, were declared acts of murder and punishable as such.

Organized bands of *thags* (from which we get "thugs"), in devotion to the goddess Kali, traveled in disguise and murdered their victims by strangulation. Their sanction came from the myth of the great battle between Kali and the all-devouring demon. From every drop of blood that fell, another demon was born, so Kali finally resorted to giving a cloth to two men to strangle the demons. The command to go forth and overcome men by the same method became a religious sanction for these bands of *thags* who terrorized train travel in certain parts of India. During the years 1831–1837, more than three thousand *thags* were apprehended and the organized bands were suppressed at the direction of the Governor General William Bentinck.

In 1950 an act was made in the state of Madras to prohibit the sacrifice of animals in Hindu temples. This piece of legislation is only regional, since the sacrifice of goats is still part of the worship of Kali in Bengal. Animal sacrifice was an integral part of the Vedic religion, but has continued into the modern period mainly with reference to Kali. Other deities are adored through elaborate *puja* ceremonies. Sensitivities were sharpened by the image such sacrifices were creating in the minds of Westerners. In addition, there was ground for dissatisfaction in the doctrine of *ahimsa* which was responsible for spreading the practice of vegetarianism. The debate in the Madras Assembly was over the reason for prohibiting such slaughter rather than the prohibition itself.

In many temples it was the practice to dedicate young girls to the deity and to the service of the temple. They were called *devadasis* (servants of God). These girls danced in the temples and engaged in sacred prostitution. The state of Mysore abolished such dedicatory practices as early as 1909, and Madras followed in 1927. The Madras Act 31 of 1947 goes so far as to eliminate certain practices commonly associated with the *devadasis,* such as dancing in the temple.

> *Dancing by a woman, with or without* kumbhaharathy (*the ceremony of* devadasi *dedication*) *in the precincts of any temple or other religious institution, or in any procession of a Hindu deity, idol or object of worship . . . or at any festival or ceremony . . . is hereby declared unlawful.*[23]

Regulation of Religious Practices

Where governmental legislation has stepped into the religious picture and effected change, it has not always acted to prohibit practice. Frequently the government has regulated religious practices in the interests of the people at large. The Indian Constitution guarantees the freedom to profess, practice, and propagate religion "subject to public order, morality, and health." [24] It is these last qualifications that permit the government to intervene in religious matters when they seem detrimental to the public good.

For both Hindus and Muslims, festivals and processions are important religious expressions. Pilgrimages and festivals attract huge crowds of devotees. In order to minimize the possibility of disease, epidemic, and injury, the government has regulated such events. Every twelve years at the confluence of the Ganges and Jumna rivers in Allahabad, there is a festival which attracts millions of pilgrims. The government has set up officers in charge of this Khumbha Mela with appointed subofficials. In 1954 the police force totaled 2,882 in addition to 250 watchmen. Some 550 additional policemen were attached to the cholera inoculation barriers. Eight hospitals and eight first-aid posts were staffed with seventeen medical officers, three women doctors, twenty nurses, and a host of ward boys, cooks, and stretcher bearers. Sanitary arrangements were covered by forty medical officers of health, nine chief sanitary inspectors, thirty-three sanitary inspectors, and nine hundred and twenty-six provincial armed constabulary men. More than six thousand sweepers were employed. In all, the government spent over 1,700,000 rupees ($360,000). A pilgrim tax was used to defray expenses, and this tax has been extended to other pilgrimage sites as well.

An important part of Muslim faith is the pilgrimage to Mecca which each Muslim should take at least once in a lifetime. Some fifteen thousand Indians make the trek each year. The Indian govern-

---

23. Quoted in Donald Eugene Smith, *India as a Secular State,* Princeton, N.J., Princeton University Press, 1963, p. 239.
24. Ibid., p. 216.

Bathing at the Ghats, Benaras. (Courtesy of the Government of India Tourist Office.)

ment has taken certain precautions for their protection on this trip. Medical teams are sent by the government to Saudi Arabia to give medical assistance to Indian pilgrims. Pilgrim passes make the obtaining of international passports unnecessary and income tax clearance certificates have become unnecessary for deck class Haj pilgrims. Given the difficulty in getting permission for foreign travel and the care taken in regulating foreign exchange, these concessions are quite significant.

With the crowds and the emotional pitch common at processions in which the deity is carried through the streets of the town, the possibility of riots or injury is always present. If a Hindu procession plays music as it passes a Mosque, or if Muslims include the slaughter of cows, the possibility of violence is further heightened. Donald Eugene Smith relates an interesting incident of this nature and how it was diplomatically resolved.

> *A Muslim procession at Benares during the Muharram festival had to pass under a peepal tree which belonged to a nearby Hindu temple. A low branch of the tree obstructed the passing of the ta-zias (wood and paper representations of the tombs of the martyrs Hasan and Hussain) borne by the procession. Because the peepal tree is regarded by Hindus as holy, the Muslims were not permitted to cut down the projecting bough. The Hindus accused the leaders of the procession of having built the* tazias *bigger than usual. As the Muslims refused to take the* tazias *through in a slanting position, the procession was held up for three hours and the discussion became heated. With a communal clash imminent, a resourceful police officer ordered the road under the tree to be dug to the depth of one foot so that the* tazias *could pass in an upright position.*[25]

Indian law has required the licensing of processions which demands an account of the extract course of the procession and the provision for police accompaniment.

Reform of Religion

One of the areas in which legislation has effected religious change through direct reform is in the administration of temples. Many Hindu temples had accumulated vast wealth in the form of money, jewels, or land holdings which had been bequeathed by kings or wealthy devotees. The administration of such temples had been seen as a function of the state, but in the middle of the nineteenth century the British abandoned such religious involvement. Without governmental supervision, the misappropriation of funds was not uncommon. In the state of Madras, several attempts at legislation led to the Madras Hindu Religious and Charitable Endowments Act of 1951. This provided for an executive department under a cabinet minister, and the appointment of three deputy commissioners who were assigned territorial jurisdictions. Part of the Act reads,

> *Subject to the provisions of this act, the administration of all religious endowments shall be subject to the general superintendence and control of the commissioner; . . . the power to pass any orders which may be deemed necessary to ensure that endowments are properly administered and that their income is duly appropriated for the purpose for which they were founded or exist.*[26]

The commissioners had power to enter the premises of the temples, to dismiss trustees, and even to appoint others in their places. If convinced that the temple or math was mismanaged, commissioners could take it over completely and appoint their own officer over it. These commissioners were required to be Hindus. Smith points out,

> *It is no exaggeration to assert that the commissioner for Hindu religious endowments, a public servant of the secular state, today*

25. Ibid., p. 222.
26. Ibid., pp. 245–246.

exercises far greater authority over Hindu religion in Madras state than the archbishop of Canterbury does over the Church of England.[27]

In 1959 an act exempted maths from such control. Sometimes commissioners have directed funds away from religious purposes to more social ends, such as orphanages, hospitals, schools, and even universities. The *Hindu,* a Madras daily, in 1961 wrote:

> Existing state legislation governing Hindu endowments has erred on the side of stretching the doctrine of cy pres *to such an extent that surplus resources of temples could be diverted to a variety of purposes, far removed from the intentions of the original donors. Such diversion could have little justification when, as against a few religious institutions with a surplus, there are thousands of others that have not the wherewithal for even the conduct of the daily* pujas, *or still worse, stand desolate or in ruins.*[28]

The central government has also appointed a commission to examine the administration of religious endowments and recommend measures for its improvement. In May 1962 the commission submitted its report which suggested regional legislation in states where such was lacking and reported that it saw no problem in enacting uniform legislation which would cover the administration of religious endowments all over India within all religious communities. The commission also recommended the creation of four Hindu theological colleges where the study of religion and the humanities could be pursued and the level of the Hindu "clergy" could be raised.

Legislation has also reformed religion in the area of caste. This is partially a direct reform, partially a suppression of certain practices and regulation of others, and partially due to the increasing tendency to limit religion to the personal dimension, thereby making the social order the concern of the state.

The discussion of caste usually includes the question of whether caste is inextricably bound up with religion or whether it can be treated as a social matter which would be under the rightful control of a secular state. Much of this discussion is not well-placed if one is asking the role of legislation in the modification of religious practices and beliefs. While reformers might want to separate caste from religion so that they can modify or eliminate aspects of the caste system while claiming they have not touched a religious matter, the fact remains that traditionally, and for many Indians today, religion is understood in terms of caste responsibilities.

It is commonly held that the more than three thousand castes (*jati*) existent in India today are merely subdivisions of the four ancient classes (*varnas*), and that they are predominantly the result of intermarriage among the classes. This "confusion of class" led to the thousands of "subcastes." We do not know exactly how the modern caste system developed, but "it did not develop out of the

27. Ibid., p. 246.
28. Ibid., p. 251.

four Aryan varnas, and the two systems have never been thoroughly harmonized."[29]

The term "caste" is derived from the word *castas* which the Portuguese applied to the social divisions they found when they came to India in the sixteenth century. However, castes developed religious responsibilities and these were perhaps more important than the responsibilities deliniated for the traditional four *varnas*.

> To the present day the life of the lower orders is much more affected by caste than by varṇa—it is not being a vaiśya or a śūdra, but being an ahīr, a kayāsth, or a sonār which matters, and corporate feeling is centered around this caste group, whether based on region, race, profession or religion.[30]

It is well to remember that even the "untouchables" or "scheduled castes" have a complicated hierarchy of divisions. Most such groups believe that there are other "scheduled castes" that are lower than they are on the social scale.

By holding that the numerous castes are only developments from the original four classes (*varnas*), the religious sanction for the *varnas* was used to attribute religious sanction for the thousands of castes as well. In the *Purusha* hymn of the *Rigveda*, the creation of the world was seen as an original sacrifice in which the four "castes" came from the mouth, arms, thighs, and feet of the Creator. In the *Bhagavad Gita*, Lord Krishna is interpreted as assuming responsibility for the "caste" system. The *Laws of Manu*, which are taken as of divine origin, relate laws to the fourfold distinction of the classes. This also was taken as religious sanction for caste. In Manu penalties are determined not only by who commits the crime (for Brahmans the penalty is often less), but also by noting against whom the crime is committed (more serious against a Brahman than a Shudra).

Today many village Indians make no distinction between their caste duties and religious responsibility. Hence the latter extends even to the avoidance of untouchables. As one Harijan puts it,

> Much of the propaganda against untouchability is wasted. . . . The voice of reason doesn't carry because most Hindus still feel that it is their religious duty to shun the Harijan. For generations this teaching has been drilled into them by mothers and grandmothers.[31]

Because of this religious sanction, legislation which modifies one's caste duty must be seen as religious reform. The Indian Constitution guarantees equal protection before the law for all citizens. Article 17 abolished untouchability and forbade its practice. Not only does this include a pledge on the part of the government, but it makes untouchability an offense punishable by law even in the case

---

29. A. L. Basham, *The Wonder That Was India,* New York, Grove Press, Inc., 1959, pp. 149–150.
30. Ibid., p. 149.
31. Quoted in Smith, op. cit., p. 308.

of discriminatory acts of individuals against individuals. There are cases where *dhobis* (washermen) were prosecuted for not washing the clothes of Harijans, and where a barber was prosecuted for refusing to cut the hair of leather workers.

The Untouchability Act of 1955 provides penalties for preventing an individual's access to roads, wells, shops, hotels, hospitals (public), educational institutions, or employment on the grounds of untouchability. Legislation permitting intercaste marriage runs counter to the ancient *Shastras,* and permitting Harijans to enter certain temples violates certain *Agamas.* But the legislation has nevertheless been made, and it has been enforced with varying degrees of consistency. However one evaluates such events—whether from the point of view of the Hindu who feels his religion has been attacked, or from a modern human rights perspective—the fact remains that such legislation has been, is, and will continue to be a means of effecting religious change.

THE GROWTH OF HINDU CONSCIOUSNESS

The terms "Hinduism" and "Hindu," terms which we commonly associate with a system of thought and practice, come from the Sanskrit *sindhu* which means "river" and was applied particularly to the Indus river which, since the partition of India and Pakistan, empties into the Arabian Sea through West Pakistan. The Persian form of the Sanskrit was *hindu* and the Greeks, using forms based on the Persian, omitted the *h* and came up with India. The term India was used for the whole country even though the full geographical expanse was unknown.[32]

Logically, then, the term "Hindu" refers to India, and "Hinduism" could only mean the religion or religions found there. When the term was first used for *a religion,* it was not realized how diverse the religions to be found in India were.

> *The term "Hindu" as a religious designation was developed by the Muslims after they had invaded the country in the second millennium A.D. For the Muslims it served to designate these aliens whom they conquered and whose not being Muslim was of course now for the first time significant. It retained for some time its geographical reference: "Indian," "indigenous, local," virtually "native." And the indigenous groups themselves and their traditional ways from these invading Muslim foreigners. It covered all such groups: those whom we now call Hindus, but also Jains, Buddhists, and all the others.*[33]

In addition to the influence of the Muslims, Christian missionaries and the presence of the British helped to engender a growing "Hindu" consciousness. Not only do such contemporary thinkers as Radhakrishnan or Vivekananda defend "Hinduism" against any attack, but there is a new concern to indicate the overarching unity among all "Hindus."

---

32. Cf. Wilfred Cantwell Smith, *The Meaning and End of Religion,* New York, Macmillan, 1962.
33. Ibid., p. 64.

The difficulty of this should be apparent to anyone who is familiar with the vast variety in Indian religions. Nevertheless, the search for an "essence" of Hinduism symbolizes the stance of some modern believers.

D. S. Sarma, former president of Vivekananda College in Madras, discusses at some length the theme "Unity in Diversity." [34] His position is that the soul of "Hinduism" is ever the same, although its embodiments differ according to time and place. But all Hindus share common scriptures, common deities, common ideals, common beliefs, and common practices.

Prior to the Muslim period, there would have been no purpose for such an inquiry. Not only did religious diversity exist, but the diverse regional languages and political allegiances made the very concept of Indian nationalism impossible. And, if the various states were not in any sense a unity, it would hardly do to suggest that the people of "Hindustan" were religiously united. Today, however, there exists a "Hindu" consciousness which has at times supported "Hindu" political movements.

A survey of religion in India should reveal that one cannot with accuracy speak of an "Indian Mind." Religious expression in India is as varied as religious expression could possibly be. Theists and Advaitins, materialists and skeptics, secularists and nationalists, all live side by side in the subcontinent. Sometimes they exist together peacefully, on other occasions they do not. That is the condition of men.

BIBLIOGRAPHY
Religion in the Vedic Period

Works on Indian religious traditions in general:
For an examination of various aspects of Indian culture prior to the Muslim rule see:
    Basham, A. L., *The Wonder That Was India,* New York, Grove Press, paperback ed., 1959.
For an historical examination of Sanskrit literature see:
    Macdonell, A. A., *History of Sanskrit Literature,* New York, Appleton-Century-Crofts, 1900.
For numerous notes on terms and for articles on specific topics see:
    Hastings, James, ed., *Encyclopedia of Religion and Ethics,* New York, Scribner, 1908–1927.
    Walker, Benjamin, *Hindu World,* 2 vols., London, G. Allen, New York, Praeger, 1968.
For an examination of Indian philosophical themes, see the following three works (listed in order of increasing difficulty):
    Hiriyanna, M., *The Essentials of Indian Philosophy,* London, G. Allen, 1949.
    Radhakrishnan, S., *Indian Philosophy,* 2 vols., New York, Macmillan, 1927.
    Dasgupta, Sarendranath, *A History of Indian Philosophy,* 5 vols., New York, Cambridge, 1922–1955.

34. Kenneth W. Morgan, ed., *The Religion of the Hindus,* New York, Ronald, 1953.

For an examination of Indian artistic traditions see:
> Zimmer, H., *Myth and Symbol in Indian Art and Civilization,* New York, Harper & Row, paperback ed., 1962.
> Coomaraswamy, Ananda K., *History of Indian and Indonesian Art,* New York, Dover, paperback ed., 1965.
> Kramrisch, Stella, *The Hindu Temple,* 2 vols., Calcutta, University of Calcutta, 1946.

For further bibliographical suggestions see:
> Adams, Charles J., *A Reader's Guide to the Great Religions,* New York, Free Press, 1965.
> Mahar, J. Michael, *India: A Critical Bibliography,* Tucson, Ariz., University of Arizona Press, 1964.

Works specifically on the Vedic and Pre-Vedic periods.

For some of the more important texts of this period see:
> Griffith, R. T. H., *Hymns of the Rigveda,* 2 vols., Banaras, E. J. Lazarus, 1920–1936.
> Hume, R. E., trans., *The Thirteen Principal Upanishads,* New York, Oxford University Press, 1962.
> Zaehner, R. C., trans., *Hindu Scriptures,* New York, Dutton, paperback ed., 1966.

For an understanding of the Pre-Vedic Period see:
> Allchin, Bridget, and Raymond Allchin, *The Birth of Indian Civilization,* Baltimore, Penguin, paperback ed., 1968.
> Wheeler, Sir Mortimer, *The Indus Civilization,* New York, Cambridge, paperback ed., 1968.

For an authoritative study of Vedic religion, with considerable emphasis on the cultic dimension, see:
> Keith, A. B., *The Religion and Philosophy of the Veda and Upanishads,* Harvard Oriental Series, Vols. 31, 32, Cambridge, Mass., Harvard, 1925.

For a systematic treatment of the thought of the Upanishads see:
> Duessen, Paul, *The Philosophy of the Upanishads,* New York, Dover, paperback ed., 1966.

For summaries by a modern authority see:
> Louis, Renou, *Religions of Ancient India,* New York, Schocken, paperback ed., 1968.
> ———, *Vedic India,* Calcutta, Susil Gupta Private Ltd., 1957.

Religion in the Post-Vedic Period

For selections of texts in the Pali tradition see:
> Cowell, Edward B., *The Jataka: or Stories of the Buddha's Former Births,* London, Luzac, 1957.
> Davids, T. W. Rhys, trans., *The Questions of King Milinda,* 2 vols., New York, Dover, paperback ed., 1963.
> Warren, H. C., trans., *Buddhism in Translations,* New York, Atheneum, paperback ed., 1963.

For selections of Jain texts see:
> Ghoshal, Sarat C., ed., *The Sacred Books of the Jainas,* Central Jaina Publishing House, 1917–1937.
> Jacobi, H. B., trans., *Jaina Sutras,* Sacred Books of the East, Vols. 22, 45, New York, Dover, paperback ed.

For an account of the life of the Buddha see:

Foucher, A., *The Life of the Buddha,* Middletown, Conn., Wesleyan University Press, 1963.

Thomas, Edward J., *The Life of the Buddha as Legend and History,* New York, Barnes & Noble, 1952.

For an account of the development of the Buddhist monastic tradition see:

Dutt, Sukumar, *The Buddha and Five After Centuries,* London, Luzac, 1957.

———, *Early Buddhist Monachism,* Bombay, Asia Publishing House, 1960.

———, *Buddhist Monks and Monasteries of India,* London, G. Allen, 1962.

For accounts of the history and thought following the life of the Buddha see:

Bapat, P. V., ed., *2500 Years of Buddhism,* Delhi Publications Division, Ministry of Information and Broadcasting, Government of India, 1956.

Conze, Edward, *Buddhism: Its Essence and Development,* New York, Harper & Row, paperback ed., 1959.

———, *Buddhist Thought in India,* London, G. Allen, 1962.

Guenther, Herbert V., *Philosophy and Psychology in the Abhidhamma,* Lucknow, Pioneer Press, Ltd., 1957.

Jayatilleke, K. N., *Early Buddhist Theory of Knowledge,* London, G. Allen, 1963.

Keith, A. B., *Buddhist Philosophy in India and Ceylon,* Oxford, Clarendon Press, 1923.

Thomas, Edward J., *History of Buddhist Thought,* London, Routledge, 1951.

For studies of the Jaina community see:

Jaini, J. L., *Outlines of Jainism,* New York, Cambridge, 1940.

Sangrove, Vilas A., *Jaina Community: A Social Survey,* Bombay, Popular Book Depot, 1959.

Schubring, Walther, *The Doctrine of the Jainas,* Delhi, Motilal Banarasidass, 1962.

Stevenson, Margaret Sinclair, *The Heart of Jainism,* New York, Oxford University Press, 1915.

Bhakti Movements

For important *bhakti* texts see:

Deutsch, Eliot, trans., *The Bhagavad Gītā,* New York, Holt, Rinehart and Winston, 1968.

Dutt, M. N., *A Prose Translation of the Mahabharata,* 18 vols., Calcutta, H. C. Dass, 1895–1905.

Hill, W. D. P., *The Holy Lake of the Acts of Rāma,* New York, Oxford University Press, 1952.

Hooper, J. S. M., trans., *Hymns of the Alvars,* Calcutta, Association Press, 1929.

Kern, H., trans., *The Saddharma-Pundarika,* New York, Dover, paperback ed., 1963.

Mueller, Max F., ed., *Buddhist Mahayana Texts,* E. B. Colwell, trans., New York, Dover, paperback ed., 1967.

Sanyal, J. M., trans., *The Śrīmad-Bhāgavatam* (5 vols.), Calcutta, Oriental Publishing Company, 1952–1954.

Sastri, H. P., trans., *Nārada Sūtras,* London, S. Sadan, 1963.

Wilson, H. H., trans., *The Viṣnu Purāṇa,* Calcutta, Punthi Pustak, 1961.

For a discussion of *bhakti* movements in India see:

Bhandarkar, R. G., *Vaiṣnavism, Śaivism and Minor Religious Systems,* London, Routledge, 1913.

Carpenter, Joseph E., *Theism in Medieval India,* London, Benn, 1921.

Macnicol, Nicol, *Indian Theism from the Vedic to the Muhammadan Period,* New York, Oxford University Press, 1915.

Majumdar, A. K., *Bhakti Renaissance,* Bombay, Bharatiya Vidya Bhavan, 1965.

For specific considerations of Krishna worship see:

Archer, W. G., *The Loves of Krishna in Indian Painting and Poetry,* New York, Grove Press, paperback ed., 1960.

De, S. K., *Early History of the Vaishnava Faith and Movement in Bengal,* Calcutta, K. L. Mukhopadhyay, 1942.

Dimock, Edward C., *The Place of the Hidden Moon,* Chicago, University of Chicago Press, 1966.

Singer, Milton, ed., *Krishna: Myths, Rites and Attitudes,* Honolulu, East-West Center Press, 1966.

Religious Systems

For an examination of texts contributing to the Madhyamika position and for expositions of that position see:

Conze, Edward, *Aṣṭasāhasrikā Prajñāpāramitā,* Calcutta, The Asiatic Society, 1958.

———, *Buddhist Wisdom Books,* London, G. Allen, 1958.

———, *The Prajñāpāramitā Literature,* the Hague, Mouten & Co., 1960.

Murti, T. R. V., *The Central Philosophy of Buddhism: A Study of the Mādhyamika System,* London, G. Allen, 1955.

Streng, Frederick J., *Emptiness: A Study in Religious Meaning,* Nashville, Tenn., Abingdon, 1967.

For an examination of texts contributing to the Yogacara position and for expositions of that position see:

Chatterjee, Ashok K., *The Yogācāra Idealism,* Banaras, Banaras Hindu University Press, 1961.

Suzuki, D. T., *The Lankāvatāra Sūtra,* London, Routledge, 1932.

———, *Studies in the Lankāvatāra Sūtra,* London, Routledge, 1930.

For an examination of texts contributing to the Advaita position and for expositions of that position see:

Deussen, Paul, *The System of the Vedanta,* La Salle, Ill., Open Court, 1912.

Jagadananda, Swami, trans., *A Thousand Teachings,* Madras, Ramakrishna Math, 1941.

Mahadevan, T. M. P., *The Philosophy of Advaita,* Madras, Ganesh, 1957.

Thibaut, George, trans., *The Vedānta-Sūtras with the Commentary of Śānkarākārya,* New York, Dover, paperback ed., 1962.

For an examination of texts and an exposition of Vishishtadvaita see:

Kumarappa, Bharatan, *The Hindu Conception of Deity as Culminating in Rāmānjua,* London, Luzac, 1934.

Thibaut, George, trans., *The Vedānta-Sūtras with the Commentary of Rāmānuja,* New York, Dover, paperback ed., 1963.

For an examination of texts and an exposition of Dvaita see:

Narain, N., *An Outline of Madhva Philosophy,* Allahabad, Udayana Publications, 1962.

Rau, S. Subba, trans., *The Vedanta-Sutras with the Commentary by Shri Madhwacharya,* Madras, 1904.

Sharma, B. N. K., *Philosophy of Śrī Madhvācarya,* Bombay, Bharatiya Vida Bhavan, 1962.

For a discussion of Yoga in Indian thought see:

Eliade, Mircea, *Yoga: Immortality and Freedom,* Willard R. Trask, trans., Bollingen Series, Vol. 56, Princeton, N.J., Princeton University Press, 1958.

For a discussion of materialism in Indian thought see:

Riepe, Dale, *The Naturalistic Tradition in Indian Thought,* Delhi, Motilal Banarasidass, 1964.

Medieval Arrivals

For a discussion of Christian presence in India see:

Thomas Paul, *Christians and Christianity in India and Pakistan,* London, G. Allen, 1954.

For the history, thought, and practices of the Parsis see:

Dalla, M., *History of Zoroastrianism,* New York, Oxford University Press, 1928.

Masani, Sir Rustrom, *Zoroastrianism: The Religion of the Good Life,* New York, Collier, paperback ed., 1962.

Modi, J. J., *Religious Ceremonies and Customs of the Parsis,* London, Luzac, 1954.

Taraporewala, I. J. S., *The Religion of Zarathustra,* Bombay, Taraporewala, 1965.

Zaehner, R. C., *The Dawn and Twilight of Zoroastrianism,* New York, Putnam, 1961.

For an understanding of Islam in India see:

Arberry, Arthur J., *The Koran Interpreted,* New York, Macmillan, 1955.

Chand, Tara, *Influence of Islam on Indian Culture,* Allahabad, Indian Press, 1954.

Iqbal, Sir Muhammad, *Reconstruction of Philosophy in Islam,* London, Oxford University Press, 1934.

Smith, Wilfred Cantwell, *Modern Islam in India: A Social Analysis,* London, Gollancz, 1946.

For the history and tradition of the Sikhs see:

Macauliffe, Max A., *The Sikh Religion: Its Gurus, Sacred Writings and Authors,* 6 vols., New Delhi, S. Chand & Co., 1963.

McLoed, W. H., *Guru Nanak and the Sikh Religion,* Oxford, Clarendon Press, 1968.

Singh, Khushwant, *History of the Sikhs, 1469–1839,* Princeton, N.J., Princeton University Press, 1963.

Archer, John Clark, *The Sikhs,* Princeton, N.J., Princeton University Press, 1946.

The Modern Period

For a survey of modern Indian religion and thought see:

Farquhar, J. N., *Modern Religious Movements in India,* New York, Macmillan, 1915.

Naravane, V. S., *Modern Indian Thought,* Bombay, Asia Publishing House, 1964.

Sarma, D. S., *The Renaissance of Hinduism,* Banaras, Banaras Hindu University Press, 1944.

For an understanding of specific modern Indian thinkers see:

Chaudhuri, Haridas, and Frederick Spiegelberg, eds., *The Integral Philosophy of Sri Aurobindo,* London, G. Allen, 1960.

The Complete Works of Swami Vivekananda, Calcutta, Advaita Ashrama, 1940–1946.

Isherwood, Christopher, *Ramakrishna and His Disciples,* Calcutta, Advaita Ashrama, 1965.

Tagore, Rabindranath, *The Religion of Man,* Boston, Beacon Press, paperback ed., 1961.

Gandhi, M. K., *An Autobiography: Or the Story of My Experiments With Truth,* Boston, Beacon Press, paperback ed., 1959.

Ghose, Aurobindo, *The Life Divine,* New York, Greystone, 1949.

Nag, K., and D. Burman, eds., *The English Works of Raja Rammohun Roy,* 3 vols., Sadharan Brahmo Samaj, 1945–1951.

Radhakrishnan, S., *Eastern Religions and Western Thought,* Oxford, Clarendon Press, 1939.

———, *The Hindu View of Life,* New York, Macmillan, n.d.

———, *An Idealist View of Life,* London, G. Allen, 1932.

Radhakrishnan, S., *The Philosophy of Rabindranath Tagore,* New York, Macmillan, 1918.

For a discussion of Indian law and its relationship to religious change see:

Derrett, J. Duncan M., *Hindu Law, Past and Present,* A. Mukherjee, 1957.

Heimsath, Charles N., *Indian Nationalism and Hindu Social Reform,* Princeton, N.J., Princeton University Press, 1964.

Smith, Donald Eugene, *India as a Secular State,* Princeton, N.J., Princeton University Press, 1963.

———, *South Asian Politics and Religion,* Princeton, N.J., Princeton University Press, 1966.

PART TWO

FAR EASTERN RELIGIOUS TRADITIONS
ALFRED BLOOM

SECTION ONE

CHINA: THE QUEST FOR ULTIMATE HARMONY AND THE GREAT TRANQUILLITY

INTRODUCTION: RELIGION IN CHINA

THE CONCEPTS OF HARMONY AND TRANQUILLITY

Chinese religio-philosophical traditions are dominated by a desire to achieve and maintain harmony with the forces of the cosmos. They reveal a central concern for the proper, the fitting, the appropriate, in all areas of life. In the midst of social struggle and tensions throughout their history, the Chinese have sought the foundations of ultimate harmony.

In the earliest periods this quest was directed toward the natural forces which impinged directly on the lives of the people in their agricultural existence. Harmony was sought through very concrete ritual means in sacrifice and divination.

As society became more complex and conflicts more intense, Confucius and his successors saw that ultimate harmony rested on the character of human relations. Harmony was not merely a matter of complying with natural forces, but of finding ways to bring lives of varying stations and capacities together for the good of the whole.

The Taoists quickly perceived that placing emphasis on external human relations merely gave rise to new conflicts and competitions. They claimed that one must find harmony at the deepest level in Nature—the source of existence. Conforming one's life to cosmic principle was the only way to harmony between man and Nature and between man and man.

Buddhism, imported from India, challenged men to achieve the highest harmony by cutting through the delusions of the ego to an understanding of the nature of things. The perception of the Real aimed at transforming human personality by reducing attachments to the world. Buddhism pointed the way for later Neo-Confucianism in finding the root of harmony beyond the world of appearances.

The quest for harmony still proceeds in China, though on a political level. It is still a problem to unite the Chinese people with a common sense of destiny and meaning.

PERSPECTIVES ON CHINESE RELIGION

China occupies a large portion of the globe and has one of the largest concentrations of population. Since the Chinese have developed one of the most durable societies, their varied systems of thought and value possess great historical significance. To aid the student in assessing the importance of Chinese tradition, we shall analyze its various strands of religio-philosophical thought represented by Confucianism, Taoism, and Buddhism, focusing upon the dominant interests and insights that have given Chinese culture its distinctive character.

Religion has been a strong force in China as man's response to elements in his environment over which he had no direct control. On both the societal and individual levels the unpredictable elements stimulated activities designed to prevent or alleviate disasters. From ancient times traditional rites existed to care for such matters. Chinese theories of government and morality drew upon religious sources for their authority.

We cannot enforce on Chinese tradition a Western standard which strictly divides the sacred and profane elements of life. The Chinese, generally, have not considered religion as something apart from life, an independent activity possessing its own intrinsic value. Except perhaps for Buddhism, Chinese religio-philosophic thought and experience does not manifest any of the "tension toward the world" which characterizes Western religious perspectives. The Chinese would not share the sentiment that it is the whole duty of man to glorify God, making religion an end in itself. The instrumental nature of Chinese religion has deep roots in ancient fertility rites designed to stimulate food production and preserve the community. This background helps to explain the anthropocentric, practical, magical, and generally tolerant features of Chinese religion. It is the basis for the organic view of Nature controlling Chinese thought and the social ideal of harmony governing moral and social existence.

Religion for the Chinese is primarily a social function for the good of society as a whole. Those elements which we call religious in the sense of orientation toward the supernatural assume importance for the Chinese only when they function to strengthen social existence. The organic view of Nature includes society, so that harmony with Heaven through religious rites guarantees social existence. Religion was employed as a sanctioning force for the political and social order. Specific, institutional forms of religion were constantly controlled by the government because they were potentially independent centers of faith and allegiance which could threaten the traditional order.

Buddhists in China argued that monasticism and religious practices such as donations to the order benefited the individual but were not merely an individualistic concern. They maintained that society also profited from the aid offered to ancestors in their progress to a higher destiny and through the believer's good citizenship inspired by Buddhist piety. Further, they claimed that Buddhism augmented the magical and spiritual resources of Chinese religion through the use of Buddhist spells and incantations and through belief in numerous Indian gods which had been absorbed into Buddhism as well as the multitude of mythical Buddhas and Bodhisattvas depicted in Mahayana, Buddhist mythology.

The awareness of varying levels of understanding within Chinese society contributes to more accurate assessment of Chinese religiosity. As we shall see, the basic cleavage in the Chinese religious world has not been between the clergy and the laity, but rather between the scholar-bureaucrat (ordinarily the Confucian elite or literati) and the generally uneducated, illiterate masses of people. While the larger mass of people remained unsophisticated concerning their religious beliefs and practices, the intellectual elite became more critical and philosophical. The two levels of perception were mainly distinguished by the depth of reflection and insight achieved by individuals within their life situation.

The scholar-bureaucrats rationalized religion and opposed excesses of superstition and magic. In order to foster their outlook on the masses, they transformed the ancient myths and traditions into didactic, moralistic stories in which the gods served as anthropomorphic models of virtue to be imitated by men. They were aware, however, of the sanction and support religion gave to political and social authority, and therefore made no attempt to abolish popular cults. When such cults were kept within proper limits, they helped to maintain order through cultivating belief in the supernatural basis of events as the will of Heaven and disposing people to be more acquiescent to the demands made by society on their lives.

While China did not develop a special class of religious personnel who tended primarily to religious matters, the scholar-bureaucrats ensured cosmic and social order and harmony through teaching moral norms and performing rituals. They criticized the contemporary order when it appeared to depart from its basic function of realizing harmony and enforcing values, and they criticized religious activities when they seemed inimical to social goals and ideals. In no case did they present for the individual a way of salvation as an alternative to life in this world and society.

Confucianism, Taoism, and Buddhism have so fused that the average person may not be aware of the source of his beliefs or practices. Even the scholars and monks who were consciously committed to a specific system would not explicitly reject other systems. Confucianism and Taoism long coexisted and mutually influenced each other; in the first stages of its introduction into China, Buddhism was confused with Taoism. As the various traditions came to be better understood, they appeared more complementary than opposing. Confucianism gave guidance for the moral life; Taoism provided techniques of magic to secure longevity, to deal with spirits, and to gain benefits from alchemy. Buddhism came to be related primarily to the afterlife in the Pure Land or Heaven. Through the ceremonies of Buddhism one fulfilled filial piety for his deceased loved ones. This fusion was expressed in the popular morality text, *T'ai-shang Kan-ying P'ien,* in which a Taoist priest discoursed on religion and destiny:

> "The soul," he said, "is Tao, and Tao is soul. The soul and the Tao are not different in essence. If the Tao is separated from the soul, you will transmigrate through the six domains and keep on the three paths, but if the soul and the Tao are united, you will finally reach paradise and the land of immortals. Hell and heaven are in your own heart. Unless heaven reside within you, the mere reading or reciting of sacred books profiteth nothing." [1]

In this passage the reference to Tao and the land of immortals points to Taoism, while the concept of transmigration and the six domains and three paths is clearly Buddhist. The virtues stressed throughout the volume reflect Confucian interest.

The merging of religious traditions can be observed in the diversity of divinities to whom people appeal to fulfill their desires and needs. Of the major deities, some have a Taoist background, some a Buddhist, and one the divinized Confucius. While most of the hundreds of deities relating to every facet of human existence and nature may be located within Taoist religion, Buddhist figures such as Kuan-yin (Avalokitesvara), Ti-tsang-wang (Kshitigarbha), and Yen-lo-wang (Yama) are important in dealing with affairs of this life or the afterlife. On the practical level, the Chinese outlook on the unity of the three teachings has been succinctly stated by Francis Hsu:

> The Chinese may go to a Buddhist monastery to pray for a male heir, but he may proceed from there to a Taoist shrine where he beseeches a god to cure him of malaria. Ask any number of Chinese what their religion is and the answer of the majority will be that they have no particular religion, or that since all religions benefit man in one way or another, they are equally good.[2]

THE HISTORICAL CONTEXT OF CHINESE RELIGION

Recent historical and archeological sources have pushed back the boundaries of myth and legend to reveal ancient organized life and culture. The once legendary Shang people have been found to be historical and in possession of a highly developed culture.

The Shang (ca. 1500–1100 B.C.) had already developed advanced techniques of bronze-casting, sericulture, weaving, and most significant for Chinese culture—writing. Despite their sophistication in comparison with surrounding peoples, they were unable to defend themselves from invasions and finally fell before the onslaught of the hardier Chou tribes of Northwest China.

1. Teitaro Suzuki, Paul Carus, trans., *T'ai-shang Kan-ying P'ien,* LaSalle, Ill., The Open Court Pub. Co., 1944, p. 84.
2. Francis L. K. Hsu, *Americans and Chinese: Two Ways of Life,* p. 237, quoted in Derk Bodde, *China's Cultural Tradition,* New York, Holt, Rinehart and Winston, 1963, p. 21.

The Chou dynasty (1100–221 B.C.) witnessed the establishment and eventual decline of feudalism. The gradual dissolution of the political power of the Chou forms the background for the most creative era in Chinese thought.

Generally, the Chou era divides into three periods. The initial period of the flourishing Chou hegemony extended from the conquest of the Shang in about 1100 to 722 B.C. when the ruler was driven from his capital in Hao to Loyang in Honan. The second period was termed the time of *Ch'un-ch'iu* (Spring and Autum—722–481 B.C.). This phase was the title of a historical chronicle of the kingdom of Lu, traditionally ascribed to Confucius. During this time, numerous petty rulers attempted to extend their authority as the royal house declined. The final period, from 481 to 221 B.C., was one of constant conflict known as the age of Warring States. The continual strife among principalities ended finally when the Chou and other states came under the despotic rule of the founder of the Ch'in dynasty, Shih Huang-ti (First Emperor).

The period of the breakdown of the Chou dynasty and Warring States was one of the most intellectually creative periods that China has experienced. According to tradition, the age witnessed the flowering of a hundred schools, representing the most diverse viewpoints. From among the host of contenders six became traditionally significant. The Confucian school was represented by Confucius (K'ung Fu-tzu, 551–479 B.C.), Mencius (Meng-tzu, 371–289 B.C.), and Hsun-tzu (298–238 B.C.). Derived from the class of literati, this school supported aristocratic morality. In contrast, the Mo-ist school, founded by Mo-ti (479–439 B.C.), appeared to represent a lower-class perspective with a doctrine of universal love and egalitarianism. A different approach to morality was furnished by the Taoist philosophy of Lao-tzu (sixth–fourth century B.C.) and Chuang-tzu (c. 399–295 B.C.). Other significant philosophical schools were the School of Names, composed of men skilled in logic and debate similar to ancient Greek sophists, the Yin-yang school and the Five Elements school,[3] which together explained phenomena in more materialistic or naturalistic terms, and the Legalist school of Han Fei-tzu (d. 233 B.C.), followed by professional politicians. Confucianism and Taoism overshadowed all other schools in shaping Chinese outlook and providing significant insight into the pressing problem of establishing and maintaining a durable society and way of life.

The period of creativity came to an end with the enforced unification under the short-lived Ch'in dynasty (221–206 B.C.). Ch'in despotism, symbolized by the persecution of scholars and destruction of classical texts, was almost immediately replaced by the great Han dynasty which lasted for some four hundred years from 206 B.C. to A.D. 220. Under the Han, Confucianism became the orthodox

---

3. *Yin-yang* refers to the contrasting cosmic forces which act to produce the world of experience, while the Five Elements, which include metal, water, earth, fire, and wood, are the basic constituents from which all things are formed.

ideology of the state and the basis of education and competitive examinations for official positions. As a result of the practical supremacy of Confucianism, study of other schools of thought waned.

The next major period of intellectual ferment attended the breakdown of the Han age and the ensuing period of disunity (A.D. 221–589). Confucianism also fell into disrepute and a mystical tendency developed as a response to the disruption and anxiety of the age. In this background Neo-Taoist philosophy emerged, and Buddhism, imported from India, spread easily through Chinese society, benefiting from initial confusion with Taoist philosophy and religion.

The spread of Buddhism through Chinese society enabled it to provide the unifying element in the establishment of the Sui dynasty (A.D. 589–618). During the succeeding T'ang dynasty (A.D. 618–907) Buddhism reached the zenith of its power and prestige. This prestige ended in the great persecution of 845, and during the Sung dynasty (A.D. 960–1127) a revived Confucianism absorbing elements from Taoism and Buddhism displaced Buddhist intellectual leadership.

From the time of the Sung until the establishment of the Republic in 1912, Confucianism was the dominant intellectual force and basis of education. The Neo-Confucian philosophies taught by Chu Hsi (A.D. 1130–1200) and Wang Yang-ming (A.D. 1472–1529) were comprehensive in promoting traditional Confucian morality as well as metaphysical and mystical elements which answered needs formerly met by Taoism and Buddhism. Throughout this long period no radically new approach in the realm of thought or religion appeared except for the incursions of Islam and Christianity, neither of which was fully accepted into Chinese life. In modern times Confucianism suffered from the disrupting influences of Western culture.

Despite the many changes, Confucian tradition provided the thread linking Chinese thought. It became the basis for the most outstanding Chinese character traits and functioned as the state's political ideology over a longer period of time than any similar ideology. Its understanding of human nature and political astuteness, as well as its system of training bureaucrats (not so much with technical expertise as with moral and cultural sensitivity), has made it one of the most significant products of the human mind and spirit. On the other hand, it was also responsible for the traditionalism and conservatism of Chinese society, making it difficult to deal with new problems requiring decisive change. For this reason it has been resisted by many Chinese concerned with the task of technological modernization, even though the Confucian tradition embodied the best in the Chinese spirit.

THE CHINESE CLASSICS

The five classics of the Confucian tradition and the archeological material relating to the Shang people are primary sources of information for pre-Confucian religion. There are some obstacles to reaching a clear understanding of the ancient religion because the texts were edited to conform to the official philosophy in the Chou period and then destroyed in the Ch'in era, necessitating a reconstruction during the Han age. Disputes arose concerning the authenticity of the reconstructed texts.

The five major classics are the *Shu-ching* (*Book of Documents* or *History*), *Shih-ching* (*Book of Poems*), *I-ching* (*Book of Changes*), *Li-chi* (*Book of Ceremonies*), and *Ch'un-ch'iu* (*Spring and Autumn Annals*). A sixth text, the *Book of Music,* has been lost to history, but its existence is implied both in the importance Confucius ascribed to music and in the fact that Confucian studies were divided into six fields.

Probably composed around the ninth century B.C. when the Chou dynasty had reached its peak, the *Shu-ching* was the primary source for the legendary history of China. Through later additions to the text, the narrative reached 625 B.C. While much of the material is of late derivation, it contains the reflection of older religious ideas.

The *Shih-ching* is a collection of folk songs covering a period of more than a thousand years beginning with the Shang era. Though it is believed that more than three thousand poems once existed, tradition claims that Confucius selected three hundred and five of the best poems relating to piety, war, and love. Since many of the poems appear to have been ceremonial in origin and purpose they provide direct insight into the earliest religion of the Chinese. Confucius himself regarded poetry as a source of moral guidance and information. Consequently, Confucian tradition has overlaid the poems with orthodox interpretation.

Used for divination, the *I-ching* is perhaps one of the most important and fundamental of the classics. Through its system of interpretation of symbolic trigrams and hexagrams, it also provided a basis for philosophical and mystical speculation in later Chinese thought.

The system of hexagrams, composed of varying combinations of solid or *yang* lines and broken or *yin* lines, is traditionally thought to have been created by the ancient hero Fu Hsi in the initial trigram system of eight symbols. Later the symbols were doubled to form hexagrams giving sixty-four possible forms. Tradition attributes the expanded forms to either Fu Hsi or King Wen of Chou who is said to have composed the text of the *I-ching* while in prison in 1142 B.C. Confucius is reputed to have written a commentary to the text, and it became closely associated with his tradition.

The theory and practices based on the *I-ching* exhibit the Chinese organic view of Nature as a grand, dynamic, harmonious process of interacting yin-yang forces and interdependent elements. Since man and society are parts of the total natural order, their destinies are dependent on harmony with Nature. To achieve or maintain this harmony, it is necessary to discover the appropriate hexagrams governing the present situation. When the diagram is determined through selecting yarrow sticks or throwing coins, the practitioner may consult the manual and interpret their lines in relation to the client's contemplated choices and actions. A significant aspect of these diagrams and their use is the limitation on corruption by the diviner, since the patterns and the explanatory passages in the text are fixed.

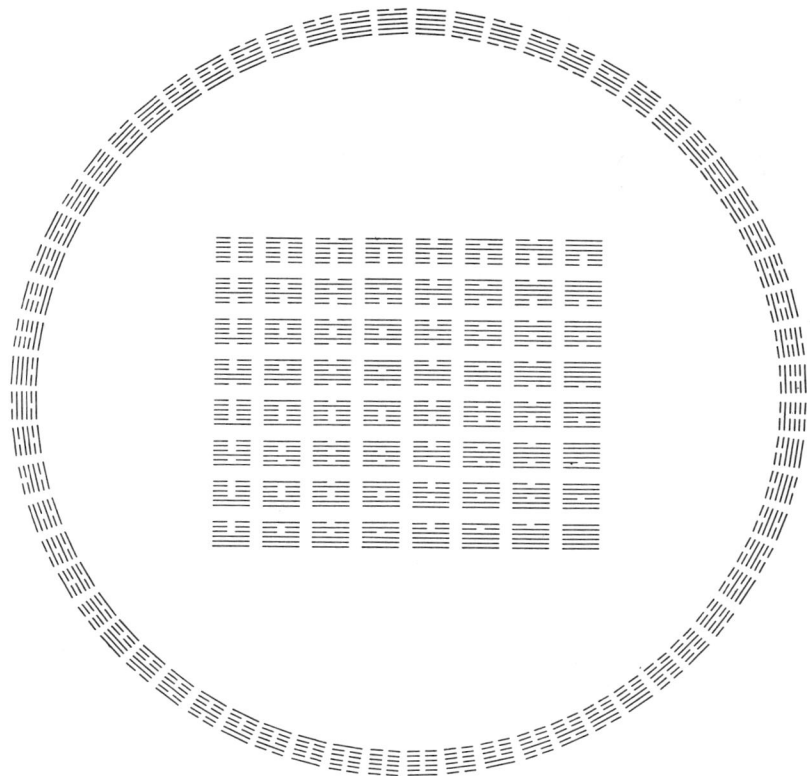

Circular diagram of the sixty-four hexagrams of the I-ching. (*From Hellmut Wilhelm,* Change: Eight Lectures on the I Ching.)

    The *Li-chi* (*Book of Ceremonies*) has considerable importance among the classics because Confucius considered ceremony and propriety essential to forming character and maintaining public peace. The work concerns ancestor worship, music, dancing, and the state sacrifices. The present version of the text derives from the second century B.C. and is clearly the work of later generations. In the twelfth century A.D. two chapters, *Ta-hsueh* (*Great Learning*) and *Chung-yung* (*Doctrine of the Mean*), were singled out for special regard in Neo-Confucianism. Other traditional texts of similar content are the *I-li* (*Ceremonies and Rituals*) and *Chou-li* (*Rituals of Chou*).
    The final text, *Ch'un-ch'iu* (*Spring and Autumn Annals*), traditionally ascribed to Confucius, concentrates on the history of the kingdom of Lu, Confucius' home state. The narration begins with the rule of Duke Yin (722–712 B.C.) and continues through a series of twelve dukes to Duke Ai (481 B.C.). It is considered one of the first accurate historical texts of China. The text itself is only a statement of fact, but in its choice of terms depicting rulers, it implies criticism of leaders who assume titles they do not deserve. The book thus appears to conform to Confucius' teaching on the rectification of names, whereby the name of a thing must correspond with its reality.

The Confucians were more interested in the meanings and morals of the classics than in the more formal literary elements of presentation. Through their interpretations, they constructed durable and creative systems of thought, although frequently obscuring ancient religious beliefs.

HARMONY IN THE CLAN AND KINGDOM: THE RELIGION OF THE SHANG AND CHOU

Archeology and the poetry of the *Book of Poems* provide the basic information for the religious outlook of the Shang and Chou eras. Behind the later official interpretations of the poems, is the basic character of the communal religion which must have been the foundation of the royal religion represented mainly in the archeological finds.[1] The emphasis on the harmonization of man and Nature, which became the controlling motif of later Chinese thought, was expressed in tribal and royal rites.

The realization of the harmony of man and Nature appeared in the *Book of Poems* in the interrelation of marriage practices and seasonal fertility themes. Within natural settings such as mountains, woods, and junctures of rivers a variety of rituals were performed in spring and autumn, including purifications, bathings, contests, sexual rites, sacrifices, banqueting, rainmaking, and flower gathering. Though later expurgated as immoral, there are hints of orgies. Concerning the significance of these religious activities Marcel Granet writes:

> Speaking generally, they are festivals of union, in which people become aware of the bonds which unite them, and, at the same

---

1. For a concise summary of the archeological discoveries relating to the religion of the Shang and Chou eras, see Jack Finegan, *The Archaeology of World Religions,* Princeton, N.J., Princeton University Press, 1965, vol. II, pp. 317–342.

time, of their oneness with their natural environment. To crown all, they also serve to guarantee, along with the prosperity of men and things, the regular working of Nature.[2]

The concern of the Shang and Chou to maintain the balance of forces in Nature indicates their awareness of interacting but unequal forces within Nature and life which could bring disaster on the community if proper means were not taken to achieve harmonization. From this awareness the yin-yang dualism which pervaded all Chinese religious and philosophical thought and the duality of *shen* (positive divine forces) and *kuei* (negative forces) have arisen.

The concept of yin-yang may have resulted from the confrontation of boys and girls in the ceremonial poetic competition preceding betrothal or from observation of meteorological phenomena, since the yin aspect is represented in Chinese by the character for raincloud and yang is represented by the symbol for the sun's rays. Consequently, yin stands for all characteristics which are dark, wet, cold, soft, and female. It is also square and even-numbered. Yang includes all qualities associated with brightness, dryness, warmth, hardness, masculinity, and is round and odd-numbered. Yang is naturally superior. It is to be noted that the duality is complementary and not conflicting. The traditional symbol implies the ultimate balance of the complementary interaction.

The contrast of positive and negative forces represented by the shen and kuei related to the development of the Chinese pantheon. The shen comprised all the good spirits which eventually came to be organized in a great hierarchy of gods headed by T'ien (Heaven) on the pattern of the feudal monarchy. Each deity had a particular function and rank within the whole.

Ancient thought regarded each person as a compound of the shen and kuei elements (also termed *hun* and *p'o*). The shen was man's superior aspect, the basis of intelligence and vital forces, while the kuei represented inferior features, the basis of physical nature. At death the shen proceeded to the palace of Shang-ti and became a beneficent deity as a result of pacification through the sacrifices of his descendants. The kuei resided in the tomb and along with the decay of the body sank to the underworld. If not appeased through sacrifices, the kuei could become a hostile spirit. The final residence of the keui was believed to be a place in the underworld called Yellow Springs.

The major deities associated with the ancient religion of the soil in China were the fertility deities Hou-t'u (Lord Soil) and Hou-chi (Lord Millet). Among the Chou the same cult was called She-chi (altar of earth and grain). The oldest and most universal cult in China, it has persisted to modern times due to the enduring importance of the soil in the life of the peasant.

In the early stages of Chinese religion the divine forces did not possess highly defined personalities. People did not attempt to relate to the deities in personal communion; they thought of them in

2. Marcel Granet, *Festivals and Songs of Ancient China,* New York, Dutton, 1932, p. 180.

P'an-ku holding in his hands the yang-yin, symbol of Heaven and Earth. (Courtesy of the British Museum.)

terms of function. All important natural objects were invested with divine power, undefined but effective. Eventually, however, the deities were historicized so that the earth deity She was identified with Yu, the reputed founder of the Hsia dynasty, and Chi, the grain deity, was identified with the founder of the Chou people. In addition to deities related to agriculture or ancestors, each home was guarded by a group of household deities who guaranteed the prosperity and security of the family. There were deities of the inner and outer doors, the well, the hearth, and the inner court. The ancient cult has continued into modern times.

The realization of harmony with Nature brought religion into close association with political power, as the king was the mediator between the total community and the forces of Nature and deities. The aim of the ritual activities of the king, like the peasants, was to secure the assistance of the ancestral deities in maintaining the continuity of the people and promoting food production. The Shang not only believed that the dead lived in the afterlife in a manner similar to this life, but that the ancestral spirits guarded the present world and guaranteed the authority of the reigning king. As imperial power grew, the supporting system of sacrifices became more elaborate.

The royal religion may be viewed as the religion of the central clan among the Shang which, as the power of the clan extended, grew to cover the entire body of associated clans. The deity Shang-ti, whose name means "Supreme Ruler" or "Supreme Ancestor," was the central deity of Shang times and may have originally been the ancestral deity of the leading clan. He was addressed as protector of the royal house and in connection with good harvests. With the transition to the Chou age, there was need for a deity who transcended tribal and clan connections. T'ien (Heaven) replaced Shang-ti. The ruler, as representative of T'ien on earth, was called T'ien-tzu (Son of Heaven), and the state defined as T'ien-hsia (Under Heaven). T'ien, in early Chinese thought, was a personal power who controlled the world.[3] There grew up about him a pantheon of deities who had various functions in maintaining the world.

The major religious practices of the Shang and Chou eras were sacrifice and divination. These practices, originally communal in nature, eventually became more individualized. Religious activities pervaded every area of life and were led by the head of the family or the ruler. The sacrifices were occasions to report to the ancestors on family matters or on the success of various ventures—military or diplomatic. Animals by the hundreds were slaughtered, as well as occasional prisoners of war. Methods included burning in open flame, drowning in rivers, or burial, depending on the occasion of the rite.

As the Chou state consolidated, sacrifice assumed central importance and the number of rites and feasts increased. The Shang were employed as ritualists, and the earlier forms of ritual were continued. The major state ceremonies, continuing until 1911, were the sacrifices made to Heaven in the spring and winter solstices. The Emperor performed them on the great altar of Heaven in the capital.

Under Chou rule the perspective on sacrifices shifted from an emphasis on clan relationships to rites centered on the personality of the founder of the dynasty, Wen-wang, to whom the divine mandate to rule had been given by the deity Shang-ti. His successors who were instrumental in the conquest of the Shang people also became

---

3. Yu-lan Fung, *History of Chinese Philosophy,* Princeton, N.J., Princeton University Press, 1952–1953, vol. I, p. 31, notes five meanings given to the term *T'ien* in Chinese thought. They should be clearly understood in order to avoid confusion in interpreting Chinese thought at various times. (1) There is the physical sky, as in the phrase "Heaven and Earth." (2) There is the anthropomorphic ruling Heaven, as "Imperial Heaven Supreme Emperor." (3) There is the fatalistic concept of Heaven applied to all events outside human control. It is equivalent to *ming,* decree, command. (4) There is Heaven used in the sense of Nature. (5) There is the ethical Heaven as the highest moral principle in the universe. In the Confucian *Analects* the anthropomorphic Heaven is most frequent.

The Altar of Heaven, Peking. (Photo by Fritz Henle, from Monkmeyer Press Photo Service.)

objects of reverence. Confucius particularly idealized the Duke of Chou for his many social and cultural achievements.

The interrelation of the religious and political was evident in the fact that only the Emperor was entitled to perform national sacrifices. For anyone else to attempt it was equivalent to a challenge to the throne. The term designating the overthrow of the state was "turning over the She-chi," which was to despoil the altars of the earth deity.

Although a more rationalistic attitude toward sacrifice developed in Chinese tradition, the basic beliefs and activities forged in the ancient period remained until recent times as the symbol of the political foundations of the state as well as the recognition of man's dependence upon the forces of Nature for his existence.

The second major practice of communal importance in ancient China was divination, since it was necessary to determine the will of the deity before engaging in activities affecting the whole society. In China the practice assumed special importance in view of the concern for the harmonization of Nature and society.

The major materials for divination among the Shang were ox bones and tortoise shells, or occasionally, sheep bones. The tortoise shells had particular significance, as they embodied in their shape the structure of the universe itself. The upper round part was like the vault of the sky, while the square lower section represented the earth. In the ancient thought tortoises were pictured as the foundation of certain islands and the world. Consequently, the ancient Chinese considered them important sources of information on worldly and heavenly affairs. The *I-ching* eventually became a major manual for acquiring counsel concerning one's future actions.

Numerous other methods of divination developed. Appeal was made to astrology; almanacs with observations on the seasons; arrangements of the five elements as earth, wood, fire, metal, and water; dreams; and the system of forms represented by phrenology. In later times coins were used in which the yang was the upper side, while the yin was the lower. Three coins were tossed at least six times and the combination was interpreted according to the *I-ching* series of sixty-four hexagrams. Also fortune-telling was performed through consideration of the correlation of the five basic elements, calendrical symbols, and one's birthdate (the year, month, and day). Divination not only pertained to matters of one's future destiny, but also to the use of the environment in placing a building. Geomancy, called *Feng-shui* (Wind and Water), was a conspicuous feature of the Chinese approach to the world.

As C. K. Yang [4] indicates, divination in earliest times was primarily a political activity dealing with war and peace. Divination gave a sacred character to political decisions and consequently contributed to their authority and popular acceptance. Yang notes that Confucian thought, though rationalistic at many points, did not alter this basic function. Only in later times was the activity extended to more private and individual concerns.

The religion of the classical period largely centered on the royal and noble clans. Through securing the support of their ancestral spirits all the land was peaceful and prosperous. Since it was the duty of the heads of the clans to perform the sacrifices, the formation of a specifically priestly caste was inhibited.

However, in connection with the sacrifices and divination performed by the king on behalf of the entire people, personnel of allied clans assisted in the prayers and sacrifices. Eventually they became specialized in function, and the performance of rites was transmitted through certain families. During the Chou period the organization of the ritual and personnel became formalized. Nevertheless, the officials of the state cult did not have mystic or magical authority.

Along with the development of official ritualists, there were functionaries termed *wu* (sorcerers or wizards). The status of these individuals in early times was quite high, sometimes second only to the king himself, who originally attained his position on the basis of magical charisma as a rainmaker. The functions of the sorcerers were divination, sacrifices, rainmaking, and ridding the community of evils. During the Chou period the status of the wu declined as a rationalistic view of government grew and the prestige of the literati advanced. Displaced through the growth of the Confucian school and its ritual functions, the wu also later faced competition from Taoist and Buddhist priests. The wu have persisted into modern times, performing fortune-telling, geomancy, prayers for the sick, exorcisms, and various forms of magic for individuals or groups out-

---

4. C. K. Yang, *Religion in Chinese Society,* Berkeley, Calif., University of California Press, 1961, pp. 107, 259–265.

Bronze ritual vessel from the Shang-Yin Dynasty, 1766–1122 B.C. (Courtesy of the British Museum.)

side the traditional religious structures. However, they are not regarded very highly.

In assessing the Chinese religion which emerged from the information available on the classical period, we may observe that it was rooted in an ancestral cult chiefly designed to maintain and unify the group by enlisting the powers of the departed members of the tribe and family. This cult with its seasonal festivals did not contain highly defined deities of concrete character, but rather an indefinite awareness of forces impressed on the imagination by natural phenomena. As the organization and function of society developed and as larger urban centers arose, the religion of the people evolved along a somewhat parallel course, resulting in the highly organized and multitudinous pantheon with each deity having its specific task in the divine bureaucracy.

During the Han period, the emergence of religious Taoism and the arrival of Buddhism spurred the proliferation of deities. The popular standing of religion as a means for attaining health, wealth, and security underlay this development and linked the modern Chinese religious perspective with its ancient precedents. There has been no significant alteration in the popular Chinese religious viewpoint, save in the scope and multiplicity of objects of worship and appeal.

The details of early Chinese religious beliefs and practices are not particularly unique when compared with other ancient religious cults revering ancestors or natural forces. Thus the specific features of the ancient cult do not explain the peculiar developments of Chinese religio-philosophic tradition. The outstanding feature of the religious history of China is the rationalization and moralization of the cult making man and the social order the central concern. This tendency was most conspicuous in the teachings of Confucius.

The basic presuppositions of Chinese religio-philosophic thought were clearly rooted in the earlier religious perspective. As we have previously noted, it was axiomatic that society was an integral part of Nature, and it was the duty of man through his ethical and moral behavior not to disturb the harmony basic to his life. Only those features of the ancient religious system which symbolized and strengthened this awareness in the people were retained and implemented in the official cult. All other elements were ignored or left to the common man for individual solution. Consequently, ancient Chinese skeptics ridiculed the rulers for their excessive attention to the spirits and superstition when the state was in danger.[5] Confucius also warned his followers not to be overly concerned about the spirits, while yet affirming the need for ceremony.

---

5. Fung, op. cit., vol. I, p. 31.

HARMONY IN SOCIETY: CONFUCIANISM

THE LIFE OF CONFUCIUS AND THE DEVELOPMENT OF HIS CULT

Confucius' life and his social ideals must be viewed against the background of the turmoil, social upheaval, and succession of intrigues and war that were destroying traditional morality, undermining old loyalties, and eroding the power of the royal house at the beginning of the Warring States period (481–221 B.C.). The magical and pragmatic traditional religion lacked sufficient moral and spiritual depth to contribute to social harmony.

In order to meet the problems of the age there appeared numerous private teachers and statesmen who offered their services to various lords. As politicians and administrators, they aided the ruler in cultivating and extending his power. These scholars were called *ju* (literati). The term itself meant weak or mild and may have first been applied sarcastically to those teachers who espoused a more pacifistic and moderate approach to human relations. Although there are numerous theories concerning their origin, they appear to have had skill in reading and writing, which enabled them to master traditional wisdom useful in administration. It is significant that Confucianism came to be known as *Ju-chiao* (the teaching of the literati) and that Confucius was perhaps most representative of that class. Undoubtedly his keen insight into human relations, the foundation of morality, and the function of leadership set the direction for later Chinese scholarship.

A major traditional source for information on the life of Confucius, apart from indications in the *Analects,* has been the *Historical Records* (*Shih-chi*) of Ssu-ma Ch'ien (d. 85 B.C.). According to his account, Confucius (K'ung Fu-tzu, 551–479 B.C.) was born in the state of Lu in the family of K'ung and given the personal name of Ch'iu and literary name Chung-ni. His parents died when he was very young. At an early age he showed great interest in sacrifice and ceremonies. Though his family was of poor and common background, the young Confucius was given responsibility in the house of Baron Chi. In the many positions which he came to hold, he had a reputation for fairness. When he was magistrate in Chung-tu, it became a model town. Under Duke Ting he became Grand Secretary of Justice, then Chief Minister. During this time, we are told, he reformed society so that mutton and pork butchers no longer sold spoiled meat; men and women used different roads;[1] things left on the street were not stolen; and foreigners were safe.

Despite his competence and moral character, Confucius ran into difficulty in the various principalities that he served, making it necessary for him to wander about seeking employment. He suffered from intrigue and slander. In the course of his travels he taught disciples the ways of a gentleman and government. Some of these pupils gained administrative positions in various states. In spite of his many problems, Confucius did not alter his ways, being convinced he had a mission which none could thwart because it was supported by Heaven. Besides carrying on his political and educational activities, Confucius also studied and edited the classics and composed the *Spring and Autumn Annals*.

His personal deportment and character are described in most eloquent terms as very much the example of what he constantly taught. Upon his death in Lu at the age of seventy-two, the Duke of Ai and his disciples deeply mourned his passing. Eventually his tomb became a shrine where his personal belongings were kept and ancestral sacrifices offered. The first Emperor of Han came to make sacrifice at the tomb in 206 B.C. At the end of his account, Ssu-ma Ch'ien poignantly contrasted the pervasiveness and lasting character of Confucius' influence with the perishability of worldly power:

> *There have been many kings, emperors and great men in history, who enjoyed fame and honor while they lived and came to nothing at their death, while Confucius, who was but a common scholar clad in a cotton gown, became the acknowledged Master of scholars for over ten generations. All people in China who discuss the six arts, from the emperors, kings and princes down, regard the master as the final authority.*[2]

Despite this legendary glorification, the life of Confucius does not suggest actions or characteristics which might lead to the formation of a religious movement or cult, and although Confucius himself was agnostic in religious matters, a cult of Confucius developed under the sponsorship of the state when Confucianism achieved supremacy as the orthodox ideology of the nation.

It should be noted, however, that this development was in line with the outlook of Chinese ancestor reverence and popular religion which, as an expression of gratitude and reward for their merit, exalted to the level of divinity individuals who benefited mankind.

---

1. In ancient Confucian thought the sexes were strictly segregated.
2. Lin Yu-tang, *The Wisdom of Confucius,* New York, Random House, 1938, p. 100.

Three sages—Shaka, Confucius, and Lao-tzu. (Courtesy of the Museum of Fine Arts, Boston, Bigelow Collection.)

Wang Chung, a critic of Chinese religion about A.D. 80, summarized the general Chinese attitude to such practices:

Two motives are underlying all sacrifices: gratitude for received benefits and ancestor worship. We show our gratitude for the efforts others have taken on our behalf, and worship our ancestors out of regard for their kindness. Special efforts, extraordinary goodness, merits and universal reforms are taken into consideration by wise emperors, and it is for this reason that they have instituted sacrifices. An oblation is offered to him who has improved the public administration, who for the public welfare has worked till his death, who has done his best to strengthen his country, who has warded off great disasters, or prevented great misfortunes.[3]

Although traditions claim that Duke Ai of Lu initiated the cult of Confucius, it did not really begin to take shape until the Han era when in A.D. 37 the Emperor Kuang Wu sponsored sacrifice at the grave of Confucius and conferred honors on his family. Even more important was the first regular cult paid to Confucius by Emperor Ming in A.D. 59, when he proclaimed that schools in the major cities should make sacrifice to Confucius. The cult became associated with education and the class of scholars in which Confucius functioned as a hero or patron saint.

Corresponding to the exaltation of the sage, there developed legends concerning his miraculous birth. While direct references to divinity were generally avoided, Confucius received honorific titles such as "Confucius, the perfectly holy teacher of antiquity." During the Ming period (A.D. 1363–1644) the cult was reformed. The image of Confucius was replaced by a tablet, and excessive titles were rejected. These changes led early Jesuit missionaries to regard the cult as reverence rather than worship.

The cult of Confucius was never a popular cult, but the reverence paid to him by the state naturally seeped down to the people so that on family and clan altars tablets, images, or pictures of Confucius were found along with Buddha, Kuan-ti, and ancestral tablets. As Hsu notes: "The popular gods in all family shrines were three: Kuan Kung (The warrior from Three Kingdoms), Confucius, and one or more Buddhas. A fourth popular figure is the Goddess of Mercy or Fertility." [4]

The Confucian cult was official instead of popular. The principle lying behind such official cults was that "the sages devised guidance by way of the gods and the (people in the) empire became obedient." [5]

In effect, the various cults receiving official authorization sanc-

---

3. John K. Shryock, *The Origin and Development of the State Cult of Confucius*, New York, Harper & Row, 1960, pp. 81–82, quoted from the *Lun Heng*.

4. Francis L. K. Hsu, *Under the Ancestor's Shadow*, New York, Doubleday, 1967, p. 184.

5. C. K. Yang, *Religion in Chinese Society*, Berkeley, Calif., University of California Press, 1961, p. 145.

tioned the ethical and political values of the society. The cult of Confucius had particular relation to the power of the state. According to C. K. Yang, it is a mistake to neglect the religious elements of this cult evident in the awe and reverence it induced among the people through its ceremonies and the dispersion of grand buildings through the country.[6]

CONFUCIUS' PHILOSOPHY OF HUMAN RELATIONS

After the death of Confucius his disciples, perhaps feeling need for his continued counsel and direction, culled from their memories his basic ideas and deposited them in a small manual now known as the *Analects* (*Lun-yu*), or "Words of Confucius."

Despite various textual problems concerning the present work, it is the most reliable source available for studying Confucius' thought. Its content is unsystematic, but there emerges a consistent system of values and insights on human behavior which have contributed to the formation of later Confucian philosophy and social theory. In order to grasp the distinctive features of his perspective, we must first consider the audience to whom the material is directed.

The audience assumed in the *Analects* was clearly the aspiring scholar-bureaucrats who sought positions in the courts of the various principalities. It was, consequently, a practical work with an aim to alert the individual to the problems of power in catering to powerful rulers and in controlling the common people. The practical advice given in the text, however, was susceptible to wider interpretation, since the problem of the man in power was only an intensified version of the problem facing all men—namely, how to develop and maintain successful human relationships.

Throughout the text there is an awareness of the limitations of sheer authoritarian compulsion and the use of force in gaining one's goals. There is also a recognition that society is structured with inevitable distinctions of superiority and inferiority. In every form of human relationship there is a leader and a follower. There is embodied in the basic philosophy the insight that individuals will accept any amount of authority provided they are permitted to retain their self respect and dignity. That government should benefit the people and that only the most morally competent should rule are two principles implied throughout the work. A basic element of governing or leading is knowing when to defer or yield. In view of these insights, the major issue confronting Confucius in the *Analects* is the formation of the appropriate moral character enabling the individual to wield power without force.

To realize the character for successful leadership Confucius advocates the cultivation of a number of principles and perspectives on human relations, all designed to contribute to harmony among men. These principles divide into interior and exterior aspects of moral life. Both dimensions are ultimately united in the ideal person. The central interior qualities of moral life essential to leadership are

6. Ibid., pp. 164–165.

jen, chung, shu, and *hsueh*,[7] while *li* and *hsiao* are the exterior elements of moral character.[8] All aspects are joined and harmonized in the ideal of the *chun-tzu* and *shih*. The power they manifest in human affairs is their *te*.

The achievement of ideal human existence requires the harmonization of the inner and outer aspects of man's life. The attainment of this harmony within himself would inevitably make the individual a leader among men through the attractiveness and magnetic quality of his character. In contrast to magical forms of charisma, Confucius asserts that the most real and effective charisma is rooted in the cultivation and expression of virtue. The durability of his thought rests on the fact that it is rational, being based on the realistic contemplation of the requirements for groups to maintain social life in the most meaningful way. It is not perfectionistic but only requires that those who subscribe to the ideal begin to move in that direction, starting where they find themselves at present. Heaven guarantees morality by responding to human actions with reward or punishment. Relying upon the classics, Confucius holds up the examples of the ancient sages and rulers such as Yao, Shun, Yu, Chou Kings Wen and Wu, and the Duke of Chou as the justification for his moral views and as models to be followed in the cultivation of virtue.

Jen stands as the supreme virtue and interior quality in Confucius' catalogue of values. As the symbol of Chinese humanism, the term embraces a wide range of meanings reflecting the importance of human relations. It may mean humaneness, humanity, human-heartedness, man-to-manness, love, benevolence, or goodness. In essence, jen is what one does when he is most truly human and implies that humanity is a task and an achievement.

As presented in the *Analects* the term jen has two dimensions. There is the level of expression in particular actions and attitudes, and a deeper dimension of perfection which can never be defined or exhausted in particular acts.

As Confucius believed that one must begin with lower things in order to arrive at the higher, we may begin to understand jen by indicating the types of action which may manifest that quality. When Jan Jung inquired about the nature of goodness, Confucius answered:

> Behave when away from home as though you were in the presence of an important guest. Deal with the common people as though you were officiating at an important sacrifice. Do not do to others what you would not like yourself.
>
> (*Analects* XII.2) [9]

---

7. Other correlative principles appearing in the *Analects* are *hsin* (faithfulness in keeping one's word) and *chi* (straightforwardness). Later, the quality *ch'eng*, usually translated as "sincerity," became a major virtue on the basis of the text of the *Chung-yung*.

8. The concept of *I* (righteousness) received greater stress in the teaching of Mencius as a correlate of *jen*.

9. Unless otherwise indicated, all quotations from the *Analects* are taken from the excellent translation by Arthur Waley, *The Analects of Confucius*, New York, Random House, 1938.

To Fan Chih he replied to the same question:

In private life, courteous, in public life, diligent, in relationships, loyal. This is a maxim that no matter where you may be, even amid the barbarians of the east or north, may never be set aside.
(*Analects* XIII.19)

In response to Tzu-chang, Confucius indicated that the good person would possess five virtues: courtesy, breadth, good faith, diligence, and clemency.

It is interesting to note in relation to the ultimacy and supremacy of jen that there are actually few passages delineating specifically the actions and qualities which constitute it. The *Analects* indicate that Confucius rarely spoke of jen, and never claimed to be good himself. As he pointed out, the man of jen is chary (jen) of speech because it is a quality difficult to attain. Confucius refused to judge the jen quality of specific persons or situations. However, it is possible to move in the direction of jen by turning one's merits to account and helping others to apply theirs, as well as using one's own feelings as a guide in helping others according to the principle of reciprocity. Everyone should compete in the pursuit of jen. One pursues it by making friends with those who manifest it.

Confucius recognized the problem of the inner reality and the external appearance. He maintained that jen came from within the man and could not be derived from someone else:

For Goodness is something that must have its source in the ruler himself; it cannot be got from others.
(*Analects* XII.1)

A true gentleman may lack jen, but all possessing jen would of necessity be true gentlemen. True jen avoids artifice as represented in clever talk and pretentious manners.

The pursuit of jen is not easy. If it is to be undertaken, it must be the primary goal of life, and, although it is a difficult task, it is the source of true happiness. While it enables one to bear up under adversity and eventually to achieve prosperity, it is an end in itself:

The Good man rests content with Goodness; he that is merely wise pursues Goodness in the belief that it pays to do so.
(*Analects* IV.2)

Finally, jen is the basis for the love of men, and it is the only means to make power durable after one's wisdom has brought him into power.

From the brief indications of jen provided in the *Analects* we can observe a studied attempt to avoid pinning the virtue down in such a way that one could assert that his superficial and limited efforts had fully expressed the quality. The nature of jen on its deepest level is a quality possessed by sages and heroes as a transcendental perfection. It is never fully present in living or historic persons.[10]

Although the political or social dimension of Confucius' thought appears to be its central interest, the ultimate indefinability of jen

---

10. Waley, ibid, p. 27.

and its crucial role in forming the basis for all successful rule and exercise of power make Confucius' thought more than mere politics or ethics. Rather, he seems to point toward a situation in which the moral order is embodied in men, enabling them to realize their full human potential.

According to Confucius, the "beads" of jen are strung on the threads of chung (conscientiousness, loyalty) and shu (reciprocity, altruism). The fulfillment of the human potential implied in jen requires a deep awareness of others and identification with them. When asked if there is a principle that would be applicable day or night, Confucius offers the quality shu expressed in the Golden Rule: Never do to others what you would not like them to do to you.

The character in Chinese for shu is a combination of the term for "like" and "similar" and the term for "mind." Behind this principle lies an idea of identification enabling persons to know the appropriate behavior for dealing with others through considering what they themselves need to live happily and securely. This principle is not to be applied mechanically. Rather, it can only be realized when there is a felt sense of oneness with others. It is in line with this principle that Confucius rejects action based on calculation of profit for oneself. The foundation for true ethical action in Confucius' view comes from contemplating what benefits all, and not merely oneself.

An ethic based on shu is more dynamic and inward than an imposed, external ethic. Shu does not exclude the existence and necessity of formal prescriptions of behavior, but it means that their application will be dictated in accord with the situation. Thus, morality is not fixed or static. Confucius is reputed to have said: "As for me, I am different from any of these. I have no 'thou shalt' or 'thou shalt not' " (*Analects* XVIII.8). Further, he was astute in noting that people with fixed principles are good when there is need for someone to take a position on an issue, but they cannot function in an emergency calling for flexibility and adaptation.

It is clear that Confucius was attempting to replace the traditional, tribal morality with an inwardly motivated morality based on one's awareness of his common humanity with others. In this view of morality he was far in advance of his time and mankind as a whole. E. R. Hughes succinctly summarizes the problem Confucius confronted:

> *It was an age of marked individualism, individualism of the dangerous egotistical kind, and Confucius' achievement was to point out to all who would listen that a man is not more of a man because he has fiercer appetites and more power to gratify them, but when he can recognize his fellow man as having equal rights with himself.*[11]

The quality chung, which generally accompanies shu, complements it. Chung represents the development of one's mind, while shu is the extension of that mind to others. According to Yu-lan

---

11. E. R. Hughes and K. Hughes, *Religion in China,* London, Hutchinson, 1950, p. 27.

Fung, though the concept chung is not defined in detail in the *Analects,* it carries the meaning of acting on behalf of others.[12] One is exhorted to be conscientious in dealing with all men, loyal to the prince one serves.

An indispensable quality or attitude in the cultivation of virtue was the desire for, and love of, hsueh (learning, study), or wisdom. While goodness (jen) is the goal of virtue, learning is its condition. It is significant that Confucius did not boast of his goodness or perfection, but rather of his love of learning. He regarded learning as an essential qualification for teaching, since only "he who by reanimating the Old can gain knowledge of the New is fit to be a teacher" (*Analects* VII.33). The learning advocated by Confucius was not restricted merely to the acquisition of information, but included the wisdom which recognized the limits of one's knowledge. Learning was to be pursued with utter seriousness and no possible source rejected, since it was only through such learning that the virtues could be kept in proper harmony without excess or distortion.

It is thus clear that for Confucius the purpose of learning was to build moral character and not merely to instruct in skill or impart information. Maintaining that "a gentleman is not an implement" (*Analects* II.12), he desired to develop leaders who were persons of broad moral quality rather than specialists in some activity. Consequently, he refused requests of disciples that he teach them farming and gardening.

Learning is for change. Confucius notes that the already wise and the stupid do not change. The wise probably do not need to, while the stupid do not want to change. The love of learning, though stated as a boast, is a confession of imperfection and openness to the future. Confucius complained that his moral power and learning remained imperfect.

Confucius' ideal of teaching was strikingly modern. He taught without discriminating according to class or economic ability. Only the desire to learn was necessary. He demanded, however, that the person who came to him for instruction must be committed and engaged in the effort to learn. He did not so much *give* education as he challenged the individual to gain his own.

> *If I hold up one corner and a man cannot come back to me with the other three, I do not continue the lesson.*
>
> (*Analects* VII.28)

He worked with students individually, adapting his approach to the student's need. He did not claim to have all wisdom, but remained open to thrashing out questions put to him even by the simplest peasant. Despite his willingness to work with all people, Confucius did not advocate indiscriminately using one's time and energy:

> *The Master said, Not to talk to one who could be talked to, is to waste a man. To talk to those who cannot be talked to, is to*

---

12. Yu-lan Fung, *History of Chinese Philosophy,* Princeton, N.J., Princeton University Press, vol. I, p. 71, n.1.

waste one's words. "He who is truly wise never wastes a man," but on the other hand, he never wastes words.

(*Analects* XV.7, VI.19, XV.15)

Since Confucius' philosophy of human relations was practical and not merely theoretical, the interior moral qualities had to find expression in supporting and complementary behavior. The concept li covered the whole range of human activities from the performance of religious rituals, such as practices of mourning, to dress, personal manners, and decorum within the family and among associates. In addition, Confucius stressed hsiao (filial piety) as an important aspect of moral behavior.

Although the Chinese character for li originally signified placing ritual vessels in proper order for sacrifice, the concept expanded to embrace all things properly done. In Confucian thought it came to represent the rationalized social order and conventions which aid in avoiding conflicts. As the practical means for achieving harmony, Confucius claimed that the people would respond to the goodness (jen) of the ruler if he would conform to li.

The necessity of li stems from the fact that the direct expression of virtue can at times be as destructive of human relations as creative. Li provides the fine polish and restraint needed to make virtue effective. Confucius states:

Courtesy not bounded by the prescriptions of ritual becomes tiresome. Caution not bounded by the prescriptions of ritual becomes timidity, daring becomes turbulence, inflexibility becomes harshness.

(*Analects* VIII.2)

Confucius is also aware that the li might become mere external show. He maintains that the inner and outer must be harmonized, since "only when ornament and substance are duly blended do you get the true gentleman" (*Analects* III.12).

Hsiao (filial piety) loomed important in Confucius' thought as a test of the actual moral character of the individual. His basic assumption was that without a deep sense of obligation toward one's parents who made his existence possible, an individual could not be trusted to have the necessary sense of obligation toward other members of society. Further, the discipline of family life was the foundation for the inculcation of the attitudes of loyalty, faithfulness, and submissiveness required for social harmony. Although Confucius regarded filial piety as essential to moral and social life, he did not consider it the supreme virtue which it later became in the *Hsiao-ching* (*Classic of Filial Piety,* written 350–250 B.C.).

Confucius held that sons should obey and defer to their parents. However, a son should also remonstrate with his parents when they fell into error. Should they fail to accept his admonitions, he must remain silent and unresentful out of respect for them.

All the virtues and qualities advanced by Confucius as the foundation and expression of moral character were combined in the ideal person termed chun-tzu. This word, originally referring to the son of a ruler or an aristocrat by birth, came to mean in the *Analects* the true gentleman or superior person as a result of his moral development. The term shih (knight, warrior) also came to signify a person of highest moral attainment rather than the virtues of warfare.

Fundamentally, the chun-tzu represents the fusion of all qualities in such a way that a person can respond to every situation benefiting mankind without sacrificing his principles. He is particularly distinguished by his faithfulness, diligence, and modesty. He neither overpowers with his knowledge, nor is afraid to admit error. He looks at all sides of any issue, is cautious and not concerned for personal recognition. Carrying himself with dignity, he appears imperturbable, resolute, and simple. He is exemplary in filial piety and generous with his kin. In his relations with others he looks for good points, though he is not uncritical. As a leader, he knows how to delegate responsibility and when to pardon or promote. He is sensitive to the feelings and expressions of others, knowing when to defer or desist. Always conciliatory, he does not merely accommodate.

In addition to the numerous qualities which depict the true gentleman, there are specific principles which govern his actions. Most important, he is committed to the good as an end in itself and to right before all else. He rejects seeking mere personal profit as well as doing wrong in order to advance or to serve an evil prince. He will not employ expediency. Honesty is essential to life. Ready to lay down his life for the good, he serves his master in faithfulness. He demands more of himself than of others. He holds to consistency (of principle), but not blind fidelity. He neither judges things by externals, nor by eloquence or status:

A gentleman does not
Accept men because of what they say,
Nor reject sayings, because the speaker is what he is.
(*Analects* XV.22)

In summary, the chun-tzu combines inner quality and spirit with outer form. He provides the harmony of substance and ornament. However, in such an ideal there is always the possibility of mere sham. Confucius notes that the gentleman may not always be good, meaning perhaps that the good could not be exhausted in any expression. Eloquence is not moral power, though they can be confused. A brave man is not necessarily good. One must be careful of those who put on solemn airs. Many passages scattered through the text criticizing the decadence of the age suggest that the true gentleman is a rarity, and Confucius almost despaired of creating or finding one.

The ideal of the chun-tzu in his nature and function created several issues which stimulated the development of later Confucian thought. These issues comprise a series of dichotomies, which, though interrelated, affect the cultivation and application of Confucian ideals. The first polarization is the conflict between devotion to self-cultivation and the ordering of society. The second dichotomy concerns the harmonization and mutual relation of inward moral capacity and the outer sphere of rules, rituals, and forms.

The third polarity was the relationship of knowledge and action. It was generally agreed that the basis of action was knowledge and learning. The problem was the nature of this knowledge and how it was developed. The earlier scholarly, historical, and factual approach of Confucius eventually developed into the more metaphysical approach of the Neo-Confucians, who sought intellectual enlightenment either by discovery of the essential harmony in the outer world or through intuiting it in the inner world of mind.[13]

As we have earlier pointed out, the fusion of moral qualities in the true gentleman endows him with profound effectiveness in creating and maintaining human relationships. The moral charisma which he generates is denoted by the term te, that peculiar efficaciousness resulting when a thing or person functions as it is designed to function. The essence of leadership is the ability to influence. Influence depends on character, in contrast to coercion which requires force. Te, as moral influence, is that power which causes people to do things on behalf of others through their own volition and desire. Confucius aptly sums up the meaning of te:

> *Govern the people by regulations, keep order among them by chastisements, and they will flee from you, and lose all self respect. Govern them by moral force, keep order among them by ritual and they will keep their self respect and come to you of their own accord.*
>
> (Analects II.3)

Although in theory te was practical, it appears that in Confucius' time men hesitated to enter fully into his way. He complained that only a few understood it and that he had not seen anyone in whom te was as strong as his sexual power. Some apparently were willing to apply te only in certain limited situations.

There were also dangers which obstruct te or destroy it. It is not to be confused with eloquence. Physical prowess is also no true indicator of te. Clever talk confounds te, while hearing the teaching and merely repeating without acting on it is to throw it away. The attempt to please everyone also undermines te.

As te is perhaps the inner force of attraction generated by the ideal ruler and official, its correlate, *wen,* is the exterior quality of culture, bearing, poise, and carriage expressed in the polite arts and ritual. Although the substance is prior to the decoration, the element of culture is indispensable. The attractive power of culture is expressed by Master Tseng:

> *The gentleman by his culture collects friends about him, and through these friends promotes Goodness.*
>
> (Analects XII.24)

Wen refers concretely to the arts of peace such as music and dancing, and literature in contrast to war. It is whatever beautifies

---

13. Benjamin Schwartz, "Some Polarities in Confucian Thought," in A. F. Wright, *Confucianism and Chinese Civilization,* New York, Atheneum, 1964, pp. 3–15.

human existence. Confucius believed that the true way to conquer a people was to spread culture. Although one may win the battle, in order to prevail completely one must have wen. Illustration of the Confucian principle appears in the Greek cultural conquest of the Romans after they themselves had been conquered militarily. The principle has frequently been tested in Chinese history where invader after invader succumbed to the allure of Chinese culture.

Before concluding the study of Confucius' thought, we should note that he employed the concepts Tao (Way) and T'ien (Heaven) in the discussion of his philosophy. In contrast to later Taoist thought, the Tao of Confucius was represented by the chun-tzu as the highest ideal of human endeavor. For him the Tao was primarily social. Aware of rival views of Tao, Confucius claimed that when his Tao prevailed, society would be ordered and authority effective. The ultimate basis for his philosophy, according to Confucius, was T'ien. Heaven was the source of moral power which guaranteed virtue. Hence, the Tao set forth by Confucius was ultimately the will of Heaven. This view was based on his conviction that his system of morality conformed to the nature of man when he functioned as a true human being.

The concept of Heaven is important in strengthening the moral commitment of the true gentleman. It gives him confidence that a power greater than his own individual strength works through his efforts to attain its ends. The belief in the ordination of Heaven mitigates disappointment when things do not go as men might desire. For this reason the true gentleman must fear and understand Heaven, since it gives perspective to his efforts and keeps the necessary balance in his deportment and attitudes.

Heaven appears in some ways to be a personal force, but it is certainly unlike spirits and ghosts. Confucius does not speculate on its nature, but attributes all events outside the control of man to the will of Heaven. Sometimes he appeals to Heaven to avert the consequences of his errors.

Confucius' contribution to the history of moral and social thought lies in his articulation of a consistent system of inner values and qualities and correlation of external actions which must be the basis for effective government. His ideal of the true gentleman is a comprehensive and universal goal which, in its humane, compassionate, sensitive, and implicitly democratic character, is worthy of serious pursuit. Its relevance for this age of moral and social confusion will be apparent to thoughtful students. Nevertheless, Confucius does not speculate on the nature of reality or the nature of man to determine precisely what basis there is in reality or man for the achievement of these aspirations. The further exploration of his thought remained for his interpreters, especially Mencius (Meng-tzu, 372–288 B.C.) and Hsun-tzu (298–238 B.C.)

INTERPRETERS OF CONFUCIUS: MENCIUS AND HSUN-TZU

In the period after Confucius the political conflicts multiplied and intensified. At the same time more challenging solutions to the problems of human relations contended for acceptance, as indicated in the so-called Hundred Schools. Social thought swung between the two poles of despair and rejection of social conventions of Yang-chu (440–369 B.C.?) and a more utopian idealism of universal love of Mo-ti (479–380 B.C.) The Confucianists followed a middle path between these extremes, applying the rational and practical outlook of the master.

Yang-chu became the symbol of social irresponsibility and indifference, espousing a hedonistic enjoyment of life. He was described by Mencius as advocating an "every man for himself" philosophy without any allegiance to a ruler and refusing to save the world even if it required only the plucking of a hair. His doctrine was pictured as a grand egoism because he put the enhancement and nurture of one's own individual existence before social obligations. The *Lu-shih Ch'un-ch'iu* quotes Yang-chu:

> *Now, my life is my own possession, and its benefit to me is also great. If we discuss what is noble and mean, even the honor of being Emperor could not compare with it. If we discuss what is unimportant and important, even the wealth of possessing the empire could not be exchanged for it. If we discuss peace and danger, were we to lose it for only one morning, we could never bring it back. These are three points on which those who have understanding are careful. There are those who care too much about life and so injure it. This is because they have not reached an understanding of the qualities of human life. Without such an understanding, of what avail is caution? . . . Among the rulers and nobles of the world, whether worthy or unworthy, there are none who do not desire to live long and see many days. Yet if they daily obstruct the course of their life, of what avail is such a desire? All long life consists in non-resistance to it. What causes such resistance are the desires. Therefore the Sage must first of all put his desires into harmony.*[14]

It is clear that Yang-chu did not promote licentiousness by his hedonism, but a principle of not being ensnared by things and affairs. Although from a later time, the sentiment of the Yang-chu chapter in the *Lieh-tzu* expressed succinctly the spirit of those ancient recluses who rejected conventional social striving as destructive to one's inner spirit and integrity:

> *Do we live for the sake of being cowed into submission by the fear of the law and penalties, now spurred to frenzied action by the promise of a reward or fame? We waste ourselves in a mad scramble, seeking to snatch the hollow praise of the hour, scheming to contrive that somehow some remnant of reputation shall outlast our lives. We move through the world in a narrow groove, pre-occupied with the petty things we see and hear, brooding over our prejudices, passing by the joys of life without even knowing that we have missed anything. Never for a moment do we taste the heady wine of freedom. We are as truly imprisoned as if we lay at the bottom of a dungeon.*[15]

---

14. Fung, op. cit., p. 137.
15. H. G. Creel, *Chinese Thought from Confucius to Mao Tse-tung*, New York, New American Library, 1953, pp. 82–83.

The tradition of iconoclasm and social criticism began very early in Chinese history. In the *Analects* (XVIII.5, 7) there appear several incidents when Confucius or his disciples encountered anarchistically inclined individualists who did not hesitate to criticize his activities. As we shall see, the Taoists, Lao-tzu and Chuang-tzu, were direct inheritors of these views, though providing them with a deeper mystical and philosophical basis.

At the opposite extreme from Yang-chu, Mo-ti advocated a utilitarian, utopian principle of universal or indiscriminate love (*ch'ien-ai*) as the ultimate solution to human problems. Although little is known of the teacher himself, he was, like Confucius, from the province of Lu and at first sought office as a Confucianist. Failing in his ambition, he turned to private teaching and developed a philosophy and way of life which criticized the Confucian emphasis on elaborate ceremonial music and uneconomic ostentation. In his own character he was an ascetic, combining intellectual acumen and moral intensity. Unlike the Confucianists, he formed a tight-knit organization by which he could direct the activities of his disciples more closely. Each student had to contribute to the master's upkeep. Through the control of his students, Mo-ti could refuse to serve rulers who did not accept his teachings.

The basic principle of his social thought by which he achieved fame was his exhortation of universal love. Although criticized by Confucianists, the concept is an extension of the Confucian principles of jen (love, humaneness) and shu (reciprocity) applied without discrimination to all people. In defense of his principle, Mo-ti appealed to the instinctive behavior of men to show that all people really accepted it, though in theory and word they might reject it. He pointed out that in a situation of crisis and disaster, people would appeal to rulers or individuals whom they knew to be inspired by generosity and social concern rather than to those they knew to be narrow and selfish. Such a reaction in his view testified to their tacit awareness of the necessity and truth of the principle of universal love. He stated:

> *It seems to me on such occasions as these there are no fools in the world. Even though he be a person who objects to universal love himself, he would choose the "universal" rulers. This is rejection of the principle in word but acceptance of it in actually making a choice—this is a contradiction between one's word and deed. It is incomprehensible, then, why the gentlemen of the world should object to universal love when they hear of it.*[16]

A corollary principle growing out of the assertion of universal love was the idea of utilitarian benefit as the basis of durable order. This concept of profit appears entirely contrary to Confucian rejection of profit, but the two perspectives may be reconciled when it is understood that Confucians denied personal profit while retaining concern for the total good. Generally Mo-ti espoused the greatest good for the greatest number as the objective of government. In re-

---

16. William Theodore De Bary, *Sources of Chinese Tradition*, New York, Columbia, 1964, vol. I, p. 43.

alizing this, rulers must promote productivity throughout the kingdom and stress frugality and simplicity in living.

Another corollary aspect of his philosophy was the rejection of aggressive warfare. Although opposed to violence, Mo-ti developed a reputation for defensive warfare and expertise in fortifications. He lent his services to besieged, weaker kingdoms.

Despite the apparent idealistic and sentimental character of the concept of universal love, Mo-ti supported strong central government to bring order to the world. He also urged the rejection of the Confucian concept of fate and the maintenance of belief in the gods and spirits in order to induce men to belief in universal love on pain of divine retribution. In addition, he preached obedience and submission to superiors, ignoring egalitarian implications of his doctrine.

The importance of Mo-ti's philosophy lies in his recognition that society must inculcate into people a broad concern for others beyond the limits of self and kin if it is to have stability. He should be credited with the astute insight that people always prefer others to be altruistic toward them, though they may act egotistically toward others. Further, in exalting material prosperity as the index of the achievement of a society he was very close to modern exponents who employ the standard of living as the basis for judging social progress.

Mencius, the St. Paul of Confucianism, lamented that the doctrines of Yang and Mo filled the world and had great appeal to the people of that time. He made it his mission to refute these philosophies and to revive the fortunes of Confucianism. Mencius' career paralleled in many ways that of Confucius. Born in the region of Tsou in Lu, he became a disciple of Confucius' grandson Tzu-ssu. In the course of his life he served numerous rulers. His thought has been preserved in the text called *Mencius*.

The *Mencius* differs conspicuously from the *Analects* in being more discursive in style. Whereas Confucius' ideas appear in epigrammatic form without elaboration, the arguments of Mencius are more fully articulated to meet the challenge of opponents. His arguments in defense of Confucianism are probably the basic reason for its eventual supremacy over other schools and its lasting influence. Though Mencius, like Confucius, is humble in attributing his views to the sages of the past, there can be no doubt concerning his creative intellectual insight.

The starting point of Mencius' thought was the Confucian assumption that to be a human being means to be a social being and that the principles of social behavior are rooted in human nature. Consequently, all theories are false which conflict with man's nature. A major consideration of Mencius and later Confucians was the definition of the nature of man.

It was from this standpoint that Mencius criticized Yang-chu for undermining allegiance to rulers, and Mo-ti for not recognizing the gradations of love in human psychology. Both, as panaceas for society, were extreme and one-sided, as well as unrealistic in understanding human nature.

With this theory of the goodness of human nature Mencius clarified the ambiguity of Confucius who simply declared without elaboration that men were "by nature, near together; by practice far apart." [17] Like Mo-ti, Mencius appeals to the spontaneous actions of people as evidence for his view. When people confront various human problems, they react with compassion, commiseration, shame, dislike, or modesty. These responses he terms "the beginnings" of the basic qualities that distinguish men from animals. When these innate potentialities of moral behavior are allowed to develop to their fullest, they express themselves in behavior embodying the qualities of jen (humaneness), I (righteousness), li (propriety), and chih (knowledge or wisdom). That men lack goodness is simply because they have not permitted their capacities to develop. Thus he argues:

> *The real kings of old were compassionate human beings, and so theirs was a government by compassionate men. And having thus brought order to the world, they turned it on the palm of their hands. It can be said that all men have a capacity for compassion because, even today, if one chances to see a toddler about to fall into a well, one becomes apprehensive and sympathetic. This is not because one knows the child's parents; it is not out of desire for the praise of neighbors and friends; and it is not out of dislike for the bad reputation that would ensue if one did not go to the rescue. In the light of all this we can conclude that without compassion one would not be a human being. And the same holds if there is no sense of shame, no ability to yield to others, no sense of what is correct and what is not correct. The sense of compassion marks the beginning of becoming man-at-his-best. The sense of shame marks the beginning of propriety. Submissiveness marks the beginning of a sense of ceremony. The sense of right and wrong is the beginning of wisdom. Every human being possesses these four beginnings just as he possesses four limbs. . . .*
> (*Mencius* II.A.6) [18]

A number of significant implications for the view of man and society flow from Mencius' theory of human goodness. He recognized the essential equality of all men in maintaining that every man could become a sage through proper cultivation of his nature. As a result of his high estimation of man, he interpreted the Mandate of Heaven as the basis for revolution against despotic kings, making government rest on the will of the people. He further insisted that the purpose of government was to benefit the people and enable them to fulfill their potentialities. To do this the ruler should provide universal education and sufficient work and income to make crime unnecessary to survive. He saw the necessity of a division of labor in society as represented in traditional class structure, but he maintained that it was functional and no real indication of the essential worth of

---

17. *Analects* XVII. 2. See also V. 12.
18. James Ware, trans., *The Sayings of Mencius,* New York, New American Library, 1960, pp. 68–69.

people. Mencius clearly understood that social institutions do not make people good, but enable them to express goodness.

In order to achieve this, it is necessary to have exemplary rulers who stimulate the people in their moral efforts. Accordingly, true kingship is realized when the ruler shares his benefits with the people and identifies with them. Through his compassion on their behalf he would be universally attractive to his own people and those beyond his borders. Ministers to kings must play the role of critic when occasion demands. A minister must never serve an evil king. Both the king and his ministers need self-scrutiny to evaluate their actions.

It is in this connection that Mencius proclaimed a type of moral mysticism which cultivated the discernment of and commitment to moral values even in difficult times. Though the precise method of meditation was not specified, it produced a state described as "being on top of oneself and the world" and embraced an intuitive conviction relating to the rightness of things. It was not a mysticism in which one lost his personality in an all-embracing reality. Rather, it related concretely to life in this world where, by moral exercise, the division of the egocentric world and the outer world was abolished through consistent goodness. Mencius related:

It is difficult to describe. As power, it is exceedingly great and exceedingly strong. If nourished by uprightness and not injured, it will fill up all between heaven and earth. As power, it is accompanied by righteousness and the Way. Without them, it will be devoid of nourishment. It is produced by the accumulation of righteous deeds but it is not obtained by incidental acts of righteousness. When one's conduct is not satisfactory to his own mind, then one will be devoid of nourishment.

(*Mencius* II.A.2) [19]

According to this passage, righteous action reinforced moral commitment, which in turn stimulated further action. Mencius forged the union of knowledge and action, later to be stressed in Neo-Confucianism, within a highly sensitive moral consciousness.

The deep moral concern of Mencius was reflected in his analysis of the profit principle which Confucianism has consistently rejected. He asserted that all ambitions motivated by desire for profit and advantage were open-ended and could never be fully satisfied until the ruler or individual had striven to attain complete possession and control. There would also be a competitive struggle for advantage once the challenge was issued. In true government, following correct procedure and propriety would naturally result in the satisfaction of all interests.

Mencius' thought in its turn received criticism from several quarters. He engaged in lengthy conversations concerning Kao-tzu, a non-Confucian who maintained the moral neutrality of human nature and asserted that one's goodness or badness depended on external

---

19. Wing-tsit Chan, *A Sourcebook in Chinese Philosophy,* Princeton, N.J., Princeton University Press, 1963, p. 63.

conditions. Within the Confucian tradition itself, the philosopher Hsun-tzu took issue directly with Mencius' thesis, declaring: "Mencius states that man is capable of learning because his nature is good, but I say that this is wrong. It indicates he has not really understood man's nature nor distinguished properly between the basic nature and conscious activity." [20]

In following out his argument, Hsun-tzu declared that man's basic nature was evil, while such goodness as he possessed was acquired. Nature, according to him, signified whatever man possessed that was neither learned nor worked for. He regarded ethical and moral conduct as determined by culture. Similar to previous thinkers, Hsun-tzu summoned the spontaneous behavior of individuals as evidence for his position. He observed that from the time of birth onward, man was egocentric and desirous of his own profit and advantage; that he possessed violent emotions of envy and hatred. Driven by desires, man naturally found himself in conflict with his fellow men. Certainly, the background of conflicts in the age of Warring States could furnish ample evidence of the thesis.

In order to deal with this fundamental selfishness in man, the sages had developed rituals and regulations in order to train (socialize) human behavior. The goodness of man was the result of restraining human nature just as "a warped piece of wood must wait until it has been laid against the straightening board, steamed and forced into shape before it can become straight. . . ." [21]

As a consequence of his view of man, Hsun-tzu, contrary to Mo-ti, regarded music, ritual, and ceremonies as indispensable in the cultivation and refinement of human emotion. He complained that Mo-ti did not understand human emotion. According to Hsun-tzu, "music is the great arbiter of the world, the key to central harmony, and a necessary requirement of human emotion. This is the manner in which the former kings created their music. And yet Mo Tzu criticises it. Why?" [22] "Therefore, I say that Mo Tzu's attempts to teach the Way may be compared to a blind man trying to distinguish black from white. . . ." [23]

As music exerted a beneficial influence on the spirit of man, bringing harmony and tranquillity, Hsun-tzu noted the function of ritual and ceremony in social control. According to him, the ancient kings established rituals in order to overcome disorder. However, the rites also had a deep root in human emotion, being a means of expressing human feeling in moments of depression, melancholy, or times of elation. He stated:

> Hence the sacrificial rites originate in the emotions of remembrance and longing, express the highest degree of loyalty, love and reverence, and embody what is finest in ritual conduct and formal bearing. Only a sage can fully understand them. The sage

---

20. Burton Watson, *Basic Writings of Mo-tzu, Hsun-tzu, Han Fei-tzu*, New York, Columbia, 1967, p. 158.
21. Ibid., p. 157.
22. Ibid., pp. 113–114.
23. Ibid., p. 114.

understands them, the gentleman finds comfort in carrying them out, the officials are careful to maintain them, and the common people accept them as custom. To the gentleman they are part of the way of man; to the common people they are something pertaining to the spirits.[24]

Hsun-tzu's perspective on religious ritual was rationalistic, distinguishing between the true understanding of the sage and gentleman and the naive belief of the common man. Further, he regarded religion as a form of art or means of beautifying life. It ennobled existence with form, order, and meaning, impressing man with his relation to the spheres of Heaven, earth, and man.

His rationalistic, antisuperstitious tendency was also expressed in his concept of Heaven, which he regarded as an amoral, naturalistic process. His view contrasted sharply with the anthropomorphic, moralistic conception of Confucius and Mencius. According to Hsun-tzu, Heaven had its regularities which, without peering into the causes of phenomena, the sage could utilize beneficially. He rejected occult interest in heavenly phenomena, for man could only affect the actions of men, not of Heaven:

You pray for rain and it rains. Why? For no particular reason, I say. It is just as though you had not prayed for rain and it rained anyway. The sun and moon undergo an eclipse and you try to save them; a drought occurs and you pray for rain; you consult the arts of divination before making a decision on some important matter. But it is not as though you could hope to accomplish anything by such ceremonies. They are done merely for ornament. Hence the gentleman regards them as ornaments, but the common people regard them as supernatural. He who considers them ornaments is fortunate; he who considers them supernatural is unfortunate.[25]

Hsun-tzu manifested a deep scholarly interest and perspective and possessed a confidence in human intellect, believing that man could control his destiny through effort and reason. However, he appears gripped by pessimism concerning man's moral capacities. His social theory based on this pessimism contributed to the development of the authoritarianism of the Ch'in dynasty. Although Hsun-tzu carried forward the rationalistic and intellectual tendencies of Confucianism, his thought fell into the shadow before the more positive and inspiring view of man of Mencius.

CONFUCIANISM IN THE TA-HSUEH AND CHUNG-YUNG

In addition to the three major figures who laid the foundation for Confucian tradition, we must also call attention to two texts which became particularly influential in the Neo-Confucian philosophy of Chu-hsi (1130–1200). The *Ta-hsueh* (*Great Learning*) and *Chung-yung* (*Doctrine of the Mean*), as we earlier noted, were sections in the Chinese classic *Li-chi* (*Book of Ceremonies*). Although the dates

24. Ibid., p. 110.
25. Ibid., p. 85.

of composition of the works remain uncertain, they revealed at an early age the two basic tendencies of Confucianism, namely, rationalism and intuitionism or mysticism.

The *Ta-hsueh* is a short chapter, presenting in capsule form a summary of the Confucian basic approach to life. Though the work is attributed to Confucius himself, the authenticity is doubtful. It is an advance over Confucius' thought in the *Analects* because it is a more systematic presentation of his basic ideas.

The text opens with a statement of the three major concerns of Confucian teaching: manifesting clear character, loving the people, and abiding in the highest good. As an outline of Confucian teaching, they indicate that the basis of life rests in cultivating the inner self, applying oneself on behalf of the people, and striving to realize the highest good or jen. The text shows that the order of the world depends on the proper ordering of the self and all human relations based on the investigation and extension of knowledge. The world rests on character and character is founded on insight.

We may summarize its philosophy briefly, following the text's chain of reasoning. In order for the ruler to make clear his character, he must bring order to the state. Order is brought to the state through order in the family, and one may regulate his family by cultivating his personal life. In order to cultivate the personal life, one must rectify his mind. When the mind is rectified, the will will be sincere. Sincerity will result when one's knowledge is extended through the investigation of things. Working back through the chain, we can see that the life of man begins with knowledge as the basis for the cultivation of character and the proper functioning of every level of social existence. Implicitly the text affirms that society is no better than the people who make it up, whether ruler or common person.

The text not only emphasizes the fact that the health of society rests on the character of those who live in that society, but it stresses that it is of utmost necessity to have a proper ordering of values. We must know what is primary and what is secondary. The principle that the primary knowledge of the highest good yields inner tranquillity reveals a basic insight into the conduct of life. Knowing the goal and foundation of one's life makes possible the detachment and confidence required to reach necessary decisions.

The *Chung-yung* (*Doctrine of the Mean*) is a work of decidedly more mystical character, elucidating themes taught earlier by Mencius. Its mystical emphasis made it popular among Taoists and Buddhists as well as Confucianists. They were attracted by its philosophical character. As the title (the terms appear in *Analects* VI. 27) indicates, it is concerned with what is central (*chung*) and universal or harmonious (*yung*). It deals with human nature and its relation to reality. According to Yu-lan Fung, the terms have the meaning of equilibrium and normality which characterize the superior man in contrast to the small, petty man. In this view the superior man performs the proper actions fitting to the situation. The concept "mean" has the sense of hitting the mark or correctness, as in common speech we say that the person is right on target.

The consideration of human action and morality is set within the framework of the great harmony which exists between man and Nature. This harmony is realized through sincerity, which is not a passive attitude in man, but involves practical efforts to manifest in human affairs the ultimate harmony of man and Nature. Pursuing the harmony of Nature within human personality, Confucian ethical perspective receives a basis in Nature which differs from its earlier emphasis on the sages as models of human behavior.

Education is the process whereby man develops the capacity to express his fundamental unity with Nature. The natural sentiments of joy, anger, sorrow, and pleasure receive expression in proper measure through instruction. The true gentleman thus attains the equilibrium and poise required to manage affairs.

A major conception in the *Chung-yung* is *ch'eng* which may be variously translated as sincerity, reality, or truth. As reality, it is the way of Heaven and the foundation of harmony. It is the only basis of successful government and may be cultivated in man through the five steps of study, inquiry, thinking, sifting, and practice.

In contrast to the ordinary conception in the West of sincerity as an attitude of a person toward his actions, the concept of *ch'eng* signifies that a man is sincere when his actions and attitudes are in harmony with the highest reality and that reality radiates through his deportment. The background of the concept is the ancient Chinese view of the universe as a grand organic harmony of Heaven and earth. All phases of the cosmic process, including human existence, have a common essence revealed in the perfect equilibrium and harmony of the cosmic process. To manifest this harmony in human affairs in every situation is to be sincere.

LATER DEVELOPMENTS IN CONFUCIAN TRADITION

As the basic perspective on life and the fundamental value system had been established in the classical period through the writings of the figures and texts studied above, there has been little decisive change in the character of Confucianism except in the direction of broadening the vistas of understanding reality and pursuing the realization of those values. After a setback in the persecution of scholars by the Ch'in despots, Confucianism, under the Han rulers, attained the position of the official ideology of the state. It never retreated from this position down to modern times. Despite the lack of great alteration in basic outlook through the centuries, there have appeared significant thinkers who amplified or refined its understanding. We may only mention them briefly here as a guideline to the further study of Confucian tradition.

Tung Chung-shu (179–104 B.C.) is noteworthy for the cosmological framework he gave to Confucianism, and his effort to relate the political order to the order of Nature. His thought was based on the *I-ching* and the theory of yin-yang. Accordingly, the universe was seen as a system of coordinated, interrelated parts in a continual process of transformation. Human life was a microcosm of the great system and the interaction between the human and natural orders was based on morality. In his concept of man Tung Chung-shu attempted to unite the theories of Mencius and Hsun-tzu.

Wang Chung (A.D. 27–100) was noted for his rationalistic approach to religion, and he was critical of the flourishing interest in divination and Taoism. He attacked the conception that Nature responds morally to man's actions by arguing that the yin-yang process was entirely impersonal, man being no more comparatively than a flea or a louse. He rejected belief in ghosts and afterlife. He appeared to be progressive in opposing reverence of the past for its own sake, and scientific in stressing factuality in assessment of the classics. In his understanding of man he attempted also to unite the theories of Mencius and Hsun-tzu.

The development of Confucian thought suffered in the decline of the Han empire and loss of confidence in the ability of Confucianism to solve pressing problems. As a consequence, Taoism revived and Buddhism began to attract intellectuals and assume spiritual leadership. After the Buddhist interlude which extended from the end of Han to the end of the T'ang dynasty, Confucianism again reasserted itself in the Neo-Confucian movement.

While we cannot go into the many reasons leading to the Confucian revival, such as the breakdown of empire, a weighty and positive cause lies in the continuing need for administrators to serve in the bureaucracy even during T'ang times. The Confucian examinations were reestablished after a long interval of neglect, and by the ninth century the intellectual class was thoroughly imbued with Confucian ideals. Consequently, the scholars expressed criticism of the religious practices of Taoism and Buddhism. Most outstanding was the famous memorial of Han Yu (768–824) who in 819 attacked the reverence given by the court to a bone of the Buddha.

The development of Neo-Confucianism, which began with such figures as Han Yu and Li Ao (c. 789), can be termed a "rediscovery" of Confucian ideals, though tailored to fit a new social situation. While its promoters intended to revive the original Confucian perspective, the movement became more metaphysical in orientation as it responded to questions posed by Buddhism. What emerged was a firmer foundation in philosophy and mystical experience for the traditional Confucian ethic. In effect, Neo-Confucianism synthesized all major thought streams which had developed in China to that time.

It is significant that the formulators of Neo-Confucianism had been either Buddhists or Taoists in their youth. Though drawing upon the experience of other traditions, Neo-Confucianism produced its own distinctive view. In particular it remained this-worldly in its concern for morality and ethic. Though influenced by *Ch'an* (*Zen*) Buddhism, it rejected Ch'an subjectivism by holding generally to the objective existence of the principle of universal order (li).

The Neo-Confucian movement can be divided into two stages or streams. These are the Reason school of the Sung era (960–1279), which culminated in the thought of Chu Hsi (1130–1200), and the Mind school of the Ming period (1368–1644), represented in the thought of Wang Yang-ming (1472–1529).

Building on numerous precedents in thought, Chu Hsi taught that everything has its li (principle or ideal prototype). The things of the world are formed through a combination of the li with the *ch'i*, a type of ether or vacuous gas providing the principle of individuation. The system of the whole exists within the Supreme Ultimate or absolute which cannot be defined and exists beyond time and space. The world is produced through a process in which the five basal elements, the yin-yang process, the li, and the ch'i interact. The embodied principle within a specific thing is its nature. It is within the Ultimate and the Ultimate is within it.

This interpretation was not developed simply for the sake of metaphysical speculation, but in order to understand man and his role in the world. The li of man consisted in the virtues of love, righteousness, propriety, and wisdom. Since he was conjoined with impure ether, man was unstable in his expression of virtue. If he purified himself, enlightenment would follow. The method to do this was to investigate things and extend knowledge according to the pattern established in the *Ta-hsueh*. Through the study of objective things and affairs one would eventually come to an understanding of the harmony of the whole which would animate his expression of virtue.

Wang Yang-ming was a scholar of broad attainments in religion, philosophy, poetry, and military and social affairs. Drawing on the thought of Lu Hsiang-shan, he emphasized three points in his Confucian philosophy. He maintained that there was a unity between li and the mind; that innate or intuitive knowledge may be cultivated without cognition or corrupting external influence; and that there was a unity of knowledge and action so that knowledge was expressed immediately in action. Whatever Buddhist influence can be discerned in his system was displaced through emphasis on selfless action in the world. In actuality, though his thought had mystical overtones, he was an activist attempting to remove the intellectualist blocks from one's commitment to action. In the background was the formalistic, rationalist Neo-Confucianism based on Chu Hsi. His thought became very popular for a time in China and was also introduced into Japan where exponents were active in the restoration of the Emperor in 1868.

In the period after the Sung and Ming philosophers there was little if any advance in the substance of Confucian thought. A major reason for the decline in the vitality of Confucian thought was the nature of the literary examinations which were the chief means to official position. Restriction of the content to Confucian dogma and authoritarianism made the system rigid. In the Ch'ing period (1644–1911) there was a reaction against Neo-Confucianism with attempted purges of the tradition of Taoist and Buddhist overtones. A major issue was the determination of the authentic texts of Confucianism giving rise to the Old Text-New Text controversy. While the movement had scientific and empiricist emphases, it did not issue in the formation of scientific theory or outlook. This limitation made the adaptation of Confucianism to modern challenges extremely difficult and contributed to the intellectual crisis in the confrontation with the West.

In the modern period, when China was challenged on all levels by Western thought, culture, and technology, there were various reactions among Chinese scholars. These reactions ranged from total rejection of the West, attempts to relate Chinese tradition to Western outlook, or total repudiation of the Chinese tradition in favor of Westernization. O. Briere has summarized succinctly the problem confronting Chinese thinkers at the end of the nineteenth century:

> *All knew that it was necessary to change something in the governmental machinery, but remained faithful to the Empire; all knew that it was necessary to borrow from the Occident its scientific spirit, its spirit of organization, whatever made for strength and material greatness; but all wanted to conserve at all costs the Confucian morality which had in the past brought about the strength and greatness of China. They reckoned that Confucianism still had its word to say in modern times, and were convinced that the welfare of humanity depended upon putting this morality into practice throughout the world.*[26]

The future of Confucian philosophy in view of the Communist takeover in 1949 remains in doubt. It is to be hoped that Marxian philosophers will better be able to assess the enduring insights of their tradition after they have recovered from the initial necessity to purge the tradition of elements inhibiting progress.

---

26. O. Briere, *Fifty Years of Chinese Philosophy 1898–1948*, New York, Praeger, 1965, p. 17.

HARMONY WITH NATURE: PHILOSOPHICAL AND RELIGIOUS TAOISM

PHILOSOPHICAL TAOISM

The "drop-out" philosophy expounded by earlier individualistic nonconformists such as Yang Chu received eloquent expression in the *Tao-te-ching,* traditionally attributed to Lao-tzu (sixth or fourth century B.C.), and the text of Chuang-tzu (between 399 and 295 B.C.). Our information concerning both sages depends on the accounts of Ssu-ma Ch'ien which are of doubtful historical value.

According to tradition, Lao-tzu, whose name means simply Old Sage, was identified by the historian with a historical individual Li Erh and the legendary archivist Lao Tan, indicating obscurity concerning the life of the teacher. Most famous in the story of Lao-tzu are the narratives of his conversations with Confucius which highlight the contrast between the Confucian and Taoist approaches to life.

In terms reflecting Taoist perspectives on morality, social responsibility, and inner freedom, Lao-tzu condemned Confucius for his attachment to the past and for excessive concern with external displaying of goodness. Then brusquely dismissing Confucius, Lao-tzu urged him:

> Get rid of that arrogance of yours, all those desires, that self-sufficient air, that overweening zeal; all that is of no use to your true person.[1]

On another occasion, Lao-tzu left Confucius with the observation that the exercise of intelligence and learning in making just criti-

1. Max Kaltenmark, *Lao Tzu and Taoism,* Stanford, Calif., Stanford University Press, 1969, p. 8.

cisms and exposing others' faults leads to an early death. He further declared that subordination to another, whether one's father or ruler, prevented a person from being his own man.

The mystery of Lao-tzu is heightened by the circumstances of his taking leave of history. After serving some time in court and witnessing its corruption, he set out in the direction of the state of Ch'in to the west. When he was about to pass through Han-ku Pass, the guard requested that he set down his teaching. He quickly composed the small volume of about 5250 characters now known as *Tao-te-ching*. His destination and place of death were unknown.

The *Tao-te-ching* itself appears to have been composed during the Warring States period and is regarded by scholars as a compilation of materials rather than the product of a single mind. Despite the implied historical priority of Taoism over Confucianism in the legendary conversations of Lao-tzu and Confucius, the *Tao-te-ching* can be understood better as criticism of the growing currency of Confucian thinking. A compact, poetical work of eighty-one sections, it has had wide influence in Chinese history, providing perspective and guidance for individuals in disturbed times. Through the centuries more than 950 commentaries have attempted to plumb its meaning, and there have been more than forty English translations, testifying to both its inherent attraction and the difficulty of rendering its sometimes obscure language. In Communist China also its thought is explored and interpreted along materialistic lines.[2]

Although the *Tao-te-ching* is commonly understood to contain a deeply personal mystical philosophy, it should be noted that it addressed itself to the problem of human relations and the functioning of society. Directed at rulers who wished to control their people, the text contains numerous passages commenting on government, the nature of the sage-ruler, criticism of society, war, and oppression. Later Legalist philosophers perceived the significance of the opportunistic political implications of the Taoist principle of acting according to Nature which discounted the past.

Although similar to the Confucian interest in morality and true leadership, there are significant differences in the Taoist approach to the problem. Where Confucianism proposes a specific system of values by which men could attain the durable society, the *Tao-te-ching* points to the requisite attitudes and personal traits which the individual must cultivate as the foundation of human relations. Confucian emphasis is on doing and acting, following specific rules of behavior. The teaching of the *Tao-te-ching* stresses one's mode of being in the world and the perspective which one must hold when dealing with the circumstances of life. The Confucians are more oriented toward the fulfillment of external obligations, while the Taoists attempt to develop their inner lives, enabling them to meet any contingency spontaneously. Although Confucius warns against

---

2. Wing-tsit Chan, trans., *The Way of Lao-tzu*, Indianapolis, Bobbs-Merrill, 1963, pp. 30–31; Holmes Welch, *Taoism, The Parting of the Way*, Boston, Beacon Press, 1966, pp. 4–5, presents a list of other major English translations.

externalism in the *Analects,* later Confucians tend to place greater stress on the exterior acts, opening the way for formalism, hypocrisy, and rigidity, which the Taoists acutely criticize.

As its name implies, the central concept of Taoism is the Tao, which means the Way or Path. Although all schools of Chinese thought had their respective Tao, for the Taoist school it refers to the process of Nature and the cosmos and to the underlying reality embracing all existence. It is the symbol of ultimate reality.

The opening passage of the *Tao-te-ching* initiates the reader immediately by means of a short, pithy statement into the metaphysical and mystical perspective of Taoism. As a warning concerning the limitation of speech to exhaust the meaning of reality, it declares unequivocally that the "*Tao* (Way) that can be told is not the eternal *Tao;* the name that can be named is not the eternal name." In a later passage, we are told that "He who knows does not speak. He who speaks does not know" (*Tao-te-ching* 56).[3]

The concept of Tao may have evolved from ancient observation of the fixed, unchanging process of Heaven or Nature. The religious beliefs concerning a female agricultural deity or the god Shang-ti may have contributed to its formation. However, in the *Tao-te-ching* the Tao has become the formless, nonactive-active reality and is essentially indefinable.

In keeping with the Taoist economy of speech in describing the nature of reality, cosmological concepts are kept to a minimum. The evolution of the world out of the Tao offers a model for the attitudes necessary in human relations and dealing with life. The concept has two aspects. It is at once the totality of the order of Heaven and Earth and at the same time the nameless, vital potentiality which is the basis of the order of Nature. As the ultimate ground of things, Tao can only be termed the nameless, or Nonbeing. It is beyond categorization, but is the necessary source of all. Among the world of things dualism is the fundamental mode of thinking. The term "Nonbeing," consequently, has two aspects. On one hand it is the basis of Being beyond thought. On the other it is the correlate of Being in the world of experience. As Nonbeing implies Being in the world of dualistic thought, so Being has mysteriously flashed forth from the midst of Nonbeing. Te is Tao manifest as the power of Being within the myriad things. It is that which makes (virtue) a thing to be what it is. Through te things fulfill their natures:

> *Tao produces them.*
> *Virtue fosters them.*
> *Matter gives them physical form.*
> *The circumstances and tendencies complete them.*
> *Therefore the ten thousand things esteem Tao and honor virtue.*
> *Tao is esteemed and virtue is honored without anyone's order.*
> *They always come spontaneously.*

---

3. Unless otherwise indicated, all quotations from the *Tao-te-ching* are from Chan, op. cit.

> *Therefore Tao produces them and virtue fosters them.*
> *They rear and develop them.*
> *They give them security and give them peace.*
> *They nurture them and protect them.*
> *(Tao) produces them but does not take possession of them.*
> *It acts, but does not rely on its own ability.*
> *It leads them but does not master them.*
> *This is called profound and secret virtue.*
>
> (*Tao-te-ching* 51) [4]

In Western terms, Taoist cosmological thinking appears grasped by the mystery of existence expressed in the ancient question: Why is there something and not nothing? Taoists are deeply aware that individual objects are not self-explainable. Things point beyond themselves to their ultimate source. At the same time, that ultimate source is mirrored in things. Each element of the world embodies a significant aspect of Tao from which man may glean wisdom for living. Thus the only true existence is that which conforms to the wisdom of Nature.

Drawing inspiration from Nature, a wide variety of natural images depict the essential qualities of the Taoist way of life. In the figure of the valley there is the suggestion of characteristics such as breadth, openness, inclusiveness, humility, and lowliness. As female, the valley expresses qualities of passivity, receptiveness, tranquillity, and productivity. The flexibility and suppleness of grass and young trees are signs of vitality, while rigidity and hardness signify death. Strength in weakness is dramatized in the invulnerability of the infant. The eroding ability of water attests to the hidden power in softness and weakness in dealing with affairs:

> *There is nothing softer and weaker than water*
> *And yet there is nothing better for attacking hard and strong things.*
> *For this reason there is no substitute for it.*
> *All the world knows that the weak overcomes the strong and the soft overcomes the hard.*
> *But none can practice it.*
>
> (*Tao-te-ching* 78)

The uncarved block suggests qualities such as genuineness, simplicity, and naturalness. It is the condition before something is imposed on it. The one who cultivates eternal virtue is described:

> *He will be proficient in eternal virtue,*
> *And returns to the state of simplicity (uncarved wood).*
> *When the uncarved wood is broken up, it is turned into concrete things.*
>
> (*Tao-te-ching* 28)

4. Other passages employing the term "virtue" (te) are 10, 21, 23, 28, 38, 41, 54, 55, 56, 60, 65, 79.

Landscape with waterfall and two figures, from the Ming Dynasty, fifteenth or sixteenth century. (*Courtesy of the Museum of Fine Arts, Boston.*)

Objects of human invention could also provide insight into the nature of reality and life strategy. In this connection the *Tao-te-ching* develops the thesis of the utility of the empty:

Thirty spokes are united around the hub to make a wheel,
  But it is on its non-being that the utility of the carriage depends.
Clay is molded to form a utensil,
  But it is on its non-being that the utility of the utensil depends.
Doors and windows are cut out to make a room,
  But it is on its non-being that the utility of the room depends.
Therefore turn being into advantage, and turn non-being into utility.

(Tao-te-ching 11)

The most famous and significant quality advanced in the *Tao-te-ching* is the trait of *wu-wei* (nonaction). Many interpretations have been given to this concept which is repeatedly set forth as the ideal way of handling affairs and governing:

Tao invariably takes no action, and yet there is nothing left undone.
If kings and barons can keep it, all things will transform spontaneously.
If, after transformation, they should desire to be active,
I would restrain them with simplicity, which has no name.
Simplicity, which has no name is free of desires.
Being free of desires, it is tranquil.
And the world will be at peace of its own accord.

(Tao-te-ching 37; also 48 and 57)

It is clear that wu-wei does not mean doing nothing. Rather, it is a special perspective on the nature of doing. Its basic meaning is to do nothing contrary to Nature or the Tao. It may also mean not to do anything with selfish motives and ends in view. However, since Nature is the model for all action, it refers to the fact that all events in Nature flow out from within Nature, and all appear to be spontaneously self-caused. They happen of themselves. The nonaction by which all is accomplished would imply that one is to cultivate his nature in order to act spontaneously from within without contriving or forcing himself or others externally in attaining a goal. If we consider that action refers to deliberate, contrived, externally imposed efforts toward some personally desired end, then nonaction is a *state of being from which* actions flow freely. Goals are not based on mere subjective desire. The difference in the two perspectives on the foundations of behavior may be illustrated in the contrast between two questions: What should I do? as against What kind of person should I be? In terms of Confucian-Taoist contrast, the Confucianist tended to specify actions which would bring a person into harmony with reality. The Taoist emphasized that harmony with reality is the basis of action.

While in relation to oneself nonaction means to act from inward and spontaneous impulse as one is harmonized with the Tao, dealing with others it also signifies that one can achieve his goals without deliberately imposing his will on others. Through the natural influence of his character, he can lead people toward desired ends in a manner corresponding to the concept te in Confucianism.

A correlative idea grows out of the understanding of nonaction. It is to let things alone. This aspect means not to intrude oneself and one's personal desires into the course of events in order to bend them to one's wishes. One should understand the course of events and allow things to work out by themselves in the light of the true way of influencing:

> *Therefore the sage manages affairs without action*
> *And spreads doctrines without words.*
> *All things arise, and he does not turn away from them.*
> *He produces them but does not take possession of them.*
> *He acts but does not rely on his own ability.*
> *He accomplishes his task but does not claim credit for it.*
> *It is precisely because he does not claim credit that his accomplishment remains with him.*
>
> (*Tao-te-ching* 2)

This passage urges the true leader to reject the ego which would attempt to dominate affairs. It is the quality of the sage that he does not intrude himself, while yet bringing to bear his influence. Letting alone may be illustrated in the image of cooking a small fish whereby, with too much poking, one may lose the fish (*Tao-te-ching* 60). Because action fails and grasping loses, the sage "supports all things in their natural state but does not take any action" (*Tao-te-ching* 64).

Two other traits are associated with letting alone. One is the noncompetitive approach to human relations, and the second is knowing when to stop. Contrary to the opinion that competition is the nature of life, hence inevitable, the sage indicates that it is willed by man, and to end it one must decide to stop it. Then there is no competition. Competition is the attempt to subjugate others to one's own ego. It is to win superiority over the other. When one has his own ego in proper perspective, however, there is no competition, as is evident in the pattern of Heaven's dealings with the world:

> *The way of Heaven does not compete, and yet it skillfully achieves victory.*
> *It does not speak, and yet it skillfully responds to things.*
> *It comes to you without your invitation.*
> *It is not anxious about things and yet it plans well.*
> *Heaven's net is indeed vast,*
> *Though its meshes are wide, it misses nothing.*
>
> (*Tao-te-ching* 73)

Knowing when to stop and discarding extremes suggest a necessary sense of moderation and balance:

> *To hold and fill a cup to overflowing*
> *Is not as good as to stop in time.*
> . . . .
> *Withdraw as soon as your work is done.*
> *Such is Heaven's Way.*
>
> (*Tao-te-ching* 9)

The sage thus "discards the extremes, the extravagant, and the excessive" (*Tao-te-ching* 29).

In addition to appeals for cultivation of various general attitudes as the basis for fruitful human relations, the *Tao-te-ching* exhorts readers with more specific and concrete principles of behavior. It declares that "much talk will of course come to a dead end" (*Tao-te-ching* 5). It recommends closing the mouth and limiting the desires.

In dealing with affairs, it counsels care and foresight. Particularly when success is in sight the greatest care is necessary:

> *If one remains as careful at the end as he was at the beginning, there will be no failure.*
>
> (*Tao-te-ching* 64)

In one's dealings with others one does not justify himself, boast, or brag. One is to be honest and good with all. Whether dealing with the big or small, many or few, hatred is to be repaid with virtue. The sage observes:

> *To patch up great hatred is surely to leave some hatred behind.*
> *How can this be regarded as good?*
> *Therefore the sage keeps the left-hand portion (obligation) of a contract*
> *And does not blame the other party.*
> *Virtuous people attend to their left-hand portions,*
> *While those without virtue attend to other people's mistakes.*
>
> (*Tao-te-ching* 79)

Again, keen insight into human relations is revealed in the admonition:

> *It is only when one does not have enough faith in others*
> *that others will have no faith in him.*
>
> (*Tao-te-ching* 23)

People's reactions to us are often reflections of our reaction to them.

The political philosophy of the *Tao-te-ching* rests on the principle that the best ruler is the one whose existence is hardly noted by the people. He rules by the principles of nonaction, letting alone, and moderation. Through the beneficent influence of his character, he brings peace and harmony to the kingdom. On this point the Taoists and the Confucianists both recommend example and moral influence over the imposition of laws as the ideal means of ordering society.

However, there are a number of passages in the *Tao-te-ching* which appear, at least on the surface, to express a despotic approach to government. They were employed later by Legalists to support their methods and outlook. While scholars agree that the passages in question have affinity with the Legalist philosophy, they also point out that the criticism of society and the Confucian system, as well as the general tendency of the Taoist perspective on human relations, would argue against their being Legalist in intent. Rather, they are paradoxical in their meaning when the value system of Taoism is kept in mind in interpreting them.

The passages in question are 3, 36, and 65. In verses 3 and 65 there is the suggestion that the ruler may despotically control the minds of his subjects by emptying their hearts, weakening ambitions, and limiting knowledge. Interpreted as advocating deceit, passage 36 has been widely condemned in Chinese tradition. While there is the suggestion of treachery, the text may also be intended to inform the king "that it is a common lot among men and kings to be built up for a fall." [5] By implication, the king should understand "that gentleness is stronger than harshness." [6]

Taoist criticism of society and war contains insights relevant in our own time. With respect to society, Taoists realized that appeals to virtue were an indication that society had already failed. Such appeals only arise when people have ceased spontaneously fulfilling virtues inspired by deep human relations.

As symptoms of a deeper problem, appeals provide no solution. Hence, calls for patriotism betray a condition in which people's patriotic fervor may be at low ebb. What is necessary is not exhortation to patriotism, but a rectification of the condition leading to a decline in the spontaneous commitment to the state. In a similar fashion laws are also seen as signs of society's failure and an attempt to gain by compulsion what should flow naturally from the human situation. The externalization of virtue and imposition of law lead only to competitive struggle, hypocrisy, and oppression in society. In essence it is a thwarting of human nature and hence society in its deepest sense. Thus the sage notes:

> *When the great Tao declined,*
>   *The doctrine of humanity and righteousness arose.*
> *When knowledge and wisdom appeared,*
>   *There emerged great hypocrisy.*
> *When the six family relationships are not in harmony,*
>   *There will be the advocacy of filial piety and deep love to children.*
> *When a country is in disorder,*
>   *There will be the praise of loyal ministers.*
>
>   (*Tao-te-ching* 18)

---

5. R. B. Blakney, *The Way of Life: Lao Tzu*, New York, New American Library, 1955, p. 89.
6. Ibid.

On the failure of law, the sage declares:

Govern the state with correctness
  Operate the army with surprise tactics.
Administer the empire by engaging in no activity.
How do I know that this should be so?
Through this:
  The more taboos and prohibitions there are in the world,
The poorer the people will be.
  The more sharp weapons the people have,
The more troubled the state will be.
  The more cunning and skill man possesses,
The more vicious things will appear.
  The more laws and orders are made prominent,
The more thieves and robbers there will be.
(Tao-te-ching 57)

In view of the people's willingness to die in resisting oppression, the sage advises rulers not to be extravagant in extracting taxes or in spending and not to "reduce the living space of their dwellings. Do not oppress their lives" (*Tao-te-ching* 72).

War is also seen as a basic failure in society, though it is recognized that war is sometimes inevitable. It brings desolation and encourages disrespect for life. When undertaken, it is to be done with sad regret. Any rejoicing in war is a sign of lack of basic humanity and understanding of existence. The sage keenly notes the results of the use of force and war:

He who assists the ruler with Tao does not dominate the world
  with force.
The use of force usually brings requital.
Wherever armies are stationed, briers and thorns grow.
Great wars are always followed by famines.
(Tao-te-ching 30)

The Taoist criticism of society made it the spokesman for the oppressed in society. Due to this feature it fostered secret societies responsible for popular uprisings aimed at political and economic reforms.[7]

The ideal state requires rejection of the superficial ways by which society measures people and demands the cultivation of awareness of the Tao rather than enforcement of externally imposed values and goals. The sage draws a picture of the ideal society which is essentially a primary group where values are spontaneously realized without legislation:

Let there be a small country with few people.
Let there be ten times and a hundred times as many utensils

---

7. C. K. Yang, *Religion in Chinese Society*, Berkeley, Calif., University of California Press, 1961, pp. 218–227.

> *But let them not be used.*
> *Let the people value their lives highly and not migrate far.*
> *Even if there are ships and carriages, none will ride in them.*
> *Even if there are arrows and weapons, none will display them.*
> *Let the people again knot cords and use them (in place of writing).*
> *Let them relish their food, beautify their clothing, be content with their homes, and delight in their customs.*
> *Though neighboring communities overlook one another and the crowing of cocks and barking of dogs can be heard,*
> *Yet the people there may grow old and die without ever visiting one another.*
>
> (*Tao-te-ching* 80)

While it may be argued whether this ideal can ever be realized in the modern context, the atmosphere and values it expresses are those which need to be cultivated wherever possible if the human spirit is not to be submerged within the structures it has created for its own protection and fulfillment. Passages like these serve to remind us that civilization extracts a price from the human spirit. With increasing civilization and organization comes the loss of spontaneity, naturalness, simplicity, and sheer delight in life itself.

The second major figure in the development of Taoist tradition is Chuang-tzu. According to the traditional biography provided by Ssu-ma Ch'ien:

> *Chuang-tzu was a native of Meng (in present Honan). His personal name was Chou. He held a small post at Ch'i-yuan, in Meng. He was a contemporary of King Hui or Liang (370–319) and Hsuan of Ch'i (319–301). His erudition was most varied, but his chief doctrines were based upon the sayings of Lao Tzu. His writings, which run to over 100,000 words, are for the most part allegorical. His literary and dialectic skill was such that the best scholars of the age were unable to refute his destructive criticism of the Confucian and Mohist schools. His teachings were like an overwhelming flood which spreads unchecked according to its own will, so that from rulers and ministers downward, none could apply them to any practical use.*[8]

Despite the presumed factuality of this account the precise date of Chuang-tzu, his relation to Lao-tzu and his teaching, and his relation to his contemporary Mencius remain unclear and uncertain. It is also a problem whether the book *Chuang-tzu* was actually authored by that individual. Nevertheless, the text reflects the work of a penetrating mind (or minds) which gave new depth and scope to Taoist teaching.

The *Chuang-tzu* advocated a decidedly mystical approach to life in contrast to the activist views of other ancient schools of thought such as the Confucianists and Mohists whom it severely criticized. Although the *Chuang-tzu* was concerned with the problem of social

---

8. Fung, op. cit., p. 221.

harmony and the fulfillment of human existence in common with the other schools, it presented a radical solution by advocating emancipation from the world instead of reforming it. According to the *Chuang-tzu*, men created their own problems by the pursuit of virtue, fame, and wisdom.

Attempting to encourage men to transcend the world, the *Chuang-tzu* makes a determined effort to shake the mind loose from its addiction to words, values, conventions, and actions which have come to be regarded as natural to man and necessary to his existence. It strives to free the mind from the conviction that what it perceives, thinks, and understands is what really is. In order to bring about this loosening, the *Chuang-tzu* employs a number of strategies such as the non sequitur, paradox, "pseudological discussion," and humor.

To achieve emancipation the *Chuang-tzu* urges the practices of "free and easy wandering," "fasting of the mind," and "forgetting." Through mystical meditation resulting in the perception of the blinding effect of words and intellection, and awareness of the illusory nature of the world and life, one arrives at a true understanding of change and death.

Through "free and easy wandering" we journey in the vast spaces of reality where one "climbs up on clouds and mist, rides a flying dragon and wanders beyond the four seas." Traveling "beyond the dust and dirt, one wanders free and easy in the service of inaction." Following "any far-away, carefree, and as-you-like-it paths," we enter into the beyond where there is nothing and where there is no trail. Borne beyond the trivialities of mundane concern in company with the Creator and great Teacher we truly govern the world as the sage notes:

> *Let your mind wander in simplicity, blend your spirit with the vastness, follow along with things the way they are, and make no room for personal views—then the world will be governed.*[9]

Not all can make this journey, for bound by benevolence and righteousness, they are blind. For small minds and spirits the freedom of the sage is as incomprehensible as the flight of ninety thousand leagues by the great P'eng bird is to the cicada and the dove. To have evident skills and capacities means slavery:

> *In comparison to the sage, a man like this is a drudging slave, a craftsman bound to his calling, wearing out his body, grieving his mind. They say it is the beautiful markings of the tiger and the leopard that call out the hunters, the nimbleness of the monkey and the ability of the dog to catch rats that make them end up chained.*[10]

To wander in the world means neither to submerge oneself in mere conformity, nor to reject or withdraw from affairs. Rather, the

---

9. Burton Watson, *Chuang Tzu: Basic Writings*, New York, Columbia, 1964, pp. 90–94.
10. Ibid., p. 91.

true sage, flexible in confronting circumstance, is "able to wander in the world without taking sides, can follow along with men without losing himself." [11]

Embarking upon the path of free and easy wandering requires that "you strip away not your fine fur only, but every impediment of the body, scour your heart till it is free from all desire, and travel through the desolate wilds." [12] Through the "fasting of the mind" we transcend the intellect and enter the emptiness of the Tao. By means of true forgetting we attain union with the Tao as we "drive out perception and intellect, cast off form, do away with understanding." [13]

The spiritual ascent to enlightenment and the realization of the unity of all differences is a process of progressive emptying of the self:

> *So I began explaining and kept at him for three days, and after that he was able to put the world outside himself. When he had put the world outside himself, I kept at him for seven days more, and after that he was able to put things outside himself. When he had put things outside himself, I kept at him for nine days more, and after that he was able to put life outside himself. After he had put life outside himself, he was able to achieve the brightness of dawn, and when he had achieved the brightness of dawn, he could see his aloneness. After he had managed to see his aloneness, he could do away with past and present, he was able to enter where there is no life and no death. That which kills life does not die; that which gives life to life does not live. This is the kind of thing it is: there's nothing it doesn't send off, nothing it doesn't welcome, nothing it doesn't destroy, nothing it doesn't complete. Its name is Peace-in-Strife. After the strife, it attains completion.*[14]

This passage is noteworthy in that the stages outlined conform generally to the pattern of mystical experience throughout the world. Devotees pass through the stages of *purgation,* freeing them from bondage to the external world, *concentration,* leading to unification of the self, and *enlightenment* or union with reality.

Although the mystic path outlined in the *Chuang-tzu* implies disregard for the affairs of ordinary men, there is no call for rejecting any particular life context in order to become the perfect man. Rather, there is recognition that a man cannot always control the conditions of life about him:

> *But though you may be one time a ruler, another time a subject, this is merely a matter of the times. Such distinctions change with*

---

11. Ibid., pp. 137–138.
12. Arthur Waley, *Three Ways of Thought in Ancient China,* New York, Doubleday, 1956, p. 39.
13. Watson, op. cit., pp. 86–87.
14. Ibid., p. 79. The alternative translation in Fung, op. cit., pp. 238–239, suggests a vision of the One which enables the sage to transcend all distinctions, past-present, life-death, tranquillity-strife.

the age and you cannot call either one or the other lowly. Therefore I say, the Perfect Man is never a stickler in his actions.[15]

It even suggests that mystic endeavor enables the ideal ruler to manage affairs successfully. Rejecting the quest for fame or imposing schemes and projects as evidence of his wisdom, his mind will be like a mirror: "going after nothing, welcoming nothing, responding but not storing. Therefore, he can win out over things and not hurt himself." [16] He can call out troops and conquer nations without losing the hearts of the people, and he benefits countless ages, though not having love for men.[17]

While the mystical pursuit appears useless from the conventional standpoint, it actually provides man with his footing in the world:

A man has to understand the useless before you can talk to him about the useful. The earth is certainly vast and broad, though a man uses no more of it than the area he puts his feet on. If however, you were to dig away all the earth from around his feet until you reached the Yellow Springs, then would the man still be able to make use of it? [18]

The concept of the "usefulness of the useless" in the *Chuang-tzu* corresponds to the idea of the utility of the empty in the *Tao-te-ching*. As a practical approach to life, it suggests that the truly wise person avoids grief and pain and fulfills his life by following a simple, quiet, obscure life which the world passes over as insignificant just as the woodcutter and carpenter ignore the gnarled and bumpy ailanthus or oak tree.

Free and easy wandering in the boundless beyond in meditative endeavor produces keen awareness of the contrast of the heavenly and the human. The heavenly is the natural, original, or fated endowment of any being just as horses and oxen naturally have four feet. In contrast the human refers to man's intentional imposition on, and manipulation of, Nature.

Heaven, like the nameless, formless Tao is beyond human categories and determinations. However, just as men cut a road through a trackless field, they attempt to impose order on Heaven, making it conform to their scheme of values:

What is acceptable we call acceptable; what is unacceptable we call unacceptable. A road is made by people walking on it; things are so because they are called so. What makes them so? Making them so makes them so. What makes them not so? Making them not so makes them not so. . . .[19]

Further, Heaven stands for what is essential and inward, while the human is the external, artificial, and manipulative. Thus, while it is

15. Watson, op. cit., p. 137.
16. Ibid., pp. 94–95.
17. For eloquent description of the demeanor and bearing of the ideal man, see ibid., pp. 75, 99–100.
18. Ibid., pp. 136–137.
19. Ibid., pp. 35–36.

according to Heaven that horses have four legs, it is the result of human intentions that horses wear halters and oxen have pierced noses. The timely word of the sage urges:

> *I say: do not let what is human wipe out what is Heavenly; do not let what is purposeful wipe out what is fated.*[20]

Against the background of this distinction we must observe the attack which the *Chuang-tzu* launches against words and language. Fundamentally, words represent man's intellectual effort to order reality. When his words are believed to represent reality as it really is, they become a barrier to the full realization of his existence.

Perceiving that the preachments of moralists, i.e., Confucianists and Mohists, permit people to consider themselves superior to others or that the subtle word play of logicians deludes people into believing they truly understand reality, the *Chuang-tzu* emphasizes the relativity of words and views. Differences among people are only matters of degree and standpoint, not substance or reality:

> *If a man sleeps in a damp place, his back aches and he ends up half paralyzed, but is this true of a loach? If he lives in a tree, he is terrified and shakes with fright, but is this true of a monkey? . . . Men claim that Mao-ch'ing and Lady Li were beautiful, but if fish saw them they would fly away. . . . Of these four, which knows how to fix the standard of beauty for the world? The way I see it, the rules of benevolence and righteousness and the paths of right and wrong are all hopelessly snarled and jumbled. How could I know anything about such discriminations?* [21]

The evaluations which men make of their experiences create endless dissatisfactions and struggles for more and more achievement. Man's life is bound and overwhelmed by fears and anxieties. Failing to see that human life is simply part of the ever-transforming process of Nature, change becomes threatening. Confusion and frustration in life result from not perceiving man's pettiness within the cosmic order.

To be able to accept and harmonize with change and to confront death with equanimity, one must press beyond the world of contrary distinctions and arbitrary evaluations. Attaining a vision of the unity of the Tao which unifies all the dualities of existence, one may keep his spirit whole, and his response to life will be like the hinge well-fitted to its socket or like a mirror which embraces and reflects all without stain. The person not touched by good or bad "just lets things be the way they are and doesn't try to help life along." [22]

It is important to notice that the man who perceives the Tao does not abolish the world of things. He understands its nature. Those who are close to attaining truth, according to the *Chuang-tzu,* are those who do not reject what pertains to Heaven nor neglect what pertains to man. He does not use "the mind to repel the Way" nor

20. Ibid., p. 104.
21. Ibid., p. 41.
22. Ibid., p. 72.

"man to help out Heaven."[23] "When man and Heaven do not defeat each other, then he may be said to have the True Man."[24]

Making a perfect adjustment to life, those who understand the Tao develop a skill in life and never exhaust their spiritual power just as the expert cook was able to use his knife for nineteen years without sharpening it because he merely passed his knife through the empty space between joints when butchering a cow.

It is clear that the major problem of existence is egoism and ego attachment. If one can attain a detachment from the self and world, one's spirit would not be disturbed by dramatic shifts in affairs. In order to drive home the relativity of existence and ego experience, the *Chuang-tzu* emphasizes that the line between dream and reality is difficult to maintain and the solidity of our ego may be merely the solidity of a dream from which we shall awake.

> *What's more, we go around telling each other, I do this, I do that —but how do we know that this "I" we talk about has any "I" to it? You dream you're a bird and soar up into the sky; you dream you're a fish and dive down in the pool. But now when you tell me about it, I don't know whether you are awake or whether you are dreaming. Running around accusing others is not as good as laughing, and enjoying a good laugh is not as good as going along with things. Be content to go along and forget about change and then you can enter the mysterious oneness of Heaven.*[25]

Concerning life and death, the *Chuang-tzu* emphasizes that the distinction is meaningless in the light of the dream nature of existence and the fact that the duality of life and death is wrongly evaluated by man. Both must be accepted as part of the nature of things. Death, particularly, is merely one of the many changes the individual undergoes through his process of living. They should not perturb his spirit.

When the spirit of Chuang-tzu's philosophy is apprehended, it enables the individual to approach life with a grand indifference. Although he is not entirely disinterested, the true man views with detachment all affairs as part of the same process whose secret he knows. He therefore refrains from trying to force it to conform to his desires.

We may compare Chuang-tzu's attitude toward fate and death with the stoic attitude of accepting everything as the working out of a universal reason. His philosophy does not guarantee success in every situation. Rather it teaches how to face every situation. When one loses, he has fortitude; when he wins, he is not prone to presumption or pride. Unless the person is certain of himself within, he cannot be sure facing the world. The nurture of the inner man, which is the foundation of all life's activities, forms the central concern of the *Chuang-tzu*.

23. Ibid., p. 74.
24. Ibid., p. 76.
25. Ibid., pp. 84–85.

NEO-TAOISM At the end of the Han era the loss of prestige of Confucianism and the upheaval of society led to revived interest in Taoist philosophy. Two distinct trends appeared in the movement. On the one hand there was a group of philosophers with Confucian leanings and devoted to reconciling Taoism with the established teaching of Confucius. The other group appears more interested in the life-style engendered by Taoist principles. The Neo-Taoist movement was termed "Pure Talk" because of its concentration on philosophical issues and rejection of worldly advantage. It was also called "Dark Learning" because it focused on the relation of the abstruse and mysterious Tao to the world.

Those concerned mainly with philosophical issues included such philosophers as Wang Pi (A.D. 225–249), who is considered the founder of the movement, Hsiang Hsiu (c. 221–c. 300), Kuo Hsiang (d. 312), and Chi K'ang (223–262). These philosophers wrote commentaries to the *I-ching*, the *Tao-te-ching,* and the *Chuang-tzu*. Through their commentaries they reinterpreted Taoism in the light of their own age and manifested considerable originality in the application of Taoist principles.

A distinctive feature of these later Taoist philosophers was their attitude to Confucius, whom Taoists generally criticized and identified with sham and hypocrisy. The latter-day Taoists regarded Confucius as the greatest sage, even superior to Lao-tzu and Chuang-tzu. The reason for this was that according to Taoist principle, he who knows does not speak and he who speaks does not know. Since Confucius did not speak of Tao and its mysterious operations, he must know it, while the Taoist sages, who spoke about it, must not know it. The motivation behind this peculiar reconciliation was the fact that Confucianism was the official philosophy of the state, and one could hardly advance in any position without coming to terms with the sage. Taoist philosophers reinterpreted the Taoist sages in order to provide a basis for participation in society. Thus the reconciliation of the perspectives of both philosophies proceeded from two directions: the exaltation of Confucius and the interpretation of his thought in terms of Taoism, and the reinterpretation of Taoist principle to make it amenable to Confucian outlook.

In general, Neo-Taoist philosophy focused attention on the problem of metaphysics, the relation of things to the source of their being and the relation of Being and Nonbeing which had been raised in the *Lao-tzu* and the *Chuang-tzu*. This type of inquiry was part of a wider interest at that time in analyzing terms and developing principles growing out of the School of Names tradition. By investigating the distinctions and meanings involved in names and terms, the principles governing reality could be discerned. Much discussion was devoted to these terms and principles, and little attention was paid to concrete actualities.[26]

The second group, known as the Seven Sages of the Bamboo Grove, appear more significant for the attitude and style of life they embodied than for the contribution they made to Taoist thought.

---

26. For detailed discussion, see Fung, op. cit., vol. II, pp. 175–179.

Their philosophy was hedonistic in its exaltation of the enjoyment of life and pursuit of pleasure. Like Yang Chu earlier, they sought enjoyment and freedom from cares. They refused office, glorified drinking, and believed that following impulse was the expression of integrity. They were also sensitive to Nature. Their care-nothing attitude was represented by Liu Ling who, unabashed at criticisms of his nakedness at home, retorted:

> *I take the whole universe as my house and my own room as my clothing. Why, then, do you enter here into my trousers?* [27]

The sense of equality of all things was demonstrated in the practice of the Juan family who enjoyed their drinking bouts by sharing the same large wine bottle, even to the extent of permitting the pigs to join in. Sympathy for animals was depicted in Chih-tun's freeing a captured crane. Sheer impulsiveness was represented in the tale of Wang Hui-chi. In the middle of the night he got the urge to visit his friend Tai K'uei, even though it was snowing. However, when he got to the door he did not knock. When asked why, he replied that the urge had passed and there was no need to knock.

RELIGIOUS TAOISM

While philosophical Taoism has provided the bureaucrat, scholar, or artist with a profound understanding of existence upon which to base his life and seek his satisfactions, it is religious Taoism which has functioned among the hosts of ordinary people to fulfill their desires for satisfaction in life and a bright destiny beyond this life.

Religious Taoism, as an institution, began about A.D. 143, established by one Chang Ling. However, the diverse beliefs and practices which make up the religion originated in more ancient times with the evolution of Chinese folk religion. Although Chinese folk religion employed elements from both Confucianism and Buddhism, religious Taoism has been the central element as the vehicle of folk beliefs. It has, however, never been supported officially by the state or advocated by scholars in the same fashion as Confucianism. At times individual rulers favored it as in the case of Emperor Kao Tsung of the T'ang who in 666 designated Lao-tzu the "Most High Emperor of Mystic Origin," a status above Confucius and Buddha.[28]

The origin or roots of religious Taoism may be traced to four sources which merged to form the complex of religious Taoism in the fourth century B.C. before any institutional establishment appeared. These sources include the philosophical Taoism of Lao-tzu, Chuang-tzu, and Lieh-tzu; a school of hygiene; the Five Element school of Tsou Yen, which later came to be regarded as a school of alchemy; and belief in the Isles of the Blest where the secret of immortality could be obtained.

The unifying element fusing these varied beliefs was the quest for

---

27. Ibid., p. 235.
28. Wing-tsit Chan, *Religious Trends in Modern China,* New York, Columbia, 1953, pp. 138–139.

immortality. It appears that magicians (*fang-shih*) were largely instrumental in promoting them. After unifying China, the first Ch'in Emperor sought his own immortality by turning cinnabar into gold in 133 B.C.

In the early centuries of the Christian era the quest for immortality developed in a hygienic direction. It became a quest for achieving longevity in this world through care of the body and deities within. According to the theory, everyone had thirty-six thousand deities dwelling within. Arranged in a hierarchy, these gods also ruled the universe. In order to maintain life, the deities must remain in the body. To assure this, certain rules of diet had to be undertaken, such as abstaining from wine, meat, and grain. Circulation was to be improved through gymnastics and breathing exercises termed "embryonic respiration," which meant to breathe like the baby in the womb. One held his breath as long as he could and directed the inhaled air to various parts of the body.

The hygienic practices, which required considerable expenditure of effort and time by the devotee, were also linked to performance of good works in order to achieve complete fulfillment. The devotee's actions contributed to his destiny from their resulting rewards or punishments.

The popular work entitled *T'ai-Shang Kan-ying P'ien* [29] illustrates the moralistic character of religious Taoism. Developed in the eleventh century, it became one of the most widely read religious books in China. Through a combination of Taoist, Confucian, and Buddhist ideas it reveals how morality and religious concepts were made available to the common people and enabled the Confucian elite to maintain their control over the people through fears of punishment inculcated by its text and drawings.

A conspicuous feature of Chinese popular religion and religious Taoism is its complex and multitudinous pantheon. For detailed study of this profusion of divinities, the reader may be referred to the study of Chinese peasant deities by Clarence Burton Day.[30] Among the most important Taoist deities, he notes the Jade Emperor, who is regarded as the father of the gods in Taoist lore. His palace is in the constellation above the North Pole where all the powers of Nature which influence earth are concentrated.

Below the more exalted deities are the popular Eight Immortals who work to bring blessings to mankind. Other widely revered deities are the Great God of Five Roads (also known as General of the Five Brigands) of evil omen and the positive God of the Five Bless-

---

29. Translated by Teitaro Suzuki and Paul Carus; discussions in Holmes Welch, *Taoism, the Parting of the Way,* Boston, Beacon Press, 1966, pp. 139–141. For a detailed study of this type of literature the reader may refer to Wolfram Eberhard, *Guilt and Sin in Traditional China,* Berkeley, Calif., University of California Press, 1967; also, C. J. Yang, *Religion in Chinese Society,* Berkeley, Calif., University of California Press, 1961, pp. 286–289.

30. Clarence Burton Day, *Chinese Peasant Cults,* Shanghai, Kelly and Walsh Limited, 1940. Also on the historical development of the pantheon, see Welch, op. cit., pp. 135–141.

ings. Very important is the god of the hearth, who keeps track of family doings and annually reports to the Jade Emperor.

As a survey of the many functions of the hosts of Chinese deities indicates, every aspect of the physical and social environment is overseen by a deity who assumes his office by appointment of the Jade Emperor (concretely through designation of the government, which regulated religious matters). The divine world is a replica of the bureaucratic world of the Chinese state.

Interaction with Buddhism imported from India contributed to the development of religious Taoism. Beliefs in Heaven and Hell, karma and transmigration, and Buddhist divinities expanded Chinese perspectives on human destiny.

The previously outlined beliefs took more concrete shape with the establishment of religious Taoism by Chang Ling in A.D. 143. Religion and politics were mixed in his work, resulting in the formation of a semi-independent state in the regions of Szechuan and Shensi. His group was called Five Bushels of Rice Taoism, since he charged that amount for membership. He also initiated a health cult to cure diseases by charms and spells, and emphasized abstention from alcohol, giving of charity, moral deeds, filial piety, meditation, repentance, and the reading of the *Tao-te-ching*. The movement continued to modern times, headed by descendants of Chang.

It is to be noted that during the period of the breakdown of the Han dynasty, the dissatisfactions of the people grew as the power of Confucianism waned. Land became concentrated in the hands of the few, and frequent floods, droughts, ruinous taxation, and banditry imperiled life.

Taoist religious organization provided a refuge for people seeking stability through a hierarchical system and offered the benefits of magic. In A.D. 184 Chang Chueh led the revolt of the Yellow Turbans, who promoted T'ai-p'ing Tao (Great Peace Taoism) in the region of Hopeh. According to this movement the age of Great Peace, the millennium, had come when all men would be equal. Yellow turbans, the color of the earth element, were their badge. Although it was put down with great effort by the Han government, the movement seriously disrupted the government itself.

In 189 Chang Ling's followers led a rebellion, gaining control over wide areas in Szechuan and Shensi. Taoist priests performed the functions of government administrators and collected taxes. In 215 they capitulated to the central government, but in return the government recognized the Taoist religion.

In the course of Chinese history numerous other rebellions have had a religious foundation in Taoism. Against the Chin and Mongols appeared the Chuan-chen-chiao (Complete Truth Religion). During the Ch'ing period there were rebellions of Taoist and Buddhist origins. The T'ai-p'ing rebellion of the nineteenth century, however, had Christian influence.

While Taoism as a religious and clerical organization has never shown an interest directly in politics, Taoist philosophy as expressed in the *Tao-te-ching* and the *Chuang-tzu* criticizes tyranny and oppressive government and society. Thus it appears to be on the side of the masses, upholding the principle of benefiting the people as the basis of successful rule. In times of stress and strain the people turned to Taoism for inspiration for their struggle. Also the magical notions of invulnerability and promises of immortality gave encouragement in face of danger.[31]

In modern times Taoist religion appears to be waning and heading for extinction, but at the same time it has inspired the formation of numerous religious societies. Largely secret in character, they require initiation into membership, vows, and the use of symbolic communications, chanting, and fasting.

Many societies began in the period preceding or just after World War I in the area of Shantung, a center of much civil and international conflict. Reflecting the general disillusion of the times, "they are all negative in outlook, utilitarian in purpose and superstitious in belief." Though they are rejected and attacked by intellectuals, Chan asserts they are not so easily dismissed, for they embody features which will influence the future of religious belief in China. He notes a number of tendencies latent in such organizations. It is a striking fact that Taoist schools and societies have generally begun as patriotic movements opposed to invaders. The Boxer Rebellion in 1900 was an outstanding modern example. They also opposed tyranny. They were this-worldly in attempting to obtain the fruits of salvation in this life. Though there are beliefs in Heaven and Hell, these were not the central religious concern. The quest of longevity was to increase life in this world. A strong ethical emphasis accompanied the attempt to achieve the good life on earth. Movements were laymen-oriented as each worked out his own salvation. Clergy performed ceremonies, but they did not control the people. The groups were syncretic, drawing from all major traditions of Confucianism, Buddhism, and Taoism.[32]

While Taoist religion continues to exist on Taiwan, its status on the mainland is in doubt. It faces severe problems in both regions from the rising influence of science and education and from its own emphasis on magical quests for self-benefit and lack of commanding leaders.

---

31. For discussion of the history and character of the Taoist church, see Welch, op. cit., pp. 113–123.
32. Chan, *Religious Trends in Modern China*, pp. 168–185.

HARMONY WITH REALITY: BUDDHISM

THE ASSIMILATION OF A FOREIGN TRADITION

Buddhism represents the first major foreign religio-philosophical tradition to penetrate and seriously influence Chinese religious and cultural outlook. Buddhism, in its Theravada (Hinayana) or Mahayana forms, promoted an essentially Indian view of reality and life which at once contradicted the Chinese understanding and also amplified it.

Buddhism contradicted Chinese interpretations of existence by generally regarding the common world of human experience as a delusive product of passion-infected minds. Hence, truth lay beyond this world in a transcendent experience of enlightenment which would reveal things as unsubstantial and valueless. This effort was to be carried out by individuals within special communities devoted to the goal of emancipation apart from common social life. Monasticism and the rigorous discipline to control the mind and passions aimed at inducing an awareness of the voidness of things, leading to detachment, tranquillity, and egolessness. These qualities marked emancipation from bondage to finitude in this life and hereafter. The individualistic character of the Buddhist quest for enlightenment collided sharply with the Chinese sense of social or communal obligation and filial piety, as well as the positive acceptance and enjoyment of this world.

The interaction between the Indian and Chinese perspectives on the world took place on various levels of Chinese society. As a consequence, distinctive forms of Chinese Buddhism (such as Ch'an) emerged, advocating acceptance of this world and supporting participation in it.

Buddhism also broadened the scope of Chinese understanding of human destiny through the concepts of karma, transmigration, and mythical cosmology. The moralism of the karmic system fitted well with Confucian social concern. Confucian tradition showed little interest in the aspirations and hopes of ordinary individuals, and Taoist philosophy primarily enabled individuals to adjust to their life conditions. Taoist religion attempted to enhance the individual's prospects in this world, but it was mainly Buddhism which attempted to console ordinary people with hope for their future well-being beyond this life through Pure Land teaching.

Although Buddhism contained aspects alien to the Chinese outlook, it had a wide attraction for people on all levels of Chinese society. On the popular level Buddhism resembled religious Taoism which could confer benefits of long life, good luck, and help in misfortune by means of magical power. Buddha was early ranked with the Yellow Emperor (Huang-ti) and Lao-tzu as an important divine personage. Emperor Huan set up an altar to these three divinities in the capital at Loyang in the period A.D. 147–167.

While the popular masses looked upon Buddhism as a means to enhance their worldly fortunes, on higher levels of society it appealed to more cultured individuals who yearned for freedom and release from worldly burdens resulting from the collapse of the Han empire. Along with the resurgence of interest in Taoist philosophy, the life of retirement and withdrawal afforded by Buddhist monasticism invited the gentry of that time.

Buddhist teachers took advantage of the similarities between Buddhist and Taoist metaphysics through a practice of matching or paralleling terms rendering Buddhism more intelligible to the Chinese mind. Consequently, the Buddhist concepts of the Absolute (*Bhutatathata*) and the phenomenal world of change were paired with the Taoist terms *Wu* (Nonbeing) and *Yu* (Being). The distinction *Nirvana-Samsara* was interpreted in terms of *wu-wei* (nonaction) and *yu-wei* (activity). The Buddhist religious ideal of the Arhat was related to the Taoist immortal Chen-jen. The five precepts of Buddhism were matched with the five virtues of Confucianism. Buddhist texts were also translated in conformity with Confucian moral sentiments. The text *Mou-tzu on the Settling of Doubts,* the first apology for Buddhism by a Chinese composed sometime between the second and fifth centuries, employed traditional Chinese texts in order to demonstrate that there was no essential contradiction between Confucianism, Taoism, and Buddhism.

Despite initial efforts of early Chinese Buddhists to commend Buddhism to the Chinese people on the basis of the similarity of its thought and practices to traditional Chinese ways, the production of more accurate translations of Buddhist texts and more penetrating studies of Buddhist philosophy revealed its basic differences with Chinese thought. As a result, numerous Taoist and Confucian spokesmen throughout subsequent Chinese history criticized and challenged the religious and social implications of Buddhism in order to advance their own religious or social interests.

Taoists charged that Buddhism was inappropriate for Chinese society because of its foreign dress, ritual, and burial customs, as well as its strange rules for food and family. They objected to Buddhist celibacy, to the use of impure materials for medicine, and to the

Kneeling Bodhisattva, from the Northern Wei Dynasty, early sixth century. (Courtesy of the Museum of Fine Arts, Boston, Hoyt Collection.)

practice of begging. Taoists followed Confucianists in criticizing the unproductive labor and wealth of the monks. They also argued about the historical priority of Lao-tzu and Buddha or superiority of Taoist and Buddhist teachings. Forged texts and misrepresentation were widely used on both sides.

The Confucianists had two main objections to Buddhism which continually recurred in memorials to the throne. They claimed that Buddhism was contrary to the basic pattern of ruler-subject relationship and that the existence of a class of nonproductive priests meant less revenue for the state. Buddhism was charged with the decline of the government and society and had to be rooted out. Such indictments often became the pretext for persecution as illustrated in the attack on the order in 446 by Emperor Shih Tsu of the Wei dynasty.

In a memorial to Emperor Liang Wu-ti (502–549), Hsun-chi, a Confucian scholar, made seven charges against Buddhism of which sedition was the central issue:

(1) the Buddhists were imitating the imperial quarters with their monasteries and temples; (2) they were translating and circulating seditious works in disrespect of the imperial mandates; (3) they were soliciting contributions for exemption from punishment in hell, thus usurping the sovereign's power of imposing penalties and punishment; (4) the Buddhist designation of the three months for fasting each year, and six days each month, was an attempt to set up another calendar in opposition to that of the dynasty; (5) they implied the existence of hardship and suffering in the royal domain by portraying the peace and joy of the Buddha lands; (6) they regarded the great bell in the temple courtyard as a substitute for the clepsydra in the imperial palace; and (7) they hoisted banners and pennants that imitated the imperial insignias.[1]

Criticisms of monastic life and superstitions were made by Fu-yi (544–639) and Han Yu (768–824). Intellectual objections centered on the existence of the soul and transmigration which the Confucians denied, mainly on the ground that this opened the people to exploitation. Confucianists were interested in ideas which had social utility.

Buddhists countered the various criticisms of both Confucianists and Taoists by maintaining that Buddhism was not contradictory to Chinese social and moral concerns. Philosophically they asserted that Buddhism was universalistic while Taoism and Confucianism were inferior in being concerned only with this world and its petty affairs. The interdependence of all beings taught in Buddhism reduced selfishness and competition, according to Buddhists.

While the attacks on Buddhism were substantial and involved many forms of argument, Buddhism spread among the people by offering glorious salvation and many benefits. The attacks sometimes resulted in persecutions of the order and restriction of its activities and numbers of monks. Sometimes wealth was expropriated in land, money, or art treasures. However, the persecutions were never of long duration, because the restlessness of the common people who supported Buddhism caused the rulers to relent.

Further, Buddhism was able to answer objections in deed as well as word. The Buddhists engaged in social work and contributed to the economy of the country through its rolling mills, oil processing facilities, hostels, and the "inexhaustible" treasury used for welfare. Buddhism brought medicine to the poor, aided the sick and starving, built roads, wells, bridges, and planted trees. In the capital the only places for recreation were the open spaces provided by temples. Buddhism grew in the face of bureaucratic and official opposition, appealing to the common man with compassion and to the intellectual with a profound vision of wisdom and spiritual emancipation.

1. Kenneth Ch'en, *Buddhism in China,* Princeton, N.J., Princeton University Press, 1964, pp. 143–144.

From the early beginnings of the Buddhist movement in China some of the best Chinese minds devoted themselves to understanding, interpreting, and elaborating the content of Buddhist thought and experience. A brief role call will serve to remind us of the personal labors behind Buddhist growth. Tao-an (312–385) studied metaphysics and meditation. His interests extended to problems of translation, cataloguing sutras and rules of discipline. Hui-yuan (344–416) was noted for his discussions on karma and the indestructibility of the soul. He argued for the independence of the Buddhist Order, maintaining that monks should not bow before kings. He also promoted meditative practices based on faith in Amitabha Buddha. The monk Tao-sheng (360–434) advanced theories which eventually became hallmarks of Chinese Buddhism, such as the doctrines of instantaneous enlightenment and universal Buddha nature. Seng-chao (374–414) was an outstanding interpreter of the philosophy of Nagarjuna which he had learned as a disciple of the famous Indian missionary Kumarajiva (in Chang-an, 401–413). Hsuan-tsang (596–664) achieved eminence as a pilgrim to India, translator, and commentator. Chi-tsang (549–623) systematized the Madhyamika philosophy of Nagarjuna and earned the reputation of being one of the most virtuous monks.

THE SCHOOLS OF CHINESE BUDDHISM

As Buddhist teachings flowed into China from India, their many tendencies gave rise to a diversity of schools and interpretations. The history of the formation of Buddhist schools divides into two periods. The initial period was known as the age of the "Six Schools and Seven Branches." During the second stage, the encouragement and support of Buddhist scholarship by the Sui and T'ang emperors led to the formation of more distinct and well-defined systems of Buddhist teaching which had enduring significance as the zenith of Buddhist intellectual leadership and influence in Chinese culture. As these schools developed, they reflected the gradual assimilation of Buddhism to the Chinese mind.

The first scholarly movement in the "Six Schools and Seven Branches" exhibited the two basic interests of early Chinese Buddhism in meditation and *Prajna,* or Wisdom. Influenced by the contemporary ascendancy of Neo-Taoism, there was a concern for the nature of ultimate reality and its relation to things. The names of the individual schools reflected rudimentary traces of Indian Buddhist philosophical tendencies.

The later major schools of Chinese Buddhism developed during the T'ang age in an endeavor to interpret Buddhism on its own terms. Efforts were made to ensure orthodoxy by the construction of doctrinal lineages. Ten schools emerged of which five had distinct Indian character and were limited in their overall influence on the Chinese mentality. These schools represented the Hinayanistic Satyasiddhi, Abhidharma Kosa, and Vinaya teachings and the Mahayanistic Yogacara and Madhyamika philosophies. More consonant with Chinese spirit were the T'ien-t'ai, Hua-yen, Ch'an, and Ching-t'u schools, which have had wide influence in Japan as well as

Eleven-headed Kuan-yin from the T'ang Dynasty, early eighth century. (Courtesy of the Cleveland Museum of Art, gift of Mr. and Mrs. Severance A Millikin.)

China. The Mantra or Cheng-yen school, transmitting Tantric teachings, did not become fully systematized in China but was absorbed into the traditions of other schools.

The transformation of Indian Buddhism into Chinese Buddhism appeared as early as Seng-chao, the famous Madhyamika teacher, when he asserted: "Reality is wherever there is contact with things." [2] This statement contrasted with the Indian emphasis on the delusive character of the world motivating withdrawal. Chinese Buddhists were critical of the Indian tradition for attempting to abolish the spiritual domination of the world over man by doing away with the world. For the Chinese, wisdom was not divorced from the

---

2. Wing-tsit Chan, *A Sourcebook in Chinese Philosophy,* Princeton, N.J., Princeton University Press, 1963, p. 356.

things of the world but rather wisdom revealed their true nature. Seng-chao declared:

> *Hence the sage is like an empty hollow. He cherishes no knowledge. He dwells in the world of change and utility, yet he holds himself to the realm of non-activity (wu-wei). He rests within the walls of the nameable, yet lives in the open country of what transcends speech. He is silent and alone, void and open, where his state of being cannot be clothed in language. Nothing more can be said of him.*[3]

With reminiscences of Taoist terminology and thought, Buddhism took up the cause of world affirmation.

The Hua-yen School

The development of a more this-worldly interpretation of Buddhism received a strong philosophical support in the thought of Fa-tsang (643–712) who expounded a complex system based on the *Avatamsaka (Hua-yen) Sutra*. In his famous parable of the golden lion presented before Empress Wu (684–705) we have a striking illustration of the ability of Buddhist teachers to render abstruse doctrines intelligible through analogies from the everyday world. Commanded to demonstrate the truth of his school, Fa-tsang explained the ten basic principles of Hua-yen philosophy concerning the relationship of ultimate reality to things by referring to a golden lion standing in the hall.

According to Fa-tsang, the ultimate teaching of Buddhism was the principle of the mutual interpenetration of all things as a result of their being manifestations of the one, all-embracing Buddha-mind. Things in the world had a degree of reality as expressions of the absolute Buddha-mind within things. Corresponding to aspects of objective idealism in the West, the teaching combined logical and psychological insight, making it one of the most influential philosophies in Chinese and Japanese Buddhism. It not only synthesized major philosophical currents in Mahayana thought, but its universal vision and ideal of mutuality within the whole inspired mystical endeavor and contained sociopolitical implications.

The T'ien-t'ai School

The face of Chinese Buddhism began to show itself in the formation of the T'ien-t'ai school, whose name was taken from the mountain in South China where the founder Chi-i (531–597) resided. This fact suggests the Chinese concern and interest in this world.

The central texts for this sect were the *Lotus Sutra (Fa-hua-ching)*. Its teaching combined in a unified system the central Mahayana doctrines of universal Buddha nature, mutual interpenetration of all things, and the theory of instantaneous enlightenment. Although there were several predecessors in the development of the school, Chi-i was the pivotal figure in completing the doctrinal system. His character, depth of learning, and intellectual power have been unparalleled in Chinese Buddhist history.

---

3. Yu-lan Fung, *History of Chinese Philosophy,* Princeton, N.J., Princeton University Press, 1953, vol. II, p. 268.

The T'ien-t'ai school attempted to confront the increasingly difficult problem of the diversity of teachings attributed to the Buddha flowing into China from India. Each doctrinal system claimed to be the direct teaching of the Buddha because all sutras opened with an affirmation that they had been originally recited by Ananda, Buddha's companion and original transmitter of his teachings.

It was Chi-i's contribution to develop a comprehensive historical-doctrinal organization of Buddhist texts and doctrine covering Buddha's lifetime which set the pattern for later thought in Chinese and Japanese Buddhism. He gave an account of the order of appearance of Buddhist teachings involving a theory of progression to the ultimate truth of the *Lotus* and *Nirvana Sutras.* His system came to be known as the theory of "Five Periods and Eight Doctrines."

Briefly stated, during the first period of twenty-one days the Buddha attempted to teach the profound doctrine of the *Hua-yen-ching.* However, his disciples did not have the capacity to understand. Consequently, he had to devote himself during the next twelve years to the propagation of Hinayana doctrine. In this time he hoped to induce individuals to higher aspirations by using a simple doctrine. In the third period, covering eight years, some individuals converted to elementary Mahayana teaching, while others were rebuked for rejecting this doctrine. The fourth stage of twenty-two years centered on the propagation of the *Prajna (Wisdom) Sutras.* The Mahayana concept of Voidness was stressed. In the fifth and final period of eight years the Buddha proclaimed the doctrine of the *Lotus* and *Nirvana Sutras* as the supreme way of Buddhism. Correlated with the different periods of Buddha's life and teachings Chi-i developed a set of criteria for distinguishing various forms of doctrine with the aim of showing the superiority of full Mahayana teaching over earlier Hinayana or elementary expressions of Mahayana philosophy.

The theory of five periods represented a quasi-historical attempt to place the Buddhist texts in their approximate historical order based on the perception of growth in the depth and breadth of Buddhist insight on the nature of salvation and the world in the development from Hinayana to Mahayana philosophy. The criteria for evaluating doctrines reflected pedagogical and mystical insight. Its major contribution to the development of Buddhist thought lay in its systematic and scholarly approach, drive for unity and coherence, and theory of religious development. Further, its universalistic philosophy, expressed in the theory of "three thousand in one moment (or instant) of thought," proclaimed, like the Hua-yen philosophy, that everything is the essence of every other thing from the standpoint of ultimate reality. Consequently, this philosophy also asserted the importance and reality of the things of this world as embodiments of the universal Buddha-nature.

The Ch'an (Zen) School

Ch'an (Zen) Buddhism appeared as the culmination of several trends within Chinese Buddhism. Combining with Taoist iconoclasm, it was, in a measure, a reaction to the scholasticism and lifeless formalism of T'ang Buddhism. It attempted, through the discipline of meditation, to bring to full practical and experiential realization the principles of universal Buddha-nature and instantaneous enlightenment. It also focused attention on life in this world, fusing with Taoist love of Nature. The emphasis on egolessness and nonduality (Buddhism) together with the resulting qualities of naturalness and spontaneity (Taoism) achieved the complete assimilation of Buddhism within the Chinese spirit.

The term Ch'an or Zen was derived from the word *dhyana,* meaning "meditation" in Sanskrit. In the sense that meditation is the heart of Buddhism, Ch'an claimed to be the most essential aspect of Buddhist life. Originally meditation was a discipline of regulated sitting, breathing exercises, and mental exercises designed to still the passions and bring discursive thought to a halt. Indian Yoga techniques provided the basic elements for this endeavor. In China, India's elaborate system of meditation underwent considerable modification in its adaptation to Chinese ways. Influenced by Taoist nature mysticism and Chinese interest in this life, meditation aimed at instantaneous enlightenment. Rather than merely bringing discursive thought to a halt, Chinese Buddhists directed their effort at realizing their fundamental identity with the absolute reality surrounding them in the world of Nature. This identity produced a new awareness of the world in which the singularity of things in the given world at the same time revealed the allness of the Buddha-nature.

As a specific tradition in Chinese Buddhism, Ch'an had a long history. Though shrouded in conflicting legends there appeared numerous schools claiming to transmit the true doctrine and practice of Ch'an. The main divisions were the Northern school, derived from the monk Shen-hsiu (605–706) who is described as maintaining a gradualist approach to enlightenment, while the Southern school, stemming from Hui-neng (638–713), emphasized instantaneous enlightenment. In the contest between these two factions the Southern school became the main stream of tradition for present schools. The basic text for this tradition was the *Platform Sutra* attributed to Hui-neng.

The story of Hui-neng and the teaching given in the *Platform Sutra* manifests certain religious characteristics of Ch'an noteworthy for their social implications. The account of Hui-neng's entrance into the monastic life and his eventual assumption of spiritual leadership depicts the democratic principle in Ch'an in which all beings equally possess the potentiality to manifest Buddha-nature. Lowly people are not to be despised. Thus Hui-neng, an illiterate woodcutter, attains enlightenment and displaces Shen-hsiu who, by virtue of training and background, is in line for leadership. The stress on illiteracy and lowly background of Hui-neng may be a comment on the scholasticism and formality in the great schools in much of Chinese Buddhism of that time. Hui-neng retorts to his master Hung-jen's assertion that he was a barbarian:

> *I replied: "Although people from the south and people from the north differ, there is no north and south in Buddha nature. Al-*

> though my barbarian's body and your body are not the same, what difference is there in our Buddha nature?" [4]

The spiritual revolution urged by Hui-neng discounted the external religious activities of building temples, giving alms or offerings, or mechanically reciting sutras. Merit in Ch'an Buddhism meant "inwardly [to] see the Buddha nature; outwardly, practice reverence." [5]

The rejection of externality and formality was carried further by the monk I-hsuan (d. 867) who declared the essence of Buddhism as the natural way of life:

> The Master told the congregation: "Seekers of the Way. In Buddhism no effort is necessary. All one has to do is to do nothing, except to move his bowels, urinate, put on his clothing, eat his meals, and lie down if he is tired. The stupid will laugh at him, but the wise one will understand. An ancient person said, 'One who makes effort externally is surely a fool.'" [6]

The radicality of I-hsuan's rejection of the obstructive attachment to externalities and forms burst forth in his demand to his disciples to "Kill the Buddha if you happen to meet him. Kill a patriarch or an arhat if you happen to meet him. Kill your parents or relatives if you happen to meet them. Only then can you be free, not bound by material things, and absolutely free and at ease.[7]

As the Southern school of Ch'an developed after Hui-neng and his disciple Shen-hui (670–762), who led the attack on the Northern school, two other schools appeared which became most influential in the progress of Ch'an in China and in Japan to the present day. These two important streams were that of Lin-chi, established by the monk I-hsuan, and the Ts'ao-tung, formed by the monk Liang-chieh (807–869). The major difference between these two schools united in aim and philosophy was the method undertaken to attain enlightenment. The Lin-chi (Japanese *Rinzai*) employed a method whereby the disciple was catapulted into enlightenment through pondering a riddle (*kung-an, koan*) and subjection to physical shock by means of a shout or blow causing the individual to release his grip on reason. The Ts'ao-tung (*Sodo*) school was more tranquil and emphasized quiet meditation under the direction of a master which would lead to the realization of one's Buddha-nature.

As the Ch'an perspective took shape, five basic principles emerged to guide its basic way of life.[8] These principles were frequently dramatically presented in the many stories used in the training of the monk as the basis of his meditation.

The first principle, that "the highest truth or first principle is inexpressible," indicates that Ch'an strives for an experience of reality beyond words and is not satisfied with merely conceptual knowl-

---

4. Philip B. Yampolsky, *The Platform Sutra of the Sixth Patriarch,* New York, Columbia, 1967, pp. 127–128.
5. Ibid., p. 156.
6. Chan, op. cit., p. 445.
7. Ibid., pp. 447–448.
8. Based on the discussion provided by Fung, op. cit., pp. 388–406.

Hui-neng, sixth patriarch of the Ch'an sect, chopping bamboo at the moment of enlightenment, from the Southern Sung Dynasty, probably end of the twelfth century. (Courtesy of the Tokyo National Museum.)

edge. This experience is called Void because it cannot be defined, but it is also called Buddha-nature or Original-nature as a symbol of union with the root of our being.

Buddhist philosophy, unlike some contemporary philosophies, is one of experience, a self-evidential experience. Consequently Ch'annists generally refuse to engage in merely rational argument and appear pretentious in their retort: "Try it yourself."

The second principle, that "spiritual cultivation cannot be cultivated," is a paradoxical assertion emphasizing the fact that religious endeavors which may begin on the conscious level must eventually be made second nature and part of the instinctive, spontaneous reactions of our personalities. When this aim is attained, one does not practice Buddhism; one is in his deepest being Buddhist. The conquest of conscious goodness abolishes affectedness and competition from religious life.

The third principle, that "in the last resort nothing is gained," refers to the fact that the world is not abolished, nor are we transferred to another realm by the fact of enlightenment. The true existence of this world is affirmed in all its depth. However, our understanding is transformed: "When I began to study Zen, mountains were mountains; when I thought I understood Zen, mountains were not mountains; but when I came to full knowledge of Zen, mountains were again mountains." [9]

The fourth principle states: "There is not much in Buddhist teaching." This is not to be taken as an expression of doubt or unbelief. Rather, it is a declaration that concepts, doctrines, and words are inferior to the experience of enlightenment itself. From the highest perspective there is really neither Buddha, Buddhists, nor Buddhism. We noted above I-hsuan's instruction to his disciples that if they meet Buddha, they should kill him. If one perceives Buddha over against himself, he is still caught in the net of discriminating abstractions. The whole attempt of Buddhist discipline, generally, is to actualize in experience what is learned in concept.

Related to this principle also is the claim that Ch'an Buddhism is a transmission beyond scriptures. There are, of course, scriptures and important texts, but the experience to which Ch'an aspires is not gained from books but through persons. Famous stories of insight gained by disciples through striking encounters with the master under whom they were training emphasize the person-to-person contact which accounts for some of Ch'an's modern appeal.

The fifth principle declares that "in carrying water and chopping wood: therein lies the wonderful Tao." It is a vivid comment on the texture of religious existence. Ch'annists have developed their specific forms of education and monastic life. Nevertheless, the sentiment exists that enlightenment is not itself confined to definite practices but may come instantly in the course of carrying out the most menial tasks. As the world is the world, and Buddha-nature is universal, one may realize it anywhere. Such a viewpoint intensifies the

---

9. D. T. Suzuki, *Studies in Zen,* New York, Dell, 1955, p. 187.

significance of even the most elementary acts. Hence, Ch'an has had extraordinary influence in art. In an age when the significance of individuals and persons appears to be declining in mass society, Ch'an stresses one's inner and ultimate identity in deep interpersonal relation with others. Artificialities are to be swept away. The emphasis on the validity of daily life as the sphere of ultimate reality and meaning also supports the individual in his quest for self-understanding.

The final major tradition of Chinese Buddhism which we must consider is the Pure Land tradition (Chinese *Ching t'u,* Japanese *Jodo*). This teaching attracted the popular masses through its offer of a simple way to salvation through reciting the name of *Amitabha* Buddha (Chinese *O-mi-to-fo,* Japanese *Amida*). The faith and practice of recitation would permit the individual to be born in the Pure Land, from which state he would eventually be assured the achievement of Nirvana or realization of Buddhahood.

The Pure Land School

The Pure Land in Buddhist mythology was created by Amitabha Buddha as the result of his vows to save all beings and the infinite merit he acquired through aeons of practice. In the Chinese mind it represented a glorious heaven beyond the travail of this world and easily accessible through reciting the Buddha's name in faith. In order to stimulate faith in the Pure Land, there were Buddhist texts which depicted the alternative destiny of birth in one of many hells for those who ignored or despised that faith. These teachings coincided with belief in heavens and the quest of immortality which had developed in religious Taoist tradition.

Like other schools, the Pure Land teachers sought in Buddhist tradition for texts and teachers in order to construct an orthodox lineage for the doctrine. They believed Buddha Sakyamuni taught the doctrine in three central texts, the *Wu-liang-shou-ching* (*Great Sukhavati-vyuha Sutra*), the *O-mi-t'o'ching* (*Short Sukhavati-vyuha Sutra*), and the *Kuan-wu-liang-shou-ching* (*Amitayur-dhyana Sutra*). It was then reputedly passed on through the famous Indian Mahayana teachers Nagarjuna and Vasubandhu. Eventually it made its way to China, where it was practiced by such outstanding monks as Hui-yuan who formed the White Lotus Society for the purpose of meditating on Amitabha Buddha.

T'an-luan (476–542) was responsible for the popular development of the doctrine. He was followed by Tao-cho (c. 645) and Shan-tao (613–681). In addition to this line of transmission, other teachers promoted the doctrine either as a subsidiary aspect to one of the more philosophical schools such as Ch'an or T'ien-t'ai or as the central teaching.

The first major figure in the Chinese tradition was T'an-luan from the area of Wu-t'ai-shan in North China. Living in an environment infiltrated with magical religion, T'an-luan engaged upon a search for the elixir of immortality following a long illness. Having obtained texts containing formulas from a Taoist master in the south of China, he returned home. On the way, legend relates, he met the Indian monk Bodhiruci who convinced him that true everlasting life was attained through Pure Land teaching. Casting aside his Taoist texts, he became a teacher of Pure Land doctrine.

T'an-luan popularized Pure Land doctrine by joining it to the theory of the decline of Buddhism. According to this theory, which became basic to Pure Land doctrine in China and Japan, the purity of the Buddhist Order, doctrine, and discipline and the ability to achieve enlightenment decreased as the inspiration of Buddha receded into the historical past. Finally, the last age of the decline and disappearance of Buddhism arrived when no Buddha was present and extremes of egoism, passion, stupidity, anger, pride, and doubt dominated human life. During this age, men did not practice or attain Buddhist ideals, though the doctrine was taught.

On the background of the degeneracy of Buddhism, T'an-luan held that ordinary mortals could achieve salvation through the recitation of Amitabha's name. Rather than depending on one's own power (self-power), mortals had to rely on the saving power of Amitabha deposited in his name. This method of salvation was designated the "easy" way in contrast to the "difficult" ways of meditation and austerities of earlier Buddhism.

The teaching was later systematically organized by Shan-tao, who made the practice of recitation of Buddha's name the central Buddhist discipline. Analyzing the doctrine into the method of meditation, attitudes, and conditions of practice, he developed a comprehensive interpretation of religious life. Through his writings he defended Pure Land doctrine against proponents of the more traditional modes of Buddhist discipline and set the stage for its later flourishing in Japan.

The evolution of Pure Land teaching coincided with the Chinese tendency to affirm life in this world, despite its other-worldly emphasis, because it opened the doors of salvation to the lowliest common man. Through the simple vocal recitation, and without arduous or strict regimentation, individuals could achieve salvation, while fulfilling their family and social obligations.

BUDDHISM IN CHINESE SOCIETY

As Buddhism spread through Chinese society it met sporadic opposition from either Confucian or Taoist exponents who regarded it as inimical to the health and progress of Chinese society and culture. As a consequence of their criticisms and the traditional control over religion maintained by the Chinese government, Buddhism was constantly under the surveillance of the state even when officials patronized the order for the sake of merit. The result of these conditions was to keep Buddhism institutionally weak but not to interfere with its permeation of the masses. Buddhism reached the peak of its influence in the Sui and T'ang periods, where it blossomed with great intellectual and spiritual creativity witnessed in the various schools.

The comparison of the state of Buddhism after the T'ang period with its prosperity during that age gives the impression that Buddhism entered into a state of continuing decline and lethargy with few signs of vitality. The persecution of Buddhism in 845, which was most severe and damaging, signaled the end of Buddhist influence on the higher levels of society. In addition, Confucian knowledge had begun to revive and spread during the T'ang age. Confucian scholars eventually displaced Buddhist intellectual leadership. Beginning with the memorial of the scholar Han Yu (786–824) against Buddhist superstition, the criticism of Buddhism mounted and reached its zenith in the Sung and Ming Neo-Confucian schools which attempted to deal with issues raised by Buddhism from a Confucian standpoint. In contrast to the other-worldly and mystical tendencies of Buddhism, the Confucianists stressed practical efforts in the world.

Further, Ch'an emphasis on practice and discipline and its anti-intellectualism limited efforts to educate monks and contributed to the waning intellectual influence of Buddhism. Buddhist scholarship did not progress beyond the lines established by the major schools of the T'ang era. In modern times reformist monks such as T'ai Hsu have advocated the education of monks and have endeavored to revive scholarly traditions, particularly the study of the Wei-shih (Consciousness-only) school of subjective idealism which T'ai Hsu thought was most compatible with the scientific era.

With the change of circumstance Buddhism lost prestige among the wealthy classes, which also meant a loss of income. The increased intellectual competition and resistance led to more government control. On the popular level the government permitted the spread of concepts and practices which aided in pacifying the people, but the aspects of asceticism and other-worldliness were made to conform to Chinese interest in this world. Nevertheless, Buddhist influence in Chinese society and culture has been extensive through its two thousand-year history, and it can be discerned in language, popular ideas, beliefs about afterlife, festivals, arts, literature, and philosophy.

Buddhism as a specific faith became relegated to a popular religion on the level of religious Taoism with which it generally fused. Among the common people the Buddhas and Bodhisattvas together with Taoist deities became the protectors of the common man in his struggle for existence. He implored divinities for aid in avoiding disaster and recovery from disease or misfortune. Buddhism became largely associated with the performance of funerals as a consequence of the promise of a glorious destiny promoted by the Pure Land cult. It also developed masses and memorials for the dead, such as the Avalambana festival designed to save ancestors as far back as seven generations from suffering. Such celebrations enabled Buddhists to fulfill filial piety demanded by Chinese morality. Although Buddhism entered into a comparative state of decline because of its changing fortunes in society, there were some positive features. During the Sung period the development of printing aided diffusion of Buddhist texts. The founder of the Ming dynasty (1368–1644), Chu Yuan-chang (1328–1398), had originally been a Buddhist. He placed Buddhism under strict regulation, knowing its hold on the masses, and also reorganized the order, testing the scholarship of priests, building and repairing temples, and contributing to publishing the canon of scriptures. Further, there were a number of Buddhist scholars during the Ming period such as Yun-ch'i Chu-hung (1535–1615) who advocated the unity of the three teachings of Buddhism, Confucianism, and Taoism as well as combining Ch'an and Pure Land teaching. He also defended Buddhism against Christianity.

During the three hundred year domination of the Manchus in the Ch'ing dynasty, Buddhism suffered from oppression and strict control under the influence of Confucian orthodoxy. Also the T'ai-ping rebellion (1864) resulted in a great destruction of Buddhist temples in southern China. Nevertheless, some emperors had personal interest in Buddhism and favored it.

With the confrontation of China and the West, like the Confucians the Buddhists have also had to struggle to discover ways to cope with the cultural crisis. In addition, Buddhists have had to deal with skeptical and reform-minded officials who wished to seize their institutions and transform them to schools or museums. While the founders of the republic in 1911 appreciated the high moral outlook of Buddhism, they did not believe it supported democracy, since it was apolitical and too passive. The crisis, however, served to awaken interest in Buddhism among laymen as well as clerics. This interest was also stimulated by a religious desire to acquire merit for their future destinies. Thus laymen sponsored Buddhist publications, lectures, and societies for the study of Buddhism. They were also moved by a desire to unite Chinese society based on Buddhist ideals as a means of meeting the modern challenge.

Although materials are now becoming more accessible for the assessment of the role of Buddhism in modern China, it has suffered from widespread misrepresentation by Christian missionaries, Chinese Confucianists, the Japanese, and Communists. The Christians regarded Buddhism as superstition and the priests lazy and ignorant, while the Confucianists looked on it as parasitic. The Japanese tended to despise it as inferior to their own forms of Buddhism, while the Communists saw it as exploitive and reactionary to social and political progress.

Due to the general negative views of Buddhism put forth by modern observers, there has been a tendency to interpret Buddhism since T'ang times as one of complete decline, degradation, and loss of vitality until a revival took place at the end of the nineteenth century and early twentieth century. This view has been challenged through detailed studies of Buddhist institutions and history in the modern period. In some measure the serious practice of Buddhism has always been carried on by a few dedicated monks in a number of monasteries widely respected for their purity and rigor. Buddhism has performed a positive role among the people in caring for their spiritual needs. The revival represented by the flurry of activity largely developed by laymen can be regarded as a shift away from the central core of Buddhism, since the major element of Buddhism was its system of meditation and discipline whose function was to provide an alternative for the human spirit to the tedium, anxiety, and struggles of conventional social life. The attempt to adjust Bud-

Kuan-yin seated in the "royal ease" pose, from the Sung Dynasty. (Courtesy of the Museum of Fine Arts, Boston, Hervey Edward Wetzel Fund.)

dhism to modern conditions in the effort to make it relevant may represent the secularization of Buddhism and signal a true loss of vitality and meaning for the religion.

In the present situation the future of Buddhism in China hangs in doubt. Though initially rejecting religion in 1949, the 1954 Constitution guarantees freedom of religion. Nevertheless, the Communist regime has seized property and forced monks in great numbers to become laymen and join the work force. In comparison to its treatment of Christianity, also a foreign and international religion, the Chinese Communists have recognized the cultural contributions of Buddhism and its utility as an instrument of foreign policy in dealing with the Buddhist countries of Asia. They have maintained the Chinese Buddhist Association which engages in studies of Buddhist tradition as well as serving as a spokesman for government policy to Buddhists outside of China. Whether the Buddhist spiritual outlook can survive its complete subordination and subjugation to the interests of a totally secular political order remains to be seen.

SECTION TWO

JAPAN: RELIGION OF A SACRED PEOPLE IN A SACRED LAND

INTRODUCTION: RELIGION IN JAPAN

The emergence of Japan as a major world power after centuries of isolation has focused world attention on her peculiar combination of old and new, conservative and progressive, particular and universal. A strong historical awareness has been coupled with a sense of the unchanging essence of her people.

Though these characteristics do not differ essentially from features previously noted in Chinese tradition, they have attained remarkable durability as a result of Japan's relative geographic isolation and racial homogeneity. Consequently, Japanese native traditions and spirit have survived waves of foreign cultural inundation from China and the West.

Japanese folk religion, as the piety of ordinary people, shares characteristics in common with other cultures in its this-worldly, communal, pragmatic, magical, and adaptive features. However, the Japanese folk religion also embodies a sense of the sacredness of the land and the people, nourished by the beauty, fertility, and relative security of the environment. As a result of this strong racial sentiment which asserts Japan's central role in the cosmic order, all freely accepted foreign cultural elements are transformed to bring them in harmony with Japanese sensitivities.

This process is clearly evident in the adoption by the Japanese of Confucian, Buddhist, and Taoist beliefs and practices. Christianity has had great difficulty in gaining broad acceptance, unlike Buddhism, despite popular fascination with and the overwhelming pressure of Western culture in all areas of social and cultural life.

The highly variegated elements of Japanese religious tradition drawn from early native religion, Buddhism, religious Taoism, and Confucianism have been fused into a complex whole. The superstructure of Japanese religious tradition rested on, and was nourished by, folk sentiment and religious piety expressed in the manifold festivals and other spontaneous religious activities. The qualities and attitudes of the Japanese outlook derived initially from the masses who lived close to the soil and reveled in its abundance and glory. While folk piety has sustained the superstructure, manifest social expressions of religion in Japan have played significant roles in the history of the people.

In the interaction of these traditions the Japanese, like the Chinese, did not sense any essential contradiction. In a somewhat simplistic way it has been true that Shinto and religious Taoism advanced human interests in this life, while Buddhism came to be concerned mainly with death and afterlife in addition to aiding endeavors of this life. Confucianism focused upon social and individual morality.

THE JAPANESE PERSPECTIVE ON RELIGION

The integration of the various components of Japanese religious tradition can be more easily understood through a brief discussion of the Japanese perspective on religion. We can approach this perspective from three angles: this-worldly realism, communalism, and emphasis on purity.

The dominant feature of this-worldly realism has manifested itself throughout Japanese history in frank acceptance and enjoyment of life and the world. Japanese landscape with its great diversity and beauty inspired ancient inhabitants with the belief that it was truly a land of gods. This faith was further borne out by the abundant fertility of the soil. The sense of sacredness of the land and its productivity banished any deep disillusionment with existence as implied in the mystical philosophy of Buddhism. The awareness of the goodness of the land stimulated all forms of art and efforts to transform even the most lowly object into a thing of beauty. There has been a conscious attempt to harmonize man-made structures with their natural surroundings, attesting to a sense of kinship and unity with Nature.

The sense of awe and wonder aroused by the creative forces of Nature has also provided the basis for accompanying traits of pragmatism, eclecticism, tolerance, and a more intuitive, sentimental and nonintellectual approach to religion among the Japanese.[1]

Ancient Japanese awareness that gods and spirits resided in natural objects which particularly arrested their attention led them to exalt the concrete phenomenon and made them especially open to novelty and influences from all areas of their world. Hence they not only welcomed Chinese culture with its religious beliefs and practices, but they continued the transformation of other-worldly Buddhism which had begun in China. Further, it is clear that eclecticism and tolerance resulted from the need to find alternative effective ways to cope with the erratic and unpredictable aspects of Nature.

---

1. H. Nakamura, *Ways of Thinking of Eastern Peoples,* Honolulu, East-West Center Press, 1964, pp. 350–406, 531–576.

The Japanese were receptive to claims that Buddhism possessed superior magic powers for dealing with divine forces.

The intuitive approach has expressed itself in the widespread Japanese sentiment that Buddhism and religion in general is mysterious and profound. Concern for the mood and beauty of a ritual outweighs in significance any intellectual consideration in its evaluation. Also group sentiment has played a great role in determining thought.

A good illustration of the predominance of intuition over intellectualization in Japanese thought is the contrast in the ways of understanding the nature of divinity in Japanese and Western tradition. In the West philosophers and theologians attempt to define what God is; then they seek the evidences of his existence in the world. The Japanese, however, regard the impressions of beauty, mystery, awe, goodness, or ugliness which arise in encounters with things in the world as signs of the presence of divinity within those things. Thus the idea of divinity begins with the recognition of the special character of the object which points beyond itself to a more fundamental reality behind and within. There is no need to define or prove divinity in this context as in the Western mode of thinking, because the recognition of the peculiar significance of the object constitutes its quality of divinity. Divinity is not limited to a specific class of objects nor to one set of attributes. Aesthetically, this perspective encourages art and the exaltation of the common and menial. Ethically, it may be criticized that religion becomes morally irrelevant when goodness and badness, beauty and ugliness, are equally divine. However, Japanese tradition emphasizes the aspects of productivity, growth, and creativity in Nature as the prime qualities in life. This stress has moral implications which counter the apparent indifference to values in the awareness of divinity.

Japanese communal feeling began with primary commitment to the clan and family in ancient times. Eventually this commitment extended to the central Imperial clan which gradually grew more powerful as the government transformed into a centralized bureaucratic state on the Chinese model. Supported by similar Confucian principles, the Japanese came to view their country as a great family headed by the Imperial parent.

As the family-nation concept indicates, religion throughout Japanese history has been inextricably interwoven with kinship, group, and national concerns and relationships. On the village level the Dozoku kinship unit (a group of related, nuclear families in hierarchical arrangement involving status and obligations) has been the major religious unit. The concrete activities of religious festivals generated a cohesive spirit as all the members, aware of their common destiny, strove to secure the life of the group through ceremonies designed to stimulate fertility or pacify the spirits of the dead. The centrality of the kinship group was expressed in ancestor reverence, which has been an essential feature in every tradition, native or foreign, in Japanese history.

A significant implication of the importance of the kinship group in social and religious matters has been the priority of the group over the individual in all vital social matters. As a consequence, religious commitment and belief have not been emphasized, though conscious voluntary adherence to a specific religious system is not entirely absent. In general, one's religion and religious activity depended on his group obligations. The social organization required in food production in ancient times imposed limitations on individual expression, since the good was not sought for oneself but for one's group.

In the sphere of politics and government the Emperor came to symbolize the unity of the people as the supreme mediator between the gods and the people. He was the concrete expression of the divinity of the nation being a direct descendant of the Sun Goddess. Because of the unique status of the Emperor, the Japanese differed from the Chinese in placing loyalty to the Emperor and nation ahead of one's family. The theory of Japanese society gradually crystallized in the concept of *Kokutai* (National Essence), which provided the ideology of modern Japanese nationalism.

Emperor reverence also relates to the tendency of Japanese to form strong bonds of devotion to concrete individuals, whether Emperor, Lord, or teacher. This characteristic contributed to factionalism and sectarianism in later developments of Japanese Buddhism.

Japanese emphasis on purity initially centered on the avoidance of actions giving rise to physical or ritual pollution or uncleanness which could threaten the well-being of the community and the individual. In common with other lesser developed peoples, the early Japanese focused their attention on the external, concrete act. Eventually consideration was given to motivation and inner character.

The Japanese concern for purification was early observed by the Chinese and a central ceremony was the *Oharae*, whose text is contained in the *Norito* (ritual prayers) of the *Engishiki*. From this passage we gain concrete indications of the idea of sin or pollution among the early Japanese. According to the prayer, sins were divided into heavenly and earthly. The heavenly sins were

> *Breaking down the ridges,*
> *Covering up the ditches,*
> *Releasing the irrigation sluices,*
> *Double planting,*
> *Setting up stakes,*
> *Skinning alive, skinning backwards,*
> *Defecation—*
> *Many sins (such as these) are distinguished and called the heavenly sins.*[2]

The earthly sins were:

> *Cutting living flesh, cutting dead flesh,*
> *White leprosy, skin excrescences,*

---

2. Donald L. Philippi, trans., *Norito*, Tokyo, The Institute for Japanese Culture and Classics, Kokugakuin University, 1959, p. 46.

> *The sin of violating one's own mother*
> *The sin of violating one's own child,*
> *The sin of violating a mother and her child,*
> *The sin of violating a child and her mother,*
> *The sin of transgression with animals,*
> *Woes from creeping insects,*
> *Woes from the birds of on high (sic),*
> *Woes from the deities of on high (sic),*
> *Killing animals, the sin of witchcraft—*
> *Many sins (such as these) shall appear.*[3]

The performance of the rite of purification caused the gods to take away all the sins recounted above. According to the ritual, the Goddess Se-ori-tu-hime who dwelled in the fast-flowing rivers carried the sins to the briny ocean where they were swallowed by the Goddess Haya-aki-tu-hime. When she swallowed them at a gulp, the deity Ibuki-do then blew them all to the underworld. With the sins gone, tranquillity reigned.[4]

As can be seen in this early listing, sins were primarily social in character. Good and evil were completely distinguished according to whether an act was beneficial for the community or dangerous. The term good (*yoshi*) covered a wide area such as beauty, excellence, good fortune, and nobility. Bad (*ashi*) signified something evil-omened, inferior, and unlucky. In the mythology the polarization of good and evil was expressed in the *Magatsubi-no-kami* (bending Kami) and the *Naobi-no-kami* (straightening Kami). The former were gods of pollution and disaster, while the latter were those who restored things to a normal condition.

Although early Shinto possessed awareness of purity and pollution and good and evil, it did not enunciate a formal value system. Rather than setting up a scale of values, it sought unity with the Kami in each action. To attain unity with the Kami meant to cultivate a bright, pure, correct, and straight mind. The characters *mei-jo-sei-choku* (brightness-purity-correctness-uprightness) provided an outline of the basic values eventually employed to express the Shinto ethic. It also contained the potentiality for a more spiritual ethic of inward purity.

Though the Japanese concern for purity became more inward, it was not guilt-oriented nor ascetic since it believed in the essential goodness of man and was optimistic. Many Imperial edicts stressed purity of heart or the honest and sincere heart. In the fulfillment of vows, an important element was the declaration that one's heart and intention was pure. This perspective in Japanese religion can be observed in the vow ascribed to the divinity Hachiman Bosatsu:

> *Though much I see as I tramp back and forth*
> *Shall I ever forget the heart of a man*
> *Who is innocent and pure!* [5]

3. Ibid., pp. 46–47.
4. Ibid., p. 48. See also poem of Motoori Norinaga, in Tsunetsugu Muraoka, *Studies in Shinto Thought*, Tokyo, Japanese Ministry of Education, 1964, p. 152.
5. Muraoka, op. cit., p. 33.

Among the symbols of Imperial authority, the mirror represented the pure heart as interpreted by the Shinto thinker Kitabatake Chikafusa:

> *The Mirror harbors nothing within itself. As it reflects all phenomena without a selfish heart, there is never an instance when the forms of right and wrong, or good and evil fail to show up. Its virtue consists in responding to these forms as they come. This is the basic source of correctness and uprightness.*[6]

In addition to the ideals of purity of body and spirit which pervaded Japanese religious tradition, the principles of filial piety, loyalty, gratitude, and sincerity have been key elements in Japanese moral existence. A keen sense of duty and obligation has inspired individuals with serious purpose. These fundamental social values have received support and reinforcement from the religious traditions through the inculcation of ancestor reverence and the teachings of the various religious communities. Confucianism particularly strengthened Japanese moral sentiments and provided the theoretical structure for native morality.

As an outgrowth of the maintenance of purity and correctness, buttressed by the Confucian principle of li (propriety and decorum), the Japanese have developed a highly ceremonial and ritualistic culture. The necessities of recognizing status have shaped language, as well as social activities, extending from everyday ordinary affairs to major social and religious events.

The Japanese religious perspective harmonized well with religio-philosophical elements imported from China. Confucianism implemented moral and political tendencies through affirming hierarchy, authority, monarchy, filial piety, and duty. Religious Taoism amplified magical techniques and divination practices, while Buddhism expanded the scope of the Japanese understanding of human life and offered gorgeous imagery, ceremony, and pageantry appealing to Japanese aesthetic sentiment.

RELIGION IN JAPANESE HISTORY

The study of the manifold characteristics and tenor of Japanese religious perspective may be further amplified through a brief survey of the basic trends arising from the mutual interaction of the various components of the tradition within the changing conditions of Japanese society.

The indigenous Japanese religion emerging out of the obscurity of prehistoric times faced the subtle complexity and pageantry of Mahayana Buddhism which appealed to many facets of Japanese character. However, rather than fading from history before the pronounced sophistication and practicality of Buddhism, the two religions merged on the folk level, and the native tradition became more self-conscious through the compilation of its myths in the *Kojiki* (712) and the *Nihonshoki* (abbrev. *Nihongi,* 720) as a result of Imperial demand. Borrowing Chinese terminology, the native tradition came to be known as Shinto (the Way of the Gods).

---

6. Ibid., p. 39.

Despite the formalization of Shinto, Buddhist perspectives and activity dominated the Japanese religious world on institutional and intellectual levels, as witnessed by the great temples and Buddhist schools of the Nara (710–784) and Heian (794–1185) eras.

However, the national sentiment, grounded in Shinto faith in the divinity of the country and people, never permitted leaders to neglect their obligations to the gods of the people. While on the surface the foreign culture appeared stronger, the folk sentiment nourished the roots as an underground stream. Eventually, the foreign tradition transformed into the national image.

As a consequence of the combination of national sentiment and Buddhist tolerance, Shinto ritual and outlook on life persevered. In the Kamakura era (1185–1333) and in the later Tokugawa period (1600–1867) Shinto tradition became reawakened alongside the flourishing of numerous popular, lay-oriented Buddhists sects. Scholarly exponents of a pure Shinto without foreign accretions and associations appeared one after the other to lay the foundation for the restoration of the Emperor Meiji to political authority by appealing to the ancient Shinto awareness in the people. The modern political use of Shinto as the basis of Japanese nationalism depended on the latent sentiments in the minds of the people. Modern popular religious cults have drawn upon either Shinto or Buddhist traditions, taking advantage of the deep-rooted association of these traditions in the hearts of the people.

Despite tension and conflict in modern times, the two traditions complement each other, corresponding to the tension of universal and particular elements in the Japanese spirit. The universal, cosmic philosophy of Buddhism provides a vision of Japan as the kingdom of Buddha radiating Buddhist wisdom and compassion to the world. Shinto supports that sense of uniqueness and particularity in the Japanese which has prevented them from losing their identity in the midst of floods of foreign influence. It is perhaps not without significance that the Nichiren Buddhist tradition which incorporates both facets has burst forth, nationally and internationally, with some of the most active religious communities.

SHINTO: A DIVINE WORLD AND A DIVINE PEOPLE

EARLY JAPANESE RELIGION

The Shinto religious tradition has deep roots going back to the remotest times when the Japanese people established themselves on the islands, becoming enamored with their climate, beauty, and fertility. We have already noted that Japanese native beliefs mingled and fused with elements from China such as Confucianism, Buddhism, and religious Taoism, drawing from them moral, metaphysical, and magical features which supported their inner feeling of the essential sacredness of the land and its people. Traditional Shinto as it has come down in history has become a complex religion, making it difficult to separate native and foreign aspects. In this short summary we simply attempt to focus upon elements of Shinto belief, its thought and history, as background for understanding Shinto influence in modern times and its potentiality for the future.

The durability of Shinto religion can be highlighted by calling attention to features of that tradition which have maintained themselves from the earliest times. We gain our first glimpse of the religion in Chinese sources from the third century which describe Japanese religious and political conditions.

According to these texts, a major element in the ancient religion was concern for purification, achieved through water rites and maintaining taboos. The still-existing practice of clapping the hands when summoning or dismissing a deity was noted as well as the practice of divination. An outstanding feature of the religion of this time was the presence of a female shaman, Pimiko (Himeko, Sun Daughter), who acted to bring peace and order to the community after protracted strife. Her activity may have provided the model for the myth of the central female Sun Goddess, Amaterasu-o-mikami.

As with other ancient societies, the early Japanese were concerned with securing food and maintaining the continuity of the group, or otherwise prospering their lives. As means to achieve these ends, the Japanese early came to revere mountains, worship spirits, and resort to shamans.

In relation to mountains, Japanese religious tradition reveals three types of beliefs concerning their sacredness. Conically shaped dormant volcanoes, supremely represented by Mount Fuji, have been objects of reverence. Mountains have also been associated with fertility as the sources of the vital water. They have also been conceived as either residences of the dead or the way the dead ascend to heaven.

The belief in mountains as the abode of the dead or the meeting place between this world and the other can be seen in the ancient practice of burying kings in natural or artificial mounds (*yama*). In the poems of the ancient classic *Man'yo-shu* some fifty-one view the dead as living on a mountain, while twenty-three place the dead in the sky or clouds.

Ancestor worship and concern for the spirits of the dead became especially prominent in Japanese religious life from the eighth to the twelfth century and appeared in the literature of the age. As Hori points out:

> *All social and personal crises such as political changes, civil wars, epidemics, famines, droughts, earthquakes, thunderstorms and typhoons, as well as difficult childbirth, diseases, and deaths, were believed to be the result of revenge by the angry spirits of the dead. Sometimes they were believed to be caused by the angry or jealous souls of living men and women.*[1]

Such beliefs have persisted to the present time and ceremonies must be held to pacify spirits of people who have suffered untimely death.

The origin of such beliefs and their gradual penetration to all levels of society perhaps lies in the interaction with early beliefs in shamans whom a deity had possessed, the deification of nobles after death, and the beliefs in spirits of the dead and the belief in the essential equality of all people transmitted through Buddhism and Taoism. The association of the spirits of the dead with Kami of ancient Shinto was a gradual development brought about through linking the activities of reverence for the dead and worship of Kami as a result of political interests. Initially the worship of the souls of the dead and ancestors was not really central to Shinto. When it appeared, it was promoted by political leaders rather than by popular religious feeling. In Buddhism the belief attained its strongest expression.[2]

1. Ichiro Hori, "Japanese Folk Beliefs," *American Anthropologist*, June, 1959, pp. 61–63, 419.
2. Delmer M. Brown, "Kami, Death, and Ancestral Kami," in *The Proceedings of the Second International Conference for Shinto Studies*, Tokyo, Institute of Japanese Culture and Classics, Kokugakuin University, n.d., pp. 169–182.

The reason for the eventual predominance of Buddhism in such matters can easily be understood in the light of its development in India and China. The myths of India concerning the hungry ghosts, *Preta,* became the basis by which Buddhism enforced and stimulated practices of filial piety on behalf of the dead as a way of accommodating Buddhism to Chinese and Japanese outlook. These practices with their pageantry and variety also appealed to the Japanese imagination.[3]

Like mountain worship and worship of spirits, the phenomenon of shamanism has deep roots in Japanese religion. The earliest evidence from outside sources concerning Japan indicate the presence of shamanesses as in the case of Queen Pimiko (see p. 343). Though it has never been institutionalized, it has persisted to the present, appearing even in contemporary religions. Lacking institutionalization, it has also penetrated and combined with alien traditions such as Buddhism and Taoism.

Shamanism in Japan has generally centered upon shamanesses, though shamans are also present. In addition, the Emperor possessed a shamanic charisma both through his descent from the Sun Goddess and as the head of the Imperial clan. Although the Emperor himself might receive divine words through dreams or ecstatic experience, he frequently received communications through other shamans and diviners.[4]

The Shugendo system of religious practices, carried out on mountains and generally associated with Buddhism, functions on the popular level as the virtual amalgamation of all the elements of early Japanese religion. The practitioners, who devote themselves to ascetic exercises on the mountains, combine Japanese reverence for mountains and beliefs in spirits, Buddhist esoterism, and Taoist wizardry and magic. Since the Heian period the movement has largely become associated with Buddhism because of the monasteries located on mountains.

The complex of Shinto tradition with many forms and nuances has emerged from the stream of Japanese religious and social history and can be studied from a variety of angles, none of which are sufficient to elicit a full understanding of its outlook and function in Japanese society. One may view it in terms of the various types of cults in the Japanese environment, such as an agricultural-fertility cult, local cults of mountains or other features of the natural environment, or aversive cults centered on attempts to appease the spirits of important personages whose death was considered unfortunate as illustrated in the cult of Sugawara Michizane. In addition, forms of Shinto can be classified as Shrine Shinto, Sect Shinto, Folk Shinto, Imperial House Shinto, or Domestic Shinto.

3. The comprehensive study of the use of Buddhist texts in ancient Japanese Buddhism by M. W. De Visser, *Ancient Buddhism in Japan,* 2 vols., Leiden, E. J. Brill, 1935, illumines the character of early Japanese Buddhism and provides ample illustration of such magical use of texts. Also, Shoko Watanabe, *Japanese Buddhism: A Critical Appraisal,* Tokyo, Kokusai Bunka Shinkokai, 1964, pp. 82–99, discusses the background and development of Buddhist ceremonies for the dead.

4. Joseph M. Kitagawa, *Religion in Japanese History,* New York, Columbia, 1966, pp. 17–19.

The term "Shrine Shinto" is a relatively modern one for that aspect of Shinto which was supported by the state in its efforts since the Meiji period to provide a basis for national integration and feeling. In earlier times it was simply called Shinto.

Over against the political use of Shinto to reinforce national sentiment, "Sect Shinto" refers to individually founded modern religious orders based on Shinto beliefs and practices. "Folk Shinto" is applied to the magico-religious beliefs which are the substratum of beliefs and sentiment in all other aspects of Shinto. These folk beliefs serve individual or communal purposes. Through Folk Shinto practices the individual attempts to satisfy his various needs for health, wealth, and security in life, while the communal cult is the focus for harmonization of the local society, politically and culturally. "Imperial House Shinto" refers specifically to those rites carried out by the Emperor and his family, while "Domestic Shinto" signifies the worship centered on the god-shelf in the ordinary home.

Further, as a consequence of the intimate relation to society and its needs, we find that Shinto, as the religion of natural groupings, has functions connected to blood-related groups such as the Dozoku and represented by the *Ujigami,* or Clan deity, land-related groups such as the village community and symbolized in the tutelary deity of the area, age-related groups in which young and old have various responsibilities in the cult, and occupation-related groups in which deities care for the interests of various trades and crafts. In addition, groups termed "Ko" have a more voluntaristic character in which people become associated for some spiritual purpose such as a pilgrimage to a famous shrine like Ise. The influence of location remains strong in the relationship of people to Shinto shrines. A distinction is made between the *Ujiko,* who are believers living in the general area, and the *Sukeisha,* who are believers from outside that region.

Beside the various structural forms and practices which can be discerned within Shinto, its mythology and beliefs reveal the nature of the folk beliefs and also provide the basis for the cult of the Imperial house and national self-understanding. A history of Shinto thought results from interaction with many influences in Japanese history. Because of the multiplicity of factors in this development, it is difficult to uncover the precise nature of early Shinto, since even its mythology, given in the *Kojiki* and *Nihonshoki* (abbrev. *Nihongi*), was organized and recorded under foreign influence. Though the popular religion is very conservative and is perhaps a good source for viewing what may have been the ancient Japanese outlook on the world, it is difficult to isolate foreign elements.

Although the various elements of ancient Japanese religion have become associated with Buddhism as well as Shinto on the folk level, it is Shinto which, through all changes, has continued to provide the foundation of the Japanese religious consciousness as a sacred people in a sacred land. As the basis of their awareness of being a particular people, Shinto has evolved into a complex system paralleling the transformation of the people from a motley group of clans to a modern industrial state. Just as the Japanese became more self-conscious through the impact of Chinese culture, so also Shinto became awakened and sought formulation of its tradition distinct from the foreign systems permeating the culture.

In view of the many aspects of the study of Shinto, rather than being exhaustive we shall simply attempt to survey several significant aspects of Shinto tradition which may enable the student to better appreciate this oft-misunderstood and inadequately known religion.

We shall first give an account of the conception of deity and the character of mythology which set the direction for the tradition. Second, we shall observe the way in which the foreign traditions of Buddhism and Confucianism came to terms and appropriated Shinto. Third, in the face of the prestige of foreign religio-philosophical traditions, we shall inquire into the struggle for a pure interpretation of Shinto. Finally, in modern times we witness the expression of Shinto as a patriotic cult and as the basis of religious communities. Through the study of Shinto in interaction with its environment we become aware of its profundity and its strength, refusing merely to be absorbed into more highly articulate traditions.

KAMI: MYTH AND RITUAL IN TRADITIONAL SHINTO

In approaching the discussion of Shinto we must rely mainly on the materials provided by the *Kojiki* and *Nihongi*, though we recognize that they were the product of a specific class of people pursuing special interests. In addition, we gain important insight from the ritual prayers called *Norito* in the *Engishiki* and such texts as the *Kujiki* and *Kogoshui*. In all probability the great deities depicted in the texts had little relation to the popular masses, but they do reflect something of awareness and understanding of deities among the people. It is also necessary to recognize that Shinto was not consciously cultivated in early times nor systematically organized. Such religious activity and thought as were present constituted the Japanese response to their surrounding environment. Wonder at the mystery of the universe inspired the Japanese from earliest times. It is this awe of the suprahuman powers in nature that penetrates all areas of religion and is the basis of their conception of deity.

The central core of Shinto lies in its peculiar awareness of divinity which, from the ethnological view, points in the direction of a mana-like conception common to the Polynesians, and from the religio-philosophical view, is the basis for the more pantheistic tendency observable in the development of Shinto theology as it is elaborated in interaction with Buddhism and Confucianism.

Unlike the conception of deity in Western tradition, the concept "Kami" in Shinto does not refer to an absolute being who stands distinct from the world and beings he has created. Rather, "Kami" refers more to a quality in things, persons, and forces, whether good or evil, which raises them above the ordinary level of evaluation through the sense of awe, wonder, fear, attraction, or repulsion which the object arouses in the person. The Shinto scholar Motoori Norinaga (1730–1801) summarizes most clearly the understanding of "Kami" in Japanese tradition:

> *I do not yet understand the meaning of the term,* kami. *Speaking in general, however, it may be said that* kami *signifies, in the first place, the deities of heaven and earth that appear in the ancient records and also the spirits of the shrines where they are worshipped.*
>
> *It is hardly necessary to say that it includes human beings. It also includes such objects as birds, beasts, trees, plants, seas, mountains, and so forth. In ancient usage, anything whatsoever which was outside the ordinary, which possessed superior power or which was awe-inspiring was called* kami. *It is needless to say that among human beings who are called* kami *the successive generations of sacred emperors are all included.* . . .[5]

Further included in this category by Norinaga are not only spirits of emperors or people of the past, but some people in villages in the present. Among nonhuman Kami are dragons, echoes, foxes, tigers, wolves, peaches, rocks, stumps, leaves, and thunder. These all may awaken awe and wonder in the human mind.

The permeation of the cosmos by deity even to the lowest form of life has made the division between divinity and profane existence difficult to draw in Japanese experience. Not only the spirits of the dead may be treated as divine, but living persons may also manifest divinity. An outstanding illustration is the Emperor himself who is termed *Arahito-gami* or "Manifest Kami."

The awareness of the divine activating Japanese religiosity has been crystallized in the mythological tradition in the conception of the *Yao-yorozu-no-kami,* the eight hundred myriads of deities (eight million deities). This conception embodied the sense of the Japanese of the abundance and pervasiveness of the divine power through the whole of the cosmos and life. According to Holtom, the number of deities, many nameless, reached untold numbers, while at the time of his research 214 deities were acknowledged in state shrines.[6]

Though Shinto is a clear polytheism, its belief may be positively evaluated in the light of its awareness of the creativity and abundance in life. As one scholar of Japanese religion states:

> *Life, by its very nature, tends to be infinite. Historians of religion, by penetrating more profoundly into the religious reality, have come to recognize that former generations have misjudged polytheism. What they understood to be "idolatry," was never practised in this manner by any religion. Religious people, by worshipping a variety of objects, always intended one thing, the SACRED, which they expressed in many forms.*[7]

From among the superabundance of divinity acknowledged by the Japanese, the myths of the *Kojiki* and *Nihongi* focus on a modest

---

5. Quoted in D. C. Holtom, *National Faith of Japan*, New York, Paragon, 1947, p. 23.

6. Ibid.

7. Heinrich DuMoulin, "The Aspect of Creation in the Shinto Concept of Kami," in *The Proceedings of the Second International Conference for Shinto Studies,* Tokyo, Institute of Japanese Culture and Classics, Kokugakuin University, n.d., p. 26.

number of deities significant for Japanese religious tradition. In general, two groupings are important in the development of Shinto: (1) a triad of deities who are responsible for the creation of the cosmos and who initiate the cosmogonic process; and (2) deities directly related to the creation of Japan and the Imperial line.

The three deities—*Ame-no-mi-naka-nushi-no-Kami* (Kami Master of the Center of Heaven), *Taka-mi-musubi-no-Kami* (High Sacred Creating Kami), and *Kami-musubi* (Sacred Creating Kami)—began creation when there was still nothing but primordial chaos and no shapes had appeared. Unlike many other deities, they had no genealogy but appeared spontaneously and later disappeared. From the young earth which they had originated there eventually appeared a whole host of deities who make up the genealogical succession resulting in the creation of Japan and the Japanese people.

The very abstract and remote character of these deities made it possible in later times to employ them as more philosophical principles. Thus Hirata Atsutane in his interpretation of Shinto placed *Ame-no-mi-naka-nushi-no-Kami* as the central divinity, existing before Heaven and Earth. The elevation of this deity to absolute status, supported by the two assisting deities, had repercussions in the modern attempt to promote Shintoism politically.

The deities who initiated the process of creation or production of growth and life in the universe do not have highly concrete imagery reflecting the folk consciousness. However, the subsequent stories concerning the sexual activity, death, births, and conflicts of deities possess a vividness suggesting that originally those deities were once centers of cultic life. The myths were important in ancient Japanese attempts to secure food and the continuity of the group through ritual action. Analysis of various myths in the cycle in the light of myths of other cultures suggests that they reflect the conditions of the environment through their symbolism.

While these myths had their original locus in the cult concerned with food and sex, as they appear in the ancient texts of the *Kojiki* and *Nihongi,* they have a different function. In this context the original nature deities are transformed into ancestors and made the basis for the faith in the divinity of the Imperial house and the associated nobility. The narratives of the Age of the Gods lead to the history of the Age of Man which is carried almost to the point when the texts were composed.

As the society developed, the originally unorganized cult took firmer shape with more concrete conceptions of deity, formation of priestly functionaries, and establishment of shrines and rituals. In time various distinctions and nuances have grown up.

In the sphere of the divine a variety of classifications appeared. There were those Kami who represented the spirits of heroes or emperors of the past. These have had political and moral significance in the education of the people. There were deities which symbolized natural phenomena. Another category stressed functional deity. The creation deities could be viewed as the divinization of the power in growth. Certain objects came also to have the value of deity as the body of the deity (*shintai*). There were also divinities which resisted classification as illustrated in the head of the Idzumo pantheon, *Okuni-nushi-no-Kami*. Some deities were classified in terms of the region they oversaw, such as the *Ubusuna-Kami* or *Chinju-no-Kami*. Classifications also appeared in the types of spirits recognized in Shinto:

> *Traditionally, Shinto acknowledged four kinds of spirits—ara-mi-tama, those which rule with authority and power; nigi-mi-tama, those which bring about union, harmony, and recollection; kushi-mi-tama, those which cause mysterious transformation; and saki-mi-tama, those which impart blessings. There are suggestions that one and the same kami might have more than one tama. Spirits of enemies and those who might have met an unfortunate death, later known as go-ryo, were also believed to have potency. Moreover, the mono or mononoke (sometimes spirits of animals) were widely feared and venerated. All those kami and spirits could "possess" men and women, and those who were thus possessed were called* kami-gakari (*kami-possessed*) *and* mono-tsuki (*mono-possessed*), *respectively.*[8]

Originally priesthood was controlled by the head of the clan in group worship. Hence, initially there was no special priesthood. At a later time, now unclear, four classes of functionaries appeared. These were ritualists called the *nakatomi*, abstainers termed *imibe*, diviners or *urabe*, and musicians and dancers or *sarume*.[9] As early as the eighth century A.D. the control of the priesthood was located in the *jingi-kan* or office of Divine affairs.

The festivals of Shinto represented the people's active response to environmental changes in the quest for food and group survival. Many were thus seasonal. The major seasonal festivals of official Shinto were the Kinen-sai on February 4 with the object of praying for the year's crops, Niiname-sai on November 23–24 which was the harvest festival, and the Rei-sai or festival of the local shrine. Many of the national holidays celebrated in the system before the war were closely related to Shinto tradition.[10] According to Sokyo Ono the purpose of the festivals was:

> to ward off or ameliorate any misfortune and secure or augment the cooperation of the kami in promoting the happiness and peace of the individual and community. They include prayer for divine protection, communion with the kami, praise of the kami's virtue, comfort for the kami's mind, reports to the kami on the affairs of daily life, and pledges offering the whole life to the kami.[11]

The major elements of the shrine ceremony were purification, carried out by both priests and devotees. Offerings, prayer, and a symbolic feast composed the *matsuri* or service to the deity. In the

---

8. Kitagawa, op. cit., p. 14.
9. Holtom, op. cit., pp. 27–29.
10. Ibid., pp. 157–158.
11. Sokyo Ono, *Shinto the Kami Way*, Tokyo, Bridgeway Press, 1962, p. 50.

The creation of Japan. Izanagi and Izanami, Shinto gods, standing in the clouds creating islands out of sea water. Late nineteenth century. (Courtesy of the Museum of Fine Arts, Boston.)

deepest sense *matsuri* enveloped all life which was lived in awareness and communion with the gods. It also referred to specific occasions when the individual or community sought blessings from the gods or the prosperity of the people.

The more than eighty thousand shrines were formerly integrated into an overall system of classification. The status of a particular shrine depended on its national, regional, and local significance and received support accordingly. Presently, without government control or support, the shrines have become independent, though priests and shrines are generally related through the Association of Shinto Shrines.

Shinto mythological narratives and understanding of the nature of Japanese society have provided Shinto tradition with several theological themes which have been the subject of discussion in the development of Shinto thought. These were the distinction between the hidden and the manifest, the concept of *musubi* (growth, productivity), and the principle of *saisei-itchi* (union of religion and government).

The distinction of the hidden and manifest was important in the political and religious spheres of thought. On the political side, it suggested that the deities resided in the hidden world but gave the visible world over to men to govern. In religion it related to the contrast between the visible world of this life and the hidden world of the dead.

The concept musubi, generally rendered "creativity" or "productivity," has significant philosophical and ethical aspects as a basic value in the Shinto interpretation of life. Its fundamental importance is evident in the fact there are a number of deities whose name includes the term. The two assisting deities of *Ame-no-mi-naka-nushi-no-Kami* are *Taka-mi-musubi-no-Kami* and *Kami-musubi-no-Kami*. These three are considered the source of all creation according to the mythology. In addition, there are *Ho-musubi-no-Kami* (Fire-Creating Deity), *Waku-musubi-no-Kami* (Young-Creating Deity), *Iku-musubi-no-Kami* (Life-Creating Deity), *Taru-musubi-no-Kami* (Plentiful-Creating Deity). Further, the prolific generation of the gods depicted in the mythology directs our attention to Japanese awareness of growth, productivity, and vitality as the essential feature of the surrounding Nature.

The awareness of the productive goodness of Nature is the basis for the Japanese ethical recognition of *on*, the obligation one has to his benefactor and the gratitude which expresses it. To repay *on* is central to Japanese ethical outlook. Japanese concepts of purity and pollution are also related to the awareness of musubi in Nature. Emphasis on life and productivity leads to the identification of pollution with death as dramatically presented in the horrified flight of Izanagi from the decayed corpse of his wife Izanami in the land of Yomi. Life wins out over death and pollution. When Izanami declares she will strangle one thousand people every day, Izanagi promises that he will cause fifteen hundred children to be born every day.

Drawing upon these implicit themes within the tradition, contemporary exponents of Shinto have attempted to show that it can provide modern man with a viable view of life. Beginning with the affirmation of the life force, they hold that it becomes embodied in history through man's work and effort. There is frank recognition that religion cannot ignore the existential anxieties of modern life and it must seek voluntary commitment.

Another important theme which Shinto thinkers drew from the mythical tradition was the principle of saisei-itchi (union of government and religion). Forming the basis of the self-understanding of the nation, this concept teaches that the religious and political dimensions of life are essentially one, because the leader of the nation and its high priest before the gods is the Emperor. Commitment to the nation is an ultimate commitment and has manifested itself in modern times in the extremes of patriotic sentiment and sacrifice for which Japan has become famous in the reputation of the Kamikaze pilots of World War II. It has been manifested in traditional thought concerning religion and government in the word *matsurigoto*, which refers both to actions performed toward the gods (*matsuri*) and civil affairs. The term *miya* also means shrine and Imperial court.

Although this principle was not strongly enforced during the periods when the Shogunate (military dictatorship) was operative, during the Meiji period the principle was stressed and attempts were made to establish Shinto as the state religion. The object of the effort was to develop national consciousness and cohesion in face of the transitions needed to industrialize and modernize the state. The principle was enunciated in the proclamation defining the relation of Shinto and the state as the basis for a broad effort of indoctrination:

> We solemnly announce: The Heavenly Deities and the Great Ancestress (Amaterasu-Omikami) established the throne and made the succession sure. The line of Emperors in unbroken succession entered into possession thereof and handed it on. Religious ceremonies and government were one and the same (saisei-itchi) and the innumerable subjects were united. Government and education were clear to those above while below them the manners and customs of the people were beautiful. Beginning with the Middle Ages, however, there were sometimes seasons of decay alternating with seasons of progress. Sometimes the Way was plain, sometimes, darkened; and the period in which government and education failed to flourish was long.
>
> Now in the cycle of fate, all things have become new polity and education must be made clear to the nation and the Great Way of obedience to the gods must be promulgated. Therefore we newly appoint propagandists to proclaim this to the nation. Do you our subjects keep this commandment in mind.[12]

This principle has had to be set aside as a result of the Shinto directive issued in 1945 declaring absolute separation of Church

---

12. D. C. Holtom, *Modern Japan and Shinto Nationalism,* New York, Paragon, 1947, p. 6. Quotation taken from Imperial Rescript of February 3, 1870.

and State in Japan. Despite the abuses of the concept in modern times, it does hold the ideal that human society is not only an organized secular arrangement, but a spiritual reality in which mundane and divine affairs are completely integrated and harmonious.

Shinto religion has displayed through the centuries a capacity for adaptation and a potentiality for philosophical and religious development, stimulated by interaction with Confucianism and Buddhism. It is this factor which has given hope to adherents that it will adapt to the necessities of the modern age.

BUDDHIST AND CONFUCIAN ACCOMMODATIONS

When Buddhism and Confucianism entered Japan from China, they gradually came to terms and fused with the Shinto awareness of Japan as a sacred people and sacred land headed by a divine Emperor. The Buddhist accommodation to Shinto was perhaps more outstanding because of the cosmic, metaphysical, and other-worldly character of Buddhist tradition. Confucian morality with its own hierarchial, social theory harmonized easily with Japanese sentiments. Some differences between the Confucian outlook and the Japanese appeared in their rejection of Mencius' implicit principle of the right of revolution in his concept of the Mandate of Heaven and the Japanese tendency to place the interest of the nation, ruler, or lord above the family, though it was generally viewed that these elements would never be in conflict. Also, Confucianism was not theological or speculative. However, it was chiefly among Buddhists that more detailed theories of the relation of Buddhas and gods had to be worked out.

Though Buddhism has easily adapted itself to native traditions in other lesser developed countries, in Japan it faced a problem of a more profound nature in attempting to harmonize itself with the deep-rooted sentiment of the sacredness of Japan. On the popular level of folk piety, Buddhism merged with the life of the people much as in other places. The latent awareness of the more fundamental issue of the true superiority of the Buddha over the gods was reflected in the development of more sophisticated and philosophical theories, grounded in Mahayana metaphysics, which attempted to demonstrate the essential equality of the Japanese deities with the Buddhist divinities.

In order to spell out the relationship of the two traditions, two theories gradually grew up within the major schools of Buddhism in the Heian period and attained full expression in the succeeding Kamakura era. The system of *Ryobu Shinto* (Double Aspect Shinto) was formulated on the basis of the Shingon esoteric doctrine promoted in Japan by Kobo Daishi (Kukai, 773–835). *Ichijitsu Shinto* (One Truth Shinto) or *Sanno Shinto* (Mountain King Shinto) embodied the theory of the Tendai school established on Mount Hiei by Dengyo Daishi (Saicho, 766–822).

The essential idea contained in both theories held that Shinto deities were fundamentally manifestations in the world of the universal Buddha-nature. Although the Buddha-nature was the source of fundamental reality (*honji*), and the deities were trace manifestations (*suijaku*), the relationship was virtually an identification, since the essence of the manifestation is the original source and the two could never be separated. On the practical and concrete level the theory maintained that specific deities such as the Sun Goddess (Amaterasu-o-mikami) and Toyo-uke-o-mikami of Ise shrine were identical with the great Sun Buddha Mahavairocana (Dainichi-nyorai). It was not without significance that the concept of the Sun Buddha was used as the symbol for the unity of the people in the construction of Todaiji in Nara as Japan grew into a centralized state.

Confucian Shinto refers to the interpretation given to Shinto by the exponents of Neo-Confucian philosophy during the Tokugawa period. In a similar fashion with Buddhist thinkers, Confucian teachers maintained the harmony of Shinto and Confucian thought. The most outstanding advocate was Hayashi Razan (1583–1657), a counselor to numerous Shoguns and an outstanding figure in promoting Chinese culture.

In maintaining the harmony of Shinto and Confucianism, Razan was continuing the work of his teacher Fujiwara Seika. According to Seika, Confucianism was but another name for Shinto, since in their respective countries both were teachings expressing mercy and compassion for all the people.

However, Hayashi Razan carried the ideas forward in a more positive way. He criticized both the Buddhist views based on honji-suijaku and teachings which attempted to set forth pure Shinto. His version of Shinto emphasized one's obligation to principle (li) or sense of duty. He interpreted Shinto as the Imperial Way along Confucian lines whose essence lay in conformity to the rule of the Emperor. He identified the virtues present in the three sacred regalia in accordance with the virtues of the Confucian classic of the *Chung-yung:* the mirror was wisdom; the jewel, humaneness; the sword, courage. His theory had great influence on all Confucianists despite their varying tendencies.

THE STRUGGLE FOR PURE SHINTO

Concurrent with the assimilation of Shinto in Buddhism and the unification of Confucian morality and political theory with Shinto beliefs in the divinity of the Imperial line and sacredness of the nation, there were exponents of pure Shinto who wished to keep the national traditions free from alien influence. In their interpretations they utilized ways of thought borrowed from foreign traditions but always in the name of Shinto itself. The effort to express a pure Shinto reached its culmination in the teachings of the National Learning (*kokugaku*) scholars, particularly Kamo Mabuchi, Motoori Norinaga, and Hirata Atsutane.

The reason for the emergence of a self-conscious Shinto polemic and apologetic may stem from what was believed to be remarkable interventions of the gods saving Japan from the Mongol invasions in 1274 and 1281 through great winds (*kamikaze*). As G. B. Sansom points out, Shinto religion flourished in times of danger when the rulers called upon the national deities to aid the nation.[13] The clan-centered character of the Kamakura regime also contributed to strengthening of Shinto clan cults. Additional influences came later from the development of historical studies by Confucian scholars and the increasing dissatisfaction with the Tokugawa leadership and its failure to solve pressing political and economic problems.

A variety of schools of thought attempted to give a pure Shinto interpretation to Japanese tradition through relying on Buddhist or Confucian philosophy for the exposition of Shinto theology. Buddhism contributed to the development of pantheism in Shinto thought, while Confucianism provided an ethical orientation and reinforcement for patriotic themes centering on reverence for the Imperial house.

In the background of the struggle for a pure Shinto, there were a number of contributory streams. *Ise* Shinto, developed by Watari Tsuneyoshi (d. 1339) and Watari Iyeyuki (d. 1355), aimed to purify Shinto of Buddhist influences, based on the *Shinto Gobusho* (*The Five Books of Shinto,* forged texts represented as ancient classics) which exalted the Sun Goddess as supreme. The famous Shinto scholar Kitabatake Chikafusa (1293–1354) continued this work in his important text: *Jinno Shotoki* (*The History of the True Succession of the Divine Emperors*). Though applying Confucian virtues to the interpretation of the three sacred Imperial regalia, he maintained the superiority of the Japanese way to the Indian and Chinese. The *Yuiitsu* (Unique, One and Only) Shinto was a reaction to the Double Aspect theory of Buddhism and reversed the relationship of gods and Buddhas. Buddhas became manifestations of the absolute Kami. *Suiga* Shinto, set forth by Yamazaki Ansai (1618–1682), employed Neo-Confucianism in order to exalt the nation and give a basis for patriotism. Ansai stressed strongly loyalty and reverence for the Emperor. The basic virtue advocated by Ansai was *tsutsushimi,* defined as "a circumspect attitude; an attitude carefully obeying precepts and rules; an attitude careful not to be guilty of disrespect or failure."[14] Other lesser trends directed attention to the practical application of morality, rituals, divination, or ceremonies for the dead.

The most important development for the evolution of Shinto thought was the emergence of the National Learning school which, as seen in the parallel term "Restoration Shinto," aimed at reawakening and purifying the national consciousness based in Shinto against Buddhist, Confucian, or Christian influences which had penetrated Japanese culture. Not only does the movement reveal the intellectual potentialities of Japanese thinkers and Shinto theology, but its patriotic fervor also sets the stage for the modern employment of Shinto as the ideological basis for nationalism and national cohesion.

13. G. B. Sansom, *A History of Japan,* Stanford, Calif., Stanford University Press, 1958–1963, vol. I, p. 445.

14. *Basic Terms of Shinto,* compiled by Shinto Committee for the 12th International Congress for the History of Religions, Jinja Honcho, Tokyo, Institute for Japanese Culture and Classics, Kokugakuin University, 1958, p. 75.

Portion of the Shinto Ise Shrine, dedicated to the Great Sun Goddess. (Courtesy of the Japan National Tourist Organization.)

In the development of this tradition of scholarship there were several important individuals whose accomplishments built one on the other, leading to greater refinement of thought. Keichu (1640–1701) developed philological studies in connection with the classic *Man'yoshu* and turned attention from Chinese ancient learning to Japanese ancient learning. Kada Azumamaro (1669–1736) developed the concept of National Learning (*kokugaku*). He was particularly concerned with the lack of interest in Shinto studies in his time. Kamo Mabuchi (1697–1769), as a poet, attempted to grasp the ancient spirit in the *Man'yoshu* and strove to clarify the Japanese outlook before Buddhism and Confucianism came to obscure it. He turned the anti-intellectual and intuitive perspective of Taoism to use in criticizing Chinese tradition. Motoori Norinaga (1730–1801) and Hirata Atsutane (1776–1843) were the key figures in the background of modern Shinto thought and scholarship.

Motoori Norinaga brought the National Learning school to its highest development in purging Japanese and Shinto thought from its Confucian and Buddhist influences. In his attempt to revive ancient Shinto, he employed the studies of philology and concentrated his attention on interpreting the ancient traditions in the *Kojiki, Nihongi,* and *Norito* in the light of linguistic study and on the basis of their internal thought. He also studied deeply the *Man'yoshu*. Though he was scholarly in his method, a pious faith inspired his devotion to study. This faith resulted from his contact with three intellectual movements penetrating his time, namely *Dazai* Learning,[15] *Suiga* Shinto, and Pure Land Buddhism.

Building on the foundations of earlier scholars of National Learning, Norinaga explored every sphere of that study and wrote prolifically in prose and poetry. His most important writing was his commentary on the Age of Kami period in the *Kojiki* (*Kojiki-den*).

15. A more independent trend of Confucian studies set forth by Dazai Shundai (1680–1747) in the tradition of Confucian Ancient Learning was developed by followers of the Wang Yang-ming wing of Neo-Confucianism.

Itsukushima Shrine, dedicated to Ichikishimahime Goddess, niece of the Great Sun Goddess. Located on "Shrine Island" in Hiroshima, this shrine is part of the Shinto nature worship. (Courtesy of the Japan National Tourist Organization.)

Norinaga particularly focused his attention upon the *Kojiki* for understanding the Japanese spirit, where earlier scholars drew from the *Man'yoshu*. Despite its limitations as a spiritual document, it provided Norinaga with a basis for cultivating spiritual sentiment in the adoration of the Sun Goddess and the elevation of the deities Taka-mi-musubi-no-Kami and Kami-musubi-no-Kami as symbols of the life force.

Norinaga gave expression in a telling fashion to the intuitive, emotional side of the Japanese spirit in his attempt to displace the dominant Confucian rationalism. Appealing to the myth of creation in the *Kojiki*, he emphasized the mystery which lay at the heart of creativity. On the same basis he asserted the superiority of Japan over other nations, pointing to the unbroken line of emperors as witness to the fact. He suggested a messianic destiny for Japan, because she possessed the ancient way of the Sun Goddess. His sentimentalism was expressed most clearly in his claim that the Buddhist monastic discipline was in contradiction to man's natural disposition and essentially insincere, though correct from a Buddhist standpoint. According to him, truth lay in the expression of human feeling and sentiment. Hence, Buddhist rejection of sexual relations was erroneous. The spontaneous outpouring of love and compassion in the Ancient Way contrasted with the formalized, external ways of the Chinese. The primary value for Norinaga was sincerity (*magokoro*):

The heart that can be moved
Is a Sincere Heart.

> Those who boast
> That they cannot be moved—
> Are they made of stone and wood?
>
> To veil and hide
> The Sincere Heart,
> To put on airs
> To pretend—
> Such are the ways of China [16]

Hirata Atsutane represented the more intellectual side of the Japanese mind. He was unusual for his knowledge of Chinese thought and contact with Christianity and Western knowledge. His Shinto theology was influenced by ideas drawn from the writings of Matthew Ricci and Didacus de Pantoja, both Jesuit theologians. In general, his notions of creation and eschatology were derived from Christian sources.

Despite the Christian influences in his thought, Hirata was committed to the revival of Shinto and at the grave of Motoori he made a vow to be his disciple and to strive for the Ancient Way. He wrote numerous works including "treatises on maritime defense, Chinese philosophy, Buddhism, Shinto, medicine, and the art of poetry as well as elaborate commentaries on the Japanese classics and discussion of Japanese political institutions and history." [17] All his knowledge was permeated and woven together by his exaltation of Shinto as the highest knowledge. His major works were *Koshi Seibun* (*Composition of Ancient History*) and *Koshiden* (*A Commentary on "Composition of Ancient History"*).

Like Norinaga and other Shinto scholars before him, Hirata was an exponent of the superiority of the Japanese people in all areas, whether material, religious, moral, intellectual, or dynastic.[18] Particularly, the unbroken dynastic succession evidenced the superiority of the Japanese and their destiny to rule over all others.

Historically, Hirata's thought was of great significance as the basis for the establishment of Shinto in the Meiji era and a major influence in modern Japanese nationalism. This approach to Shinto did not differ greatly from his predecessors, except perhaps in the intensity of antiforeignism and nationalism. Though despising the West, he appreciated the value of Western science and the influence of Christian thought was evident in his concept of deity and afterlife.

According to Hirata the deities of Shinto were universal gods. Ame-no-mi-naka-nushi-no-Kami was the highest personified deity. The deity Taka-mi-musubi-no-Kami was the supreme creator of all. He used evidences from other religions concerning the existence of a supreme creator to support his contention of the truth of the Shinto teaching of creation. He wrote:

---

16. Tsunetsugu Muraoka, *Studies in Shinto Thought*, Tokyo, Japanese Ministry of Education, 1964, pp. 158–159.
17. Holtom, *National Faith of Japan*, p. 50.
18. Ibid.

> *Thus, in all countries, as if by common consent, there are traditions of a divine being who dwells in Heaven and who created all things. These traditions have sometimes become distorted, but when we examine them they afford proof of the authenticity of the ancient traditions of the Imperial Land. There are many gods but this god stands at the center of them and is holiest of all.*[19]

He took great comfort in advocating his position from the Copernican revolution which recognized that the earth revolved about the sun. According to Hirata, Japanese tradition had always recognized the centrality of the sun.

Hirata revealed his own independent thought in his conceptions of the afterlife. Stimulated by Christian conceptions, he went beyond his teacher Norinaga to give a comparable Shinto view. For him, the concealed and mysterious Kami world, which Norinaga had identified merely with the amoral Yomi or the land of darkness, was a world of souls where individuals who had become Kami on their death resided. Kami possessed various capacities and powers to reveal the future. This world was a place of testing, and all accounts would be squared in the world of souls. He also believed that souls lived in the vicinity of their graves and the spirit of Motoori Norinaga lived at Mount Yamamuro.

His contribution to the establishment of Shinto as a patriotic and national cult in the Meiji period lay in his interpretation of the genealogies given in the mythology and the association of the general ancestor worship of the Japanese to the worship of the deities of the Imperial House. He gave some attention to the problems of rites and ceremonies.

In summary, the National Learning school of Shinto provided the emotional, spiritual, and intellectual foundation of modern Japanese national consciousness. It involved elements of sentimentalism, rational criticism, a logic of its own based on faith in the uniqueness of Japan and her people, antiforeignism, and chauvinism. Though penetrated by a religious faith, it was political in centering devotion on reverence of the unbroken Imperial line, believed to be divine in origin.

When the intention of the scholars of this tradition is seen in the light of their nationalist faith, their scholarly capacity is more readily appreciated despite its distortions. They excelled in philology, classics, and literature. They frequently combined a wide knowledge of Chinese and Japanese tradition, and in the case of Hirata, knowledge of Western religion and science. The most pertinent criticism of their endeavor lay in the subordination of their scholarship to the goal of exalting the supremacy of a particular national and cultural tradition. This effort often resulted in the distortion of historical and religious understanding. Nevertheless, when viewed within the context of the changing fortunes of the Tokugawa era, they believed deeply that they were restoring the truth of their tradition which had been obscured through foreign influence resulting in

---

19. William Theodore De Bary, *Sources of Japanese Tradition*, New York, Columbia, 1958, p. 546.

the social decline then becoming more and more evident. The later fortunes of Shinto in the Meiji period suggest, however, that nationalist and particularistic fervor were no real substitutes for a foundation in universal truth supported by sound scholarship in the solution of problems facing the nation.

SHINTO—PATRIOTISM OR RELIGION?

In modern times the most significant outcome of the National Learning movement which stirred Japan during the Tokugawa period was the restoration of Imperial authority under Emperor Meiji and the establishment of Shinto as the official ideology and expression of patriotism. Japanese leaders responsible for preparing Japan to take its position in the modern world politically and industrially sought in Shinto the basis of national cohesion. They proclaimed that the restoration of the Emperor was the revival of the ancient Imperial way and the continuation of the creative work of Emperor Jimmu. Success in the effort depended on the citizen's revering the Emperor and worshiping the Kami and ancestors and on uniting religion and government.

To realize the goals of the new regime, Shinto was proclaimed the state religion, and Buddhism was purged from any association with Shinto shrines and ceremonies. The motto was *shimbutsu-bunri* (the separation of Kami and Buddha). The antiforeign and anti-Buddhist feeling which the restoration engendered appeared at times in violent ways. Temples were burned and destroyed and the slogan *haibutsu-kishaku* (abolish Buddha, cut down Sakyamuni [icons]) was heard through the land.

Doctrinally, official Shinto did not go beyond that already presaged in the National Learning school, and it was based largely on the thought of Hirata Atsutane.

With the establishment of the Office of Shinto Affairs there was set up a Board of Shinto Missionaries to propagandize and indoctrinate the people concerning Shinto and patriotism. It aimed also to check the spread of Christianity, particularly in the area of Kyushu. Eventually Buddhists also came to participate in the effort of indoctrination centering on three major points: (1) Compliance with the spirit of reverence for Kami and love of country; (2) Clarification of "the principle of Heaven and the Way of man"; (3) Exalting the Emperor and obeying the Imperial Court.[20] Various teaching institutes for indoctrination on a variety of religious and political themes were set up throughout the country, with the central one being the Daikyoin in Tokyo.

This effort was a history of failure for numerous reasons, symbolized in the successive governmental bureaus charged with responsibility for Shinto affairs. The propaganda effort also went through repeated changes which indicate the problems encountered by the government, until finally the whole effort was abandoned in 1882.

Numerous factors led to the collapse of the endeavor. Among them was the growing dependence on Buddhist priests to carry out

---

20. Muraoka, op. cit., p. 206.

the teaching of essentially anti-Buddhist doctrine. Also, the existence of numerous Shinto bodies which sought more independence as separate churches revealed the fragmentation of the Shinto world. Other more fundamental reasons centered on the fact that this attempt to institutionalize an ancient religious tradition uncritically was not in harmony with the demands of modernization and the need for Japan to measure up to the West as indicated by Fukuzawa Yukichi (1834–1901). In addition, there was the theological weakness of Shinto itself.

Fundamentally, such Shinto theology as had developed could not be entirely free from dependence on foreign modes of thought in order to meet the challenge of those systems. Buddhist, Confucian, and even Christian influences had been turned to the defense of Shinto. However, in the period of the establishment of Shinto this factor ultimately worked against it, particularly in that Hirata theology was the basis of the political effort to ground patriotism in Shinto. Hirata's views of creation and afterlife became focal points of attack in demonstrating that Shinto was a religion which lacked an adequate theology. Further, Hirata's theology was not without criticism within Shinto itself.

Progressives and conservatives among Shintoists also disagreed. It was also realized that it was unwise to subject religion to political control. The attempt to establish Shinto religion politically led to a cry for religious freedom and the separation of Church and State. Buddhists were outstanding in this effort to establish religious freedom, since they were forced by their promotion of Shinto often to contradict their own basic Buddhist convictions. Representatives sent abroad to observe conditions in modern nations informed the Japanese government that establishment of a state religion contradicted the trend in modern nations to separate the political and religious aspects of life because of the conflict between those areas.

A leader in the effort to achieve freedom of religion was Mori Arinori (1847–1889) who had studied in the United States and put his thoughts on religious freedom into a text, *Religious Freedom of Japan,* which he presented to Prince Sanjo. His basic point was that religious freedom and freedom of conscience was a prerequisite to human progress and civilization. He predicted the failure of government policy in compelling religious belief and activity. Another was Shimaji Mokurai (1838–1911), a Buddhist of the Jodo Shinshu school, who noted that while the government might feel a threat to the National Polity (Kokutai) in modern thought, one could not actually compel belief.

Despite the fact that religion and government were officially separated in the Meiji period, Shinto, defined as a patriotic cult rather than a religion, continued to play a part in the government's efforts to inculcate national feeling. As a consequence of defeat in World War II, the new Constitution made it explicit that the government must henceforth refrain from any religious involvements. The Shinto Directive set forth by the allied powers demanded that the militaristic and ultranationalist doctrines, supposedly found in Shinto, be abolished.

The problems of Shinto within the modern development of Japan have raised the question whether it is a religion or merely a patriotic cult. In the postwar period since 1945 voices claiming a non-religious status for Shinto similar to that applied in the Meiji era have attempted to secure revision of the Constitution and financial support from the government for Ise and Yasukuni shrines, both shrines central to nationalistic concern.

Other Shinto thinkers have maintained that the future development of Shinto as a factor in the construction of a new and modern Japanese society lies in deepening the faith and theology of Shinto following the true intentions of Norinaga and Hirata. They have welcomed the loss of privileged status because it opens the door to free and voluntary commitment to the ideals of Shinto and is the only way to harmonize Shinto with the needs of contemporary Japan.

Although on the official levels of government and scholarship, Shinto was artificially established as the state cult in the Meiji era, during the Tokugawa period and into more recent times there have appeared numerous explicitly religious movements inspired by charismatic individuals and based on Shinto beliefs and outlook. The sociological and religious characteristics of these popular movements are important as part of the background of post-World War II movements commonly termed "New Religions."

The social background of these sects was the political and economic decline of the later Tokugawa period. Internal problems arose from economic and political conditions within the feudal system. Rising taxation and higher prices pressured the peasants and exacerbated the continuing economic decline of the samurai class. Increasing dissatisfaction with the Tokugawa regime was expressed in local uprisings. Confrontation with the West symbolized in the appearance of Commodore Perry's black ship off Japan in 1853 complicated the problems. Eventually a royalist movement succeeded in abolishing the Shogunate and restoring the Emperor to power in 1868. He set about reorganizing the government and meeting Japan's many problems.

The disturbed political and social conditions reflected themselves in religion in the emergence of sects emphasizing morality, nationalism, or ways of salvation. Some sects criticized contemporary conditions and issued proclamations of a coming age where all evils would be corrected.

The Japanese appear to respond religiously to times of crisis. This tendency can be observed at the time when the Shamaness Queen Pimiko was made the ruler in ancient Japan. It appears also during the Kamakura period in the revival of Buddhism, at the end of Tokugawa in the sects presently under discussion, and after World War II with the New Religions. Recent studies of mass movements represented by the Communist-Socialist movements and the Buddhist Soka Gakkai movement reveal clearly the religious orientation of Japanese in their approach to problems. Although the Leftist movement confronts problems in Japanese society, it is highly intellectual and divorced from the feelings and needs of the common man, where the many popular religious movements not only attempt to deal with current problems, but also provide for the emotional and spiritual needs of the people.

In the later Tokugawa period the most significant of the popular movements which have maintained their existence to the present, such as Tenri-kyo and Konko-kyo, originated with people of peasant origin. In the cases of Tenri, Konotabi, and Omoto-kyo the founders were sensitive women sharing characteristics derived from the shamanistic tradition of Japanese folk religion. While these movements were purely religious, they instilled in the pious devotee a sense that his faith would sustain him during upheaval, and they prepared people to accept the changes in society. Through advocating a broadly altruistic morality, emphasizing loyalty to the nation and Emperor and instilling confidence that one could better his life situation through the cultivation of one's spirit, these sects contributed to the orderly process of modernization which enabled Japan to confront the West with minimum disruption to her own way of life.

The most detailed analysis of these sects is provided by D. C. Holtom who classifies the thirteen officially recognized sects of Shinto into five categories. In addition to those thirteen, Anesaki adds the Konotabi sect founded by the peasant woman Kino (1756–1826), while Kitagawa mentions Omoto-kyo, Seicho-no-Ie, and Hito-no michi which developed later in the Meiji and Taisho periods.

For the sake of convenience, we shall follow the general categories given by Holtom in depicting the significant aspects of these movements. The group designated as Pure Shinto includes Shinto Honkyoku (Main Bureau of Shinto), Shinri-kyo (Divine Reason Teaching), and Taisha-kyo (Teaching of the Great Shrine). These sects were called Pure Shinto because they worshiped deities central to ancient Shinto Tradition and were devoted to the realization of the ideals of Shinto religion. Based on a pantheistic interpretation of divinity, they all promoted a universal ethic regarded generally as the fulfillment of the divine will in man and the expression of the true nature of man. In some cases it was claimed that the ills encountered in life, physical, social, and mental, were all due to the failure to cultivate the true spirit. They also included elements from folk religious practices and ceremony. Though the teachings were altruistic and universalist, all groups were committed to cultivating nationalism through adherence to the three principles set forth by the government's propaganda.

The sects described as Confucian also followed the basic tenets of Shinto, but they buttressed these teachings with moral and social concepts derived from Confucian tradition. Representative of this trend were the Shusei-ha and Taisei-kyo. Shusei was a term derived from the words *shuri,* meaning to repair, strengthen, or improve, and *kosei,* meaning to consolidate and make secure. These terms, taken from the myth of the creative actions of Izanagi and Izanami, set the perspective for moral cultivation in the interests of the development of Japanese society. *Taisei* meant Great Accomplishment and combined Confucian teaching, Shinto religion, and encouragement of science in the service of the nation.

The Mountain sects consisted of Jikko-kyo (Practice-Conduct teaching), Fuso-kyo, and Mitake-kyo. These sects were based on traditional Japanese reverence for mountains. The two former sects had Mount Fuji as their object of worship, while the latter had Mount Ontake. Their aim, like others, was the security and prosperity of the nation.

The Purification sects, which include Shinshu-kyo (Divine Learning) and Misogi-kyo (Purification), emphasized ritualism as the means to attain the goals of national, individual, and human existence. Particularly, they supported the practices of ancient Shinto.

The Faith-healing groups such as Kurozumi-kyo, founded by Kurozumi Munetada (b. 1780), and Konko-kyo (Metal Luster Teaching) were distinguished by their stress on material and bodily welfare through cultivating the spirit. They were significant also in that their founders believed they received their teaching through divine inspiration or were possessed by deity. The revelations put in writing have become the sacred texts of the sect.

In the case of Mrs. Miki Nakayama (1798–1826), who founded the Tenri-kyo sect, and Deguchi Nao (1836–1918), foundress of the Omoto-kyo, a prophetic quality was present. Through her revelations Miki foretold the coming of a new age when the world would return to the paradisiac conditions of the age of the Kami, while Nao proclaimed the coming transformation of the world and a new age of eternal peace.

The Sect Shinto religious organizations have maintained their existence down to the present time. Some of them have split into subgroups so that they now total about seventy-five groups. Those with the largest following are the Taisha-kyo, now known as the Izumo Oyashiro-kyo, and the Tenri-kyo, which is the most active of all. However, their development since the war has been affected by the formation of other "New Religions" which have many similar traits but are less conservative than the older groups.

In the postwar period after 1945 and the granting of complete religious freedom, there was another outburst of religious activity stimulated by the anxieties, upheavals, and turmoils of the war. In their overall character the new groups resembled those religious societies which originated in the earlier period. However, the freedom of the postwar age permitted the flowering of such groups in unprecedented numbers reaching several hundreds and including many fraudulent groups. An early listing indicates 735 sects. After some sifting of fraudulent organizations, the number was reduced to 377 as of 1956. Among this large grouping, those of Buddhist orientation mounted to 170, while Shinto-oriented sects reached 142. A miscellany of others had Christian (36) or other (29 unclassified) background.

It has been pointed out that though many groups are incorporated as independent sects, they are really subdivisions of the three traditional religions and only about twenty-nine can be accepted as

"New Religions."[21] According to one recent study, 171 groups are potentially religiously significant, and the author describes twenty-two of the most important organizations.[22]

Apart from the sects of primarily Buddhist derivation among the "New Religions" we may simply take note that the Tenri-kyo, which was earlier placed among the Shinto sects of the Meiji era, also continued to expand with vitality in the most recent period. The Omoto-kyo, also a Shintoistic organization developed in the early part of this century, continued to attract attention. Several sects developed out of Omoto-kyo and attained widespread notoriety. Among these were the Seicho-no-Ie, Sekai Kyusei-kyo, and P. L. Kyodan. A widely known group of mixed background was Ittoen.

The phenomenal growth of religious mass movements has attracted the attention of scholars in view of the slow, plodding growth of political mass movements such as Communism and Socialism which in actuality have not been very successful. The religious mass movements are a combination of ancient and modern themes. Five common factors which have led to the appearance of these organizations are (1) a social crisis, or upheaval in the cultural situation; (2) a charismatic leader or inspired personality; (3) performance of miracles and wonders; (4) forms of ecstatic behavior as trance; and (5) syncretic doctrines. The combination of these elements in the modern context has led Margaret Mead to describe the phenomena as "the ferment of the half abandoned old and the half understood new."[23]

In contrast to the highly intellectual, alien, and radical pronouncements of political mass movements which are out of touch with the feelings of the majority of people, the "New Religions" have been very successful in concentrating attention on the concrete needs of the people for health, wealth, and security in the highly competitive mass society. A major element in the appeal of most groups is the promise of benefits through magical practices and faith. In addition, they support popular aspirations for democracy and peace. They emphasize youth and attempt to win the minds of people through comprehensible indoctrination and publishing efforts. This element contrasts sharply with traditional endeavors in religious education and with the abstract and intellectualistic approach of the political ideologies. Further, they cater to the need of individuals for recognition and status through offering means of mobility within the organization for ordinary people of devotion and zeal. A quasi-intellectual cast is frequently given to the organization by titling leaders as lecturers, professors, and assistant professors. A democratic flavor is often present in the society through discussion groups where believers may raise questions and witness their faith. However, in many instances the charismatic leader is the final voice of authority. De-

---

21. *Japan's Religions: New Religions: Directory No. 4,* International Institute for the Study of Religions, February, 1958, pp. iii–iv.

22. Harry Thomsen, *The New Religions of Japan,* Rutland, Vt., Charles E. Tuttle Co., 1963, pp. 11–12.

23. H. Neill MacFarland, "Japan's New Religions," *Contemporary Religions in Japan,* December, 1960, 1–4, p. 60.

votion to the leader and loyalty to the group frequently supply the necessary ethical guidance for individuals whose family relations have weakened in the modern context. The modernity of such organizations is often symbolized through the construction of enormous centers for worship or administration.

Despite the use of all forms of modern media to reach people, the basic teachings of most groups are reconstitutions of traditional Japanese values drawn from Shinto and Buddhist background and reformulations of the general metaphysical outlook largely derived from Buddhism. The traditional characteristics of such societies often lead critics to regard them as reactionary, retrogressive, and fundamentally conservative. Nevertheless, it is clear that they have functioned to provide the individual with a stable and familiar basis on which he may stand to cope with the pressing problems of contemporary existence.

Our survey of Shinto tradition reveals that the ancient religion had a durability and vitality through the ages, and though permeated by various influences such as Buddhism and Confucianism has been able to provide spiritual orientation in the face of perplexing problems on the level of intellectual leadership as well as on the popular level. Its close association with the Imperial political institutions as the basis for their sanction created a situation in which the permanence of the Imperial line was supported by its religious foundation, and the religious ideology persisted through the prestige gained in the recognition of the unbroken line of emperors. Consequently, in recent times Shinto became the spiritual and ideological vehicle for the expression of nationalism. While this was consciously cultivated on the part of government, it was not unnatural in the consciousness of the Japanese. In the present postwar period Shinto has suffered from the shock of defeat, but as a whole it was more than a cult of nationalism and through its symbolism it could be reinterpreted to provide a philosophy of life adequate to attract modern intellectuals. The spiritual tradition also displayed great potentiality as a resource for the emergence of new religious communities, which could orient men and women in a difficult world and constantly renewed their sense of being a sacred people in a sacred land.

BUDDHISM IN THE LAND OF THE GODS

INTRODUCTION

Though Buddhism initially entered Japan from the Asian continent by way of Korea and later through transmissions from China, it did not remain merely a foreign religion. Rather, it became absorbed into the Japanese way of life, adapting to the spiritual needs and social demands of the Japanese people, and became the second major religious tradition in Japanese culture.

The attitude of the Japanese toward Buddhism differed considerably from the Chinese who already possessed a highly developed and articulated cultural system. In China, Buddhism was always regarded as a foreign religion, at times subject to political persecution or criticism by Confucianists or Taoists, as well as favor by rulers. Buddhism, however, came to Japan as part of Chinese civilization, and its acceptance was thought to be a mark of a progressive nation. While Chinese Buddhism remained throughout its history institutionally weak, Japanese Buddhism developed firm organization and institutions which sometimes became formidable threats to the established order.

A key to the understanding of Japanese Buddhist history is the recognition that the Japanese awareness of being a sacred people in a sacred land eventually placed its stamp on the universal tradition of Buddhism itself. Our present study will attempt to trace Buddhist involvement in the political affairs of the nation, its fusion with the indigenous folk religious and magical perspectives, and the emergence of Buddhist schools or sects dominated by the Japanese spirit.

These various aspects of Buddhism have been interrelated and interdependent. The construction of temples, dissemination of Buddhist texts, and ceremonies of national Buddhism contributed to the spread of Buddhism among the people and supported the various technical schools whose leaders and teachers often functioned as the personnel of the national Buddhism. Popular Buddhism provided means of support and basis for the further development of the popular Buddhist schools, while the various schools and their associated temples provided the context for the development of Buddhist insight and experience and the maintenance of Buddhist tradition within Japanese society.

In contrast to the emphasis on ideological issues present in the development of Buddhism in China, our study of Japanese Buddhism will concentrate on social-cultural relations in order to provide a background for understanding the state of Buddhism in modern Japan. A survey of the various facets of Japanese Buddhism reveals the conditions which have contributed to the passivity and detachment of the Buddhist communities in the face of modern problems and the resultant criticisms by nonreligious intellectuals as well as by thoughtful devotees. The exploitation and political manipulation of Buddhism by the ruling classes in history as they attempted to unify and control the people, the magical and otherworldly outlook of traditional Buddhism, and the pronounced divisive sectarianism which dominates the tradition have created doubts in the minds of many modern people concerning its ability to contribute to the modernization of Japan or to turn back the growing secularization of the society.

NATIONAL BUDDHISM

According to the account recorded in the *Nihon Shoki,* Buddhism officially entered Japan during the reign of Emperor Kimmei in 552, though it may actually have been 538. On this occasion the king of Kudara (Paekche) in Korea presented the court with Buddhist images and texts. He declared that Buddhism would benefit the Japanese people and that it had been accepted by such leading countries as China. Though Buddhism had earlier infiltrated Japan carried by Chinese and Korean immigrants, its spread was greatly facilitated by the recognition of its political utility for promoting national interests.

Immediately upon its introduction it became involved in the political rivalry between the Soga and Mononobe clans, though neither side understood the true nature of the religion. The Soga, who supported Buddhism and adopted it as its own clan religion, represented the more internationalist and progressive leadership among the Japanese, while the Mononobe represented the particularistic interests of the clans.

The first major figure to appear in the formation of national Buddhism was Prince Shotoku (573–621). He implemented the Soga aim of establishing a strong central authority as the regent of the Soga-sponsored Empress Suiko (592–628). Admiration of China and a desire to restore Japanese fortunes in Korea also motivated him.

Because the Prince was deeply devoted to the teachings of Buddhism and recognized its spiritual role in the development of a unified nation, he was credited in history with the promulgation of a seventeen-point constitution which advocated reverence for the

Horyuji Temple, an early Japanese Buddhist temple. (Courtesy of the Japan National Tourist Organization.)

three treasures of Buddhism by all the people as the basis of social harmony. In addition, the Prince was thought to have composed commentaries on three major Mahayana sutras which reflected his critical and independent thought as he transformed Buddhism from an other-worldly religion to one promoting social harmony in this world. His emphasis on Buddhism as a religion of laymen greatly influenced later generations.

The Prince also encouraged Buddhism by inviting visiting priests to lecture, cultivating Buddhist scholarship, and commissioning the construction of numerous temples and works of art. Most prominent of the temples established by the Prince were the Shitennoji, which included social welfare facilities, Horyuji, and Chuguji.

Though Buddhism was supported by the court after Shotoku, it was subjected to greater control as a result of the Taika reform in 645 when the T'ang law codes were adopted in Japan. Private temples were prohibited, and monks had to be licensed. In addition, they could not work among the people.

A more positive approach to the Buddhist Order appeared, however, in the provincial temple system set up in 741 by Emperor Shomu who devoted himself to the prosperity of Buddhism. Symbolic of his efforts was the construction of the great Buddha of Todaiji (consecrated in 752). The Buddha selected for representation was Mahavairocana Buddha (Dainichi Nyorai), the great Sun Buddha. This Buddha symbolized the philosophy of the *Kegon Sutra* (Sanskrit *Avatamsaka,* Chinese *Hua-yen*), which taught that the essence of each thing contained the essence of every other thing. All reality was interdependent and mutually permeating. Hence, the world manifested the Buddha nature combined in a grand harmony.

The symbolism of the image and its many surrounding Buddhas carried a political message of the interdependence of the Japanese people and the Imperial house.

Emperor Shomu viewed Buddhism as a magical religion founded on the belief that the proper recitation of various nation-protecting sutras would bring prosperity and security to the nation. It was not the principles of Buddhist philosophy which brought harmony, but the use of Buddhist texts and institutions which granted security. According to these "nation-protecting" sutras the divine heavenly kings protected any country that materially supported Buddhism or copied and recited such texts. Eventually a whole system of provincial temples equipped with sutras, monks, and nuns was constructed with Todaiji as the head temple for the purpose of benefiting the nation through spiritual protection.

As a result of the efforts lavished on the construction of the system of national and provincial temples, corruption appeared when the official temples acquired great properties and wealth. The situation reached a climax when the monk Dokyo became the Prime Minister with apparent designs on the throne. However, at the death of Empress Shotoku (764–770) he was banished and the Buddhist Order was subjected again to strict regulation.

Another stage in the political relations of Buddhism opened when the monks Saicho (767–822) and Kukai (774–835) attempted to free themselves from the influence of the Nara temples after studying in China. The establishment of the Chinese Tendai and Shingon schools of Buddhism were in some measure attempts to reform and reestablish the true principles of Buddhism in Japan.

The reforming aspect was particularly strong in Saicho who asked the court for permission to set up his own Tendai ordination platform on Mount Hiei, which would then qualify his monks to serve in the provincial temples. Because the temples in Nara only followed the Buddha's instruction in words, Saicho maintained that Tendai Buddhism would provide monks who would be true national treasures and that the nation would be better protected spiritually. The court granted approval soon after his death in 822.

With the removal of the capital from Nara to Kyoto (794), Mount Hiei became continually involved with national politics. As its own economic and political power grew, organized warrior monks fought in the interests of the order. The problems of violence and corruption created by these militant monks became notorious in Japanese history. The *Heike Monogatari* depicted numerous instances of the terror which the monks of Hiei aroused in the people as they preyed upon the religious sensibilities of the people and court.

Kukai, who introduced the Shingon school to Japan (Sanskrit *Mantra,* Chinese *Chen-yen*), was at first allied with Saicho, but later they separated when Kukai taught that the esoterism of Shingon was really superior to the exoterism of Tendai. In addition, Kukai did not strongly oppose the temples of Nara and soon attained high rank in the official organization, becoming the abbot of the Toji temple in Kyoto. Here he performed the rite of *kanjo* (a form of ordination), as well as ceremonies for the pacification of the nation. Supported by the court, Kukai and his order attained wide influence. Even emperors received instruction in Buddhism under the tutelage of Shingon monks.

The relation of these schools to the Imperial house in the Heian age took a special form called Insei (Cloister) government, which involved the monasteries more deeply in politics. It became the custom for emperors to retire from active rule and to enter a monastery. This system was based on the principle that men of responsibility might retire to devote themselves to religious concerns, transferring their worldly burdens to others. In the political sphere it might also mean an escape from conspiracy. The purpose of the retirement was thus not always religiously motivated. In some instances the retired Emperor had more political power in this status than he had as actual Emperor. The involvement of Buddhism in political conflicts during this period tended to degrade it and to stimulate those forces of reform which later appeared in the Kamakura period.

The Buddhist schools of Nara and Heian held little concern for the ordinary person. Although individual monks engaged in social welfare and religious work among the people, the various official schools were more concerned with promoting their power and influence through the manipulation of spiritual forces and catering to the demands of the aristocracy.

Against the background of the corruption and spiritual decline of Mount Hiei and Mount Koya as well as the earlier Nara temples, a number of sects emerged during the Kamakura age which differed in their views of the relation of Buddhism and society and its function in providing spiritual protection for the state. On the one hand the Pure Land schools of Ryonin, Honen, Shinran, and Ippen were other-worldly and designed chiefly to bring birth in the Pure Land for individuals. On the other hand Eisai, who introduced the Rinzai (Lin-chi) Zen (Ch'an) tradition from China, maintained in his treatise *Kozengokokuron* (*Treatise on Spiritually Protecting the Nation through Prospering Zen*) that the nation could be spiritually protected only through promoting the true practice of Zen.

Dogen, Eisai's disciple and the founder of the Soto Zen sect, asserted that Buddhism was superior to the state. According to his view, human laws were merely based on precedents and ancient laws whose origins were uncertain. However, Buddhism had a clear transmission from the beginning. Thus the state was not absolute. Claiming extraterritoriality for the monk who did his duty by performing his discipline, Dogen refused to associate with the government and established his temple in a distant province.

Perhaps the most important expression of the relation between the nation and Buddhism in the Kamakura era was the teaching of the Buddhist prophet Nichiren. According to his basic work *Risshoankokuron* (*Treatise on the Attainment of Peace in the Country through the Establishment of the True Teaching*), the security of the nation depended on strict adherence to the true form of Buddhism. The true Buddhism was the Tendai school based on the *Lotus Sutra* as interpreted by Nichiren himself.

Insisting on the supremacy of the Lotus Sutra over all other teachings of Buddhism, he demanded that the government establish it as the national religion to the exclusion of all other forms of Buddhism. His intolerance was the result of his conviction that the many natural disasters and political upheavals which Japan had experienced had been prophesied by the Buddha as punishment for not adhering to the truth. Very soon, he taught, the final punishment would come with the invasion of the Mongols. He pointed to the prosperity of Pure Land teaching, Zen Buddhism, the use of Shingon practices, and the fame of Ritsu priests as evidence that the people had ignored and were blind to the truth originally declared by Saicho. Even traditional Tendai teachers had strayed from the truth by adopting Pure Land teaching and Shingon practices into their own system.

Although Nichiren employed traditional concepts of the relation of state and Buddhism, he held strongly to the primacy of Buddhism over the state in contrast to the traditional political subservience of Buddhism. His outspokenness and uncompromising attitude brought him persecution and banishment.

The period of civil wars and strife following the fall of the Kamakura Shogunate in 1334 until the establishment of the Tokugawa regime in 1615 frequently involved Buddhist orders as they carried on sectarian rivalry or attempted to protect their own interests. As Sansom points out: "Although most of the numerous sects of Buddhism in Japan were tolerant to the point of indifference in matters of doctrine, they were very jealous of their rights, and would fight hard on a point of privilege." [1]

The various dictators engaged in armed struggles to reduce the political and military threats of the great Buddhist institutions. While Ashikaga Takauji (Shogun, 1338–1358) had to retrench before the militant reaction of the forces of Mount Hiei, Oda Nobunaga (1534–1582) was eventually able to subdue the hosts of the Ikko (Single-minded sect of Pure Land devotees) and Mount Hiei. He even encouraged the propagation of Christianity to counter the influence of the Buddhists. Hideyoshi (1536–1598) pursued the monks of Kumano and Mount Koya. As the monks turned from warlike activities to works of piety, Hideyoshi began to restrain the Christians, ordering missionaries to leave the country in 1587. Oppression of Christians mounted under Hideyoshi and reached its peak with the martyrdom of twenty-six persons at Nagasaki in 1597. The persecutions and martyrdoms of Christians increased under the Tokugawas, reaching a climax in the Shimabara revolt which precipitated the policy of total isolation from foreign relations for the next 250 years.

The importance of the Christian persecutions lies in their relationship to the political control of the Buddhist Orders during the Tokugawa era. As a measure in the abolition of Christianity, Buddhist clergy began to function as police. In 1640 an investigating agency was formed in Edo and extended throughout the country. In

---

1. G. B. Sansom, *A History of Japan,* Stanford, Calif., Stanford University Press, 1958–1963, vol. II, p. 153.

order to seek out Christians, citizens were made to trample the cross, and local Buddhist temples were required to register all persons in their district on such matters as their personal history and activities.

The Buddhist religion declined because of the earlier attacks on its institutions and its reduction to a mere political tool in the Tokugawa effort to achieve total social stability and harmony. The dominant ideologies of the Tokugawa age were Confucianism and a renascent Shintoism, both of which were critical and negative to Buddhism. Buddhist institutions continued to function, and members of the government associated with it through their families as a matter of custom. However, it exerted little control or influence over the intellectual outlook or personal conduct of the national leaders.

Buddhist scholars regard the change brought about in Buddhism, resulting from the activities of Nobunaga, Hideyoshi, and the later Tokugawas, as a turning point in Buddhist history. During this period Buddhism completely capitulated to secular authority. The establishment of the parish system (*Danka Seido*) irrespective of doctrinal convictions, as well as the imposed clerical control, effectively cut Buddhism off spiritually from the people. Despite the fact that Buddhism had permeated daily life or that scholarship had developed within the monastic communities, the real vitality of Buddhism was lost when compared with its impact in the medieval periods of Heian and Kamakura. The position of Buddhism in the feudal period resembled only externally its role in the earlier period when the state was institutionalized. The important difference was that rulers in the earlier ages believed in Buddhist spiritual experience, and revering the three treasures (*Buddha, Dharma, Sangha*) prayed for the welfare of the nation. In the later period the Edo warriors, dominated by Confucianism, regarded Buddhism simply as a useful instrument of social control.

When the Tokugawa regime ended with the restoration of Imperial rule under Meiji in 1868, Buddhism was rudely awakened by the shout of "Expel Buddha, cut down Sakyamuni." The renascent Shinto sentiment held by leaders of government quickly overthrew the trappings of state support of Buddhism, and the new nationalism claimed it was merely a foreign religion. The attack failed because of the faith of the ordinary people in Buddhism which had given them some hope for their meager existences.

As we have seen in the study of Shinto, Buddhist leaders joined with Shintoists in promoting the new nationalism and thus linked themselves to the political absolutism of the new regime. Government officials welcomed the assistance of Buddhist clergy, since they had traditionally the closest relation to the people. While promoting religious freedom in order to gain its own autonomy, Buddhism was soon faced with the new threat of a spreading Christianity. In modern times in numerous ways, the various Buddhist Orders have attempted to commend themselves as supporters of the national destiny reinforcing the awareness of the sacredness of the land and people. However, institutional lethargy has inhibited serious grappling with the problems of modernization and social progress. Thus a major issue confronting the Buddhist sects has been their own relevance in a rapidly changing and more highly sophisticated, complex, industrial society.

POPULAR BUDDHISM

Merely recounting the history of Buddhist institutions in Japanese society would be insufficient to convey the significance of Buddhism in the life of the people. The description of formal and external relations cannot replace an understanding of the impact on the people which has sustained the religion through periods of great social change. Buddhist influence, widespread in all areas of culture, is readily evident in the arts and literature. It is apparent in language where colloquial terms reflect Buddhist background. For example, "to drop dead" is *tachiojo-suru*. Literally it means to attain rebirth while standing. Rebirth refers to the Buddhist belief in transmigration. *Kara-nembutsu*, which means "vain talk," refers to an empty mouthing of the recitation of Buddha's name. The common phrase *jigo-jitoku*, which means "it's your own fault," summarizes the Buddhist karmic principle that what one sows one reaps.

Buddhism infiltrated into Japan when immigrants from China or Korea carried their faith with them. However, official recognition of Buddhism also spurred the spread of Buddhism among the people as the more wealthy families built private temples in their domains. They tended to view the Buddhas as analogous to their ancestral and tutelary deities. From the death of Prince Shotoku in 622 when there were 46 temples in the country, the number grew to 545 in the time of Empress Jito (687–697).

As a rule, the growth of Buddhism was largely concentrated within the ruling class who displayed their social power through building temples, sponsoring images, and copying sutras. However, a few monks traveled about the country and preached Buddhism to the common people, despite government restrictions on such activity. In their alliance with the people such unauthorized and shamanistic priests naturally became critical of political exploitation and religious corruption,[2] having deep concern for the spiritual and material welfare of the common man.

Representative popular priests in the Nara period were Dosho (629–700) and Gyogi Bosatsu (670–749). Dosho was highly regarded as an ideal Buddhist monk and scholar of the Hosso school. Among his many contributions, he is credited with the introduction of cremation as the proper Buddhist way to dispose of the dead. During the later years of his life he gave himself to the welfare of mankind by constructing wells, bridges, almshouses and ferries, as well as monasteries.

Gyogi's efforts on behalf of mankind were so outstanding that he was given the title *Bosatsu* (*Bodhisattva*), which testified to the depth of his compassion for man. Although he was learned in Buddhist philosophy and meditation discipline, he engaged in works

---

2. Joseph M. Kitagawa, *Religion in Japanese History*, New York, Columbia, 1966, pp. 40–41.

of mercy by building bridges and river dykes, planting fruit trees, and constructing way houses for travelers, reservoirs, irrigation canals, ferries, and harbors. In addition, he was credited with opening thirty-four monasteries and fifteen nunneries. His popularity grew to such dimensions that the government prohibited his activity and banished him. However, because of his great influence the government sought his assistance in soliciting funds to construct the great Buddha of Nara, and in 745 he was elevated to the rank of *Daisojo* (Great High Priest).

In the succeeding Heian period several noted compassionate monks traveled through the country offering the hope of salvation to the common man through the recitation of the name of Amida Buddha. The simplicity of the Pure Land doctrine appealed to ordinary people and influenced all levels of society. The attraction of the other-worldly faith increased along with the social turmoil and upheavals at the end of the Heian era. During this period the popular preachers laid stress on the fact that it was the Last Age (Mappo) of corruption and strife, dramatizing the anxieties of the age.

Several priests drew particular attention in promoting the spread of Pure Land doctrine during this time. Kuya Shonin (903–972) was called "the Saint of the Market" as he went about proclaiming Pure Land faith and using a melodic form of recitation. The preaching of these priests was augmented by the work of Genshin (942–1017), a high-ranking monk and scholar on Mount Hiei, through his treatise on the essentials for rebirth in the Pure Land (*Ojoyoshu*). The text became a handbook for preachers by bringing together all scriptural passages relating to the Pure Land and Hell. The monk Ryonin (1071–1132) taught a doctrine of mutual salvation (*Yuzu-nembutsu*) which gave a social dimension to efforts for salvation. During the later Kamakura period, the priest Ippen (1238–1289) taught a distinctive interpretation of Pure Land doctrine which advocated reciting the *Nembutsu* at six specific times during the day and emphasizing that one should regard each moment of life as his last in reciting the sacred name.

Although the Pure Land teaching based on faith in Amida Buddha became the dominant Buddhist belief among the common people during the Heian era, other Buddhist divinities also were objects of devotion. Jizo (Sanskrit *Kshitigarbha,* Chinese *Ti-tsang*) assisted men in the afterlife and helped them to avoid going to hell. Merging with beliefs of folk religion, he was also regarded as a savior for those in trouble, particularly women in childbirth and children. Kannon (Sanskrit *Avalokitesvara,* Chinese *Kuan-yin*), the Goddess of Mercy, was widely revered. Tradition held that even Prince Shotoku was an ardent devotee. Emperors sponsored lectures and ceremonies on the *Kannon Sutra* and promoted the popularity of the cult. According to this text, Kannon symbolized the depth of Buddha's compassion. She promised to save men from all forms of calamity and to grant them health, wealth and security in life. Other popular deities were Kangiten (Sanskrit *Ganesa*), the elephant-headed deity dispensing wisdom, and Kishimojin (Sanskrit *Hariti*), a goddess of childbirth.

Amida Raigo triptych of the Pure Land school, from the Heian Period, late eleventh century. (Courtesy of the Koyasan Museum, Wakayama.)

Together with the beliefs in great Buddhist divinities there were numerous practices designed to gain desired benefits. Most popular and easiest was the recitation of magical phrases such as *Namu-Amida-Butsu* (*Hail Amida Buddha*) or *Namu-Myoho-Renge-Kyo* (*Hail Lotus of the Wonderful Law*). Shingon teaching became very influential because of the potent magical *Dharani* spells and incantations of Indian origin which it offered for every possible contingency. There were also mystic ceremonies such as the fire ritual, *goma,* which was thought to burn away impurity and to remove curses of demons. The ceremony was much used in the Heian period.

During the period when the manifold Chinese religious beliefs and practices spread into Japan with Buddhism, religious Taoism also came, though not in an institutional form. Whereas the teachings of Confucianism were first regarded as the required learning for rulers and politicians, religious Taoism had a wider influence and import, offering various methods for advancing one's life in this world and attaining longevity or good fortune. In addition to religious Taoism, yin-yang magic and divination, astrology, geomancy, and calendrical computations were combined with Buddhism. Taoist belief in sage-hermits contributed also to the formation of the Shugendo movement of Buddho-Shinto mountain ascetics. The practitioners of Shugendo functioned among the people as exorcists and shamans.

Ceremonies for the dead were also a prominent aspect of Japanese Buddhism. Not only was there the fear of dead spirits which emerged in the Heian period (see pp. 344–345), but there was also reverencing of the dead in filial piety. Masses for the dead helped to assure the good destiny of the departed. A calendar of memorials provided the dead with periodic assistance until they faded from living memory to become part of the general host of ancestors.

An important annual festival was the Urabon-e (Sanskrit *Avalambana, Ullambana*), based on the story of Buddha's disciple Mokuren (Sanskrit *Maudgalyayana*) who saw that his mother had become a hungry ghost. Thereupon began the rite of offering food for one's parents and ancestors. Related to the Urabon-e but of different origin was the Segaki ceremony of feeding the hungry ghosts. This ceremony is still regularly performed.[3] Other ceremonies connected with the dead occurred at the spring and autumn equinox and were called Higan-e.

Ancestors are venerated through masses and entertainments. Most important are visits to the grave which, despite the decline in religious activity among modern people, are still commonly carried out even by those of no specific religious commitment. Considerable criticism has been directed to Buddhism because of its predominant association with death. Watanabe states:

> It is clear that funeral services were not the work of monks in Sakyamuni's Order. They were the task of hereditary Brahmins. In

---

3. S. Watanabe, *Japanese Buddhism: A Critical Appraisal,* Tokyo, Kokusai Bunka Shinkokai, 1964, pp. 88–91.

Jizo Bodhisattva, patron of the world of death, late twelfth century. (Courtesy of the Museum of Fine Arts, Boston.)

> *East Asia such was not the case. When Buddhism came to act as agent for the folk religion, it became responsible even for funeral rites. . . .*
>
> *If one considers that Buddhism has a living road in the future, there is probably nothing else to do but to advance in the direction of rejecting the cloak of funeral rites which is satisfied with mere form, and both to have confidence itself concerning life and death and to indicate it to others.*[4]

The elements of popular religion have penetrated all sects to secure support from the masses. The Shugendo movement was very instrumental in carrying these beliefs and ceremonies to the people, particularly in the Tokugawa period when the traditional sects had largely been deprived of their spiritual influence among the people.

In the modern era a gap frequently exists between critical intellectual priests and the ordinary persons in relation to the magical and pragmatic features of Buddhism. Despite the calls for reformation and modernization within Buddhism today, the great source of support and strength in the orders still derives from the magical and pragmatic faith which, for lack of a better alternative, supports individuals in dealing with the problems and anxieties of modern life.

DOCTRINAL BUDDHISM

Though Buddhism has functioned in the social and political sphere as a support for the state and ruling class, and on the popular level has fused with native folk religion with stress on magic and pragmatic, this-worldly interests, it also established its own thought tradition in which Japanese monks studied and researched Buddhist texts and principles and applied themselves to the practice of Buddhist disciplines in the effort to achieve their own enlightenment. Thus, while it is easy to criticize Buddhism for its political exploitation and superstitious elements, it is necessary to balance these judgments with the recognition of serious efforts to understand Buddhism and to realize its own distinctive ideals.

The development of Buddhist thought in Japan follows largely the major historical periods of Nara (710–784), Heian (794–1185), and Kamakura (1185–1333). In general we may describe each period as a step in the gradual assimilation or Japanization of Buddhism.

In the Nara period the highly scholastic and philosophic schools current at the time in T'ang China (618–907) commanded the center of interest. The schools in this introductory period had little relation to the common man and were little more than academic trends, representing the various alternative Buddhist perspectives which had developed in India and then China. Commonly referred to as the Six Schools of Nara Buddhism, they were Jojitsu (Sanskrit *Satyasiddhi*), Kusha (Sanskrit *Abhidharma Kosa*), Hosso (Sanskrit *Dharmalakshana, Yogacara*), Sanron (Three Treatise, Sanskrit *Madhyamika*), Kegon (Sanskrit *Avatamsaka*), and Ritsu (Sanskrit *Vinaya*). They were introduced at various times by Chinese or Japanese monks from about 625 to 754.

---

4. Ibid., pp. 98–99.

Of greater religious and historical significance was the introduction of the Tendai (Chinese *T'ien-t'ai*) school by Saicho and the Shingon (Sanskrit *Mantra,* Chinese *Chen-yen*) by Kukai. The doctrines and scholarship within these traditions laid the foundation for the flowering of Japanese Buddhism in the Kamakura period. Stressing the idea that there was really only one truth among the diversity of teachings in Buddhist tradition, they opened the way for greater sectarianism as later teachers asserted that they taught the "One Vehicle," or one truth necessary for salvation. In addition, they taught the universality of salvation based on the theory of mutual interpenetration of the Kegon school. The development of Pure Land teaching, particularly within the Tendai school, and the increasing emphasis on mystic rites and pageantry contributed to the broadening impact of Buddhism on all classes in the Heian era. These trends assured that Japan would be a Mahayana Buddhist country.

Against the background of dramatic social change and the deepening penetration of Buddhism into Japanese life, the flourishing of novel and creative movements in Buddhist tradition mark the Kamakura era in Japanese history as one of the most significant periods in the history of religion. While Buddhism reflected native aspirations and needs, closely identifying with the common man, it also offered universal paths of salvation unique in Buddhism.

With the rise to political dominance of the warrior clans, headed first by the Taira and then the Minamoto who established their center of power at Kamakura, a new virile and martial ethos displaced the formalistic and aesthetic outlook of the Heian nobility. The life of delicate beauty, peace, and ease of Heian changed to a way of life based on bravery and loyalty.

The repercussions of the transformation reverberated through all aspects of culture, whether art, literature, or religion. In religion the new era expressed itself in the emergence of several Buddhist leaders: Honen (1133–1212), Shinran (1173–1262), Dogen (1200–1253), and Nichiren (1222–1282). Their critical spirit and search for truth enable us to view them as reformers, much on the order of their European counterparts.

Each of these individuals attempted to achieve the ideals of Buddhism through the study of traditional doctrine and discipline either on Mount Hiei or in Nara. The general decline of studies and discipline and the activities of turbulent, warlike monks did not provide an atmosphere conducive to sincere religious pursuits. In each case, religious dissatisfaction stimulated the search for a new approach to Buddhist enlightenment. As a result of their various quests, these men were inevitably led to reject the traditional ecclesiastical system which had become formalized, sterile, ritualistic, doctrinally sterile, superstitious, and inwardly corrupt. Each found his solution in some aspect or tendency within Buddhist tradition which he elevated to a supreme position and proclaimed as the superior or true way to reach the goal of enlightenment.

In contrast to earlier Buddhism which was largely dominated by the interests and outlook of the nobility and Imperial house, the new movements appealed to the common man. Aristocratic support and outlook were rejected. In offering Buddhism to the common man, each of the major teachers strove for a simplified doctrine and religious discipline within the capabilities of the ordinary person. Drawing on the tradition of One Vehicle Buddhism which had developed within the Tendai tradition, out of which all these individuals had come, there was a strong tendency to sectarianism based on the conviction that each teacher had discovered the one fundamental truth of Buddhism.

As illustration of these various tendencies, there was Honen who wrote his "Testimony on One Sheet of Paper" just before his death, and Shinran who asserted that only faith was required for salvation. They represented the ultimate perhaps in the simplification of the abstruse and complicated systems of Buddhist philosophy and discipline. The rejection of the aristocratic life and political connections was portrayed in Dogen's rejection of favor with the Shogun and the construction of his monastery far from centers of power in distant Echizen province. He is said to have excommunicated the monk who brought him the message of the Shogun's gift of land. The sectarianism of the new Buddhism of Kamakura appeared most decisively in the four denunciations of Nichiren concerning the other contemporary schools. He declared emphatically that believers in the Pure Land teaching would go to hell; that the Zen sect had been created by devils; that Shingon was the ruination of the state; and that the Ritsu sect betrayed the country. Only the teaching proclaimed by Nichiren would save the nation from destruction.

It was the teacher Honen who, slightly before the onset of the Kamakura period, first gave himself to the attempt to discover in Buddhism a solid foundation for the spiritual life. According to his biography, his religious dissatisfaction was expressed in anxiety for his future destiny. Though having studied at the great Japanese centers of Buddhism, he had no spiritual peace until he happened on the Chinese teacher Shan Tao's Pure Land doctrine. Struck by this teaching, he abandoned religious life on Mount Hiei and eventually established his own school in 1175, later known as Jodo-shu.

The main characteristic of his school was the rejection of manifold practices of Buddhist tradition and the selection of the single practice of recitation of Amida Buddha's name as the only means of salvation. When he published his major work, *Senjakuhongannembutsushu* (*Treatise on the Nembutsu of the Select Original Vow*), for the regent Fujiwara Kanezane in 1198, the true nature of his doctrine became clear and eventually resulted in persecution and banishment.

Through analyzing traditional Buddhist doctrines in the light of the dawn of the Last Age in the decline of Buddhist teachings, Honen made it clear that the only certain way for ordinary persons in this age to achieve salvation was the recitation of the Buddha's name alone. Implicitly, the exaltation of this practice rendered all other Buddhist disciplines meaningless.

Apart from the theoretical foundations of his teaching, Honen was also motivated by a deep compassion for the common man, and he eloquently attacked the aristocratic Buddhism of his time which made salvation contingent on wealth or learning:

> And so Amida seemed to have made his Original Vow the rejection of the hard and the choice of the easy way, in order to enable all sentient beings, without distinction, to attain birth into the Pure Land. If the Original Vow required the making of images and the building of pagodas, then the poor and destitute could have no hope of attaining it. But the fact is that the wealthy and noble are few in number, whereas the number of the poor and ignoble is extremely large. If the Original Vow required wisdom and great talents, there would be no hope of that birth for the foolish and ignorant at all, but the wise are few in number, while the foolish are very many.[5]

The essence of his faith and practice were given concisely in the famous "Testament on One Sheet of Paper":

> The method of final salvation that I have propounded is neither a sort of meditation, such as has been practiced by many scholars in China and Japan, nor is it the repetition of the Buddha's name by those who have studied and understood the deep meaning of it. It is nothing but the mere repetition of the "Namu Amida Butsu," without a doubt of his mercy, whereby one may be born into the Land of Perfect Bliss. The mere repetition with firm faith includes all the practical details, such as the three-fold preparation of mind and the four practical rules. If I as an individual had any doctrine more profound than this, I should miss the mercy of the two Honorable Ones, Amida and Shaka, and be left out of the Vow of the Amida Buddha. Those who believe this, though they clearly understand all the teachings Shaka taught throughout his whole life, should behave themselves like simple-minded folk, who know not a single letter, or like ignorant nuns or monks whose faith is implicitly simple. Thus without pedantic airs, they should fervently practice the repetition of the name of Amida, and that alone.[6]

Shinran was a disciple of Honen and followed him in promoting Pure Land doctrine (Jodo-shinshu, true sect of the Pure Land). After a period of exile as a result of the persecution of Honen's band, Shinran taught in the eastern province of Kanto. In his latter years he returned to Kyoto and lived in retirement. During this period he produced various texts which are major sources for his thought. Among them are *Kyogyoshinsho* (*Treatise on the Doctrine, Practice, Faith and Realization*), various groups of hymns, some interpretative texts, and letters to his disciples. In addition, his disciple Yuiembo wrote the popular little text *Tannisho* (*Deploring the Heresies*), giving the essence of Shinran's thought.

---

5. Harper H. Coates and Ryugaku Ishizuka, *Honen the Buddhist Saint*, Kyoto, Society for the Publication of Sacred Books of the World, 1949, vol. II, p. 344.

6. Ibid., pp. 728–729.

While Shinran was in harmony with the spirit of Honen's teaching and motivation to aid spiritually the common man, his Pure Land doctrine went beyond Honen's in several important respects. Honen had concentrated attention on the adequacy of the practice of vocal recitation to bring salvation in comparison with traditional Buddhist disciplines, while Shinran directed attention to the foundation of the efficacy of this practice. He found its effectiveness rooted in the transfer of merit made by Amida Buddha as the result of his arduous effort to create a way of salvation for all beings. The transfer of merit gave potency to the name, and it also was the basic cause for the resultant faith in the Buddha's Vow and Work within the person. Shinran placed major emphasis on the experience of faith. He criticized all forms of Buddhism, including those advocating the repetition of Buddha's name, as expressions of man's egoism through attempting to achieve salvation by his own effort.

Since the experience of faith reveals that one's salvation has been assured by Amida Buddha, one may attain spiritual peace in contrast to the self-powered disciplines which always involve an anxiety of not knowing whether one has sufficiently purified himself in order to gain salvation. Consequently, the religious life undergoes a dramatic reinterpretation in which our lives and religious practice are to be viewed as expressions of gratitude for the salvation already assured rather than as desperate attempts to achieve spiritual security.

The life of gratitude had several social implications which eventually became clear in the history of the tradition. In contrast to traditional Buddhism Shinran rejected the magical principle of performing Buddhist practices in order to gain benefits in this world and salvation in the next. In the doctrines of Bodhisattvic return to this world after death (*Genso*), Shinran made the goal of religion the salvation of others. In rejecting self-powered, egocentric religious attitudes, all superstitious practices which had such a prominent role in popular Buddhism were cast aside. Further, with the assurance that one's status in the next world was already determined, one might give more attention to developing himself in this world. Abandoning the disciplines and precepts regulating the lives of monks in earlier Buddhist orders, Shinran's clerical followers were noted because they ate meat and married. Believers could also engage in occupations of their choice. With the decline of magic and a more ethically oriented interpretation of faith developed later by the patriarch Rennyo, Shinran's teachings assisted in the development of the merchant class in the Tokugawa period.[7]

Although Eisai is credited with introducing the Zen sect into Japan, it was the aristocratic and highly intellectual form of Rinzai (Lin-chi) Zen which employed the rigorous, demanding Koan or riddle method of revealing one's attainment of enlightenment. The characteristics of Kamakura Buddhism appear more within the Soto (Chinese *Tsao-tung*) tradition of Zen which Dogen introduced to Japan after his study in China.

7. Robert N. Bellah, *Tokugawa Religion,* New York, Free Press, 1967, pp. 117–122.

Like other Kamakura Buddhists, the priest Dogen had become dissatisfied with the religious discipline he encountered on Mount Hiei and at first went to study under Eisai. Because this did not meet his need either, he went to China where he studied under the master Ju Ching. There he discovered a form of Zen, which was based not only on monastic existence but also could be expanded to allow men of all walks of life—great ministers, woodsmen, hunters, and even women—to gain enlightenment. He rejected the Koan practice, enabling his form of Zen, based on the meditation practice itself, to spread more easily among the common people. While the popular spread of Zen could not compare with that of the Pure Land, it gained the name "Farmers' Zen" because of its greater adaptability to ordinary life.

Dogen inherited his master Ju Ching's insistence on the centrality of the practice of *Zazen* over all other Buddhist practices. According to his interpretation in such works as the *Shobogenzo* (*The Repository of Buddhist Teaching*), Zazen was the process wherein Buddha himself had attained the bliss of enlightenment. There was no temporal, cause-effect relation between meditation and enlightenment. To perform Zazen was thus in a mysterious manner to participate in the enlightenment of the Buddha. Practice and realization were identical.

The identity of the practice and attainment led Dogen to criticize other approaches to Zen which made the practice secondary and instrumental, merely a means to the effort to attain Buddhahood through perceiving one's true nature (as Buddha). He also rejected the Zen principle of a special transmission beyond scripture. He criticized the dichotomy this view implied between the Buddha's mind and his teaching as represented in the sutras. Thus Dogen was more scripturally oriented than the Zen of the Rinzai tradition. Further, because the doctrine of the Buddha's "one mind" did not allow dualities, everything was embraced within his enlightenment. The world, as it is, was Buddha's mind.

In addition to criticizing other Zen teachings, Dogen also denied the theory of the three periods in the decline of Buddhist teaching (Mappo) as emphasized in the Pure Land tradition. Buddha's enlightenment and the possibility of realizing it were not affected by time.

The attitude toward life and the world generated in Zen discipline of whatever school has made it significant in the development of Japanese society and culture. It has been the basis of such military arts as Kendo (swordsmanship) and Judo. The discipline and traits of character it cultivated made it attractive to the samurai (warrior) class. It influenced broadly such arts as architecture, gardens, literature, drama, painting, and calligraphy. Its experience was expressed profoundly in such activities as the tea ceremony and flower arranging.

Perhaps the most fiery and striking personality among the Kamakura Buddhist reformers was Nichiren. Unlike the other thinkers who appear to have had aristocratic or warrior background, Nichiren was the offspring of a fisherman's family in the eastern province of Awa. Impressed early by the impermanence of life, he decided to enter nearby Kiyozumi-dera monastery which belonged to the Tendai sect. While studying, he visited Kamakura, Kyoto, Hiei, and Nara. At first he became attracted to Pure Land teaching, but soon began to doubt its efficacy to assure salvation. Other doubts also began to assail his spirit and motivate his study. He was concerned about the problems of peace in the country, particularly in relation to the death of the boy-Emperor Antoku, whose divine personage should have assured him assistance from the gods. He knew also of other Emperors, such as Go-Toba, who had been exiled by the Hojo regents. He was also perturbed by the numerous Buddhist sects existing in the country. He believed that just as there may be only one rightful ruler in a country, there could be only one true teaching of Buddhism. After studying all the various schools, he concluded that only the *Lotus Sutra* (*Hokkekyo*) taught the supreme truth of Buddhism as Saicho had earlier proclaimed.

In a unique manner he connected the fortunes of the country with the nation's lack of clear support for the true form of Buddhism. Rather than the *Lotus Sutra* being the center of faith, the land was overrun by Pure Land teaching. In his work *Risshoankokuron* he pointed out that Japan had already suffered numerous penalties for failing to adhere to true Buddhism, but a final major one, namely invasion by a foreign country, would bring an end to the nation unless she adopted the true teaching. Implicitly Nichiren advocated the abolition of all other sects and the establishment of his own doctrine. He characterized himself as "the pillar of Japan." Although Nichiren claimed merely to be restoring the truth of Tendai, since the age of Mappo had arrived and the successors of Saicho had themselves perverted the tradition, he did not simply desire a return to an exact replication of traditional Tendai Buddhist teaching.

Nichiren, who believed he was the *Jogyo Bosatsu* promised by Buddha Sakyamuni in the Last Age in the *Lotus Sutra,* brought his missionary zeal to bear in challenging the government, people, and contemporary religious institutions, now including Zen, Shingon, and Ritsu, as well as Pure Land. As he began to win supporters, he soon experienced persecution. He was attacked by mobs, chased from temples, banished several times, and even once nearly met death. These events only strengthened his confidence that he had the truth. In addition to street preaching and other varied activities, Nichiren wrote voluminously.[8]

Nichiren's teaching embodied a response to a time of crisis in Japanese society. Though his predictive powers are not entirely clear, his admonitions concerning the invasion of the country as a final punishment by the Buddha and the gods appeared to be borne out when the Mongols attempted to invade Japan in 1274 and 1281. These events provided him with a greater following, though the nation did not turn as a whole to his teaching nor was it destroyed.

8. Five texts are basic for Nichiren's thought: *Risshoankokuron* (*Treatise on Attaining Peace in the Country Through Establishing True Buddhism*), *Kaimokusho* (*Treatise on Opening the Eyes*), *Hoonsho* (*Treatise on Requiting Gratitude*), *Senjisho* (*Treatise on Selection of the Time*), and *Kanjinhonzonsho* (*Treatise on the Meditation of the True Effect of Worship*).

Although along with other Buddhist schools Nichiren was concerned with providing a way of individual salvation, he was also moved by a strong national feeling. Buddhism was not purely an individual matter but of utmost importance to the life of the whole society. In relating Buddhism and the state, he differed from traditional thinkers in placing Buddhism above the state. He believed the destiny of the state depended on its adherence to the true form of Buddhism. In contrast to Pure Land other-worldly indifference to the state, and Dogen's rejection of the seductive influence of political connections, Nichiren sought to influence state policy through his religious views.

In view of the importance of maintaining true Buddhism, Nichiren's intolerance went beyond that of other schools in seeking the abolition of all other schools. The method of *Shakubuku,* forced conversion or a way of aggressively conquering evil, was widely employed by Nichiren, and by his later followers to the present day. His personal involvement in his teaching and his sense of divine mission gave greater intensity to his teaching so that the tradition stemming from him bears his own name.

Though he is doctrinally related to the Tendai tradition, he modified it by establishing his own Mandala (sacred symbolic diagram) based on the view of the eternal Buddha presented in chapter 16 of the *Lotus Sutra.* This is the ultimate Buddha who stands behind the historical Sakyamuni Buddha. The true Buddha is the timeless reality, not a person who at a specific time and place attained enlightenment. That mode of expression was only to accommodate men and guide them to deeper faith. In the Last Age in the decline of the Buddhist teaching the most profound teaching must be given just as a very ill person must be given the most effective and powerful medicine. On this point Nichiren differed with the Pure Land tradition in that the means of salvation must be correlated directly with the capacities of the people of that time. As it was a corrupt age, an easy way to salvation was necessary. Nevertheless, the religious practice of Nichiren was the recitation of the title of the *Lotus Sutra, Namu-Myoho-Renge-kyo.* This practice was probably influenced by the development of Pure Land, though the supporting philosophy differed.

Like Saicho, Nichiren wanted to establish the true ordination platform based on his teaching. Within the context of Japanese Buddhism this would signify state acceptance of his doctrine as a recognized religion and a participant in the effort to maintain the spiritual security of the state. In this case the ordination platform would represent official adherence only to Nichiren's interpretation of Buddhism, rather than the mere inclusion of his teaching with others.

With the acceptance of the Tendai philosophy of "Three thousand in one thought" by which all things in this world express the Buddha-mind itself, his interpretation of human existence is this-worldly rather than other-worldly in emphasis. One's mystic unity with the reality within things is achieved through the recitation of the *Daimoku* (title of the *Lotus Sutra*) rather than the elaborate meditations in Tendai. Nichiren is significant for the way in which he adapted the abstruse Tendai philosophy to the needs of ordinary men. As a result, his tradition has revitalized today with the outcropping of a multitude of sects drawing on his fervor and his thought in attempting to deal with modern problems.

The new impetus given to Buddhist thought by the Kamakura teachers determined the direction of Buddhist tradition down to the present day. Because of social circumstance, it became increasingly separated from the life of the people and largely functioned to attain health, wealth, and security, to dispense one's duties toward the dead, or become an instrument of the state in the pursuit of its ends. Nevertheless its fundamental insights were preserved in the scholarly, priestly traditions.

In the postwar period Buddhism shares significantly in the religious fermentation, with statistics indicating the establishment of some 170 Buddhist sects in contrast to the 56 prewar sects distributed within the thirteen traditional schools. The statistics are deceptive because the increase is largely due to secessions resulting from the freedom of religious competition granted by the new Constitution. Whether there is really a revitalization of Buddhism or religion in general may be questioned when one compares studies concerning the actual participation and interest in religion with the official statistics recorded by religious organizations. According to a recent study of religion in the urban context, hardly one third of the adult population expressed interest in religion, while the remainder affirmed the need for religion but would not presently join any group.[9]

Nevertheless, within the shifting urban situation of the postwar period, two Buddhist organizations have shown phenomenal growth corresponding to conditions of rising urban populations. The Rissho Koseikai and Soka Gakkai, both derivative from the Nichiren tradition, have attracted the attention of social scientists as well as religionists.

There are numerous reasons given for the striking progress of these sects. A major reason is that they have addressed themselves aggressively to meeting the needs of the new urban dwellers and their problems. In contrast to the traditional Buddhist organizations whose foundations are largely rural and familial, the new sects attempt to provide a personal ethic and sense of meaning for people released from traditional bonds of community and family. They provide a focus for positive dealing with the sense of frustration and dissatisfaction that attends the competitive life of the city. Where other sects wait for people to come when there is need, the newer groups reach out and contact the socially disorganized urbanite. The method of their spread emphasizes the personal aspect in that believers contact prospects and draw them into fellowship. Through educational programs and frequent meetings loyalty to the group

---

9. Fujio Ikado, "Trend and Problems of New Religions: Religion in Urban Society," in *The Sociology of Japanese Religion,* Kiyomi Morioka and William H. Newell, eds., Leiden, E. J. Brill, 1968, pp. 101–117.

and solidarity develop. These less tradition-bound groups have benefited from the experience of other organizations in propagandizing for they have borrowed tactics from such diverse sources as the Christian Church and the theories of Saul Alinsky.

Despite the roots which Rissho Koseikai and Soka Gakkai have in Nichiren tradition and in the *Lotus Sutra,* the styles of the groups contrast sharply. As a consequence they also appeal to different segments of the urban population. The former relies upon the rural middle class and the small businessman of the city for support, while the latter attracts laborers and the urban lower middle class.

The approach to the problems of contemporary life of these supporters helps to account for the differing attitudes represented by the sect. Rissho Koseikai is more tolerant, striving for a Buddhist ecumenicity as well as positive interfaith relations. Great emphasis is laid on filial piety as the prime ethical value. Soka Gakkai embodies the dogmatic and intolerant attitudes of the prophet Nichiren himself and holds itself aloof from any compromise with other forms of Buddhism. For individuals strongly dissatisfied with the prevailing social conditions, this form of religious outlook provides a rationalization that social ills are due to a failure to follow the true religion. Its zeal for bringing about change in society in conformity with its own ideals has led the Soka Gakkai movement to enter into politics by forming the Clean Government party (Komeito), whose name symbolizes its reformist attitudes. This party's meteoric rise to prominence and importance in the various local and national elections has led to apprehensions among other religious groups which fear its religious intolerance.

The Rissho Koseikai in its general orientation tends to be more individualistic in its emphasis on the development of one's personal life through faith in Buddhism and practice of filial piety. It is also interested in society at large and has developed numerous social welfare projects such as hospitals, schools, old age homes, and cemeteries. The Hoza group meeting is significant in bringing believers into active participation in a religious and social gathering of mutual fellowship and assistance.

The Soka Gakkai provides for the satisfaction of individual needs through the emphasis on the benefits which the devotee receives from the concentrated practice of reciting the *Daimoku; Namu-Myoho-Renge-Kyo.* It is most renowned for the practice of *Shakubuku,* which refers to the forceful exhortation and strong insistence on the truth of Soka Gakkai teaching. It is the obligation of each member to win his family and friends to this faith.

The effort is inspired by an eschatological perspective based on the doctrine of the Last Age in the Decline of Buddhist Teaching at which time the strong medicine of the *Lotus Sutra,* as taught by Nichiren and further elaborated through the recent teachers and leaders of Soka Gakkai, Tsunesaburo Makiguchi, Josei Toda, and Daisaku Ikeda, is required for the solution of modern social problems of peace, justice, and social welfare. The quasi-political concept of the true ordination platform (*Hommon Kaidan*) advocated by Saicho in Tendai Buddhism and Nichiren in his time symbolizes the perfect union of religion and the state for the promotion of universal human good. It is this theory imbedded in the doctrine of Soka Gakkai that arouses the fears of a religious totalitarianism and intolerance should it become the dominant political force in Japan. Each devotee is to work for realization of this ideal. This theory has not only motivated the political activity of the group, but recently has caused it to turn attention to the fields of labor and education to achieve its goals in society.

It should be noted also that its universalist goals extend beyond Japan. Soka Gakkai has experienced a rapid spread among Americans, first among servicemen with Japanese wives, but in more recent times on the basis of its own religious appeal. In the missionary context the political implications of the doctrine are muted.

While the development of Rissho Koseikai and Soka Gakkai has commanded the major attention of students of the Japanese religious world in recent years, the efforts of the traditional schools to adapt themselves to contemporary conditions should not be overlooked. In the many schools supported by these sects scholarly study of Buddhism in all aspects has rapidly progressed. The education of clergy has attained higher standards. Lectures, publications, and broadcasting bring the claims of Buddhism to a wide audience. Nationwide Buddhist organizations of lay persons and clergy attempt to unite the sects of Buddhism around common projects. There are also efforts to engage the interest of young people.

Despite the wealth of activities carried on in the various sects and chronicled in the many religious papers and periodicals, the traditional organizations are hindered in making an impact by the general stereotype that Buddhism is only for funerals and by the lack in the past of a concerted effort in religious education. Since intellectual commitment was never an essential part of the mode of religious belonging in the community or family, the average lay person understands little of the essential teachings of Buddhism. Statistics indicating that Shinto claims some seventy-nine million followers and Buddhism about seventy-eight million in a nation of ninety million people reveal that most Japanese appear not to sense any contradiction between the two traditions, and they show little consciousness of belonging to a particular religion.

In an age when customary and familial foundations for religion are weakening, the traditional Buddhist sects are at a disadvantage in maintaining social and economic support. With decreased income priests must often work as teachers or run kindergartens to maintain their livelihood. The result is that they lack adequate time for religious cultivation and evangelism.

Further, a hereditary clergy and a hierarchical organizational structure has tended to work against needed reforms urged by scholars and younger priests. As a consequence of these various factors, the older orders cannot match the vitality of the newer groups.

Although facing great difficulties, as the religious world stabilizes, the older organizations may benefit from their greater maturity and scholarship, as well as from the prestige that attends a lengthy history in Japan. A new age may be dawning when Buddhism will attain intellectual leadership as it comes to more adequate terms with the forces of secularism and modernization. In this connection, the understanding of Buddhism in the newer sects does not go beyond the traditional insight, though a greater attempt may be made to make those doctrines relevant to the contemporary situation. Thus from the intellectual standpoint the new and old sects are on much the same footing. The clash of claims, however, will encourage the refining and clarifying of views which will benefit the entire Buddhist tradition in Japan.

BIBLIOGRAPHY
Chinese Religio-Philosophical Tradition

General historical works:
 Creel, H. C., *Chinese Thought from Confucius to Mao Tse-tung*, New York, New American Library, 1953.
 Hughes, E. R., and K. Hughes, *Religion in China*, London, Hutchinson, 1950.
 Li, Dun J., *The Ageless Chinese: A History*, New York, Scribner, 1965.

Sourcebooks:
 Chan, Wing-tsit, *A Sourcebook in Chinese Philosophy*, Princeton, N.J., Princeton University Press, 1963.
 De Bary, William Theodore, et al., *Sources of Chinese Tradition*, 2 vols., New York, Columbia, paperback ed., 1964.
 Hughes, E. R., *Chinese Philosophy in Classical Times*, London, Hutchinson's University Library, 1950.

General works on Chinese perspectives in religion and philosophy:
 Eberhard, Wolfram, *Guilt and Sin in Traditional China*, Berkeley, Calif., University of California Press, 1967.
 Hsu, Francis L. K., *Under the Ancestor's Shadow*, New York, Doubleday, 1967.
 Nakamura, Hajime, *Ways of Thinking of Eastern Peoples*, Honolulu, East-West Center Press, 1964.
 Thompson, Laurence G., *Chinese Religion: An Introduction*, Belmont, Calif., Dickenson, 1969.
 Yang, C. K., *Religion in Chinese Society*, Berkeley, Calif., University of California Press, 1961.

Works on Chinese popular religion:
 Day, Clarence Burton, *Chinese Peasant Cults*, Shanghai, Kelly and Walsh Limited, 1940.
 Finegan, Jack, *The Archaeology of World Religions*, Vol. 2, Princeton, N.J., Princeton University Press, paperback ed., 1965.
 Granet, Marcel, *Festivals and Songs of Ancient China*, New York, Dutton, 1932.

General works on Chinese philosophy:
 Fung, Yu-lan, *A Short History of Chinese Philosophy*, ed. D. Bodde, New York, Macmillan, paperback ed., 1966.
 ———, *The Spirit of Chinese Philosophy*, trans. E. R. Hughes, Boston, Beacon Press, 1967.

Waley, Arthur, *Three Ways of Thought in Ancient China,* New York, Doubleday, paperback ed., 1956.

Works on Confucianism:
   Creel, H. C., *Confucianism and the Chinese Way,* New York, Harper & Row, paperback ed., 1960.
   Levenson, Joseph R., *Confucian China and its Modern Fate,* 3 vols., Berkeley, Calif., University of California Press, 1968.
   Lin, Yu-tang, *The Wisdom of Confucius,* New York, Random House, 1938.
   Shryock, John K., *The Origin and Development of the State Cult of Confucius,* New York, Appleton-Century-Crofts, 1932.
   Verwilghen, Albert Felix, *Mencius: The Man and His Ideas,* New York, St. John's University Press, 1967.
   Waley, Arthur, *The Analects of Confucius,* New York, Random House, 1938.
   Ware, James, trans., *The Sayings of Mencius,* New York, New American Library, 1960.
   Watson, Burton, *The Basic Writings of Mo-tzu, Hsun-tzu, Han Fei-tzu,* New York, Columbia, 1967.
   Wright, Arthur F., *Confucianism and Chinese Civilization,* New York, Atheneum Publishers, 1964.

Works on Taoism:
   Chan, Wing-tsit, trans., *The Way of Lao-tzu,* Indianapolis, Bobbs-Merrill, 1963.
   Kaltenmark, Max, *Lao-tzu and Taoism,* Stanford, Calif., Stanford University Press, 1969.
   Watson, Burton, *Chuang Tzu: Basic Writings,* New York, Columbia, 1964.
   Welch, Holmes, *Taoism, the Parting of the Way,* Boston, Beacon Press, paperback ed., 1966.

Works on Buddhism:
   Ch'en, Kenneth, *Buddhism in China: A Historical Survey,* Princeton, N.J., Princeton University Press, 1964.
   Fung, Yu-lan, *History of Chinese Philosophy,* Vol. 2, Princeton, N.J., Princeton University Press, 1952–1953.
   Suzuki, Daisetsu T., *Studies in Zen,* New York, Dell, paperback ed., 1955.
   Welch, Holmes, *The Practice of Chinese Buddhism, 1900–1950,* Cambridge, Mass., Harvard, 1967.
   Wright, Arthur F., *Buddhism in Chinese History,* Stanford, Calif., Stanford University Press, 1959.
   Yampolsky, Philip B., *The Platform Sutra of the Sixth Patriarch,* New York, Columbia, 1967.

Works on modern China:
   Briere, O., *Fifty Years of Chinese Philosophy (1898–1948),* New York, Praeger, paperback ed., 1965.
   Chan, Wing-tsit, *Religious Trends in Modern China,* New York, Octagon, 1968.

Japanese Religious Tradition

Works on the historical backgrounds of Japanese culture:
De Bary, William Theodore, *Sources of Japanese Tradition,* New York, Columbia, 1958.
Sansom, G. B., *A History of Japan,* 3 vols., Stanford, Calif., Stanford University Press, 1958–1963.
———, *Japan: A Short Cultural History,* New York, Appleton-Century-Crofts, rev. ed., 1962.

Works on Japanese religious history:
Anesaki, Masaharu, *History of Japanese Religion,* Rutland, Vt., Charles E. Tuttle Co., 1963.
Kitagawa, Joseph M., *Religion in Japanese History,* New York, Columbia, 1966.
Kishimoto, Hideo, ed., *Japanese Religion in the Meiji Era,* Tokyo, Obunsha, 1956.

Works on Japanese religious perspectives and value orientations:
Anesaki, Masaharu, *Religious Life of the Japanese People,* Tokyo, Kokusai Bunka Shinkokai, 1961.
Bellah, Robert N., *Tokugawa Religion,* New York, Free Press, 1957.
Benedict, Ruth, *The Chrysanthemum and the Sword,* Rutland, Vt., Charles E. Tuttle Co., 1965.
Earhart, H. Byron, *Japanese Religion: Unity and Diversity,* Belmont, Calif., Dickenson, 1969.
Hori, Ichiro, *Folk Religion in Japan,* Chicago, University of Chicago Press, 1968.
Morioka, Kiyomi, and William H. Newell, eds., *The Sociology of Japanese Religion,* Leiden, E. J. Brill, 1968.
Moore, Charles A., ed., *The Japanese Mind,* Honolulu, East-West Center Press, 1967.
Nakamura, H., *Ways of Thinking of Eastern Peoples,* Honolulu, East-West Center Press, 1964.
Philippi, Donald L., trans., *Norito,* Tokyo, The Institute for Japanese Culture and Classics, Kokugakuin University, 1959.

Works on the Shinto tradition:
Aston, W. G., *Nihongi,* London, G. Allen, reprint, 1956.
Brown, Delmer, "Kami, Death, and Ancestral Kami," *The Proceedings of the Second International Conference for Shinto Studies,* Tokyo, Institute of Japanese Culture and Classics, Kokugakuin University, n.d.
Creemers, Wilhelmus H. M., *Shrine Shinto After World War II,* Leiden, E. J. Brill, 1968.
Holtom, D. C., *Modern Japan and Shinto Nationalism,* New York, Paragon, 2d ed., 1947.
———, *National Faith of Japan,* New York, Paragon, 1965.
Matsumoto, Shigeru, *Motoori Norinaga: 1730–1801,* Cambridge, Mass., Harvard, 1970.
Muraoka, Tsunetsugu, *Studies in Shinto Thought,* Tokyo, Japanese Ministry of Education, 1964.

Ono, Sokyo, *Shinto the Kami Way,* Tokyo, Bridgeway Press, 1962.

Philippi, Donald L., *Kojiki,* Princeton, N.J., Princeton University Press, 1969.

Ross, Floyd H., *Shinto: The Way of Japan,* Boston, Beacon Press, 1965.

Works on the Buddhist tradition:

Anesaki, Masaharu, *Nichiren the Buddhist Prophet,* Cambridge, Mass., Harvard, 1916.

Bloom, Alfred, *Shinran's Gospel of Pure Grace,* Tucson, Ariz., University of Arizona Press, 1965.

Coates, Harper H., and Ryugaku Ishizuka, *Honen the Buddhist Saint,* 5 vols., Kyoto, Society for the Publication of Sacred Books of the World, 1949.

DeVisser, M. W., *Ancient Buddhism in Japan,* 2 vols., Leiden, E. J. Brill, 1935.

Dumoulin, Heinrich, *A History of Zen Buddhism,* New York, Pantheon, 1963.

Matsunaga, Alicia, *The Buddhist Philosophy of Assimilation,* Rutland, Vt., Charles E. Tuttle Co., 1969.

Saunders, E. Dale, *Buddhism in Japan, with an Outline of Its Origins in India,* Philadelphia, University of Pennsylvania Press, 1964.

Watanabe, Shoko, *Japanese Buddhism: A Critical Appraisal,* Tokyo, Kokusai Bunka Shinkokai, 1964.

Works on new religions:

MacFarland, H. Neill, "Japan's New Religions," *Contemporary Religions in Japan,* 1, no. 4 (December, 1960), pp. 57–69.

MacFarland, H. Neill, *The Rush Hour of the Gods,* New York, Macmillan, 1967.

Murata, Kiyoaki, *Japan's New Buddhism,* New York, Walker-Weatherhill, 1969.

Offner, C. B., and H. Van Straelen, *Modern Japanese Religions,* Leiden, E. J. Brill, 1963.

A Short History of Tenrikyo, Tenri, Japan, 1958.

Thomsen, Harry, *The New Religions of Japan,* Rutland, Vt., Charles E. Tuttle Co., 1963.

GLOSSARY

A NOTE ON TRANSLITERATION
The simplest English transliterations of Sanskrit, Pali, Chinese, and Japanese, without diacritical marks, have been used in the text to make reading easier for the student unfamiliar with these languages. The more linguistically correct forms, with diacritics, have been used in the Glossary.

PART 1

Pronunciation of Sanskrit

Accent the first syllable of two syllable words. In longer words accent the penult when it is long vowel, otherwise the antepenult. A long syllable is one which contains a long vowel or diphthong. The vowels e and o are diphthongs, as are ai and au. For introductory purposes, one can ignore the dots that are sometimes found beneath certain consonants (ṭ, ḍ, etc.). The following can be taken as a general guide to pronunciation:

ā	as the a in father
a	(short) as the u in but
e	(long) as the a in say
ī	as i in machine
i	(short) i as in pin
o	as in go
ū	as in rule
u	(short) as in full
ṛ	(a vowel) usually as ri in river
c	as ch in church
g	as in get
ṣ or ś	as sh in shun
bh	as in abhor
th	as in anthill (not as in that)

Abhidhamma Piṭaka (*Abhidhamma Pitaka*). The third basket of the Pali Canon, containing doctrinal refinements.

Acharyas (*Āchāryas*). Teachers; those who, like Ramanuja, provided a philosophical base for theism.

Adhvaryu. Those priests of the Vedic sacrifices who are responsible for the manual operations of the sacrifices.

Adi Granth. The sacred book of the Sikh Community.

Advaita. Lit. "non-dual"; a philosophical system associated with Shankara.

Agni. The Vedic god of the fire, the priestly archetype.

Agnishtoma (*Agniṣṭoma*). Soma sacrifice, performed annually in the Spring.

Ahimsa (*Ahiṁsā*). Non-violence; non-injury to any living being.

Ahura Mazda. The one supreme being of Zoroaster.

Ajiva (*Ajīva*). The unconscious, matter; one of the two Jaina categories which compose the universe.

Alaya-vijnana (*Ālaya-vijñāna*). Yogacara doctrine of store-consciousness, accounting for deeds which do not reach immediate fruition.

Alvars (*Ālvārs*). Lit. "those who are immersed in God"; the twelve successive poet-saints of South India who were devoted to Krishna.

Amesha Spentas. Six divine abstractions which, for Zoroaster, were aspects of Ahura Mazda. They later became deities in their own right.

Amitabha. Lit. "Infinite Light"; Buddha of the Western Paradise.

Anatta (Pali; Skt. **Anātman**). Denial of Atman, the concept of a permanent self.

Anicca (Pali; Skt. **Anitya**). Impermanence.

Apramanani (*Apramāṇāni*). The four immeasurables of Theravada morality: loving kindness (*mettā*); compassion (*karuṇā*); sympathetic joy (*mudita*); and equanimity (*upekha*).

Apsaras. Water nymphs, wives of *gandharvas*.

Aranyakas (*Araṇyakas*). Lit. "forest texts"; the third part of the Vedas, secret and private sayings which later led into the Upanishads.

Arhat. One who is worthy to be honored, one who is enlightened; the ideal of the Pali Canon.

Asha. The Parsi concept of truth or justice; counterpart of the Rigvedic *Rita*.

Ashram (*Aśram*). A monastery.

Ashramas (*Aśramas*). The four stages in life: student (*brahmacarin*), householder (*gṛhastha*), forest dweller (*vanaprasthya*), and wanderer (*sannyasin*).

Ashvamedha (*Aśvamedha*). The Vedic rite of horse sacrifice, made by a king to signify that he was a universal monarch.

Ashvins (*Aśvins*). The heavenly twins, Vedic deities; possessors of horses.

Asuras. Vedic demons, enemies of the *devas*; good deities to the Parsis.

Atharvaveda (or **Atharvasaṁhitā**). The fourth collection of the Vedas, consisting mostly of magical formulae.

Ātman (*Atman*). The essence within man which is identical with the essence of the universe (*Brahman*).

Atyashramin (*Atyaśramin*). Lit. "he who is beyond the ashrams"; the fourth stage of life, later called sannyasin.

Avataras (*Avatāras*). Incarnations or descents, particularly the descents of Vishnu.

Avesta. The sacred text of the Parsis.

Avidya (*Avidyā*). Ignorance.

Ayatanas (*Āyatanas*). The classification of sense organs and sense data, analyzed in the *Abhidhamma Pitaka*.

Bhagavad Gita (*Bhagavad Gītā*). Part of the great epic the *Mahabharata*. The *Bhagavad Gita* is a book of devotion to Krishna as the Supreme deity.

Bhagavan (*Bhagavān*). Lit. "the Adorable One"; an epithet of personal devotion used of various deities, particularly of Krishna and the Buddha.

Bhajans. Hymns.

Bhakta. An adept who practices *bhakti*.

Bhakti. Lit. "Devotion"; a religious orientation including faith, love, surrender and devotional attachment, most often expressed to a personal deity.

Bhikkhu (Pali; Skt. **Bhikṣu**). Almsmen; the title for the followers of the Buddha who entered

the *Sangha* and lived by the rules of the *Vinaya*.
Bhikkunis (Pali; Skt. **Bhikṣunis**). Members of the monastic order for female devotees of the Buddha.
Bodhisattva. A Buddha-to-be.
Brahma (*Brahmā*). The creator god; sometimes placed in a triad with Siva (destroyer) and Vishnu (preserver).
Brahmacarin (*Brahmacārin*). The first stage of life, that of student.
Brahman. Devotion; food for the food offering; chant of the Sama singer; magical formula or text; great; the essence which pervades the universe; pure consciousness devoid of all attributes and categories of the intellect. Also, the highest class.
Brahmanas (*Brāhmaṇas*). Prose commentaries on the Samhitas or basic collections of the Vedas.
Buddha. Lit. "Enlightened One"; the title of Siddhattha Gotama.
Cakra. Wheel, circle; *cakra-puja* is left-handed tantric worship in which worshipers sit in a circle.
Dakmas. Towers of silence for the disposal of Parsi dead.
Dasyas. Dark-skinned worshipers of the phallus; foes of the Vedic Aryans.
Devadasis. Lit. "servants of God"; girls who were dedicated to temple deities and engaged in dancing and temple prostitution.
Devas. Lit. "gods"; a class of Vedic deities; "demons" to the Parsis.
Dhamma (Pali; Skt. **Dharma**). Law; the principle of order in society and in the universe; the teaching of the Buddha.
Dhatus (*Dhātus*). The irreducible elements of the universe: earth, fire, water, air, space (*akasha*), and consciousness.
Digambaras. Lit., "clothed in space"; a Jaina sect which gave up all attachments including clothes.
Din Ilahi. "The Divine Faith," promulgated by Akbar, which was intended to be a synthesis of "the best" of several Indian faiths.
Drishti (*Dṛṣti*). Dogmatism, viewpoints.
Druj. The Parsi personification of the Lie.
Dukkha. Suffering or "ill."
Dvaita. Dualism, the philosophical position of Madhva.
Gandharvas. Cloud spirits, husbands of the *apsaras*.
Gayatri (*Gāyatrī*). A verse to Savitri, recited daily by Brahmans.
Gopis. Cowherd lasses who are the lovers of Krishna in the *Bhagavata Purana*.
Grihapati (*Gṛhapati*). Lit. "lord of the house"; used as both an epithet of Agni and a term for a domestic priest.
Grihastha (*Gṛhastha*). The second stage of life, that of householder.

Gurdwaras. Lit. "gates of the Guru"; Sikh temples.
Guru. A spiritual teacher; a cult of the guru involves devotion to him as a divine manifestation.
Hanuman (*Hanumān*). The monkey god of the *Ramayana*.
Harihara. The deity who is a combination of Vishnu and Shiva.
Harijans. Children of Hari; people of god; Gandhi's term for the "untouchables."
Hinayana (*Hinayāna*). The "Little Vehicle"; a pejorative name given to the Theravada ("Way of the Elders") by the Mahayana, or followers of the "Great Vehicle."
Hotri (*Hotṛ*). Lit. "pourer of oblation"; a reciter of the verses of the *Rigveda*.
Indra. One of the principal deities of the *Rigveda*, a storm god attendant to the Buddha.
Ishvara (*Iśvara*). A supreme personal deity, Ultimate Reality for Ramanuja; in *advaita*, Brahman as qualified Lord or Saguna Brahman.
Jainas. Followers of the *jinas* who attained release and enlightenment; religion stemming from Mahavira.
Japji. Morning devotional prayer of the Sikhs.
Jinas. "Conquerors" or "victors."
Jiva (*Jīva*). The conscious or living principle, one of two Jain categories which compose the universe; the phenomenal personality in Shankara.
Jivan-mukti (*Jīvan-mukti*). Liberated while living; the state of perfection in this life after realization of unity with Brahman in the thought of Shankara.
Jnanamarga (*Jñānamārga* or *Jñānayoga*). Lit. "the way through knowledge", i.e., through meditation and discriminative thought.
Karma (Pali **Kamma**). "Deed" or "act"; causal connection within the spiritual order; results of actions; the law which governs the regrouping of the khandhas and rebirth in the Pali Canon and which weights the *jivas* down in Jaina thought.
Karmamarga (*Karmamārga* or *Karmayoga*). Lit. "the way through works"; the way through sacrifice in the Vedic period, and through disciplined action in the *Gita*.
Karuna (*Karuṇā*). Compassion, sympathy without attachment.
Kevalin. "Omniscient One"; a Jaina term for the individual whose influx of karma has stopped and whose permeating karma is worked out.
Khalsa (*Khālsā*). "Community of the Pure"; a Sikh term for those initiated into the community by drinking and being sprinkled with *amrit*, sweetened water.
Khandhas (Pali; Skt. **Skhandhas**). The components of phenomenal individual existence.
Krishna (*Kṛṣna*). Lit. "the Dark One"; a human hero in the *Mahabharata*; supreme deity in the *Bhagavad Gita*; avatar of Vishnu.

Kshatriyas (*Kṣatriyas*). A warrior, the second highest class.
Kusti. Parsi sacred thread.
Lakkhana (*Lakkhaṇa*). The three marks of existence in the Pali Canon: impermanence (*anicca*), no self (*anatta*), and suffering (*dukkha*).
Lokakasha (*Lokākaśa*). For the Jainas, the top of the universe, where purified *jivas* live in eternal bliss.
Linga (*Liṅga*). The male reproductive organ; symbol of Shiva.
Madhyamika (*Mādhyamika*). "The Middle Way" between realism and nihilism; a philosophical school associated with Nagarjuna; a system of logic which reduces ontological systems to absurdity.
Mahabharata (*Mahābhārata*). One of the two Indian epics; it contains the *Bhagavad Gita.*
Mahavira (*Mahāvīra*). "Great Hero," an epithet of Vardhamana, the Jaina saint.
Mahayana (*Mahāyāna*). "The Great Vehicle," the so-called Northern School of Buddhism.
Mahayogi (*Mahāyogī*). "Great ascetic," an epithet of Shiva.
Mandalas (*Maṇḍalas*). Diagrams of mystic import.
Mantras. Short verses; mystic syllables often containing unintelligible sounds.
Math. Monastery.
Maya (*Māyā*). Occult, superhuman; in *advaita*, cosmic illusion.
Metta (*mettā*). Loving kindness, benevolent harmlessness.
Milindapanha (*Milindapañhā*). Lit. "Questions of King Milinda"; a Theravada text not actually in the Pali Canon.
Moksha (*Mokṣa*). Emancipation, release, enlightenment.
Mudita (*Muditā*). Sympathetic joy.
Mudras (*Mūdrās*). Ritual gestures with the fingers.
Nibbana (Pali; Skt. **Nirvāṇa**). The blowing out; state of enlightenment and bliss; the attainment of the Buddha.
Naojote. "One who offers prayers new"; initiation ceremony for the Parsi boy or girl.
Nataputta (*Nātaputta*). "Son of the Nath"; an epithet of Mahavira.
Nataraja (*Naṭarāja*). "Lord of dance"; an epithet of Shiva.
Nayanars (*Nāyanārs*). South Indian devotees to Shiva whose hymns form the *Devaram.*
Niganthas (*Nigaṇṭhas*). Followers of Mahavira.
Nyasa (*Nyāsa*). Ritual movements of the hands.
Pabbajja. "Outgoing" from the world; a preparatory ordination for followers of the Buddha who sought to join the Sangha.
Panna (Pali *Paññā*) or **Prajna** (Skt. *Prajñā*). Insight or wisdom; for Nagarjuna, a non-dual intuition of the Real.
Parajikas (*Pārajikas*). The four offenses, any of which would cause expulsion of a bhikshu from the Sangha: sexual intercourse, theft, knowingly depriving a creature of life, boasting of some superhuman perfection.
Parinibbana (Pali; Skt. **Parinirvāṇa**). Complete escape from chain of causation; the release or liberation that occurs at death.
Patijnana (*Patijñāna*). Lit. "Knowledge of the father"; divine knowledge given by Shiva.
Patimokkha (Pali; Skt. **Prātimokṣa**). The 252 rules of the Sangha.
Pitris (*Pitṛs*). Distant and somewhat mythical male ancestors.
Prajapati (*Prajāpati*). "Lord of Beings"; originally a title of many Rigvedic deities, later used for the Rigvedic deity conceived to be above all others.
Prana (*Prāṇa*). Breath; the vital force in man that was considered for a time to be the unifying substance of the universe.
Prapatti. Surrender, absolute humility, a willingness to give up anything that is against God's will. *Prapatti* is an attitude that expresses itself in *bhakti.*
Prasada (*Prasāda*). Divine grace.
Pretas. Spirits of recently dead male ancestors.
Puja (*Pūjā*). Adoration and worship; rites of offerings and circumambulation of the temple or image.
Puranas (*Purāṇas*). A group of scriptures dating from the medieval period that emphasize bhakti.
Purdah. The Muslim practice of the veiling and seclusion of women.
Purusha (*Puruṣa*). Lit. "Man"; primordial sacrifice; the permanent and spiritual aspect of man in Samkhya and Yoga philosophies.
Radha (*Rādhā*). The consort of Krishna; one of the cowherd lasses.
Rakshas (*Rakṣas*). Demons.
Rama (*Rāma*). The great hero in the *Ramayana*; he is the incarnation of Vishnu, supreme deity of the Ramanandi or Ramawat sect.
Ramadan (*Ramadān*). The Muslim month of fasting.
Ramayana (*Rāmāyaṇa*). One of the two great Indian epics, centering around Rama and Sita.
Rigveda (*Ṛgveda*); also **Riksamita**. The first of the four Vedic collections.
Rishis (*Ṛṣis*). Seers; those who apprehend eternal truth.
Rita (*Ṛta*). A cosmic and ethical order, the later extension of which is *dharma*.
Saddharmapundarika (*Saddharmapuṇḍarīka*). Lit. "Lotus of the True Law"; a Mahayana sutra with strong *bhakti* emphasis.
Sadhana (*Sādhanā*). Meditative exercises or discipline.
Samadhi (*Samādhi*). Concentration.
Samaveda (also *Samasaṁhitā*). A collection of melodies (*samans*) to be sung at the Soma sacrifice; the third of the four Vedic collections.

Samhitas (Saṁhitās). Collections of basic verses, including the *Rigveda*.
Samsara (Saṁsāra). Successive states of rebirth.
Samskaras. Life cycle of sacred events; ceremonies to secure divine favor from birth to death.
Sanatana Dharma (Sanātana Dharma). Lit. "Eternal religion"; a term used by Radhakrishnan and others to refer to Hinduism.
Sangha. The monastic order of the followers of the Buddha.
Sannyasin. Later term for the fourth stage of life, that of the "wanderer," or one who has renounced the world.
Sarasvati. The goddess of the river, one of the few female deities in the *Rigveda*.
Sati. Lit. "a virtuous or chaste woman"; the immolation of a widow on her husband's funeral pyre.
Satyagraha (Sātyāgraha). Lit. "holding on to truth"; the refusal, as by Gandhi, to participate in the working of an unjust system.
Savitri (Savitṛ). A Vedic solar deity.
Shakti (Śakti). Lit. "power"; a deity's power in form of his consort.
Shakyamuni (Śakyamuni). "Sage of the Shakyas"; an epithet of the Buddha.
Shiva (Śiva). An epithet of the Rigvedic Rudra, lit. "auspicious"; the destroyer; the great ascetic; lord of animals; and lord of the dance.
Shramanas (Śramanas). Ascetics.
Shravakas (Śrāvakas). Lit. "hearers"; Jaina lay followers.
Shruti (Śruti). Lit. "that which is heard"; hence, not of human origin, i.e., the Vedas.
Shuddhi (Śuddhi). The ceremony used by Arya Samaj to reclaim those who had left "Hinduism."
Shudras (Śudras). Members of the fourth class, who performed manual labors; not of the twice-born.
Shunyata (Śūnyatā). Void or emptiness.
Shvetambaras (Śvetāmbaras) Lit. "white-clothed"; a Jaina sect of monks who believed it possible to attain perfection even if one wore clothes.
Sikhs. Lit. "disciples"; followers of the True Name, a movement initiated by Nanak.
Sila (Śīla). Pali morality, as represented by the ten precepts for *bhikkhus* and the five precepts for laymen.
Sita (Sītā). In the *Ramayana*, the wife of Rama.
Smriti (Smṛti). Lit. "that which is remembered"; commentaries on *shruti* that are only authoritative for advaitins to the extent that they agree with *shruti*.
Soma. A plant and the exhilarating beverage made from it; the heavenly nectar of the gods; also, a Vedic deity.
Spenta Mainyu. Lit. "Holy or Bounteous Spirit"; a Parsi deity.
Sthanakavasis. A Jaina sect opposed to the use of images.
Sudrah. The sacred shirt used in the Parsi initiation ceremony.
Surya (Sūrya). The sun; a solar deity; an all-seeing deity.
Sutta Pitaka (Sutta Piṭaka). The second basket of the *Tipitaka,* containing collections of reputed sayings of the Buddha.
Sutra (Sūtra; Pali **Sutta**). Lit. "thread"; short statements; discourses of the Buddha.
Swadesi. Gandhi's term for the use of only those things produced in one's immediate neighborhood.
Swaraj. Gandhi's ideal of self-rule.
Syadvada (Syādvāda). The Jaina doctrine of maybe, a sevenfold logic of affirmation and denial.
Tanha (Taṇha). Grasping; desire.
Tantras. Texts connected with Saktism.
Tapas. Heat; austerities.
Tathagata (Tathāgata). "One who has thus come," an epithet of the Buddha; an enlightened being.
Tathata (Tathatā). Lit. "thatness" or "suchness"; the Real as void of all views.
Tattvas. The five forbidden things that are used in left-handed tantric ritual: wine, meat, fish, parched grain, and sexual intercourse.
Thags. Organized bands of devotees to Kali who murdered victims by strangulation; hence the English word "thugs."
Theravada (Theravāda). Lit. "Way of the Elders"; followers of Buddha who follow the Pali Canon.
Tilak. Symbolic marks on the body showing devotion to a particular deity.
Tipitaka (Pali; Skt. **Tripiṭaka**). Three baskets; the scriptures of the Theravadins (*Vinaya, Sutta,* and *Abhidhamma*).
Tirthankaras (Tīrthaṅkaras). "Fordfinders," a long line of great *jinas* who have achieved release; objects of worship of the Jainas.
Trikaya (Trikāya). The doctrine of the "three bodies" of the Buddha: the cosmic body (*Dharmakaya*), the body of bliss (*Sambhogakaya*), and the apparitional body (*Nirmanakaya*).
Trimurti (Trimūrti). The synthesis of Brahma, Vishnu, and Shiva into one deity.
Udgatri (Udgatṛ). A priest of the Samaveda ritual; a singer at Soma sacrifice.
Upanayana (Upanāyana). A rite of initiation that can only be performed by the three highest classes.
Upanishad (Upaniṣad). Lit. "to sit nearby devotedly"; mystical, philosophical texts and secret sayings; the texts that come at the end of the *Vedas* and are important for *Vedanta*.
Upasakas (Upāsakas). Male lay devotees of the Buddha; householders.
Upasikas (Upāsikās). Female lay devotees of the Buddha.
Upasampada (Upasaṁpadā). Lit. "the arrival"; ordination into full membership in the Sangha.

Upaya (*Upāya*). Device; skill in means.
Upekha (*Upakhā*). Equanimity, the quality of neutrality and non-attachment.
Uposatha. The fortnightly service of confession for *Bhikkhus*.
Vaishya (*Vaiśya*). The commercial class, the third of the four classes.
Vajra. A thunderbolt, the weapon of Indra.
Vajrasattva. Lit. "being of diamond essence"; the fourth body whereby the Buddha embraced his Shakti, Tara, or Bhagavati.
Vanaprasthya (*Vānaprasthya*). A forest dweller, the third stage of life.
Vardhamana (*Vardhamāna*). A Kshatriya who became Mahavira and pointed the way to enlightenment for the Jainas.
Varna (*Varṇa*). Lit. "color"; the class system that evolved from the Aryan conquest of Dasyas, the fourfold division of society into Brahmans, Kshatriyas, Vaishyas, and Shudras.
Varuna (*Varuṇa*). A Vedic deity, sovereign of the cosmic order, ruling with *Rita*.
Veda. Lit. "knowledge"; sacred knowledge. Also, a group of sacred texts considered *shruti* and hence not of human origination.
Vedi. The fire pit where Agni dwells.
Videhamukti. In Shankara's thought, a state of disembodied liberation following Jivanmukti.
Vijnanavada (*Vijñānavāda*). Yogacara (q.v.).
Vinaya Pitaka (*Vinaya Piṭaka*). The first basket of the *Tipiṭaka*, containing the rules for the Sangha.
Vishishtadvaita (*Viśiṣtadvaita*). A philosophical position of qualified non-dualism advocated by Ramanuja. The Absolute is qualified by diversity of interrelated elements.
Vishnu (*Viṣṇu*). A minor solar deity of the Rigveda who later became an important deity with numerous *avataras*.
Vishvakarman (*Viśvakarman*). Lit. "All Creator"; a late Rigvedic deity conceived to be above others.
Yajurveda (also *Yajurṣaṁhitā*). One of the four Vedas, a collection of sacrificial formulae.
Yasna. A liturgical book of the Parsis.
Yatis. Lit. "strivers"; Jaina monastic order comprised of those who give up the life of the householder.
Yogacara (*Yogācāra*). A philosophical school of the followers of the Buddha which held that only consciousness is Real; a method of withdrawal of the senses from supposed external objects until there is Thought only; the goal of pure subjectivity.
Yoni. Vulva, the symbol of female principle.

PART 2

Chinese Terms

Chen-jen. A Taoist immortal.
Ch'eng. Sincerity, truth, reality.
Ch'i. A Neo-Confucian term meaning ether or vacuous gas; the principle of individuation.
Ch'ien-ai. Universal love: in the philosophy of Mo ti, indiscriminant love.
Chih. Knowledge, wisdom.
Chung. Conscientiousness, loyalty.
Chun-tzu. Lit. "son of an aristocrat"; the true gentleman, superior person, or ideal man in Confucian thought.
Feng-shui. Wind and water: a term for geomancy.
Five Elements. The basic constituents of all things: metal, water, earth, fire, and wood.
Hou-chi. Lord Millet, the grain deity.
Hou-t'u. Lord Soil, the earth deity.
Hsiao. Filial piety.
Hsueh. Learning, study.
I. Righteousness.
Jen. A basic Confucian virtue: benevolence, love, humaneness.
Ju. Literati.
Ju-chiao. The teaching of the Literati: a traditional term for Confucius.
Kuei. The negative, demonic forces that are the basis of physical nature in man.
Li. Principle, reason.
Li. Propriety, courtesy, etiquette; principles of conduct.
Shang-ti. Supreme rule: Supreme Ancestor, the central deity of Shang people.
She-chi. The altar of earth and grain in ancient Chinese folk religion.
Shen. Positive, divine forces: good spirits; the superior aspect of human person: basis of intelligence and vital forces.
Shih. A knight, an ideal person similar to *chun-tzu* in Confucian thought.
Shu. Reciprocity, altruism.
Tao. The way, road, or path. In Taoism, the way of nature, the cosmic order or reality; in Confucianism, the way of society and human behavior.
Te. In Taoism, the manifestation of Tao in nature and affairs; in Confucian thought, moral force and influence.
T'ien. Heaven. This term has numerous meanings, extending from personalized divine force to the impersonal order of nature.
T'ien-ming. The mandate or decree of Heaven, implying a moral order running through the universe and human affairs.
Wen. Culture, decoration, bearing, poise.
Wu. Sorcerer, wizard, or shaman in Chinese popular religion.
Wu-wei. Non-action, by which all actions are completed. *Wu-wei* is a basic doctrine of Taoism.
Yin-yang. The contrasting cosmic forces making up the universe. Yin represents such negative features as dark, moist, cold, soft, female, etc., and yang the bright, dry, warm, hard, male characteristics in things.

Japanese Terms

Daimoku. The title of the *Lotus Sutra,* associated with the Nichiren Buddhist tradition.

Dōzoku. A group of related, nuclear families in a hierarchical arrangement involving status and obligations.

Gensō. The doctrine of the return of the Bodhisattva to this world to work for the salvation of beings, stressed in Shinran's Pure Land doctrine.

Hommon Kaidan. The ordination platform emphasized in Nichiren tradition.

Honji-suijaku. Fundamental-reality-trace-manifestation, basic terminology for the Buddhist philosophical theory developed in Japan, showing the gods as manifestations of the Buddha.

Hōza. Group meetings for mutual spiritual support in the Japanese Rissho-kosei-kai Buddhist organization.

Kami. In the Japanese Shinto tradition, divinity.

Kokugaku. National Learning, a term associated with the intellectual movement in Shinto tradition.

Kokutai. National Essence, National Polity, a term referring to the unique character and structure of the Japanese people in Shinto tradition.

Makoto. Sincerity, truth; a basic value in Shinto tradition.

Mappō. In Buddhist eschatology, the Last Age in the decline and disappearance of the *dharma.*

Matsuri. In Shinto tradition, a festival, service of a deity.

Musubi. In Shinto tradition, growth, creativity, productivity.

Norito. Shinto ritual prayers.

Oharae. Shinto prayer for purification.

On. Favor, goodness, kindness; to repay *on* is to be grateful and mindful of one's obligations.

Saisei-itchi. The union of religion and government in Japanese tradition.

Shakubuku. Forceful, aggressive efforts to convert someone, a term prominently associated with the Nichiren Buddhist tradition.

Sūkeisha. A voluntary member of a Shinto shrine because of belief or interest.

Ujiko. Lit. "son of the clan"; a member of a Shinto shrine because of birth or territorial relationship.

Zazen. In Zen Buddhism, the practice of sitting in meditation.

INDEX

Abhidhamma-Pitaka, 26, 37, 40, 70
Abhidharma Kosa Buddhism, *see* Kusha Buddhism
Abkar, 97–98
Absolute
   Buddhist concept of, 74, 206
   in Theosophy, 115
Absolute Power, the, *see* Khshathra Vairva
abstainers, *see* imibe
Acharyas, 54
actions, *see Karma; Yu-wei*
adepts, 116
Adhvaryu, 8, 14
Adi Brahma Samaj, 108–109
Adi Granth, 100, 101
Adorable One, *see* Bhagavan
advaita
   and Madhva, 82
   in Ramakrishna movement, 113
   Shankara on, 77
   and Shiva *bhakti,* 64
   and Sikhs, 101
   See also Advaita Vedanta
afterlife
   in Shang religions, 153–154
   in Shinto, 250
   in Vedic religion, 22
   Wang Chung on, 181
Agamas, 132
age of Great Peace, 203
Agni, 11–12, 15
   hymn to, 6–7
agnishtoma, see soma sacrifice
ahimsa, doctrine of, 44, 85
   Gandhi on, 119
   and vegetarianism, 126–127
Ahura Mazda, 14, 92, 93, 94

Ai, Duke of Lu, 149, 160, 162
ajiva, 43
Akbar, Emperor, 101
alaya-vijnana, 76
alchemy, 202
Alexander the Great, 91
All Creator, *see* Vishvakarman
almsmen, *see* bhikshus
altruism, *see* shu
Alvars, 53–54, 62
Amaterasu-o-mikami, 232, 241, 243
Ame-no-mi-naka-nushi-no-Kami, 237, 240, 247
ameretat, 93
Amesha Spentas, 93
Amida Buddha, 51, 217, 218, 264, 266, 270, 272
Amitabha, *see* Amida Buddha
Amitayur-dhyana Sutra, see Kuan-wu-liang-shou-ching
Amitayus, *see* Amida Buddha
amrit, 103
Amrita, 59
Analects, 159, 163–171, 179
ananda, 115
Ananda, 212
anatman, see anatta
anatta, doctrine of, 32, 37, 76
ancestor worship, 92
   in ancient Shinto, 232
   and Confucianism, 160, 162
   in Shang religion, 154
   See also ancestors
ancestors
   in ancient Chinese religions, 157
   in Popular Buddhism, 266
   in Vedic ritual, 17
Anesaki, 252

Angad, 101
Angra Mainyu, 93
Anguttara-nikaya, 26, 31
anicca, 31
animal sacrifice,
   laws against, 126
animal worship, in pre-Vedic religion, 4
animals
   in ancient Shinto, 236
   in Neo-Taoist thought, 201
   spirits of, 238
anitya, see anicca
Ansai, Yamazaki, 244
Antoku, Emperor, 274
aparigraha, 85
Appeal to the Christian Public, 107
apramanani, 40–41
apsaras, 14
Aquinas, Saint Thomas, 89
Arahito-gami, 236
ara-mi-tama spirits, 238
Aranyakas, 6, 8
Arhat, 27, 32–33, 37, 45, 206
Arinori, Mori, 250
aristocracy
   and Confucianism, 146
   and Doctrinal Buddhism, 270
Arjan, 101
Arjuna, 52
Armaiti, 93
art
   Buddha in, 49–50
   influence of Ch'an Buddhism on, 216–217
   and Zen discipline, 273
artha, 124
Arya Samaj, 109–110

292 INDEX

Aryan varnas, 131
Aryans, and Indus Valley civilization, 4–5
Aryas, 18, 121
asamprajnata, 86
asana, 85
Asanga, 74
asat, 78
asceticism
  and Sikhs, 101
  See also tapas
ascetics, *see* asceticism; *shramanas*
Asha, 92–93
Asha Vahishta, 92–93
ashes, 61
ashi, 228
Ashoka, King, 26
ashramas, doctrine of, 18, 120
Ashtasahasrika Prajnaparamita Sutra, 69
ashvamedha, see horse sacrifice
Ashvins, 12–13
Association of Shinto Shrines, 240
asteya, 85
astrology, 156, 266
Asuras, 14, 92
atharvan, 7
Atharvasamhita, see Atharvaveda
Atharvaveda, 7
Atman, concept of, 32, 36
  and Advaita Vedanta, 78–79
  and Jainas, 43
  Real as, 70
  supreme, *see* Paramatman
attachment, *see upadana*
attention, *see dharana*
atyashramin, 18
Aurangzeb, Emperor, 96, 98–99, 103
  See also Awrangzeb
Aurobindo, Sri, *see* Ghose, Sri Aurobindo
austerities, *see tapas*
Avalambana festival, 219
  See also Urabon-e festival
Avalokitesvara, *see* Kannon; Kuan-yin
Avatamsaka Buddhism, *see* Kegon Buddhism
Avatamsaka Sutra, see Kegon Sutra
avataras, 48
  doctrine of, 58
  of Shiva, 61
  of Vishnu, 58, 59
Avesta, 91–92
avidya, 74, 81
avijja, 33
ayatanas, 70
Ayodhyakanda, 57–58
Azumamaro, Kada, 245

Badarinath Monastery, 76
badha, 78
Bali, 59
Banaras Hindu University, 115
baptism, of Sikhs, 103
Baroda College, 121
bathing rituals
  in Ramakrishna movement, 113
  in Shang and Chou religions, 151
becoming, *see bhava*
behavior, in Taoist thought, 189
  See also morality

Being
  in Neo-Taoist thought, 200
  in Taoist thought, 186
  See also sat
Belur Math, 112
bending Kami, *see* Magatsubi-no-kami
Bengal
  Kali worship in, 66
  Krishna worship in, 54
  religious laws in, 126
Bentinck, William, 126
Bergson, Henri, 117
Besant, Annie, 114, 115
Best Order, the, *see* Asha Vahista
betel chewing, 54, 54*n*
Bhagavad Gita, 46, 49, 72, 77
  and caste system, 131
  influence on Gandhi, 119
  Krishna in, 52
  and Radhakrishnan, 123
Bhagavan, 48, 80
Bhagavata Purana, 52, 54
  and Dvaita, 82
bhakti movements, 48–49, 66–67
  attempts at synthesis of, 66–67
  definitions of, 56
  influence on Sikhs, 101
  and Ramakrishna movement, 111
  and Shankara, 80
  and Theosophy, 116
  and Vishtishtadvaita, 81
  See also Buddha *bhakti;* Krishna *bhakti;* Rama *bhakti;* Shakti *bhakti;* Vishnu *bhakti*
bhava, 33
Bhikku-Sangha, 39
bhikkhunis, 39
bhikkus, 38–39
  moral precepts of, 40–41
bhikshunis, see bhikkhunis
Bhutatathata, 206
biblical religion, *see* Christianity
birth
  determination of abode of, 35
  and Vedic rituals, 16
birth control, Gandhi on, 120
black age, *see* Kali
Blavatsky, Madame, 114
bliss, *see ananda*
Boar, the, *see* Varaha
Board of Shinto Missionaries, 249
Bodhiruci, 218
Bodhisattvas
  in *bhakti* sutras, 51
  and return after death, *see* Genso
  vows of, 27
  wives of, 65
  See also Bosatsu
"body of bliss," *see* Sambhogakaya
body markings, 83, 103
Book of Ceremonies, see Li-chi
Book of Changes, see I-ching
Book of Documents, see Shu-ching
Book of Music, 148
Book of Poems, see Shih-ching
Bosatsu, Gyogi, 263–264
Boxer Rebellion, 204
Brahma, 13, 67
  and Buddha, 50
  in triad of gods, 67
  wife of, *see* Sarasvati

Brahma Covenant, 108
Brahma Samaj, 107–109
Brahma Sutra
  and Radhakrishnan, 123
  Shankara's commentaries on, 76–77
  and Vishtishtadvaita, 80
brahmacarin, 18
brahmacarya, 85
  Gandhi on, 120
"Brahmana of the hundred ways," *see* Shatapatha Brahmana
Brahmanas
  and Dvaita, 82
  Vishnu in, 58
Brahmans, 18
  and Advaita Vedanta, 77–78
  and ethics, 80
  interpretations of Vedic texts by, 8–9
  and Krishna, 54
  and Muslim invasion, 97
  in Pali Canon, 70
  and Ramakrishna movement, 114
  after Rigvedic period, 21–22
  and sacrifice rituals, 14–15
  theistic trends of, 58
  and Vishtishtadvaita, 81
Brahmanical religious system, *see* Vedic religion
Brahmanization, 58–59
breath, *see prana*
breath control, *see pranayama*
Briere, O., 183, 183*n*
Brihadaranyaka Upanishad, 21, 77
Brihaspati, 86
British, in India, 106–107
Buddha, 45, 47, 262
  according to T'ien-t'ai school, 212
  as *avatara,* 60
  birth of, 27
  bodies of, 65
  Chinese attitude toward, 206
  death of, 26, 30
  images of, 162
  life of, 27–30, 50–51
  as manifestation of absolute Kami, 144
  multiplicity of, 72
  and Pali tradition, 25–27
  remains of, 49
  silence of, 69–70
  Vishnu in form of, 60
  and Zazen, 273
  Buddha *bhakti,* 49–51
Buddha of Nara, 164
Buddha-nature, 216
Buddha Sakyamuni, 217, 274
Buddha of Todaiji, 258
Buddhaghosha, 26
Buddhism
  in China, *see* Chinese Buddhism
  compared with Jaina doctrine, 43
  and doctrines of Buddha's life, 27–30
  and harmony in human relations, 142
  influence on Confucianism, 182
  in Japan, *see* Japanese Buddhism
  moral precepts of, 30–41
  Pali doctrines of, *see* Pali doctrine
  and Pure Shinto, 244, 245

Buddhism (continued)
  and Religious Taoism, 202, 203
  and Sangha, 38–40
  and Shakti worship, 65
  and shamanism, 233
  and Shinto, 242–243
  and social function of religion, 143–144
  and worship of souls of dead, 232–233
Budhgaya, temple of Buddha at, 60
Burma, religious law in, 125
butchering, in Jaina doctrine, 44

cakra-puja, 65
Calcutta
  Kalighat Temple in, 66
  sati in, 126
calendar(s)
  Buddhist, 208
  of memorials, 266
car festival of Lord Jagannath, 60
Carey, William, 90
Carvaka, 68, 86–88
caste system
  Gandhi on, 119
  and government legislation, 130–132
  Radhakrishnan on, 124–125
  and Rama *bhakti*, 56, 57
  in *Rigveda*, 122
cat view, 82
Catholic Church, *see* Roman Catholic Church
causation, doctrine of, 70, 71, 72
  See also paticcasumuppada
Central Hindu College, 115
ceremonial bath, 16
Ceremonies and Rituals, *see I-li*
Ceylon, 26, 55
Chaitanya, 54–55
Ch'an Buddhism, 181, 209, 212–214, 216–217
  See also Rinzai Zen Buddhism
Chandogya Upanishad, 23, 77
Chang Chueh, 203
Chang Ling, 203
charms, in Vedic texts, 7
  See also magic
Chen-jen, 206
Chen-yen Buddhism, *see* Shingon Buddhism
ch'eng, 164n, 180
chi, 164n
ch'i, 182
Chi, Baron, 160
Chi-i, 211, 212
Chi K'ang, 200
Chi-tsang, 209
Chikafusa, Kitabatake, 229, 244
child marriage, 106
  and Arya Samaj, 110
  and Brahma Samaj, 107
child sacrifice, 126
Ch'in dynasty, 146, 147, 178
Chinese Buddhism, 144–145
  beginnings of, 205–209
  and *Chung-yung*, 179
  compared with Japanese Buddhism, 256–257
  Confucianist criticisms of, 219
  emergence of, 157–158
  fusion with religious Taoism, 219
  growth of, 208–209
  during Han dynasty, 181
  historic view of, 218–221
  in modern China, 220–221
  relationship to Taoism, 206–207
  schools of, 209–211
    Chu'an school, 212–214, 216–217
    Hua-Yen school, 211
    Pure Land school, 217–218
  spread of, 147
  Taoist and Confucian attacks against, 206–208
  and Western culture, 220
Chinese Buddhist Association, 221
Chinese folk religion, 201
Chinese religions
  ancient, 157–158
  Buddhism, *see* Chinese Buddhism
  during Chou dynasty, 145–146
  classics of, 147–150
  compared with Western religions, 143
  Confucianism, *see* Confucianism
  harmony and tranquillity as goals of, 142–143
  historical stages of, 145–147
  influence on Japanese religion, 266
  merging of, 144–145
  and Mo-ti, 173–174
  Neo-Taoism, 200–201
  Philosophical Taoism, 184–197
  and politics, 155
  Religious Taoism, 201–204
  role of scholar-bureaucrat in, 144
  in Shang and Chou eras, 145, 151–158
  social function of, 143–144
  and Yang-chu, 172–173
Chinese scholars, *see* Ju
Ch'ing period, 182
Ching t'u, *see* Pure Land School
Chinju-no-Kami, 238
Chinvat Bridge, 94
Ch'iu, *see* Confucius
Chou, *see* Chuang-tzu
Chou dynasty, 138, 145–146, 156
Chou-li, 149
Chou religions, 151, 151n, 154
Christ, *see* Jesus Christ
Christian Church, *see* Christianity
Christian missionaries
  and "Hindu" consciousness, 132
  in India, 106–107
  and Theosophical Society, 114
Christianity
  and Brahma Samaj, 108, 109
  in China, 147
  and Chinese Buddhism, 220
  and Gandhi, 119
  in India, 89–90
  in Japan, 224, 249
  and National Buddhism, 261–262
  and quest for immortality, 202
  Radhakrishnan on, 123
  and Shinto, 247
  Tagore on, 117
  See also Christians, Protestantism, Roman Catholic Church
Christians, Indian, 89–90
"Christians of Saint Thomas," 89
Chu Hsi, 147, 181–182
Chuan-chen-chiao, 203
Chuang-tzu, 146, 155–156, 164, 184, 194–201
Chuguji temple, 258
Ch'un-ch'iu, time of, 146, 148, 149
chung, 164, 166, 167
Chung-ni, *see* Confucius
Chung-yung, 149, 178, 179–180, 243
chun-tzu, ideal of, 164, 169–170
Church of England, 106
Church-state conflict
  and Buddhism, 275
  in India, 125–126
    and reform of religion, 129–132
    and regulation of religious practices, 127–129
    and suppression of religious practices, 126–127
  and Japanese religion, 250
Chu Yuan-chang, 219–220
circle worship, *see cakra-puja*
circumambulation of temple, 48
cit, 115
citta, 84
civil disobedience, 120
civilization, *see also* specific names of, e.g., Indus Valley Civilization
clans
  in Japanese society, 226
  of Shang people, 154
  See also sects
class
  and caste, 130–131
  Radhakrishnan on, 124–125
  in Vedic religion, 18
Classic of Filial Piety, *see Hsiao-ching*
Clean Government party, *see* Komeito
Cloister government, *see* Insei government
clothing, in Jaina religion, 46
Cochin, Jewish settlement at, 90
coins, divination with, 156
color
  as class distinction, 18
  of Kali, 66
Commentary on "Composition of Ancient History," A, *see Koshiden*
Common man, *see* masses
communal feeling, in Japanese religions, 226–227
Communism
  and Chinese Buddhism, 220, 221
  and Confucian philosophy, 183
  in Japan, 251–252, 254
Community of the Pure, *see* Khalsa
compassion, *see karuna*
Complete Truth Religion, *see* Chuan-chen-chiao
Composition of Ancient History, *see Koshi Seibun*
concentration, 196
  See also samadhi
confession, in Buddhism, 39
Confucian Shinto, 243, 252–253

Confucianism, 146
  and Buddhism, 218–219
  and Chuang-tzu, 194–195
  compared with Japanese Buddhism, 256–257
  compared with Taoism, 191–192
  and criticisms of Buddhism, 207–208
  and divination, 156
  early development of, 160, 162–163
  fusion with Taoism, 144–145
  during Han dynasty, 146–147
  and Hsun-tzu, 177–178
  and human relations, 163–171
  in Japan, 224, 266
  and Japanese Buddhism, 262
  and karmic system, 205–206
  and life of Confucius, 159–160
  and Mencius, 174–177
  in modern times, 180–183
  and Mo-ti, 173
  and Neo-Taoism, 200–201
  and Old Text-New Text controversy, 182
  and Philosophical Taoism, 185–186, 198
  polarities in thought of, 170
  religious literature of, 147–150
  and Shinto, see Confucian Shinto
  and *Ta-hsueh*, 178–179
  and Western culture, 147
  See also Neo-Confucianism
Confucius, 146
  on Duke of Chou, 155
  on externalism, 185–186
  on harmony in human relations, 142
  on Lao-tzu, 184, 185
  life of, 159–160
  philosophy of, see Confucianism
  on poetry, 148
  Yang-Chu's interpretations of, 171–173
conscientiousness, see *chung*
conscious, see *jiva*
consciousness, see *vinnana*
Consciousness-only school, see Wei-shih school
contact, see *phassa*
contentment, see *santosha*
conversion, see converts
converts
  Buddha's first, 30
  and Parsis, 96
  of Zoroaster, 92
Copernican revolution, 248
corruption, in National Buddhism, 259
cow, sanctity of, 119
cowherd element of Krishna *bhakti*, 54
creation myth, of Shinto, 250
Creator, the, see Brahma
cremation, in Buddhism, 263
Croce, Benedetto, 117
"crypto-Buddhism," 77, 82
cullavagga, 25
cults
  ancestral, 157
  of Chang Ling, 203
  of Confucius, see Confucianism
  in Japanese religion, 233

  of Sugawara Michizane, 233
  in Vedic religion, 14–19
  See also under individual names of
cy pres, doctrine of, 130

Dabu, Dastur Khurshed S., 95–96, 96n
Daikyoin, 249
Daimoku, recitation of, 275, 276
Dainishi Nyorai, see Mahavairocana Buddha
Daishi, Dengyo, see Saicho
Daishi, Kobo, 242
Daisojo, 264
dakmas, 95
dancers, see *sarume*
dancing in temple, laws against, 127
Danka Seido, 262
Dark Learning, see Neo-Taoism
Das, Amar, 101
Das Gupta, Surendranath, 20, 20n
Dasas, see Dasyus
Dasharatha, 55
dasya, 54
Dasyas, 11
Dasyus, 18
Dawn, 12
Day, Clarence Burton, 202, 202n
Dayananda Saraswati, 109–110
Dazai learning, 245
dead
  Buddhist masses and memorials for, 219
  cremation of, 263
  in mountain worship, 232
  in Popular Buddhism, 266
  See also death
death
  in ancient Chinese religions, 152
  of Arjan, 102
  of Buddha, 30
  in Jaina doctrine, 43–44
  of Mahavira, 41
  of Nanak, 103–104
  and Parsis, 94–96
  and Popular Buddhism, 266, 268
  and reincarnation, 36
  and Shinto, 240
  Tagore on, 118
  Taoist thought on, 198, 199
  in Vedic religion, 17–19
  See also dead; *jaramarana*
Deer Park Sermon, 30, 33
deities
  of Arya Samaj, 109
  of Buddhism and Shinto compared, 243
  Chinese, 145, 152–153, 162, 219
  of early Christian era, 202
  female, 4, 12
  inanimate, 13–14
  of Jaina religion, 47
  Japanese, 226, 228, 236
  of pre-Vedic religion, 3–4
  of Religious Taoism, 202–203
  in *Rigveda*, 92

  of Shang religion, 154
  of Popular Buddhism, 264
  of Pure Shinto, 252
  of Shinto, 240, 247–248
  of Vishnu *bhakti*, 59–60
  of Traditional Shinto, 235–238
  See also gods; and individual names of
demons
  asuras and *devas* as, 92
  Bali, 59
  and *goma*, 266
  Hiranyaksha, 59
  Kamsa, 60
  Ravana, 60
  in Vedic religion, 14
  in Vishnu *bhakti*, 59–60
dependent origination, see *patticcasamuppada*
Deploring the Heresies, see *Tanisho*
desire, see *tanha*
destroyer, the, see Shiva
devadasis, 127
Devaki, 52
devaluation, principle of, see *badha*
Devaram, 63
devas, 14, 92
Devendranath, 108–109
Devotion, see Armaiti; *dasya*; *Ishvarapranidhana*
Dewey, John, 117
Dhamma, 30
Dhammapada, 26
dharana, 85
Dharani spells, 266
dharma, 22, 124
Dharma, 262
Dharmakaya, 72–73
Dharmalakshana Buddhism, see Hosso Buddhism
Dharmashastras, 80
dhatus, 70
dhitthi-vada, 69–70
dhobis, 132
dhyana, 85, 213
Diamond Cutter Sutra, see *Vajracchedika*
dietary laws
  of Buddha, 28–29
  in early Christian era, 202
  of Ramakrishna movement, 113
  of Sikhs, 103
Digambaras, 46
Dighanikaya, 25–26
Din Ilahi, 97
Dipavamsa, 26
disciples, Sikhs as, 101
divination
  in ancient Chinese religions, 155–156
  and Popular Buddhism, 266
  during Shang and Chou eras, 154
divine abstractions, see Amesha Spentas
Divine Faith, see Din Ilahi
Divine Learning, see Shinshu-kyo
"Divine Plan The," 116
Divine Reason Teaching, see Shinrikyo Shinto
diviners, see *urabe*
divinities, see deities; gods
Doctrinal Buddhism, 268–279

Doctrine of the Mean, see Chung-yung
Dogen, 260, 269, 270, 272–273
dogmatism, *see dhitthi-vada; drishti*
Dokyo, 259
domestic rites, 15–16
Domestic Shinto, 233, 234
Dosho, 263
Double Aspect Shinto, *see Ryobu Shinto*
Double Aspect theory of Buddhism, 244
Dozoku, 234
  kinship unit of, 226
dreams, 199
dress, *see clothing*
drishti, 74
Druz, 92–93
dualism
  and Taoism, 186
  and Yoga system, 84
  See also dvaita; moksha
dukkha, 30, 32
Durga, *see Shakti*
dvaita view, 82–83
Dwaraka monastery, 76
Dwarf, the, *see Vamana*
Dyaus Pitar, 12

Edo warriors, 262
education
  and Confucianism, 180
  and Indian Christianity, 90
egoism
  and repetition of Buddha's name, 272
  in Taoist thought, 89, 199
Eight immortals, 202
Eisai, 260, 272, 273
elements of existence, *see dhatus*
elephant, in Buddhism, 27
emancipation, *see liberation*
emotions, Hsun-tzu on, 177
emperor
  in ancient Shinto, 236, 237
  divine, 242
  religious role of, 154–155, 227
  and shamanism, 233
  and Shinto, 241
  See also under names of
Engishiki, 227, 235
enlightenment
  and Chinese Buddhism, 214
  and Taoism, 196
  riddle method of testing, 272
epics, Indian, 55
  See also myths; tales
equanimity, *see upekha*
erotic practices of Shakti *bhakti*, 64
eternal religion, *see Sanatana Dharma*
ethics
  of Advaita Vedanta, 80
  of Arya Samaj movement, 110
  of Parsis, 92–93
  See also morality
evil
  in Japanese religion, 228
  and Parsis, 93
evolution, concept of, 121–122
existence
  in Advaita Vedanta, 77–78

  Buddhist interpretations of, 205
existence
  in Jaina doctrine, 42
  three marks of, *see Lakkhana*
exorcisms, 156
externalism, Confucius on, 185–186

Fa-hua-ching, see Lotus Sutra
Fa-tsang, 211
Faith-healing groups of Shinto, 252
family life, in Confucianism, 168
family-nation concept, 226
Fan Chih, 165
fang-shih, 202
Farmers' Zen, 273
fashion, *see clothing*
fasting, Gandhi on, 110
"fasting of the mind," 195–196
feeling, *see vedana*
female, 4, 12
Feng-shui, 156
fertility, and mountain worship, 232
fertility deities, 152
festivals
  government regulation of, 127–129
  Japanese, 226
  of Popular Buddhism, 266
  of Shinto, 238
  at Sravanabelgola, 47
  See also under specific names of
filial piety
  and Popular Buddhism, 266
  and Rissho Koseikai sect, 277
  See also hsiao
Fire-Creating Deity, *see Ho-musubi-no-Kami*
fire ritual, *see goma*
fire worship, 92, 94–95
Fish, the, *see Matsya*
fishing, in Jaina doctrine, 44
Five Blessings, 202–203
Five Books of Shinto, The, see Shinto Gobusho
Five Elements school, 146, 146*n*, 201
five K's, 103
five M's, *see tattvas*
"Five Periods and Eight Doctrines," theory of, 212
flowering of one hundred schools, 146
folk religion, Japanese, 224–225
Folk Shinto, 233, 234
forest dweller, *see vanaprasthya*
"forest texts," *see Aranyakas*
fortune-telling, 156
Foucher, A., 29, 29*n*
fourteen Inexpressibles, 69–70
free kitchens, of Sikhs, 101
freedom, Yang-chu on, 172
friendly love, *see sakhya*
Fu Hsi, 148
Fu-yi, 208
funeral pyre, in Vedic religion, 17
funeral rites
  Buddhist, 219, 266, 268
  Parsi, 95–96
Fuso-kyo Shinto, 253

Gadadhar Chatterji, *see Ramakrishna*
gandharvas, 14

Gandhi, Mohandas Karamchand, 118–120
Ganesa, *see Kangiten*
Ganges river, 61, 126
Garuda, 60
Gathas, 91, 92, 93
Gautama, *see Buddha*
Gaya, 30
"Gayatri," 13
General of the Five Brigands, 202
Genshin, 264
Genso, 272
geomancy, 156, 266
Ghose, Sri Aurobindo, 121–123
ghosts
  hungry, 266
  Wang Chung on, 181
  See also soul; spirits
Gitagovinda of Jayadeva, 54
giving, *see dana-sila*
go-ryo spirits, 238
Go-Toba, Emperor, 274
God, *see gods*
Goddess of Fertility, 162
Goddess of Mercy, 162
gods
  Ahura Mazda, 14
  of Bhagavan, 80
  Chinese, 152
  synthesis of, 66–67
  Tirthankaras, 41–42
  of *Rigveda*, 10–14
Gokhale, 118
Golden Temple, 101, 103, 105
goma, 266
good
  in Japanese religion, 228
  and Parsis, 93
  See also goodness
goodness
  in Confucianism, 164–166
  Mencius on, 175
  in Taoist thought, 191
  See also good; jen
gopis, 52, 55
Gospel of Sri Ramakrishna, The, 111
Gotama, Siddhattha, *see Buddha*
government
  and Chinese Buddhism, 207
  and Confucianism, 163, 179
  and Japanese Buddhism, 257–263
  and Japanese religion, 249–251
  Mencius on, 175
  Mo-ti on, 173–174
  and Taoist thought, 191–193
  See also church-state conflict; religious law
Govind Singh, 103
grace, in Shiva *bhakti*, 63
Granet, Marcel, 151–152, 152*n*
Granth, 103, 105
graves, visits to, 266
Great Gods of Five Roads, 202
"Great Hierarchy," 116
Great High Priest, *see Daisojo*
Great Learning, see Ta-hsueh
Great Mother Goddess, Pre-Vedic statues of, 3–4
Great Peace Taoism, *see T'ai-p'ing Tao*
Great Sukhavati-vyuha Sutra, see Wu-liang-shou-ching

Great White Brotherhood, see Great Hierarchy
greed, see aparigraha
grihastha, 18
Grihya Sutras, 14
Guadapada, 77
Gujarat, 47
Gurdwaras, 101, 103
Gurmukhi, 101
guru(s)
 of Krishna *bhakti* sect, 54
 Nanak, 99–101
 and *pranayama* training, 85
 and Shiva *bhakti*, 61
 of Sikhs, 101–103
Gyogi Bosatsu, 263–264

Hachiman Bosatsu, 228
haibutsu-kishaku, 249
hair
 of Buddha, 28
 of Shiva, 61
 in Sikh religion, 104–105
Hamestakan, 94
Han dynasty, 146–148, 157, 181, 200, 203
Han-Fei-tzu, 146
Han Yu, 181, 208, 219
Hanuman, 55, 56, 111
hand clapping, in Shinto, 231
Har Govind, 102, 103
Har K'ishan, 103
Har Rai, 103
Harappa, 3
 Aryan invasion of, 5
Harihara, 66
Harijan, see untouchables
Harivamsa, 52, 66
harmony
 as Chinese religio-philosophical tradition, 142–143
 in Confucianism, 164, 180
 in Japanese Buddhism, 258–259
 in Shang and Chou religions, 151–154
haurvatat, 93
Haya-aki-tu-hime, 228
health, Vedic charm for, 7
health cult of Chang Ling, 203
Heaven, concept of
 in Confucianism, 171
 Hsun-tzu on, 178
 in Taoist thought, 186, 197–198, 199
heavenly sins, 227
hedonism
 and Neo-Taoism, 201
 of Yang-chu, 172
Heian period, 230, 242, 260, 264
"henotheism," 10
"heterodox" religious systems, 68
hexagrams, 148, 156
hidden-manifest distinction, 240
Hideyoshi, 262
Higan-e ceremonies, 266
High Sacred Creating Kami, see Taka-mi-musubi-no-Kami
High Thought, see Armaiti
Himeko, see Pimiko
Hinayana community, 25
Hinayana doctrine, 212
Hinayanistic Satyasiddhi, 209
"Hindu" consciousness, 132–133

Hindu-Muslim conflict, 99–104, 128–129
 and Sikhs, 99–105
"Hinduism"
 origin of word, 132
 Radhakrishnan on, 123–125
 and Theosophy, 114–115
Hindus
 attitude toward Christian missions, 90
 in Aurangzeb's reign, 99
 and Sikh community, 56–57
Hiranyaksha, 59
Hirata Atsutane, 237, 243–245, 247–248, 249
Historical Records, see Shih-chi
History of the True Succession of the Divine Emperor, see Jinno Shotoki
Hito-no michi Shinto, 252
Ho-musubi-no-Kami, 240
Hojo regents, 274
Holtom, D. C., 252
Homa juice, 93
Hommon Kaidan, 277
Honen, 260, 269, 270–271, 272
honesty, in Taoist thought, 191
honji, 242
honjisuijaku, 243
Hoonsho, 274n
Hori, Ichiro, 232, 232n
horoscope of Buddha, 27
horse sacrifice, 15
Horyuji temple, 258
Hosso Buddhism, 263, 268
hotri, 8
Hotri, 14
Hou-chi, 152
Hou-t'u, 152
householder, see grihastha
Hoza group meeting, 277
Hsu, Francis L. K., 145, 145n
Hsuan of Ch'i, 194
Hsüan tsang, 65, 209
hsueh, 164, 167
Hsun-chi, 207–208
Hsun-tzu, 146, 177, 181
Hsiang Hsiu, 200
hsiao, 164, 168
Hsiao-ching, 168
hsin, 164n
Hua-yen school of Buddhism, 209, 211
 See also Kegon Buddhism
Hua-yen Sutra, see Avatamsaka Sutra; Kegon Sutra
Huan, Emperor, 206
Huang-ti, see Yellow Emperor
Hui, King, 194
Hui-neng, 213–214
Hui-yuan, 209, 217
Human Hair Research Institute, 104–105
human relations
 and Advaita Vedanta, 78–79
 and Confucianism, 142, 163–171
 in Taoist thought, 185, 189, 191
human sacrifice(s)
 and Shakti *bhakti*, 65
 in Vedic religion, 14
Hume, 112
hun, see shen
Hundred Schools, 171

Hung-jen, 213
hygienic practices of Religious Taoism, 201–202
hymn(s)
 of Alvars, 54
 of Aryans, 5
 to Harihara, 66
 of Parsis, 91
 of *Rigveda*, 6–7, 11
 of Shiva *bhakti*, 62
 Vedic, 18, 19–20, 109

I, concept of, 164n
I-ching, 148, 155, 200
I-hsuan, 214, 216
I-li, 149
Ibuki-do, 228
Ichijitsu Shinto, 242
iconoclasm, in China, 173
Ideal Humanity of Jesus, The, 107
idealism, of Yogacara, 76–77
idolatry, and Brahma Samaj, 107–108
 See also, image worship; gods
ignorance, see avidya, avijja
Ikeda, Daisaku, 277
Ikko sect, 261
Iku-musubi-no-Kami, 240
illusory existent, see pratibhasika
image worship
 and Brahma Samaj, 107
 Gandhi on, 119
 in Jaina religion, 46–47
 in Krishna *bhakti* movement, 55
 in Rama *bhakti*, 56
 in Vishtishtadvaita sects, 80
 See also images; idolatry
images
 of Confucius, 162
 of Kali, 66
 of Vishnu, 60–61
imbibe, 238
immeasurables, see apramanani
immobility of Buddha, 29
immortality
 in religious Taoism, 201–202
 See also Ameretat
imperial clan, in Japanese religion, 226
Imperial House Shinto, 233, 234
Imperial rule
 restoration of, 262
 symbols of, 229
 See also emperor
impermanence, doctrine of, 32
India
 Bhakti movement in, see bhakti movement
 British influence on, 106–107
 Buddhism in, see Buddhism
 Muslim invasions of, 96–97
 in post-Vedic period, see post-Vedic religion
 pre-Vedic religion in, 3–4
 religions of, 68
  in medieval period, 89–105
  in modern world, 106–116, 126–133
  and modern Indian thinkers, 116–125
  See also Advaita Vedanta; Buddhism; Carvaka; Madhyamika; Yoga; Vishtishtadvaita

India (continued)
  religious laws in, 125–132
  Vedic period, religion in, *see* Vedic religion
  worship of the Mother in, 4
Indian Constitution, religious law in, 127
"Indian Mind," 133
Indian Thought and Its Development, 123
individualism
  and Confucius, 166
  and Taoism and Confucianism compared, 205–206
"individualization," in Theosophy, 115
Indra, 11, 18
Indus Valley Civilization, 3–5
industrial revolution, and National Buddhism, 263
Inexpressibles, *see* fourteen Inexpressibles
infallibility, of Vedas, 108
inheritance rights, in Vedic period, 19
initiation rituals
  Parsi, 96
  of Vedic religion, 16
injury to living creatures, *see* ahimsa
Insei government, 260
insight, *see* panna
intelligence, *see* cit
intermarriage
  and Parsi, 96
  Radhakrishnan on, 124
  among Vedic classes, 18
intuitive knowledge, *see* Prajna
involution, concept of, 121–122
Ippen, 260, 264
Iran
  Aryans in, 5
  daevas worship in, 92
  Parsis in, 91
  Vedic religion in, 14
Ise, pilgrimages to, 234
Ise Shinto, 244
Ishvara, 85
Ishvarapranidhana, 85
Islam
  in China, 147
  during reign of Akbar, 97–98
  See also Muslims
invisibility, 69
Ittoen sect, 254
Iyeyuki, Watari, 244
Izanagi, 240, 252
Izanami, 240, 252
Izumo Oyashiro-kyo, 253

Jade Emperor, 202, 203
Jahangir, Emperor, 98, 101–102
Jainas, 23, 41–47, 71, 119
Jagannath, Lord, 60
Jan Jung, 164
Japanese Buddhism, 230
  Ch'an school of, 214
  compared with Chinese Buddhism, 256–257
  compared with Confucianism and Taoism, 256–257
  doctrinal, *see* Doctrinal Buddhism
  effect on language, 263
  and emperor reverence, 227
  fusion with Taoism and Confucianism, 224
  Hua-Yen school of, 211
  national, *see* National Buddhism
  numbers of followers of, 278
  origins of, 226
  popular, *see* Popular Buddhism
  purge of, 249
  and Shinto, 230
  and Shugendo system, 233
Japanese Constitution, 250, 251
Japanese language, Buddhist influence on, 263
Japanese nationalism, and Shinto, 230, 247–249
Japanese religions
  blending of, 224–225
  Chinese influence on, 225
  and communal feeling, 226–227
  folk religion, 224–225
  historic view of, 229–230
  and intuition versus intellectualization, 226
  morality of, 227–229
  "New Religions," 251
  post-1945, 253–255
  sins in, 227–228
  and this-worldly realism, 225–226
  See also under individual names of
jaramarana, 34
Jataka tales, 37
jati, 34
jen, 164, 165, 166, 167
Jesus Christ
  and Brahma Samaj, 108
  and Ramakrishna, 111
  in Theosophy, 116
Jesuits, 89–90
Jews, in India, 90
jigo-jitoku, 263
Jikko-kyo, 253
Jimmu, Emperor, 249
Jina, the, 41–42, 45
jingi-kan, 238
Jinno Shotoki, 244
Jito, Empress, 263
jiva, 41, 43, 79
Jivanmukta, 79, 80
Jizo, 264
jnanamarga, 8
jnanayoga, 49, 113
Jodo, *see* Pure Land Buddhism
Jodo-shinshu, *see* Pure Land Buddhism
Jodo-shu, 270
Jogyo Bosatsu, 274
Jojitsu Buddhism, 268
ju, 159
Ju-chiao, *see* Confucianism
Ju Ching, 273
Juan family, 201
Judah, *see* Jews
Judaism, *see* Jews
judgment, and Parsis, 94
Judo, 273
Jumna river, 53
jurisprudence, *see* religious law

Kabir, 56, 101
Kach, 103
Kaimokusho, 274n
Kalama, Alara, 28
Kali, 65–66
  and Ramakrishna movement, 111
  See also Shakti *bhakti*
Kali Tantra, 66
Kalighat Temple, Calcutta, 66
Kalki *avatara,* 159
Kalkin, 60
kama, 124
Kamakura era, 230, 242, 244, 260–261, 269–276
Kamakura shogunate, fall of, 261
Kami, 235–237
  classifications of, 237–238
  Hirata on, 248
  nonhuman, 236
Kami Master of the Center of Heaven, *see* Ame-no-mi-naka-nushi-no-Kami
Kami-musubi-no-Kami, 237, 240, 246
kami-gakari, 238
kamikaze, 243
Kamikaze pilots, 241
kamma, law of, 32, 34–37
Kansa, King, 52, 60
Kanezane, Fujiwara, 270
Kangh, 103
Kangiten, 264
Kanjinhonzonsho, 274n
kanjo, rite of, 259
Kannon, 264
Kannon Sutra, 264
Kanthaka, 27
Kao Tsung, Emperor, 201
Kao-tzu, 176–177
Kara, 103
Kara-nembutsu, 263
Kariti, *see* Kishimojin
karma, 22, 43
  and Advaita Vedanta, 79–80
  and Buddha *bhakti,* 51
  and Carvaka school, 87
  and Chinese philosophy, 205–206
  Gandhi on, 119
  Ghose on, 122
  Radhakrishnan on, 124
  in Shaiva Siddhanta, 63
  and Sikh community, 100
  in Theosophy, 115
  See also kamma
karmayoga, 49
karmamarga, 8
karuna, 40
karya, 78
Kashmir Shaivism, 64
Katha Upanishad, 9, 21
Kathavatthu, 26
Kegon Buddhism, 268, 269
  See also Hua-yen school
Kegon Sutra, 211, 258
Keichu, 245
Kendo, 273
Kesh, 103
Keshab Chandra Sen, 108–109
Kevalin, 45
Khalsa, 103
khandhas, 32, 37, 76
  in Madhyamika system, 70
  in Pali Canon, 70, 71
Khshathra Vairya, 93
Khuddaka-nikaya, 26
Kimmei, Emperor, 257
Kinen-sai festival, 238

Kino, 252
kinship, in Japanese religions, 226–227
Kirpan, 103
Kishimojin, 264
Kitagawa, 252
Kiyozumi-dera monastery, 274
knight, *see shih*
"Ko" groups, 234
Koan, 272, 273
Kogoshui, 235
Kojiki, 229, 234, 235, 236–237, 246
Kojiki-den, *see Kojiki*
kokugaku, *see* National Learning
Kokutai, 227, 250
Komeito, 277
konko-kyo Shinto, 252, 253
Konotabi movement, 252
Koshi Seibun, 247
Koshiden, 247
Kozengokokuron, 260
Krishna, 46, 47, 49
  as *avatara* of Vishnu, 60
  and caste system, 131
  life of, 52–53
  Vishnu in form of, 60
Krishna *bhakti,* 52–55
Kshatriya, 18, 41, 59–60
Kshitigarbha, *see* Jizo; Ti-tsang-wang
Kuan Kung, 162
Kuan-ti, 162
Kuan-wu-liang-shou-ching, 217
Kuan-yin, 145
  See also Kannon
Kuang Wu, Emperor, 162
kuei, 152
Kujiki, 235
Kukai, 259–260, 269
  See also Daishi; Kobo
Kumarajiva, 209
kumbhaharathy, 127
kung-an, see riddle
K'ung Fu-tzu, *see* Confucius
Kuo Hsiang, 200
Kurma, 59
Kurozumi-kyo, 253
Kurozumi Munetada, 253
Kusha Buddhism, 209, 268
kushi-mi-tama spirits, 238
kusti, 92, 96
Kyogyoshinsho, 271
Kyusei-kyo sect, 254

laity
  in China, 144
  in Jaina religion, 44–46
"Lake of Rama's Deeds, The," *see Ramacharitmanas*
Lakkhana, 31–33
Lakr spirits, 238
Lakshamana, 55, 57
Lakshmi, 59, 60, 65
Lalitavistara, 50
land, sacredness of, 225
language, Taoist thought on, 198
Lanka, *see* Ceylon
Lankavatara Sutra, 76
Lao Tan, 184
Lao-tzu, 146, 184–185, 194, 201
Last Age, *see* Mappo
Last Age in the Decline of Buddhist Teaching, doctrine of, 277
laws, religious, *see* religious laws

Laws of Manu, 131
lay devotees, *see upasakas; upasikas*
learning, *see hsueh*
left-handed tantra, *see cakra-puja*
Legalist philosophy, 146, 192
legend, *see* myths; tales
li, 164, 168, 182, 229
Li Ao, 181
Li-chi, 148, 149, 178
Li Erh, 184
Liang-chieh, 124
Liang, King, 194
Liang Wu-ti, Emperor, 207–208
liberation
  and Advaita Vedanta, 79–80
  and *bhakti,* 49
  and Carvaka school, 88
  and Ch'an Buddhism, 214
  and Chuang-tzu, 195
  and Dvaita, 83
  in Jaina doctrine, 44
  in Shiva *bhakti,* 63
  in Theosophy, 116
  in Vedic religion, 23
  and Vishtishtadvaita, 81–82
  and Yoga, 84
  and Yogacara, 74–76
Lie, *see* Druz
Lie Demon, 92
Lieh-tzu, 201
life after death, *see* afterlife
Life-Creating Deity, *see* Iku-musubi-no-Kami
life cycle, in Vedic religious rituals, 16
Life Divine, The, 121
Lin-chi Buddhism, 214
  See also Rinzai Zen Buddhism
linga, 4, 61, 66
linguistics, *see* language
literati, *see* Ju
logic, Jaina, 42–44
lokayata, see Carvaka
Lord of Beings, *see* Prajapati
Lord Millet, *see* Hou-chi
Lord Soil, *see* Hou-t'u
Lotus Sutra, 211, 212, 260, 261, 274, 275, 277
Lotus of the True Law, see Saddharmapundarika
love
  in Krishna *bhakti* doctrine, 53–55
  and Parsis, 93
  various forms of, 54
loving kindness, *see metta*
lower classes, *see* masses
loyalty, *see chung*
Lu, kingdom of, 149
Lu Hsiang-shan, 182
Lu-shih Ch'un-ch'iu, 172
Lumbini, 27

Mabuchi, Kamo, 243, 245
madhurya, 54
Madhva, 54, 82–83
Madhyamika Buddhism, 50, 68–74, 209
  compared with Yogacara, 75
  in Japan, 229
  and *Trikaya* doctrine, 72–73
  See also "crypto-Buddhism"; Sanron Buddhism
Madras Act 31 of 1947, 127

Madras Christian College, 123
Madras Hindu Religious and Charitable Endowments Act of 1951, 129–130
Magatsubi-no-kami, 228
magic
  in ancient Chinese religions, 156–157
  and Buddhism, 226
  in Chinese religions, 144
  and Popular Buddhism, 258, 266
  and Yoga, 86
magical formulae, *see atharvan*
magical spells, 266
magician, and Religious Taoism, 201
magokoro, 246
Mahabharata epic, 52, 55
Mahaparinibbanasutta, 26
Mahavagga, 25
Mahavairocana Buddha, 243, 258
Mahavamsa, 26
Mahavastu, 50
Mahavira, 24, 41
  See also Jainas
Mahayana Buddhism, *see* Madhyamika; Yogacara
Mahayana sutras, 258
Mahayanistic Yogacara school, 209
Main Bureau of Shinto, *see* Shinto Honkyoku
Maitri Upanishad, 86
Majjhima-nikaya, 26
Makiguchi, Tsunesaburo, 277
Makkah, pilgrimages to, 99, 127
Malabar, Jews at, 90
Man-Lion, the, *see* Narasimha
Manchus, Buddhism and, 220
Mandala of Nichiren, 275
mandalas, 65
Mandate of Heaven, 242
Manifest Kami, *see* Arahito-gami
Mantra Buddhism, *see* Shingon Buddhism
mantras, 65
Manu, 59, 110
Man'yoshu, 245, 246
Mao-ch'ing, 198
Mappo, 264, 273, 274
Mara, 29–30
Maratha State, 99
marks of existence, *see* Lakkhana
marriage
  of Buddhist monks, 272
  Gandhi on, 120
  intercaste, 132
  in Jaina doctrine, 45
  in Shang and Chou eras, 151
  of widows and widowers, 110
  See also child marriage
Maruts, 11
Marxism, and Confucianism, 183
masses
  and Buddhism, 206
  and Buddhist monks, 263–264
  and Doctrinal Buddhism, 269–270
  and Gandhi, 119
  and Honen, 270–271
  and Mo-ist school, 146
  and Pure Land tradition, 217
  and religious Taoism, 203–204
material well-being, *see artha*
materialism, Philosophical Taoism and, 198–199

materialists, *see* Carvakas
maths of Shankara, 76
Mathura, 52, 55
matsuri, 238, 240
matsuri-goto, 241
Matsya, 59
maya, doctrine of, 11, 27, 77
    Radhakrishnan on, 123, 124
    Ramanuja's interpretation of, 81
    in Shaiva Siddhanta, 63
    and Sikhs, 100
    world as, 113
maybe, doctrine of, *see syadvada*
Mazda, 91
Mead, Margaret, 254
Mecca, *see* Makkah
meditation
    body position for, 85
    and Ch'an Buddhism, 212–213
    in Jaina religion, 45, 46
    in Krishna *bhakti*, 55
    and Taoism, 195
    in Theosophy, 116
    in Vedic religion, 8, 20, 21, 23
    in Vishtishtadvaita, 81
    and Yogacara, 75
    See also dhyana
Meiji, Emperor, 230, 249, 262
Meiji era, 247, 249, 251
melodies, *see samans*
Menander, King, 26
Mencius, 146, 174–177, 179, 181, 194, 242
    criticism of, 176–177
    on *I*, 164*n*
Mencius, the, 174–177
merchant class, Shinran's teaching and, 272
merit
    in Ch'an Buddhism, 214
    transfer of, 272
Metal Luster Teaching, *see* Konko-kyo Shinto
metaphysics
    of Buddhism and Taoism compared, 206
    and Neo-Taoist philosophy, 200
metta, 40
Meykandar, 63
Middle Ages, in India, 89–105
Milindapanha, 26, 32, 35, 36, 37
militarism, of Sikhs, 102, 103
Mill, J. S., 112
Minamoto, 269
mind and matter, *see nama-rupa*
Mind school of Neo-Confucianism, 181, 182
Ming, Emperor, 162
Ming period, 181, 182, 219–220
    cult of Confucius during, 162
miracles
    in Buddhism, 27–28
    of Krishna, 52
    and Theosophical Society, 114
    of Zoroaster, 92
    See also magic, miraculous birth
miraculous birth, of Confucius, 162
mirror, as Shinto symbol, 229, 243
Misogi-kyo Shinto, 253
missionaries
    in India, 90
    See also Christian missionaries
Mitake-kyo Shinto, 253

miya, 241
Mo-ti, 146, 173–174, 177
Mo-ist school, 146
Mo-tzu, *see* Mo-ti
Mohenjo-Daro, 3, 5
Mohists
    and Chang-tzu, 194–195
    and Philosophical Taoism, 198
moksha, 23, 41, 120, 124
    See also liberation
Mokurai, Shimaji, 250
Mokuren, 266
monasteries
    Shankara, 82
    See also maths; monks
Mongol invasions, 243, 261, 274
monkey school of Vishtishtadvaita, 81
monks
    Buddhist, 208, 209, 219
    and common man, 263–264
    in Japan, 259–260
    laity as, 45
    of Mount Hiei, *see* Mount Hiei monks
    Ramakrishna, 112
    in Shinran's order, 272
Mononobe clan, 257
monotheism
    and Parsis, 91
    and Vedic religion, 19–20
morality
    of Chinese religions, 146
    of Confucius, 163–171
    Hsun-tzu on, 177
    of Japanese religion, 228
    of Religious Taoism, 202
    of Taoism, 191
    See also dharma
Mother Goddess, in Shakti *bhakti*, 64
Motoori, 247
Mou-tzu on the Settling of Doubts, 206
Mount Fuji, worship of, 253
Mount Hiei monks, 242, 259, 261, 264, 273
Mount Otake, worship of, 253
Mountain King Shinto, *see* Sanno Shinto
Mountain sects of Shinto, 253
mountain worship, 232
mudita, 40
mudras, 65
Mughal emperors, 97–98
Mughals, in India, 96–97
Muhammad, in Theosophy, 116
Muharram festival, 129
Mula Shanker, *see* Dayananda Saraswati
Müller, Max, 10
murder, in Buddhist doctrine, 36, 39
music, Hsun-tzu on, 177
musicians, *see sarume*
Muslims
    and "Hindu" consciousness, 132–133
    in India, 96–99
    and Sikhs, 103, 104
    See also Hindu-Muslim conflict
Muslim-Hindu conflict, *see* Hindu-Muslim conflict
musubi, concept of, 240

Mutiny of 1857, 106
mystic diagrams, *see manadalas*
mysticism
    and Chuang-tzu, 194–197
    and *Chung-yung*, 179
    of Mencius, 176
    of Ramakrishna, 111–112
    and Taoism, 185
mythology, *see* myth(s)
myth(s)
    of ancient Shinto, 236–238, 240–242
    Buddhist, 144, 217
    Chinese, 144
    Japanese, 228, 232
    in *Kojiki*, 246
    of Mokuren, 266
    of Nagarjuna, 68–69
    of Rama, 55–57
    Shinto, 234, 240
    See also epics; tales

Naciketas, 9
Nagarjuna, 68–74, 209, 217
nagas, 4
Nagasaki, Christian martyrdom at, 261
Nagasena, 26, 32, 35
nakatomi, 238
Nakayama, Mrs. Miki, 253
nama-rupa, 33
name and form, *see nama-rupa*
names, rectification of, 149
Nanak, 99–101, 103–105
Nanda, 30
Nandi the bull, 61
Naobi-no-kami, 228
Naojote ceremony, 96
Nao, Deguchi, 253
Nara era, 230, 263, 268
Nara temples, 259
Narada Bhakti Sutras, 48
Narashimha, 59
Narendranath Datta, *see* Vivekananda
Nataraja, 61
National Buddhism
    decline of, 262–263
    and Emperor Shomu, 258–259
    formation of, 257–258
    in Heian age, 260
    in Kamakura age, 260–261
    and Nichiren, 260–261
    and persecution of Christians, 261–262
    political relations of, 257–263
    and Prince Shotoku, 257–258
    in Tokugawa era, 261–262
National Christian Council, 90
National Essence, *see Kokutai*
National Learning school of Shinto, 243, 244–247, 248–249
National Polity, *see Kokutai*
nationalism
    and Buddhism, 262
    in India, 118–123
    and Shinto, 244, 255
    See also Japanese nationalism
nature
    in ancient Chinese religions, 153–154
    and Ch'an Buddhism, 213
    and Confucianism, 180, 181

nature (continued)
  harmony between man and, 142–143
  and *I-ching*, 148
  in Japanese religion, 225
  in Shang religions, 151–154
  in Shinto, 240
  in Taoism, 186, 187, 198
nature deities, 237
nature worship, in Vedic religion, 10–13
Nayanars, 62
Nembutsu, 264
"neo-advaitin," 113
Neo-Confucianism, 147, 170, 181–183
  and pure Shinto, 244
  religious texts of, 149
  Wang Yang-ming wing of, 245n
Neo-Taoism, 147, 200–201
"New Religions," 251–255
Nibbana, 30, 37–38, 40
Nichiren, 260–261, 269, 273–276, 277
  four denunciations of, 270
Nichiren Buddhist tradition, 230
Nigi-mi-tama spirits, 238
nihilism, and Madhyamika system, 73–74
Nihongi, 235–237, 245
  See also Nihonshoki
Nihonshoki, 229, 234, 257
Niname-sai festival, 238
1954 Constitution of China, 220
Nirguna Brahman, 77
Nirmanakaya, 73
Nirvana
  in Buddha *bhakti*, 50, 51
  in Jaina religion, 41, 46
  in Madhyamika system, 73
  in Pure Land Buddhism, 217
  in Theosophy, 116
  See also Nibbana
Nirvana-Samsara, 206
Nirvana Sutra, 212
Nirvikalpa Samadhi, 111
niyama, 85
Nobunaga, Oda, 261, 262
nonaction, *see wu-wei*
Nonbeing, 186, 200
nonviolence
  and Gandhi, 119–120
  and Ghose, 121
Norinaga, Motoori, 235–236, 245–247, 248
Norito, 227, 235, 245
Northern school of Ch'an Buddhism, 213
Northern school of Vishtishtadvaita, *see* Vadagalai
nudity, in Jaina religion, 46
Nobili, Robert de, 89–90
nuns, 25
  See also bhikkunis
nyasa, 65

O'mi-t'o'ching, 217
O-mi-to-fo, *see* Amida Buddha
observances, *see niyama;* prayers
occult, and Theosophical Society, 114
  See also magic; mysticism

offenses, *see parajikas*
Office of Shinto Affairs, 249
Oharae ceremony, 227
Ojoyoshu, 264
Okuni-nushi-no-Kami, 238
Olcott, Colonel, 114
old age, *see jaramarana*
Old Text-New Text controversy, 182
Omoto-kyo Shinto, 252, 253, 254
on, 240
One Truth Shinto, *see* Ichijitsu Shinto
One Vehicle Buddhism, 269, 270
Ono, Sokyo, 238, 238n
oppression, Taoist thought on, 192–194
  See also persecution
ordeals, 55
orders, in Jaina religion, 44
  See also monasteries; monks; and individual names of
ordination, into Sangha, 38–39
orgies, 151
Original-nature, *see* Buddha nature
Original Vow of Amida Buddha, 271
"orthodox" religious systems, 68
outcasts, and Christian missionaries, 90
  See also Untouchables

pabbajja, 38, 69
Pahlavi books, 92
pain, and Carvaka school, 88
Pakistan, religious laws in, 125
Pali Canon, 25–27
  and Buddha *bhakti*, 51
  compared with Madhyamika thought, 69–71
  compared with Yogacara, 76
  date of, 26
  doctrine of causation in, 71
  kamma and rebirth in, 34–37
  Lakkhana in, 31–33
  moral precepts of, 40–41
  Nibanna in, 37–38
  paticcasamuppada in, 33–34
Pali language, 25
panna, 40
Pantoja, Didacus de, 247
parable of the golden lion, 211
paradox, in Ch'an Buddhist principles, 216
parajikas, 39
Paramahamsa, *see* Ramakrishna
Paramatman, 78
Parashurama, 59–60
Parinibbana, 30, 37, 51
parish system, *see* Danka Seido
Parsis, 90–96
"parting of the hair" ceremony, 16
Parvati, *see* Shakti
Patanjali, 61, 84–86
patticcasamuppada, 33–34, 71
Patimokkha, 25, 26, 38
patriotism
  and Shinto, 244, 250–251
  Taoist thought on, 192
  See also nationalism
People of God, *see* Harijans
perception, and Carvaka school, 87
perfection
  Chuang-tzu on, 196–197

  steps in attaining, 40
  See also haurvatat
Perry, Commodore, 251
persecution
  of Chinese Buddhists, 147, 207, 219
  of Honen, 270
  of Japanese Christians, 261–262
  of Nichiren, 274
  of Religious Taoists, 203
Persian Empire, Zoroastrians in, 91
phallus worship, 4
phassa, 33
phenomenally real, *see vyavaharika*
philosophical Taoism
  in China, 184–197
  and Chuang-tzu, 194–199
  compared with religious Taoism, 201
  morality of, 189–191
philosophy
  and Chinese religion, 142–143
  of Chou dynasty, 146
phrenology, 156
physical prowess, in Confucianism, 170
pilgrim tax, 127
pilgrimages
  government regulation of, 127–129
  of Muslims, 99
  of Sikhs, 105
"pillar of Japan, the," 274
Pimiko, 231–232, 251
pipal tree, 4
pitribhakti, 54
pitris, 17
Platform Sutra, 213
pleasure, and Carvaka school, 88
Plentiful-Creating Deity, *see* Taru-Musubi-no-Kami
P. L. Kyodan sect, 254
p'o, see kuei
politics
  and ancient Chinese religions, 158
  and Buddhism, 277–278
  and Chinese religions, 155
  and cult of Confucius, 162–163
  and Doctrinal Buddhism, 270
  and Gandhi, 118–119
  and Ghose, 121
  and Hindu consciousness, 133
  and Japanese religions, 227
  and National Buddhism, 257–263
  and Religious Taoism, 203–204
  and Shinto, 234, 243–244, 251
  of Taoism, 191–192
poll tax for non-Muslims, 97, 99
polygamy, 107
Popular Buddhism, 263–264, 266, 268
Portugal, and Christianity in India, 89–90
possession of marks, 73
posture, *see asana*
Practice-Conduct teaching, *see* Jikko-kyo
Prajapati, 19
Prajna, 72, 74, 75
Prajna Sutras, 212
Prajnaparamita, 72
prakriti, 84
prana, 21
pranayama, 85

prapatti, 48, 54
Prashna Upanishad, 9
pratibhasika, 78
Pratimoksha, see Patimokkha
pratityasamutpada, *see paticca-samuppada*
pratyhara, 85
prayer(s)
   Hsun-tzu on, 178
   Norito, 235
   and Rama *bhakti*, 56
   of *Rigveda*, 17–18
   Shinto, 238
   for the sick, 156
   of Sikhs, 100
   of Vedic texts, 7
   See also under individual names of
Precepts of Jesus, The, 107
pregnancy, Vedic rituals for, 16
pretas, 17
priests
   of Aryans, 5
   of Popular Buddhism, 263–264
   Shinto, 238
   Vedic, 14–15
profit
   Hsun-tzu on, 177
   Mencius on, 176
   and Mo-ti, 173–174
Prophecy, about Krishna, 52–53
prostitution, sacred, 127
Protestant missions, in India, 90
pudgala, 86
Pudgalavadins, 76
puja, 48
punarmrityu, see "re-death"
punishments
   in Japanese Buddhism, 261
   and Mongol invasion of Japan, 274
Punjabi sabha, 105
Puranas, 59, 60
Pure Land Buddhism, 217–218, 245
   and Dogen, 273
   and Honen, 271
   in Japan, 260, 261, 264
   and Japanese Buddhism, 269
   and Nichiren, 274, 275
   and Shinran, 271–272
Pure Shinto, 243–249
   Christian influence on, 247
   sects of, 252
"Pure Talk," *see* Neo-Taoism
purgation, 196
Puri monastery, 76
purification
   in Japanese religion, 227–229
   in Shang and Chou religions, 151
   in Shinto, 231
Purification Shinto, *see* Misogi-kyo Shinto
purity, in Shinto, 240
purusha, 84
purusha hymn, 18, 131

Qur'an, in Pakistani law, 125

Race, in Vedic religion, 18
Radha, 52, 54
Radhakrishnan, Sarvepalli, 107, 123–125, 132

Rahula, 28, 30
rainmaking, 151, 156
Rajagaha, First Council at, 38
rakshas, 14
Ram Mohun Roy, 107, 126
Rama, 56, 60, 111
   Vishnu in form of, 60
   See also Rama *bhakti*
Rama with the Ax, *see* Parashurama
Rama *bhakti*, 55–58
Ramacharitmanas, 57
Ramakrishna movement, 107, 110–114, 125
Ramananda, 56, 101
Ramanandis sect, 56
Ramanuja, 54, 80–82
Ramawats sect, *see* Ramanandis sect
Ramayana epic, 55
Ratri, 13
Ravana, King, 55, 57, 60
Razan, Hayashi, 243
Real
   and Advaita Vedanta, 80
   in Buddhism, 69
   in Madhyamika doctrine, 74
   upanishadic view of, 70
   See also Reality
Reality
   and Advaita Vedanta, 77–78
   and Carvaka school, 88
   and Ch'an Buddhism, 214, 216
   and Dvaita, 82–83
   in Madhyamika system, 70–72
   and Ramakrishna movement, 114
   in Shinto, 242–243
   in Taoist thought, 195, 199
reason, and Advaita Vedanta, 79
Reason school of Neo-Confucianism, 181–182
rebirth, in Theosophy, 115–116
   See also jati
reciprocity, *see shu*
recitation
   of Buddha's name, 217, 218, 264, 270
   of *Daimoku*, 277
   of magical phrases, 266
   of *Nembutsu*, 264
   of title of *Lotus Sutra*, 275
reciter of *Rigveda, see hotri*
"re-death," 22
reform, in India, 129–132
reincarnation
   in Buddhist doctrine, 34–38
   in Vedic religion, 22
Rei-sai festival, 238
religion
   and magic, *see* magic
   and myth, *see* myth
   symbols used by; *see* symbols
religious festivals, *see* festivals
Religious Freedom of Japan, 250
religious functionaries, *see* priests
religious law, 125–126
   and Chinese Buddhism, 219–220
   and Chinese Communists, 221
   in India
      and administration of temples, 129–131
      and caste system, 130–132
      and regulation of religious practices, 127–129

      and religious endowments, 130
      and suppression of religious practices, 126–127
   and Japanese Buddhism, 257, 259
   and Japanese religion, 250–251
   against sacrifice, 65
   of Sangha, 38–40
   Taoist thought on, 192–193
religious reform, *see* reform
religious studies, *see svadhyaya*
religious symbols, *see* symbols
Religious Taoism, 201–204
   fusion with Buddhism, 219
   future of, 204
   in Japan, 224, 229
   origins of, 201–202
Rennyo, 272
renunciation
   Tagore on, 118
   in Vedic religion, 17–18
repetition, of Amida Buddha's name, 272
   See also recitation
Repository of Buddhist Teaching, The, see Shobogenzo
"Restoration Shinto," 244
restraint, *see yama*
resurrection, Ghose on, 122
revolt of the Yellow Turbans, 203
revolution, Mencius on, 242
Ricci, Matthew, 247
riddles, as test of enlightenment, 214
righteousness, Mencius on, 176
   See also Asha Vahista; I
Rigveda, 4
   and caste system, 131
   date of, 10
   deities in, 92
   gods of, 10–14
   roots of *bhakti* in, 49
   social doctrines of, 17–19
   and social order, 17–19
   Vishnu in, 58
Rinzai Zen Buddhism, 214, 260, 272–273
Risshcankokuron, 260, 274, 274n
Rissho Koseikai Buddhism, 276–277, 278
rita, concept of, 13, 20
rites
   of passage, *see* initiation rituals
   of purification, 228
   of return, 16
   See also rituals
Ritsu Buddhism, 268, 270
Ritsu priests, 261
ritual(s)
   in Confucianism, 168
   gestures, *see mudras*
   Hsun-tzu on, 177, 178
   intoxication, 93
   of king, 153
   movements of hands, *see nyasa*
   of offering food for parents and ancestors, 266
   and Parsis, 93
   of Shakti *bhakti*, 64
   of Shang and Chou eras, 151
   of Sikhs, 101
   of Vedic religion, 8, 14–19
ritualists, *see nakatomi*

Rituals of Chou, see Chou-li
Roman Catholic Church
   in India, 89–90
Rudra, *see* Shiva
rules
   of Buddhism, *see Tipitaka*
   of Gandhi, 120
   in Jaina doctrine, 44
   of Sangha, 39, 39n
   of Sikhs, 103
   See also religious laws
ruling classes, Buddhism and, 257
rupa, 32
Russell, Bertrand, 117
Ryobu Shinto, 242
Ryonin, 260, 264

Sacred Creating Kami, *see* Kami-musubi
sacrifices
   in ancient Chinese religions, 156
   and Brahma Samaj, 107
   and Carvaka school, 87
   in Chinese religion, 162
   at grave of Confucius, 162
   Hsun-Tzu on, 177–178
   and Parsis, 93
   in Shakti *bhakti*, 65
   during Shang and Chou eras, 151, 154
   in Vedic religion, 8, 14–16, 20, 21
   See also animal sacrifice; human sacrifice
sacrificial formulae, *see yajus*
Saddharmapundarika, 51
Sadharan Brahma Samaj, 108
sage-hermits, 266
Saguna Brahman, 77
Saicho, 242, 259, 269, 274, 275
"Saint of the Market, the," *see* Shonin, Kuya
saki-mi-tama spirits, 238
Sakyamuni, 249, 262
saints, Jaina, 45
   See also under individual names of
saisei-itchi, 240
sakhya, 54
Sakyamuni Buddha, 275
salayatana, 33
salvation
   and Buddhism, 269
   and Doctrinal Buddhism, 270–271
   Honen on, 271
   Nichiren on, 275
   and Pure Land doctrine, 217, 218
   Shinran on, 270
   See also Yuzu-nembutsu
samadhi, 40, 86
samans, 7
Samasamhita, see Samaveda
Samaveda, 7, 8
Sambhogakaya, 73
Samhitas, 6–10
samprajnata, 86
samsara, see reincarnation
samskara, see sankara
samurai class, 251, 273
Samyutta-Nikaya, 34
Sanatana Dharma, 123, 125

Sanchi, *stupa* at, 50
Sangha, 262
   life in, 38–40
   morality of, 40–41
   rules of, 25
sanjna, see sanna
Sanjo, Prince, 250
sankara, 32, 33
Sankhya philosophy, 71, 71n
   and Yoga, 84
sanna, 32
Sanno Shinto, 242
   sannyasins, 18
   Radhakrishnan on, 124
Sanron Buddhism, 268
Sanskritization, 58–59, 59n
Sansom, G. B., 243–244, 261, 261n
santosha, 85
Saoshyans, 94
Sarasvati, 13–14, 65
Sarma, D. S., 115, 115n, 133
Sarnath, 30
sarume, 238
Sarvadarshanasamgraha, 87
Sarvastivadin school, 74, 74n
Sassanian Empire, 91
sat, 78, 115
sat paramarthika, see Reality
sati
   and Brahma Samaj, 107
   laws against, 126
satkaryavada, 78
satya, 85
satyagraha, and Gandhi, 119–120
Satyasiddhi Buddhism, *see* Jojitsu Buddhism
Savritri, 13
"scheduled" castes, 131
scholar-bureaucrat, in Chinese religion, 144
scholasticism, of Chinese Buddhism, 213
School of Names, 146, 200
Schweitzer, Albert, 117, 123
Science
   and Indian religions, 117
   and Ramakrishna movement, 113
Se-ori-tu-hime, 228
seasonal festivals, 238
seclusion of women, 101
secret societies, Taoist, 193, 204
Sect Shinto, 233, 234, 253
sectarianism, *see* sects
sects
   factors leading to appearance of, 254–255
   of Jaina religion, 146
   Shinto, 252–253
   Shri-Vaishnavism, 80
Segaki ceremony, 266
Seicho-no-Ie Shinto, 252, 254
Seika, Fujiwara, 243
"self," 32
   See also purusha
self-denial, in Jaina religion, 45
self-identity, *see* Atman
self-reality, *see purusha*
self-rule, *see swaraj*
Seng-chao, 209, 210
Senjakuhongannembutsushu, 270
Senjisho, 274n
sense fields, *see salayatana*

sense organs and sense data, *see ayatanas*
senses, control of, *see pratyahara*
Sermon on the Mount, 119
serpent, in *Rigveda*, 11
serpent deities, *see nagas*
servant of God, *see devadasis*
Seven Sages of the Bamboo Grove, 200–201
sex, of *bhakti* gods
sexes, segregation in Confucianism, 160, 160n
sexual intercourse, 39
   and *cakra-puja* ceremony, 65
   Gandhi on, 119
   with *guru*, 54
   in Jaina doctrine, 45
   and Shinto, 246
sexual organ, female, *see yoni*
sexual organ, male, *see linga*
sexual rites, in Shang and Chou religions, 151
sexuality, control of, *see brahma-carya*
Shaiva Siddhanta, *see* Shaivism
Shaivism, 62–64, 83
   See also Shiva *bhakti*
Shaktas, 65
Shakti *bhakti*, 64–66
Shaku-buku, 275, 277
Shakya clan, 27
Shakyamuni, 27
shaman(s)
   female, 231–233
   possessed by deity, 232
   See also Shamanism
Shamanism, 233
Shan-tao, 217, 270
Shang, 145, 146
   and divination, 155–156
   and sacrifice, 154
   religions of, 147–148, 151–154
Shang-ti, 186
Shankara, 76–80
   and *bhakti*, 101
   and Madhva, 82–83
   and Radhakrishnan, 123
   and Ramanuja, 80
Shankara monastery at Shringeri, 82
Shankara-Narayana, *see* Harihara
Shastras, 132
Shatapatha Brahmana, 8, 21
Shandilya Sutras, 48
She, 153
She-chi, 152
shen, 152
Shen-hsiu, 213
Shen-hui, 214
shih, 164, 170
Shih-chi, 159
Shih-ching, 148, 151
Shih Huang-ti, 146
Shih Tsu, Emperor, 207
Shimabara revolt, 261
Shimbutsu-bunri, 249
Shingon Buddhism, 210, 242, 259–261, 266, 269
Shinran, 260, 269, 270, 271, 272
Shinri-kyo Shinto, 252
Shinshu-kyo Shinto, 253
shintai, 237

Shinto
    Buddhist accommodation to, 242
    concept of purity in, 228
    and decline of Buddhism, 262
    ethics of, 228
    future of, 251
    and Japanese Buddhism, 262
    and Japanese nationalism, 247, 248–249
    Mountain sects of, 253
    numbers of followers of, 278
    officially recognized sects of, 252–254
    origins of, 229–230
    as patriotic cult, 250–251
    pure, see Pure Shinto
    and principle of saisei-itchi, 241
    sects of, 253
    and social crisis, 243–244
    as state religion, 241–242, 249–251
    traditional, see Traditional Shinto
Shinto clan cults, 244
Shinto Directive, 250
Shinto Gobusho, 244
Shinto Honkyoku, 252
shirt, sacred, see sudrah
Shitennoji temple, 258
Shiva, 11, 13, 47, 55, 66
    pre-Vedic prototype of, 4
    and Rudra, 61
    and Shakti *bhakti,* 65
    and Shankara, 76
    in triad of gods, 67
    wife of, see Shakti
Shiva *bhakti,* 61–64
Shivaguru, 76
Shiva-jnana-bodham, 63
Shobogenzo, 273
Shogunate
    abolition of, 251
    and Doctrinal Buddhism, 270
Shomu, Emperor, 258
Shonin, Kuya, 264
Short Sukhavati-vyuha Sutra, see *O-mi-t'o' ching*
Shotoku, Empress, 259
Shotoku, Prince, 257–258, 263, 264
shramanas, 24
shravakas, 44–46
Shri, 60
Shri Sampradaya sects, see Shri-Vaishnavism sects
Shri-Vaishnavism sects, 80
shrine ceremony, 238
Shrine Shinto, 233, 234, 240
Shringeri monastery, 76
shruti, 62, 79
shu, 164, 166
Shu-ching, 138
Shyddodhana, King, 27
Shugendo movement, 233, 266, 268
Shun, 164
Shunyata
    Absolute as, 74
    Dharmakaya arising from, 73
    in Madhyamika system, 73
    Real as, 74
Shusei-ha Shinto, 252
Shvetambaras, 46
Shvetashvatara Upanishad, 61
Sikhs, 56–57, 99–105
    and Muslim-Hindu conflict, 99–105
sila, 40
silence, see *prajna*
sin(s)
    earthly, 227–228
    in Japanese religion, 227–228
    and Parsis, 94
    in Vedic religion, 13
sincerity, see *ch'eng; magokoro*
Singh, 103
Single-minded sect, see Ikko sect
Sita, 55, 56, 57, 60
Siva, see Shiva
Sivaji, 99
Six Schools of Nara Buddhism, 268
"Six Schools and Seven Branches," 209
skhandhas, see *khandhas*
skill, in Taoist thought, 199
skill in means, see *upaya*
Smith, Donald Eugene, 128, 129-130
snakes, and Shiva, 61
social order
    Radhakrishnan on, 124
    and religion in China, 143–144
    and Vedic religion, 17–19
social problems
    and Buddhism, 257, 276–277
    and Japanese religion, 251–252
    and Popular Buddhism, 263–264
social theories
    and Japanese religion, 226–227
    of Mo-ti, 173
society, and Taoist thought, 192
Sodo school of Buddhism, 214
Soga clan, 257
Soka Gakkai Buddhism, 251–252, 276–278
Soma, 12, 14
Soma juice, see Homa juice
soma sacrifice, 7, 15
Son of Heaven, see T'ien-tzu
sorcerers, see *wu*
Soto Zen Buddhism, 260, 272–273
souls
    and Dvaita, 83
    in Taoism, 145
    in Theosophy, 115
    worship of, 232–233
    See also *jiva*
Southern school of Buddhism, 26
Southern school of Ch'an Buddhism, 213, 214
Southern school of Vishishtadvaita, see Tengalai
speech, and Taoism, 186
Spencer, Herbert, 112
Spenta Mainyu, 93
Spirit, see spirits
spirits
    in ancient Chinese religions, 152
    in ancient Shinto, 232, 236
    Confucius on, 158
    in Japanese religion, 226
    and Parsis, 93, 94
    in Shang religion, 154
    Shinto classifications of, 238
    in Vedic religion, 17–19
Sravanabelgola, 47
Sri Guru Granth Sahib, 103
Spring and Autumn Annals, see *Ch'un-ch'iu*
Ssu-ma Ch'ien, 160, 184
starvation, voluntary, 41
state-church conflict, see church-state conflict
state-religion
    and Japanese Buddhism, 257–263
    and *saisei-itchi,* 241
stealing, see *asteya*
Sthanakavasis, 46
Stoicism, in Taoist thought, 199
"store consciousness," doctrine of the, see *alaya-vijnana*
straightening Kami, see Naobi-no-kami
straightforwardness, see *chi*
strivers, see *yatis*
students, see *brahmacarin*
study, see *hsueh*
stupas, 49–50, 51
Subhuti, 73
sudrah, 96
suffering
    and lust, 69
    in Madhyamika system, 70
    and Nibbana, 37–38
    See also *dukkha*
Sui dynasty, 147, 218
Suiga Shinto, 244, 245
Suijaku, 243
Suiko, Empress, 257–258
Sukeisha, 234
Sukhavativyuha, 51
Sun Buddha, see Mahavairocana Buddha
Sun Daughter, see Pimiko
Sun Goddesses
    Amaterasu-o-mikami, 232, 243
    in *Ise* Shinto, 244, 246
    in Japanese religion, 227
sun gods, see Surya
Sung dynasty, 147, 180–182, 219
"Supermind," 122
supernatural events
    Hsun-tzu on, 178
    See magic, miracles
superstition
    in Chinese religions, 144
    Shinran on, 272
Supreme Lord, see Ishvara
Supreme Ultimate, 182
surrender to God, see *prapatti*
Surya, 12, 13
sutras
    nation protecting, 259
    prajnaparamita, 69
    See also under individual titles of
Sutta-Pitaka, 25
Sutta-vibhanga, 25
Suttas, 37
svadhyaya, 85
swadesi, 120
swaraj, 120
swastika symbol, 4
sword, as Confucian Shinto symbol, 243
swordsmanship, see Kendo
syadvada, doctrine of, 42–43
symbol(s)
    hexagrams, 148
    of imperial authority, 229
symbolic diagram, sacred, see Mandala

sympathetic joy, see mudita
Syriac Christians, see "Christians of Saint Thomas"

Ta-hsueh, 139, 178–179, 182
taboos
  of Parsis, 91
  Shinto, 231
tachiojo-suru, 263
Tagore, Devendranath, 107–108, 117
Tagore, Rabindranath, 107, 117–118
T'ai Hsu, 219
Tai K'uei, 201
T'ai-ping rebellion, 203, 220
T'ai-p'ing Tao, 203
T'ai-Shang Kan-ying P'ien, 145, 202
Taika reform, 258
Taira, 269
Taisei-kyo Shinto, 252–253
Taisha-kyo Shinto, 252
Taiwan, Taoism on, 204
Taka-mi-musubi-no-Kami, 237, 240, 246, 247
Takauji, Ashikaga, 261
tales
  of Kingdom of Lu, 149
  of Wang Hui-chi, 201
Tamil Shaivism, 63
T'an-luan, 217–218
T'ang dynasty, 147, 218
T'ang law codes, 258
tanha, 30, 33
Tannisho, 271
Tantra, disciplines of, 111
tantrism, 65
Tao, concept of, 186
Tao-an, 209
Tao-cho, 217
Tao-sheng, 209
Tao-te-ching, 184–187, 189–194, 200
Taoism, 146
  and Buddhism, 206–207, 256–257
  and Ch'an Buddhism, 212–213
  and Chung-yung, 179
  emergence in China of, 157–158
  fusion with Confucianism, 144–145
  during Han dynasty, 181
  and harmony in human relations, 142
  in Japan, 266
  and opposition to Buddhism, 218
  philosophical, see Philosophical Taoism
  religious, see Religious Taoism
  and Shamanism, 233
  and utility of the empty, 89
  and wu-wei, 89
tapas, 23, 85
Taraporewala, I. J. S., 94, 94n
Taru-musubi-no-Kami, 240
Tathagata, 27, 45, 72, 73
tattvas, 65
te, 164, 170, 186–187
tea ceremony, 273
teaching, Confucius on, 167–168
Teaching of the Great Shrine, see Taisha-kyo Shinto
Tegh Bahadur, 103
temple(s)
  of Brahma Samaj, 107
  Buddhist, 258

dedicated to Krishna and Radha, 55
  Jaina, 46–47
  Parsi, 94
  reform of administration of, 129–130
  of Sikhs, 105, see also gurdwaras
  and untouchables, 132
  See also under individual names of
Tendai Buddhism, 209, 211–212, 269, 274
  in Japan, 259–261
  and Nichiren, 274–276
Tendai Shinto, 242
Tengalai, 82
Tenri-kyo Shinto, 252, 253, 254
"Testament on One Sheet of Paper," 270, 271
theft, 39
theism
  and bhakti, 48–49
  and Brahmans, 58
  of Brahma Samaj, 107
Theosophical Society, 114–116
Theravada Buddhists, 25–27, 33
  morality of, 40–41
thread, sacred, see kusti
"three baskets" canon, see Tipitaka
three bodies of Buddha, doctrine of, see Trikaya doctrine
three jewels, in Jaina doctrine, 44
three periods, theory of the, 273
three treasures, see Buddha; Dharma; Sangha
Three Treatise Buddhism, see Sanron Buddhism
Ti-tsang-wang, 145
T'ien, 152, 154, 154n, 171
T'ien-hsia, 154
T'ien-t'ai Buddhism, see Tendai Buddhism
T'ien-tzu, 154
tilak marks, 83
Ting, Duke, 160
Tipitaka, 25–26, 27
  doctrines of, see Pali doctrine
  Nibbana in, 37–38
Tirthankaras, 41–42, 45–47
Tirthankara Rshabha, 41
Tirumurai, 62
Toda, Josei, 277
Todaiji temple, 243, 259
Toji temple, 259–260
Tokugawa era, 230, 244, 248, 252, 261–262
Tolstoi, 111
tomb, of Confucius, 272
Tortoise, the, see Kurma
tortoises, and divination, 155
Totapura, 111
"towers of silence," see dakmas
Toyo-uke-o-mikami, 243
Traditional Shinto
  in ancient times, 230–235
  classifications of, 233
  concept of "kami" in, 235–237
  evolution of, 234–235
  myth and ritual in, 235–238, 240–242
  and Shamanism, 233
  theological themes of, 240–241
traditionalism, and Confucianism, 147
trance

of Ramakrishna, 111
  and Yogacara, 75
tranquillity, in Chinese tradition, 142–143
transmigration of souls
  Buddhist belief in, 263
  and Chinese philosophy, 205–206
  Gandhi on, 119
  in Pali tradition, 36
  in Vedic religion, 22, 23
travel, in Jaina religion, 45
Treatise on Attaining Peace in the Country Through Establishing True Buddhism (or True Teaching), see Risshoankokuron
Treatise on the Doctrine, Practice, Faith and Realization, see Kyogoshinsho
Treatise on the Meditation of the True Effect of Worship, see Kanjinhonzonsho
Treatise on the Nembutsu of the Select Original Vow, see Senjakuhongannembutsushu
Treatise on Opening the Eyes, see Kaimokusho
Treatise on Requiting Gratitude, see Hoonsho
Treatise on Selection of the Time, see Senjisho
Treatise on Spiritually Protecting the Nation through Prospering Zen, see Kozengokokuron
triad of gods, 13, 66–67
trigrams, symbolic, 148
Trikaya doctrine,
Tripitaka, see Tipitaka
true ordination platform, see Hommon Kaidan
truth
  in Jaina doctrine, 44–45
  and Shruti, 79
  See also asha; dhamma; satya
Tsao-tung Buddhism, see Soto Zen Buddhism
Tsou Yen, 201
Tsuneyoshi, Watari, 244
tsutsushimi, 244
Tulsi Das, 57, 60
Tung Chung-shu, 180–181
Tushita heaven, 27
twelve causes, doctrine of the, 33–34
tyranny, Taoism and, 203–204
Tzu-chang, 165

Ubusuna-Kami, 238
udambara twig, 16
Udgatri, 8, 15
Ujigami, 234
Ujiko, 234
Ullambana festival, see Urabon-e festival
Ultimate Buddha, 275
Ultimate Reality, 81
Uma, see Shakti
Unconditioned Reality, 70
unconscious, see ajiva
unity
  and Brahma Samaj, 107–108
  of Buddhism, Confucianism, and Taoism, 220
  of Chinese religions, 144–145

unity (*continued*)
  among "Hindus," 132–133
  with Kami, 228
  and Ramakrishna movement, 111–112
  and Sun Buddha symbol, 243
  of Taoist thought, 201–202
"Unity in Diversity," 133
universal love, 171, 172
universal religion, 107
unreality, *see asat*
untouchables
  divisions among, 131
  Gandhi on, 120
  and Shri-Vaishnavism sects, 80
Untouchability Act of 1955, 132
upadana, 33
Upadeshasahasri, 77
upanayana rite, 16
Upanishads, 6, 8–9
  bhakti tendencies in, 49
  compared with *Tipitaka*, 31
  and sacrifice, 20–21
  Shankara's commentaries on, 76–77
  and renunciation, 18
  and Vishishtadvaita, 80, 81
upasakas, 39–41
Upasampada, 38–39
upasikas, 39–40
upaya, 51, 73
upekha, 40–41
Uposatha service, 38
urabe, 238
Urabon-e festival, 266
urban life, and Buddhism, 276–277
Ushas, *see* Dawn
"usefulness of the useless," 197
utility of the empty, Taoist theory of, 189

Vadagalai, 82
Vaishnavas, 60
Vaishya, 18
Vajracchedika, 69
vajrasattva, 65
Vallabha, 54
Valmiki, 57
Vamana, 59
vanaprasthya, 18
Varaha, 59
Vardhamana, *see* Mahavira
varnas, see classes
Varuna, 13
Vasubandhu, 74, 217
Vasuki, 59
vatsalya, 54
Vayu, 82
veda, definition of, 5
vedana, 32, 33
Vedanta
  and Radhakrishnan, 123
  and Ramakrishna movement, 113
Vedanta-sara, 107
Vedas, 5–10
  and Arya Samaj, 109
  and Brahma Samaj, 108
  and Carvaka group, 86–87
  and classification of religious systems, 68
  and Dvaita, 82
  and Vishnu, 59, 60

Vedic gods, 55
Vedic hymns, 18
Vedic religion
  challenges to, 24–25
  cult practices in, 14–19
  gods of, 10–14
  literature of, 5–10
  after Rigvedic period, 19–23
  social aspects of, 17–19
Vedic texts, 5–10
vegetarianism, 119, 126–127
veiling of women, 101
Vendidad, 91–92
Vijnana, *see vinnana*
Vijnanavada, *see* Yogacara
Vinaya Buddhism, *see* Ritsu Buddhism
Vinaya-Pitaka, 25, 38
vinnana, 32, 33
violence
  Gandhi on, 120
  and Parsis, 92
virtues
  in Buddhism, 206
  of Confucian Shinto, 243
  in Confucianism, 165–166, 206
  of Shinto, 244
Vishishtadvaita, 80–82
Vishnu, 13, 46, 47, 55, 66
  and Buddha, 50
  and Dvaita, 82, 83
  in form of Buddha, 60
  and Krishna, 52, 60
  as Supreme God, 55
  in triad of gods, 67
  various forms of, 59–60
  wife of, *see* Lakshmi
  See also Vishnu *bhakti*
Vishnu *bhakti*, 58–61
Vishnu Purana, 82
Vishtaspa, Prince, 92
Vishvakarman, 19
Vispered, 91
Visuddhimagga, 26
Vithoba, 60–61
vivarta, 77–78
Vivekananda, 107, 112–114
  and "Hinduism," 132
  and Radhakrishnan, 125
Vivekananda College, 133
Vohu Manah, 92, 93
void
  in Ch'an Buddhism, 216
  in Yogacara, 75
volitional activities, *see sankara*
vow(s)
  of Brahma Samaj, 108
  of *Brahmacarya*, 120
  in Gandhi's Ashram, 120
  of Hachiman Bosatsu, 228
  of Jaina religion, 44–45
Vrindavan, 54, 55
Vritra the serpent, 11
vyavaharika, 77, 78

Waku-musubi-no-Kami, 240
wandering, 195–197
Wang Chung, 162, 181
Wang Hui-chi, 201
Wang Pi, 200
Wang Yang-ming, 147, 181, 182
war
  Confucius on, 170–171

Mo-ti on, 174
  and Taoist thought, 192
Warring States, age of, 146, 159, 177
warrior, *see shih*
warrior class, *see* samurai class
washermen, *see dhobis*
Watanabe, S., 266–267, 266*n*
water nymphs, *see apsaras*
water rites, Shinto, 231
Way, *see* Tao
Way of the Gods, *see* Shinto
way through knowledge, *see jnana-marga*
way through works, *see karmamarga*
wealth, goddess of, *see* Shri
Wei dynasty, 207
Wei-shih school of Buddhism, 219
wen, 170–171
Wen of Chou, King, 148, 164
Western culture
  and Buddhism, 220
  and Confucianism, 147
  influence on Confucianism, 183
  influence on Tagore, 117
  and Japan, 224
  and Shinto, 250
  and Taoism, 187
wheel of causation, *see paticcasamuppada*
Wheeler, Sir Mortimer, 5, 5*n*
White Lotus Society, 217
widowers, and Arya Samaj rules, 110
widows
  and Arya Samaj rules, 110
  and Gandhi, 120
  self-immolation of, 126
  in Vedic religion, 17
wind god, *see* Vayu
witchcraft, as sin, 228
wizards, *see wu*
women
  childbirth deities for, 264
  and Japanese religious movements, 252
  in monastic orders, 46
  and Rama *bhakti* disciples, 56
  and sacred prostitution, 127
  as Shinto shamans, 231–232
  in Sikh community, 101
  in Vedic period, 19
"Words of Confucius," *see Analects*
world origins, in Vedic religion, 19–20
World Parliament of Religions (1893), 112
world view
  and Carvaka school, 87
  of Dvaita, 83
  in Jaina doctrine, 43–44
  in Madhyamika system, 70
  as *maya*, 113
  and yin-yang process, 182
worship, *see* prayer
wu, 156–157, 206
Wu, King, 164
Wu-liang-shou-ching, 217
we-wei, 189, 206

Xavier, Francis, 89

Yahweh, 13
Yajnavalkya, 21
Yajuhsamhita, *see* Yajurveda

Yajurveda, 7, 8
yajus, 7
yama, 84–85
Yama, *see* Yen-lo-wang
yang, *see* yin-yang concept
Yang, C. K., 156, 156*n*
Yang-chu, 171–174, 184, 201
Yao, 164
Yao-yorozu-no-Kami, 236
Yashodhara, 27
Yasna, 91
yatis, order of, 44–45
Yellow Emperor, 206
Yellow Springs, 152, 197
Yellow Turbans, 203
Yen-lo-wang, 145

yin, *see* yin-yang concept
Yin, Duke, 149
yin-yang concept, 148, 152, 181, 266
Yin-yang school, 146, 146*n*
Yoga, 84–86
 Aurobindo on, 122
 and Ch'an Buddhism, 213
Yoga Sutras, 84–86
Yogacara, 74–76
 See also Hosso Buddhism
Yomi, land of, 230, 248
yoni, 4, 65, 66
yoshi, 228
Young-Creating Deity, *see* Waku-musubi-no-Kami
Yu, 153, 164, 206

Yu-lan Fung, 166–167, 167*n*, 179
yu-wei, 206
Yuiembo, 271
Yuiitsu Shinto, 244
Yukichi, Fukuzawa, 250
Yun-ch'i Chu-hung, 220
Yuzu-nembutsu, 264

Zaehner, R. C., 93, 93*n*
Zazen, 273
Zen Buddhism, *see* Ch'an Buddhism
Zend-Avesta, see Avesta
Zoroaster, 90–96
Zoroastrians, *see* Parsis

DATE DUE			
NOV 26 '78			
APR 5 7 '87			
APR 3 '87			
DEC 1 '92			
DEC 10 1997			
MAR - 1 1999			
MAY 03 1999			
GAYLORD			PRINTED IN U.S.A.

72 73 74 75 7 6 5 4 3 2 1